DEVELOPING SOURCING CAPABILITIES

DEVELOPING SOURCING CAPABILITIES

Creating Strategic Change in Purchasing and Supply Management

Edited by
Björn Axelsson, Frank Rozemeijer and Finn Wynstra

John Wiley & Sons, Ltd

Copyright © 2005   John Wiley & Sons Ltd, The Atrium, Southern Gate, Chichester,
West Sussex PO19 8SQ, England

Telephone (+44) 1243 779777

Email (for orders and customer service enquiries): cs-books@wiley.co.uk
Visit our Home Page on www.wiley.com

Illustrations by Josje van Koppen. © John Wiley & Sons Ltd

This publication is designed to provide accurate and authoritative information in regard to the subject
matter covered. It is sold on the understanding that the Publisher is not engaged in rendering
professional services. If professional advice or other expert assistance is required, the services of a
competent professional should be sought.

Other Wiley Editorial Offices

John Wiley & Sons Inc., 111 River Street, Hoboken, NJ 07030, USA

Jossey-Bass, 989 Market Street, San Francisco, CA 94103-1741, USA

Wiley-VCH Verlag GmbH, Boschstr. 12, D-69469 Weinheim, Germany

John Wiley & Sons Australia Ltd, 42 McDougall Street, Milton, Queensland 4064, Australia

John Wiley & Sons (Asia) Pte Ltd, 2 Clementi Loop #02-01, Jin Xing Distripark, Singapore 129809

John Wiley & Sons Canada Ltd, 22 Worcester Road, Etobicoke, Ontario, Canada M9W 1L1

Wiley also publishes its books in a variety of electronic formats. Some content that appears
in print may not be available in electronic books.

Library of Congress Cataloging-in-Publication Data:

Developing sourcing capabilities : creating strategic change in purchasing
and supply management / edited by Björn Axelsson, Frank Rozemeijer and Finn
Wynstra.
         p. cm.
     Includes bibliographical references and index.
     ISBN-13 978-0-470-85012-1 (pbk. : alk. paper)
     ISBN-10 0-470-85012-4 (pbk. : alk. paper)
   1.   Purchasing – Management. 2.   Industrial procurement.   I. Axelsson,
Björn, 1948- II. Rozemeijer, Frank. III. Wynstra, Finn.
     HF5437.D44 2005
     658.7'2 – dc22
                                                                 2005006839

British Library Cataloguing in Publication Data

A catalogue record for this book is available from the British Library

ISBN-13 978-0-470-85012-1 (PB)
ISBN-10 0-470-85012-4 (PB)

Typeset in 10/12pt Palatino by Laserwords Private Limited, Chennai, India
Printed and bound in Great Britain by Antony Rowe Ltd, Chippenham, Wiltshire
This book is printed on acid-free paper responsibly manufactured from sustainable forestry
in which at least two trees are planted for each one used for paper production.

CONTENTS

LIST OF CONTRIBUTORS

Henrik Agndal is Research Fellow at Jönköping International Business School, Jönköping University, Sweden. His current research interests include the internationalization of SMEs and various issues relating to international purchasing/sourcing.

Björn Axelsson is a tenured professor at Stockholm School of Economics (SSE) and the first occupant of the Silf Chair of Purchasing and Supply Management at the school. He has served as Professor of Marketing at SSE and Jönköping International Business School. He started his career at Uppsala University and was for more than a decade responsible for its executive MBA programme. He has published several books on purchasing issues, one of which is *Buying Business Services* (John Wiley & Sons, Ltd, 2002), with Finn Wynstra. His research revolves around business-to-business operations within a markets-as-networks view. His book, *Industrial Networks: A New View of Reality* (Routledge, 1992), co-edited with Geoff Easton, demonstrates this.

Pieter Bouwmans graduated in 2003 from the Eindhoven University of Technology. His final thesis dealt with purchasing knowledge management at purchasing organizations of large companies. In his research he conducted case studies at five large Dutch companies. Pieter Bouwmans is currently a management trainee at NedTrain B.V., the maintenance depot of the Netherlands Railways.

Ethel Brundin is an Assistant Professor at Jönköping International Business School. In 2002 she defended her PhD on emotions and strategic leadership. Her current research interests are: emotions and family businesses; emotions and growth; and entrepreneurship among immigrants and in developing countries. She also takes a special interest in methodological issues. She is currently involved in a joint research project with the Western Cape University in South Africa. She has published articles on impression management, real-time methodologies, social entrepreneurship, immigrant entrepreneurship and ethnic entrepreneurship. Ethel Brundin also serves as a lecturer in leadership courses on different levels and for different audiences and is a member of the Editorial Advisory Board of Acta Commercii in South Africa.

Anna Dubois is Professor at the Department of Industrial Marketing, Chalmers University of Technology, Sweden, where she is director of a recently started international master's programme in 'Supply Chain Design and Management'. Anna Dubois's research interests are within the area of industrial marketing and purchasing with particular focus on business relationships and industrial networks.

Recent articles are published in *Industrial Marketing Management*, *Journal of Purchasing and Supply Management*, *Journal of Business Research*, *Journal of Management Studies* and *Journal of Customer Behaviour*.

Tony Fang is presently Assistant Professor of International Management at Stockholm University School of Business and Visiting Associate Professor, Asia Research Centre, Copenhagen Business School. He previously worked as a researcher at Linköping Institute of Technology, Stockholm School of Economics, and as a manager in Chinese and Scandinavian firms in the shipping industry. Tony Fang's research has focused on global cross-cultural management, intercultural communication behaviour, industrial marketing and purchasing (sourcing), international business negotiation and Chinese business dynamism. Tony Fang is the author of the book *Chinese Business Negotiating Style* (Thousand Oaks: Sage Publications, 1999).

Jens Hultman is a PhD candidate at the Department for Entrepreneurship, Marketing and Management at Jönköping International Business School. Jens Hultman received his master's degree in business administration from the University of Gävle, Sweden, in 2001. His thesis work and research interests include electronic commerce and information technology adoption.

Fraser Johnson is an Associate Professor at the Richard Ivey School of Business, The University of Western Ontario, where he teaches purchasing and supply, logistics and operations. Prior to accepting a faculty position, Fraser worked in the automotive parts industry where he held a number of senior management positions in both finance and operations. Professor Johnson is an active researcher in the area of purchasing and supply chain management and he is the author of several articles that have been published in a wide variety of journals and magazines. His textbook, *Purchasing and Supply Management* (with Michiel Leenders, Harold Fearon and Anna Flynn), published by McGraw-Hill Irwin, is now in its thirteenth edition. Professor Johnson has consulted for organizations in the private and public sectors, and has taught on a number of different management development programmes in Canada, the United States and Europe.

Michiel Leenders is the Leenders Purchasing Management Association of Canada Chair and Professor Emeritus at the Richard Ivey School of Business, The University of Western Ontario. Michiel is a former director of the School's PhD programme and since 1998 Director of the Ivey Purchasing Managers Index. He has written a number of articles in a variety of magazines and journals and his supply texts have been translated into nine different languages. He was the educational advisor to the Purchasing Management Association of Canada from 1961 to 1993, and received PMAC's Fellowship Award in 1975 and the Prix Guy Charette from Samson, Belair, Deloitte & Touche in 1991. Michiel held the first Canadian chair in purchasing in 1993. In 1997, Michiel received the Financial Post Leaders in Management Education Award and in 2002 the International Federation of Purchasing and Materials Management (IFPMM) Purchasing Research Award. Michiel has taught and consulted extensively both in Canada and internationally and is a director of ING Bank of Canada.

Leif Melin is Professor of Strategy and Organization at Jönköping International Business School and previously he was Professor of Strategic Management at Linköping University, Sweden. Leif Melin's international publications have covered many strategic issues, such as international strategies, strategic leadership, strategy processes, innovative forms of organizing and micro-strategizing. His PhD from 1977 focused on purchasing strategies. He serves on editorial boards for several international journals, such as *Strategic Organization, Organization Studies, Long Range Planning* and *Journal of World Business*.

Marc Reunis is currently pursuing a PhD at the Delft University of Technology, Netherlands, on the topic of behavioural interventions to increase intra-organizational adoption of e-procurement. His PhD is sponsored by NEVI (the Dutch Purchasing Management Association). He has a research interest in organizational behaviour and technological advances in the purchasing function. He has work experience at the global procurement office of a large car manufacturer and he completed his MSc on e-procurement adoption at the Eindhoven University of Technology, Netherlands.

Frank Rozemeijer is presently working as a part-time lecturer in Purchasing Management at RSM Erasmus University, Netherlands. He also runs his own purchasing consulting firm called FRConsulting, focusing on developing purchasing organizations. His books and publications in academic journals mainly focus on topics like professionalizing purchasing, organizing purchasing and supplier development and partnership. He is co-author of the books *Revolution in Purchasing* (1996), *Ondernemend Samenwerken* (1999) and *Creating Corporate Advantage in Purchasing* (2000).

Sicco Santema is Professor of Marketing, Management and Organization at the Delft University of Technology and Professor of E-Business Marketing and Procurement at the Eindhoven University of Technology. Santema's publications focus on dyadic relationships in supply chains, currently including the relationship effects of e-procurement. He sees purchasing and marketing as two sides of the same coin, called business. His field of academic application is aerospace and aviation. Sicco is also director of Scenter Management Consultants.

Arjan van Weele holds the NEVI Chair of Purchasing and Supply Management at Eindhoven University of Technology, Faculty of Technology Management. His publications cover a wide range of topics related to purchasing management and supply strategies. He is the author of *Purchasing and Supply Chain Management* (2005), which has developed into one of the leading textbooks in the field. In 2003 he received the Hans Ovelgönne Award from the International Federation of Purchasing and Materials Management (IFPMM) for his outstanding academic contribution to the field. He is member of the Editorial Board of the *Journal of Purchasing and Supply Management*. More information can be found at www.arjanvanweele.com.

Finn Wynstra is currently NEVI Professor of Purchasing and Supply Management at RSM Erasmus University, Netherlands, and has previously worked at universities in Sweden, the UK and the US. Finn Wynstra's publications mainly focus on the integration of supply and innovation processes, supplier relations and total cost of ownership, and with Björn Axelsson he co-authored the book *Buying Business Services* (John Wiley & Sons, Ltd, 2002). He is currently Editor of the *Journal of Purchasing and Supply Management*, and has been a Chairman of the International Purchasing and Supply Education and Research Association, a global organization of more than 300 practitioners and academics.

FOREWORD

Professional buying of products and services nowadays is a crucial factor for a sustainable competitive position. This is not only true for manufacturing companies, but also for large firms operating in the service sector, like KPN Royal Dutch Telecom. Although the tools and techniques of purchasing and supply management are covered by an increasing number of textbooks, the topic of managing strategic change in purchasing has until now received little explicit attention. This book aims to fill this gap and it does so in an excellent way. Not only are the specific characteristics of strategic change in purchasing and supply management dealt with by the authors, they also provide a new perspective on the role of the CPO as a change leader.

From my experience as a CPO at different large multinational companies, I learned that people are critically important in obtaining maximum value from purchasing and thereby creating a competitive advantage. The purchasing function should be staffed with the right skills, subject expertise and competencies. You need people who are able to communicate with business managers, influence buying behaviour, cope with resistance and motivate suppliers to improve their performance. This is not something you can realize overnight: it requires a clear development strategy covering elements like recruitment, training and learning-on-the-job. Since you cannot change purchasing if the rest of your company is not changing either, it also requires a great deal of learning outside the purchasing function (e.g. in Finance, HR, IT departments). This latter is a real challenge, and therefore management of strategic change in purchasing should not be left only to the CPO; top management must be involved.

By reading this book you will be able to better understand how you can manage change in purchasing and supply management. In writing this book, the authors have drawn both on their considerable academic knowledge and practitioner networks. This makes this book a unique blend of pragmatic theory and structured application. The reader will benefit from the many case examples that are included in the text. I am sure that the book generates a wealth of ideas for you on how to develop sourcing capabilities. A must read!

Willem van Oppen
Chief Procurement Officer
KPN Royal Dutch Telecom

PREFACE

Writing this book has been like a long and pleasant journey. Four years ago on a skiing holiday two of the editors, Björn Axelsson and Finn Wynstra, set out the basic framework of a book addressing strategic change in purchasing. We had met so many purchasing managers as well as managers in other positions, particularly CEOs, who claimed that they realized the very important role purchasing and supply management should play in today's and future organizations. Managers outside the purchasing function asked primarily the 'what' question: what should one do to be best able to leverage the opportunities for competitive advantage that are inherent in a professional purchasing organization? The purchasing managers, especially the chief purchasing officers (CPOs), thought they knew. Instead they asked the 'how' question: how can one make the desired improvements happen? This book addresses primarily the latter question, but the first one will also – indirectly – be dealt with.

We designed quite early on the basic ideas and structure of the book. We thought that we had a substantial load of material for most of the areas, and that with some effort over a period of one to two years or so, we should be able to finish the project. Time went by and a lot of other things happened.

At the same time, we realized that the material we had and our own abilities to address the very broad field we wanted to cover were limited. To be honest, we did not have the level of in-depth knowledge needed in all the areas we wanted to include. As a result, we invited distinguished colleagues to stand by our side and together with us create the contents. We wanted to add a 'purchasing flavour' to chapters on for example strategic change, leadership, the utilization of information and communication technologies (ICT), the role and reactions of individuals affected by processes of strategic change and so on. The experts thus took responsibility for the specialized content as such and we added the purchasing flavour.

Later, it turned out that we also could benefit from someone in a better position than us to help with this adaptation and connection to the practitioners of purchasing. Dr Frank Rozemeijer, with an academic background and several years of consultancy experience, particularly in relation to creating and managing change in purchasing and supply management, came to our aid. Frank's all-round expertise made him a perfect complement to the two original editors.

These measures turned out to be very fruitful. We are now able to present a book with, first of all, a much deeper specialist knowledge in the various fields that we could not cover by ourselves. Secondly, we have been able to harvest from many richer opportunities to make the connection to practice. Altogether, this means that we actually 'walked the talk' of strategic sourcing.

Still, we made the conscious decision that at least one of us editors should be actively involved as author in every chapter. This way we have been better able to keep our initial ideas alive and to better integrate the content than is normally the case in edited books. We know from research that complex services (such as writing a book chapter fitted to a certain set of ideas) can hardly be bought through market-like 'transactions'. They need to be dealt with as high-involvement, interactive processes. By having our intentions and fields of speciality meet with those of our writing partners, we tried to gain synergies. Again, we tried to be true to our basic beliefs in sourcing methods and to act accordingly.

It has been a pleasant and interesting journey, with interesting and pleasant companions. Even though we have invited several co-authors from *outside* the purchasing field, many of them are *within* the field, albeit with different subfields of expertise. There are a number of natural meeting places for academics involved in a certain research area. In connection with for example the annual IPSERA (International Purchasing and Supply Education and Research Association) and IMP (Industrial Marketing and Purchasing Group) conferences, we have been able to set up meetings and coordinate our efforts. Thus, the project has made important moves forward in such places as Enschede (the Netherlands), Budapest (Hungary) and Catania (Italy).

In addition to this we have had meetings with selected groups of authors in Stockholm and Jönköping in Sweden, and in Eindhoven, Rotterdam and Dordrecht in the Netherlands. The two original editors have also met at that initial skiing place at Idre in Sweden and later at Blidö in the archipelago of Sweden. The final meeting with all three editors took place in a cottage in the Ardennes in Belgium. This way we have not only had an intellectual journey, but also a physical one, full of new impressions and insights.

To conclude, we should express our appreciation to the many partners involved in the whole project.

First of all, we would like to thank all co-authors for their great work and pleasant collaboration along the way: Henrik Agndal, Ethel Brundin, Jens Hultman and Leif Melin from Jönköping International Business School, Anna Dubois from Chalmers Technical University, Tony Fang from Stockholm University (all Sweden), Fraser Johnson and Michiel Leenders from Richard Ivey Business School, London, Ontario (Canada), Pieter Bouwmans (Nedtrain Consulting), Arjan van Weele from Technische Universiteit Eindhoven, and Marc Reunis and Sicco Santema, from Delft University of Technology (all the Netherlands). You made the journey into a real learning experience for us.

Also we would like to thank all the other kind and cooperative colleagues and practitioners who have willingly shared their insights with us. We have also benefited from the knowledge and support of our 'everyday' colleagues, especially Finn and Frank's colleagues from RSM Erasmus University and Björn's colleagues from Stockholm School of Economics and Jönköping International Business School, but also all other colleagues in our field: from your publications, from our discussions in relation to conferences such as the annual IPSERA and IMP conferences, dissertation exams and so on.

Several CPOs and CEOs have been interviewed and had interesting dialogues with us on these matters during this process. We thank you for your generosity in sharing your experiences and ideas with us.

Last but not least, we gratefully acknowledge the financial support we received from ERPS (the European Centre for Research in Purchasing and Supply) in Vienna, Austria.

Finally, we really hope that we have managed to produce an inspiring and insightful book on this very relevant and important topic. We hope that CPOs, CEOs, CFOs and other managers in today's organizations, will be able to relate to it and find it useful. We also hope that our colleagues will find it a necessity to have, read and use the book, for example in their teaching. It should fit well into MBA classes as well as advanced MSc courses in purchasing and supply management/strategic sourcing and maybe also in courses and other events addressing issues of strategic change.

Björn Axelsson, Frank Rozemeijer and Finn Wynstra
14 January 2005

Part I

INTRODUCTION

Chapter 1

THE CASE FOR CHANGE

Björn Axelsson, Frank Rozemeijer and Finn Wynstra

1.1 The development of sourcing

The development of the role of the purchasing function is sometimes described as a process in which the responsibility has gone from *buying*, via *procurement* to *supply management*.[1] These various steps have meant an increase in the scope and impact of purchasing activities within the organization.

Purchasing as in 'buying' represents purchasing activities and responsibilities that deal with buying the goods and services needed and making sure that the basic function of the items bought is acquired at favourable conditions. This is a rather narrow scope with a low degree of sophistication, the conceptual development of which mainly originated in the 1950s. The implementation on a broad scale of a more commercial orientation (initial steps to 'play the market') is normally dated a decade or so later.[2]

Purchasing as in 'procurement' deals with acquisitioning and optimizing the flow of materials (materials management, logistics), implying a widened role. It means (among other things) that not only price but also volumes and time aspects are being taken into account. The optimization aspect refers to the balancing act of buying large quantities to get a low price, but not too large to avoid costly stocks and not too small to avoid shortage and production downtime. The conceptual development of procurement is often dated to the 1960–70s, and its realization on a broad scale a decade later.

Purchasing as in 'supply management' increases the scope several steps further, and includes also the formation of supplier structures, the development of suppliers' capabilities (resources, knowledge), improving administrative routines and so on. All this is done in order to reduce *total cost* – not only the price of the specific products bought, but also the costs of related activities like quality assurance and administration. In addition it includes efforts to stimulate the creation of new opportunities in terms of product and process innovation. The Japanese car and electronics industries' way of organizing their supply structures is often referred to as a role model for this view on purchasing. Concepts like 'multi-tiered supply chains' and 'early supplier involvement' are important hallmarks of this view. Purchasing as in supply management could thus be defined as 'managing the external resources of the firm, aimed at acquiring inputs at the most favourable conditions'. This definition acknowledges the possibility that a customer may be interested in more supplier inputs than just the 'core' goods and services, for example the knowledge embedded in the current and possible future offerings of the supplier. The definition also implies that purchasing may involve activities that are only indirectly concerned with ('aimed at') 'obtaining' inputs such as relationship building and supplier development programmes. The word 'acquiring' implies that the inputs may not only be bought, but could also be leased, rented, borrowed or traded (e.g. as in the case of counter-trade).[3]

There are several reasons behind this gradual increase in the importance and scope of the purchasing function. Much is due to the ongoing trend towards specialization, meaning that every organization specializes in an increasingly smaller range of value added in its production process (be it manufacturing or services production processes), which leads to an increased share of externally acquired goods and services. Nowadays, purchasing-to-sales ratios in general are in the range of 30–60% for service organizations, 50–70% for manufacturing industries and 80–95% for retailing firms – and many organizations are seeing a further rise in this percentage. Not only are organizations increasingly *outsourcing* noncore activities, for example in the form of contract manufacturing, but this frequently takes the form of *offshoring* – essentially shifting activities to lower-wage countries such as India and China.[4]

There are also other reasons behind the pattern of change described, including the development of new managerial principles and concepts such as total quality management (TQM), just-in-time (JIT), efficient consumer response (ECR) and so forth, often enabled by new information and communications technologies (ICT). These concepts naturally lead to a strong focus on the need to consider interorganizational relations in efforts to improve efficiency and effectiveness in organizations.

As part of the development towards this more 'holistic' view of purchasing, there has been an ongoing process of increasing sophistication in the concepts, techniques and human resources involved. These techniques and concepts have been applied to varying degrees, related not only to the type of organization, but also to the particular goods and services bought within each organization.

The approach described in Figures 1.1 and 1.2 illustrates very well a 'holistic' approach towards purchasing. This approach was introduced in the late 1990s by Professor Monczka and his team from Michigan State University and was based on the insights from the Global Procurement and Supply Chain Benchmark initiative. This integral framework sketches the route to purchasing excellence and includes eight key strategic processes and six strategic enablers. To run a sophisticated purchasing and supply management operation, a company should continually address the basic strategic questions related to purchasing and supply chain operations. First, it should consider whether to outsource specific processes or not, or whether it should insource processes presently performed by outside suppliers. Once that decision has been made to outsource, or keep as outsourced, the next step is to develop a commodity strategy for each specific item.

The subsequent steps, as illustrated in Figure 1.1, are to establish and leverage a world-class supply base, to develop and manage supplier relationships, then, to integrate suppliers into new product development processes and to integrate

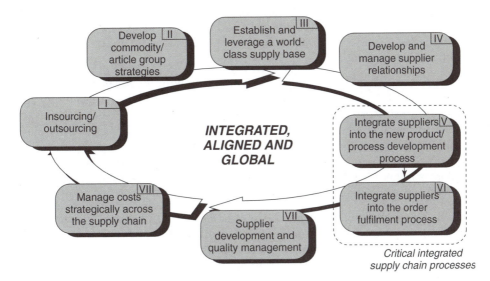

FIGURE 1.1   Purchasing and supply chain world-class excellence – strategic processes.
Source: Adapted from NEVI (2002) *Nederlandse bedrijven op weg naar Purchasing Excellence: Resultaten Project 1*, NEVI: Zoetermeer, p. 59.

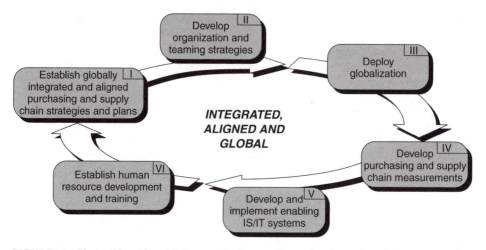

FIGURE 1.2   The enablers of world-class purchasing excellence. Source: Adapted from NEVI (2002), *Nederlandse bedrijven op weg naar Purchasing Excellence: Resultaten Project 1*, NEVI: Zoetermeer, p. 62.

them into order fulfilment processes. In order to keep improving, the company should opt for supplier development as well as successively manage costs across the supply chain.

These processes cannot be performed without relevant capabilities, or *enablers*. Therefore a second cycle is introduced. The first step is to introduce globally integrated and aligned purchasing and supply chain strategies and plans. This is followed by steps to develop proper organization and teaming strategies, deploying globalization and developing purchasing and supply chain measurements. The final two steps include to develop and implement enabling IS/IT systems and to establish human resource development and training. This way, by applying the two connected cycles, a company will manage to create an integrated and aligned as well as global operation.

These areas of capability building largely coincide with the areas of change that we discuss in this book. However, here they are not framed as areas of change in relation to processes of strategic change. They are merely framed as factors that need to be shaped and fitted to the operation in order to enable world-class operations. We agree, nevertheless, with this overall representation of purchasing and supply management and conclude that there is always a need for change in companies, otherwise they will be unable to stay competitive. All changes need not be of a strategic character, though.

We will be emphasizing that given the inherent cross-functional nature of the purchasing process, there are many actors inside a firm who act as 'part-time purchasers'. Still, the purchasing specialists themselves have experienced an increase in qualifications and recognition. This has been reflected in, among other things, an upgrade of purchasing in the corporate hierarchy. Especially in large firms, we now frequently find titles such as purchasing director, vice-president of purchasing or chief purchasing/procurement officer. Gartner expects that by the end of 2008, at least 50% of all Global 2000 firms will have a

CPO in place who is directly reporting to the CEO.[5] Also from job descriptions and recruitment processes, it is easy to infer that the profession has advanced substantially.

In this short description of the development of the purchasing function, one can also recognize an increased emphasis on nonoperational activities. Within the overall purchasing function, as for other business functions, a distinction can be made between operational, tactical and strategic tasks.

In this book from now on, we primarily use the term *sourcing* rather than purchasing, to reflect our emphasis on strategic and tactical purchasing activities.[6] Sourcing essentially is a cross-functional process, aimed at managing, developing and integrating with supplier capabilities to achieve a competitive advantage.[7] This does not only involve externally oriented activities, such as supplier performance measurement and market research, but also (primarily) internally oriented activities such as the development of organizational mechanisms like cross-functional buying teams, and human resource development. We sometimes use *purchasing and supply management* as a synonym for sourcing, also to reflect this combination of internally and externally oriented activities, which obviously in reality will be very closely connected to each other.

Strategic sourcing has also become quite a popular term among management consultants such as McKinsey, AT Kearney, Boston Consulting Group, Booz Allen & Hamilton, PricewaterhouseCoopers and OC&C.

Given the substantial challenges in moving from one type of view or orientation on purchasing to the next, many organizations and sourcing managers have been facing numerous issues regarding the creation and management of change. This book deals primarily with such change issues – not only in terms of the areas of change, but also the methods of change.

Before we continue to discuss the objectives and contents of the book further, let us consider the example of one of the world's largest firms in the computer industry in order to get a first impression of the kind of transitions or transformations we will be looking at.

1.2   An illustration: sourcing transformation at IBM

IBM's sourcing transformation story begins in the early 1990s.[8] IBM suffered from shrinking earnings and cash flows. In 1993, earnings and cash flow went negative and the stock price decreased to US $41, when it was US $117 in 1990. The fate of the entire company was at stake.

This 'near-death experience' acted as a catalyst for change. IBM embarked on a transformation of all of its key business processes, resulting in many role changes. Sourcing, or 'procurement' as it is usually referred to within IBM, was recognized as a key part of the overall IBM corporate transformation, sponsored by the chief financial officer (CFO) and chief executive officer (CEO). Procurement was becoming increasingly important as IBM's business model changed from being a hardware manufacturer towards being a service provider. Today, almost 50% of each revenue dollar is converted to supplier spend and purchasing makes up 72% of the costs of goods sold. Procurement was reaffirmed by the board as the only part of the organization allowed to commit funds for IBM (delegation of authority). The goal was to create a strategic reorientation with sustained competitive advantage. This, however, was not an easy target. IBM faced some serious gaps in procurement performance. The procurement organization was fragmented, end-users were dissatisfied with procurement performance and there was a lot of 'maverick buying' (buying without formal approval) going on. People working within procurement lacked real sourcing expertise and mainly had an operational focus. Processes were inconsistent, paper intensive and slow. For example, it took 30 days to process an order and about 6–12 days to process a contract.

It was IBM's strategy to move from a short-term to a strategic focus, which would drive long-term sustained results. To achieve and sustain procurement effectiveness, it invested in four major areas: strategy and governance, processes, technology, and people and organization. Also, IBM established a set of procurement strategic imperatives that have remained remarkably consistent over the years:

1. Perpetually drive quality improvements from suppliers.
2. Continually delivery lowest cost and greatest competitive advantage.
3. Establish premier supplier relationships that give IBM access to the latest technology, supply continuity and speed to market.
4. Grow e-procurement leadership.
5. Continually improve client perception of our value through increased influence and customer service.
6. Attract, motivate and retain the best talent within procurement.

IBM adopted a new leadership model to drive the transformation. The CFO established a global procurement office headed by a chief procurement officer (CPO) to create an organization with executive standing. The CPO was given sole responsibility, by the board of directors, for procurement. The global procurement organization consists of the global procurement staff, the global procurement services group (e.g. industry intelligence, market analysis, logistics support), the procurement executives and the procurement engineering group (e.g. early supplier involvement, emerging supplier development, technological quality). In 2002, there were more than 3700 full-time employees working in procurement in more than 70 countries and over 300 procurement resident locations – compared to 3300 employees in 1995. More importantly, the percentage of people within this group that was working on strategic issues had risen from 10% to 75% in this period!

The global commodity councils are at the core of IBM's leadership structure. There are 13 nonproduction councils (e.g. travel, marketing, telecom) and 18 production councils (e.g. LCD, Cables and Connectors, OEM and Contract Manufacturing). The permanent commodity councils perform strategic activities associated with procurement. They have the following responsibilities:

• Develop commodity strategies and implement plans.
• Gather client requirements and demand management data.

- Develop technical roadmaps.
- Provide market intelligence.
- Reduce costs and improve competitive advantage.
- Lead cross-functional evaluation of new suppliers, services and parts.
- Negotiate contracts and manage supplier relationships.
- Communicate contract guidelines to all affected parties.
- Resolve major supplier performance issues.

A critical first step performed by the councils was to rationalize IBM's global supply base. They also implemented a standardized contracting model across the enterprise to simplify the process. From a situation in which it took six months or longer to implement a 40+-page contract, it takes 30 days or less to implement the six-page standard master contract today.

In order to measure procurement's contribution to the corporation, IBM implemented a Procurement Competitive Advantage (PCA) measure. PCA measures the difference in actual price change for IBM versus industry price changes and it shows IBM's buying performance relative to the marketplace. For example, a 15% IBM price reduction in a given commodity versus an industry price reduction of 10% would yield a positive 5% PCA measurement. IBM uses multiple measures along with market intelligence to test the effectiveness of its buying.

Apart from the issues discussed so far, IBM invested heavily in its people to ensure that they have the necessary skills to implement the procurement strategy. A well-structured set of courses was designed for people in procurement:

- Basic core courses for the essential procurement skills.
- Intermediate courses for more specific knowledge like strategic outsourcing.
- Advanced courses in, among other things, strategic cost management, strategic supplier relationship management and strategy development.

In order to deliver these courses efficiently to a global procurement population, IBM uses e-learning techniques.

IBM went through multiple phases while transforming its procurement practices.

Phase 1 – Foundation (1994–95)

- IBM leverage, delegation decision, council structure, enforcement.
- Strategic sourcing, single management system.
- Skills, learning, roles, responsibilities, leadership, communications.
- Data simplification, procurement-to-payment linkage.

Phase 2 – Transforming the enterprise (1996–97)

- Link to development and employees, competitiveness measures, joint scorecard.
- Common processes.

- One procurement team, new roles: influence bid teams.
- Transaction engine, global workspace, global data management.

Phase 3 – E-business (1998–2002)

- Quick wins, fix problems, create value, build for future.
- Supplier readiness, supplier capability, hands-free process, eliminate paper.
- E-care, e-learning.
- E-procurement, web exploitation, point solutions.

Phase 4 – On demand (2003–?)

- On-demand global supply chain, vertical to horizontal, industry SCM (supply chain management) leadership.
- E2E process execution (direct electronic links between the various actors in the supply chain), supply organization, demand conditioning, real-time collaboration.
- One ISC (integrated supply chain) community, broad skills development.
- Inter/intra-enterprise integration, broader/deeper e-procurement exploitation, seamless data management.

The results of the transformation have been tangible and allow IBM to continue investing in procurement (see Table 1.1).

IBM is widely recognized for its efforts in transforming procurement. It was the 1999 winner of the *Purchasing* magazine Medal of Professional Excellence[9] and the MIT Sloan School award for Transformation of Procurement and Payables. Also, a large number of companies (more than 50 a year) come to visit IBM to benchmark procurement practices. IBM is now regarded as a world-class standard in sourcing.

IBM learned some valuable lessons that might be worthwhile to look at. When transforming procurement one should never underestimate the importance of:

- Managing organizational change.
- Inducing the right behaviour.

TABLE 1.1   Results of the sourcing transformation at IBM

	1990s	2004
Sourcing expertise in place	<10%	100%
Electronic catalogues	0	280
Maverick buying	>35%	<0.5%
End-user satisfaction	40%	82%
Acceptable business controls	55%	95%
E-enabled suppliers	<500	33,000
Electronic purchases	<20%	95%
Purchase order cycle time	30 days	<1 day

- Making significant investments.
- Taking some risks.
- Leadership.
- Innovating constantly.
- Enlisting corporate support.
- Involving all stakeholders.
- Getting help.

Many of these topics and other issues in developing sourcing as an organizational capability will return in the following chapters.

1.3   Contents of the book

In this book, we explore the topic of strategic change in sourcing. The basic notion is that it is quite commonly known what potentials and options there are to improve the contributions of the competitiveness of the organization – but *how* can it be done? Many sourcing executives sigh: 'We all know what should be done, but how can we make it happen?' It is our ambition that this book gives at least a useful overview of the potential areas and instruments of change, combined with some practical illustrations and recommendations. In the end, however, it is obviously individual organizations and managers that 'make it happen'.

The book is divided into three main parts: Part I – Introduction, Part II – Areas and Instruments of Change, and Part III – Illustrations (see Figure 1.3). In Part I, the following chapter, Exploring Change Issues in Strategic Sourcing, expands on the introduction in the current chapter. Among other things, it discusses a model of various maturity stages in sourcing, which will return in following chapters. Chapter 3, the final chapter of the Introduction part, focuses on a number of general aspects of strategic change. Henrik Agndal, Björn Axelsson and Leif Melin provide an overview of the most important issues in the field and introduce us to the present thinking in the area of strategic change and its management. They also provide some implications of their overview for strategic change in purchasing.

In Part II of the book, we turn to specific areas and instruments of change within sourcing. Chapter 4 deals with supplier relations and supplier networks, and the creation of change within those. Anna Dubois and Finn Wynstra discuss issues like transactional vs relational buying, variety in supplier relations, different patterns in changing supplier relations and the role of sourcing as an interface between internal and external parties. In Chapter 5, Frank Rozemeijer and Finn Wynstra take changes in organizational design and organizing processes as their point of departure. In Chapter 6, the creation of change through changes in leadership, culture and values is discussed by Ethel Brundin, Leif Melin and Björn Axelsson. This chapter has a very strong focus on the human resources side of change management.

Chapter 7, by Björn Axelsson, Pieter Bouwmans, Frank Rozemeijer and Finn Wynstra, deals with another aspect of human resources: management and improvement of knowledge, skills and capabilities. In Chapter 8, Jens Hultman and Björn Axelsson discuss strategic change originating from the exploitation of (new) information

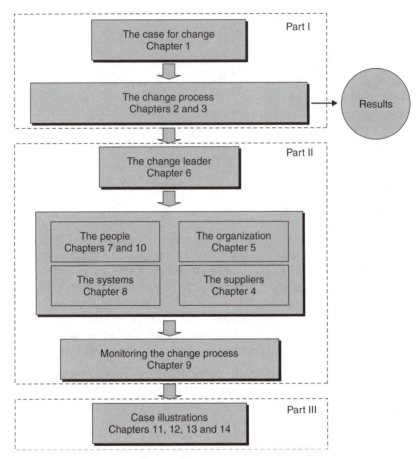

FIGURE 1.3 Overview of the book.

and communications technology. Chapter 9 looks at performance measurement and management accounting as enablers of change within sourcing. Björn Axelsson, Finn Wynstra and Frank Rozemeijer discuss various concepts and tools and their possible effects. Finally, Chapter 10 concludes Part II with a discussion of the role of individuals in strategic change processes, in particular related to sourcing. Sicco Santema, Marc Reunis and Frank Rozemeijer deal with issues such as how job characteristics and individual roles may be affected by various changes within sourcing, and the attitudes of individuals towards change.

Part III comprises a number of illustrations of specific change or transformation efforts, mainly from different worldwide-operating European companies. In Chapter 11, Arjan van Weele surveys several experiences of change processes in the Dutch purchasing community, specifically in relation to centralization vs decentralization efforts. In Chapter 12, Björn Axelsson describes a rather ambitious case study of the construction company NCC, in which the change agents have combined several of the areas and creators of change discussed in the previous chapters. In Chapter 13, Fraser Johnson and Mike Leenders analyse the role of purchasing in a dramatic corporate turnaround at Thomson. Chapter 14, finally, looks at one of the most widespread 'geographical' trends in sourcing nowadays: sourcing in China, in particular the experience of Ericsson. Tony Fang and Björn Axelsson look at the patterns, the challenges that buying firms are facing, and the ways to meet those challenges.

Last, in Chapter 15, Björn Axelsson, Frank Rozemeijer and Finn Wynstra provide a synthesis of the entire book and a discussion of what is possibly ahead.

Notes and references

[1] Axelsson, B. and Wynstra, F. (2002) *Buying Business Services*, John Wiley & Sons Ltd: Chichester. Van Weele, A.J. (2005) *Purchasing and Supply Chain Management: Analysis, Strategy, Planning and Practice*, 4th edn, Thomson Learning: London. A more detailed description of the evolution of purchasing and supply (chain) management, albeit from primarily a North American point of view, is given by Monczka, R., Trent, R. and Handfield, R. (2005) *Purchasing and Supply Chain Management*, 3rd edn, South-Western/Thomson Learning: Cincinnati, OH, Chapter 1.

[2] We primarily refer to development in regions like the EU and North America.

[3] Axelsson and Wynstra (2002) *opere citato*, Chapter 1.

[4] Offshoring and its effects on the economy was one of the central issues in the 2004 US presidential elections. See also the book by Buchholz, T.G. (2004) *Bringing the Jobs Home: How the Left Created the Outsourcing Crisis – And How We Can Fix It*, Penguin: Harmondsworth.

[5] Andriesse, F. (2004) 'Het jaar van de superinkoper', *Tijdschrift voor Inkoop en Logistiek*, January–February.

[6] See also Van Weele (2005) *opere citato*, Chapter 1. Van Weele defines sourcing to include processes like supplier selection and contracting, but to exclude the prior step of specification setting. We, however, include this step also in sourcing.

[7] See Monczka, R., Trent, R. and Handfield, R. (2002) *Purchasing and Supply Chain Management*, 2nd edn, South-Western/Thomson Learning: Cincinnati, OH, p. 11.

[8] The IBM case is based on the following presentations: Sharman, J.R. (2003) 'Best practices: Strategic transformation at IBM', http://learningcenter.ariba.com/p_resource.cfm?INIT_ID=11; Schaefer, W.S. (2003) 'Mining for gold: Turning global business intelligence into value for your enterprise', www.napm.org/Conferences/OnlineDailySupply1101.cfm.

[9] Other recent winners include Honda of America (1995), Sun Microsystems (1996), AlliedSignal (1997) (now Honeywell), American Airlines (1998), Harley Davidson (2000), John Deere (2001), Lucent Technologies (2002), Cessna Aircraft (2003) and HP (2004) (see a.o. www.purchasing.com and *Purchasing* magazine's *The Book of Winners*, 2nd edn, Cahners: Newton, MA).

Chapter 2

EXPLORING CHANGE ISSUES
IN STRATEGIC SOURCING

Björn Axelsson, Frank Rozemeijer and Finn Wynstra

This chapter serves two purposes. The first is to position the role of sourcing in the organization and thereby provide an overview of the development of this specific function. The idea is to give an orientation of the potential contribution of sourcing (or purchasing and supply management) to the firm. In doing so, the chapter discusses what are today considered to be good sourcing practices and how this understanding has come about. The second purpose of this chapter is to make the rationale for the need for strategic change in sourcing – and for the need to study and write a book on this phenomenon.

2.1 Definitions of sourcing

As already briefly described in Chapter 1, various definitions of sourcing have been used over the years. In earlier literature, sourcing – during that time most often referred to as purchasing or buying – has often been interpreted in a narrow and operational way. This has led to a strong orientation on the position of the buyer and a narrow understanding of the organizational issues pertaining to the solution and organization of purchasing tasks. One early definition, for example, refers to sourcing as 'buying materials of the right quality, in the right quantity, at the right time, at the right price, from the right source'.[1] However, following the trends of the last two decades, the definition of purchasing has broadened considerably to a more strategic understanding of the underlying processes, leading to definitions such as 'managing the external resources of the firm'.[2] Others even describe sourcing as broadly as 'a company's behaviour in relation to its suppliers'.[3]

Our earlier definition, 'managing the external resources of the firm, aimed at acquiring inputs at the most favourable conditions', is the one fitting best with the overall scope of this book. This definition focuses on the strategic aspects of resource acquisition and generation, especially when 'the most favourable conditions' is read to include both short-term and long-term aspects.

Another very pragmatic but in most situations very suitable definition, which also fits well with the contents of this book, is 'sourcing involves all activities that lead to an incoming invoice'. Many goods and services are bought without much involvement from sourcing specialists, yet those acts still result in incoming invoices. This brings us to the distinction between the sourcing function (or process) and the sourcing department.

Most organizations do have specialized sourcing departments, even though their role and their organization can differ greatly. Sometimes the departments have a strong and strategic role, maybe manifested by the sourcing manager being a member of the company's top management team and/or involved in all important supply issues. In other cases the role of the sourcing department and the sourcing professionals is limited and many of the strategic issues are taken care of by other specialists such as engineering, marketing, materials management, general management and so on. This means that other professionals in the organization act as 'part-time buyers'. Nevertheless, the *sourcing function* is being performed. In the remainder of this chapter the reference is to the sourcing function at large, thus including the 'part-time buyers'.

2.2   The contributions, objectives and roles of sourcing

The (potential) contributions, objectives and roles of sourcing for the organization can be discussed in various ways. The three main objectives for sourcing to contribute to an organization's competitive position are:

- Cost optimization (e.g. lower purchase price, transaction cost and overhead costs etc.).
- Asset utilization (e.g. outsourcing, inventory management etc.).
- Value creation (e.g. new products/process development, quality improvement etc.).

Arguably, sourcing (as 'purchasing') has traditionally been focused on cost optimization, and asset utilization has mainly been highlighted through the outsourcing/offshoring trend. Value creation is, for most organizations, the newest area in terms of sourcing strategy development, which includes not only product innovation but also the wider process of business development.

A more detailed list of sourcing contributions to competitive advantage would include[4]:

- Reduction of direct material cost (price savings).
- Reduction of net capital employed (reducing inventory).
- Reduction of quality costs.
- Product standardization.
- Contribution to product design and innovation.
- Increasing flexibility.
- Fostering purchasing synergy.

To demonstrate the ultimate 'bottom-line' contribution of sourcing practices, many organizations use the so-called DuPont chart. Specifically, the DuPont analysis illustrates the impact on return on investment or return on net assets (ROI, RONA) of a reduction in purchasing expenditure – i.e. material costs – and of a reduction in stocks or capital investment – i.e. working capital (see Figure 2.1). Expenditure may be reduced by decisions and actions such as negotiation tactics, volume bundling, standardization of products and so on, while stocks and capital investment (at least for the customer) may for example be reduced by JIT arrangements, vendor-managed inventory schemes and so on.

What this specific illustration demonstrates is that for a company with a purchasing ratio of 60% in relation to sales, an existing profit margin of 2% and fixed capital of 20, a reduction in purchasing expenditures of just over 3% will increase profit margin by the same amount, resulting in an increase in ROI of 15 percentage points (250%). In other words, the increase in ROI (and profit margin) is five times as large as the reduction in purchasing expenditure – which is due to the fact that, in the existing situation, a) purchasing expenditure relative to total cost is high

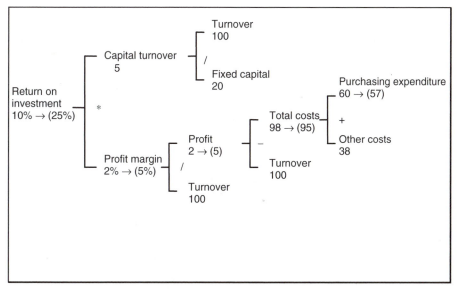

FIGURE 2.1   DuPont chart (all figures in absolute numbers, except where stated differently).

(over 60%) and b) the existing profit margin is low (2%). Similar calculations could demonstrate the effect on ROI of, say, a 5% reduction of working capital through outsourcing of production activities and the assets involved.

Purchasing decisions may, ultimately, also affect other costs. However, if there are savings in time spent, for example on invoicing processes, those savings could be attached a monetary value only when the freed time could be utilized for other value-creating processes or be deducted from the accounts payable. A similar argument applies to reductions in (working) capital investments.

More recently, discussions have indeed also focused on sourcing's possible contribution to 'top-line' as opposed to 'bottom-line' growth. In other words, sourcing may be able to contribute to revenue increases through growing market shares or raising sales prices (for final products), for example by buying superior quality inputs, or through building in 'branded ingredients' into the final product ('Intel inside'). In line with this argument, some have also proposed accounting concepts like total *value* of ownership – as opposed to 'just' looking at total *cost* of ownership.[5]

Besides (financial and non-financial) contributions of sourcing, others have defined more general objectives for the sourcing process[6]:

- To support operational requirements (providing an uninterrupted flow of high-quality goods and services that internal customers require).
- To manage the purchasing process efficiently and effectively.
- To manage the supply base (select, develop and maintain sources of supply).
- To develop strong relationships with other functional groups.
- To support organizational goals and objectives (aligning sourcing and corporate goals).
- To develop integrated purchasing strategies that support organizational strategies.

We see these objectives primarily as a set of tasks and processes that need to be organized and executed within the overall sourcing process. In that respect, most of these tasks and processes will also be dealt with in the remainder of this book. The objective of efficient process management, for example, is one of the main topics in Chapter 8, dealing with ICT implementation and usage. Supply base management is largely dealt with in Chapter 4, on supplier relations, while the topic of cross-functional relationships is discussed, among other things, in Chapter 5 on organization and organizing.

On the basis of this list, one can also recognize particular shifts in emphasis on the respective objectives. Whereas the support of operational requirements ('serve the factory') has traditionally been the main focus of purchasing and supply management, the alignment of sourcing and corporate goals and strategies has been placed at central stage in more recent years. Section 2.3 discusses these shifts in objectives and priorities in more detail. Before doing so, however, we conclude this section with a brief overview of the possible *roles* of sourcing, which may serve as an overall frame of reference for positioning and analysing its changing objectives and characteristics.

Three roles of sourcing

On a general level, sourcing can be argued to perform three roles within each organization: a rationalization role, a development role and a structure role.[7]

The *rationalization* role entails the possibilities for the purchasing function to contribute to the company's competitive advantage through acting towards keeping total costs down in production, stocks, prices of raw materials and so on. This role includes three main tasks:

- Minimizing the *direct costs* (price in relation to volume, freight, insurance etc.) of buying goods and services.
- Minimizing the *indirect costs* when purchasing a certain functionality; this could include administrative aspects such as handling invoices and costs of keeping and maintaining a supply base. It also relates to quality costs: costs of quality control and consequences of poor quality and so on.
- Keeping the *internal production costs* down by reducing the resource consumption and/or increasing the value creation.

It is obvious that the rationalization role is quite broad and that a single organization cannot handle all these measures at the same time and to the same extent. Prioritizing of what should be done is generally a matter of carefully considering the company's specific situation in terms of needs and possibilities.

The sourcing function's *development* role is about systematically matching the company's development or innovation process with those of individual suppliers and the overall supplier network.[8] Here we propose to divide the role into four main tasks[9]:

- Building, accessing and maintaining a *resource structure* of external suppliers.
- Making sure that existing *technological capabilities* of suppliers are leveraged in the internal innovation process.
- Mobilizing suppliers to *develop particular technologies, processes and products* that the buying organization needs and motivating suppliers to be involved in the buyer's innovation processes.
- Supporting *development projects in collaboration with suppliers*, together with other internal functions.

These actions can be very valuable: the kind of development resources discussed here are often very expensive. The development role is relatively complex. It is about how the supplier's development resources can best be used and integrated internally in its own operations. Furthermore, this role's tasks can easily be extended to 'business development'. In that case, the purchasing function, with or without purchasing specialists, becomes an important part of the company's development of new products, production methods, ways of working, markets and business concepts – which is again related to 'top-line' growth.

The *structure* role, finally, concerns the efforts of the sourcing function to strike an optimal balance in term of dependence vs independence on suppliers. On the one hand, the organization should not end up in situations of dependence that are difficult to handle and possibly detrimental to its position as the buying organization. On the other hand, creating situations where a buying organization is dependent on a particular supplier may be necessary in order to create unique values (products, processes, procedures etc.) in the relations with suppliers. This structure role can be described in terms of three main responsibilities:

- Activities for *identifying and monitoring developments* in supplier structures.
- Measures for *influencing the level of standardization* of supplier offerings.
- Activities related to increasing, maintaining or reducing the *number of potential suppliers*.

The three roles are complementary to each other and partially overlapping. The rationalization role focuses on matching the organization with suppliers in such a way that production and indirect costs are minimized, and the development role focuses on matching too, but now with the purpose of achieving synergetic effects in technological development. The structure role sets some conditions – restrictions – on the solutions that the other two roles may come up with. The rationalization role can, for example, be favoured in the short run by a strategy that creates an unfavourable supplier structure in the long run. Considering costs, for example, it can be beneficial to concentrate all purchases of a particular item at one supplier. When doing so, the firm should be aware that it does not become too dependent on that supplier, otherwise purchasing has neglected its structure role.

Similarly, there are overlaps between the development role and the structure role. Developing a new component in close cooperation with one particular supplier, for example, could lead to a *de facto* monopoly situation for that supplier, which may be undesirable from the point of view of the structure role.

Finally, there are potential overlaps or conflicts between the rationalization and the development role too. For instance, an important element of the development role is that purchasing participates in the design phase of new product development projects, but by choosing a design, construction methods and, consequently, components and suppliers, the rationalization role can also be affected in an important way. Suppliers that are excellent partners for technological collaboration may be less suitable as a long-term source of supply, for example because of unfavourable cost structures.

There are also issues where all three roles are overlapping. This can be seen when a firm starts to adjust the design of its final product, together with some of its suppliers, so that it can use some standard, 'catalogue' fixtures instead of customized ones, with the aim of saving assembly and material costs and increasing the number of potential suppliers. The weight of the different roles, and the extent to which there are potential conflicts between them, is contingent on the specific characteristics and objectives of the sourcing strategy and the overall competitive strategy of the organization at hand.

Having identified and discussed these three roles of purchasing and supply management, the next section returns to our earlier exploration of the changing views on purchasing and supply over time, and relates this to the different roles and tasks of sourcing in more detail.

2.3   Degrees of sourcing maturity

Individual business units or corporations – or even entire industries – will be characterized by a certain mixture of sourcing roles, or a dominance of particular objectives, at any given point in time. Often, such characterizations or *orientations* have been referred to as stages or phases, reflecting the notion that they follow a certain logical or even chronological sequence.

Against this background, there have been several attempts to classify these orientations, often in terms of different degrees of maturity. Such maturity models are helpful not only in terms of classifying organizations in terms of their current position, but are especially relevant for determining possible directions for strategic change. How could a firm develop from stage 1 to 2, or from stage 4 to 5? What measures need to be taken? What barriers are to be overcome? What potential improvements are to be harvested?

It would be beyond the scope of this book to present and discuss all available 'models' of development phases in purchasing and supply, so we focus on one particular, relatively recent version that also builds on existing models.[10]

The framework we propose distinguishes six levels of sourcing maturity (Figure 2.2.). The lowest level of maturity, or professionalism, is said to be prevalent for the *transactional orientation* phase. This is recognized in a very passive or reactive purchasing operation where the purchasing professionals, in principle, merely 'administer' the purchasing tasks. Phase 2, *commercial orientation*, regards a somewhat more developed commercial approach with regular requests for tender, comparisons of various bids from suppliers and negotiations, as well as operating with pre-qualified suppliers. This is, by the way, a purchasing

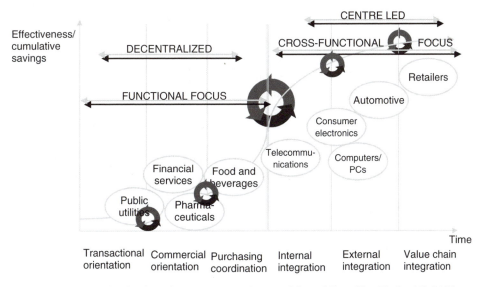

FIGURE 2.2   Six levels of purchasing maturity. Source: Adapted from: Van Weele, A.J. (2005) *Purchasing and Supply Chain Management*, 4th edn, Thomson Learning: London, p. 94.

approach that naturally follows from applications of practices in line with laws on public procurement. Phase 3, *purchasing coordination*, emphasizes a work mode where the buying company has strong control over purchased volumes, the number of suppliers and purchased items. This enables it to carry out more powerful and coordinated actions – across factories, business units and divisions (where applicable).

Common to all of these three levels is a functional approach where the purchasing department acts – more or less – on its own, while levels 2 and 3 additionally call for increased coordination or even centralization of purchasing operations.

Phase 4, *internal integration*, implies that the organization handles purchases and suppliers in a more process-oriented way, utilizing cross-functional teams with the relevant competencies and expertise, who naturally take responsibility for important goods and services (functions) bought. A natural prerequisite for such a process orientation are well-functioning and well-communicated systems (e.g. purchasing systems, enterprise resource planning (ERP) systems and management planning systems (MPS)). Furthermore, such organizations utilize not only pre-qualified but also ranked suppliers that are in various ways connected to development and improvement programmes supported by performance-based contracts.

Phase 5, *external integration*, adds one level of professionalism as it introduces synchronization and optimization of supply chains. In doing so, it requires an increased awareness of where in the supply chain the relevant business conditions are determined, and systematic efforts to coordinate suppliers on various levels upstream into a (proposed) supply chain. For this to function, there is a need for an active utilization of ICT, for example (web-based) EDI systems and collaborative planning, forecasting and replenishment (CPFR) systems. There is also a need for information to be coordinated across several levels in supply nets and for the organization to be able to apply various models to decide on the most suitable way of operating the supply chain in question.

Phase 6, *value chain integration*, which is looked on as the most sophisticated development phase, adds a clear connection to the buying organization's own customers. In other words, sourcing here means doing all of the synchronized purchasing and supply operations from the previous phases *plus* actively contributing to the creation of customer value, for example in the form of superior quality, functionality and availability of final products.[11] In-depth understanding of customer needs and willingness as well as capabilities to satisfy these are the basic requirements for reaching phase 6. This presupposes that sourcing, in addition to the demands of the previous steps, also has a global perspective on suitable suppliers and is sufficiently positioned and equipped to undertake entrepreneurial collaboration with suppliers.

In terms of the organization of the activities, there are some common ingredients for phases 4 to 6. Cross-functional teams and centre-led operations (see Chapter 5) appear to be an important prerequisite. A centre-led function could, but does not necessarily have to, imply the dominance of a centrally placed purchasing unit. What is most important is that every commodity group is coordinated from a single point and that the necessary competence is tied to the sourcing activities.

Models like these should be regarded as basically conceptual, even though they have been utilized as an instrument for diagnosis and can be translated into operational measures, as we will see in Chapters 7 and 9. Common to these models is that they focus on the following aspects as a more advanced, matured and sophisticated way to operate the sourcing function:

- Coordination and synchronization; the company is in command of its purchases. This means, among other things, that it has full control over volumes, suppliers utilized, quality issues and so on.
- Organizing around commodity groups and cross-functional teams that are able to match supplier knowledge about products, technologies involved and industry structure.
- Commodity strategies based on some kind of segmentation model.[12]
- Well-developed processes and routines.
- Competence and capabilities to carry out a continuous learning process and manage internal teams of complementary competencies.
- Solid knowledge, not only about internal user needs but also the needs of the buying company's own customers.

Taken together, a mature and sophisticated working method is very much about developing and applying a *structured* working method. The fundamental idea is that the organization will thereby establish a sustainable, improved foundation for its sourcing operations. Figure 2.3 presents a way to illustrate this.

Often, improvement measures are put into operation in nonsystematic ways. Someone identifies a problem, for example that too high a price is paid for some products. A common reaction is to try for a period of time to reach a better balance. There is nothing wrong with that, but the problem will tend to come back quite soon if no systematic effort has been made to improve some basic processes in relation to the problem identified. The latter could be issues such as how to carry out supplier analyses, how best to integrate a supply chain and so on. Systematic

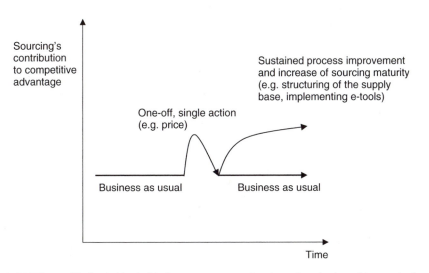

FIGURE 2.3   The basic idea behind a more structured and synchronized working method.

effort is an obvious yet (in a short-term perspective) time-consuming way to reduce and eliminate future problems.

Maturity models such as the one presented in Figure 2.2 have in common that they are good bases for discussion of how advanced a specific purchasing organization is. It should, however, be noted that a specific organization could in some aspects act on level 5 and in others on level 1.

For example, buying of *services* seems, in general, to be an area less exposed to more advanced purchasing practices. One indication of this is that large parts of all services bought are, or at least were until recently, not subject to systematic purchasing practices. Some of the reasons are that the focus has most of all been on dealing with the goods sourced for the manufacturing process. The buying of services such as market research, law services, management consultancy and many others has been looked on as the 'domain' of the specialists closest to the identified needs.

It is also worth noticing that purchasing professionals are not involved in about one third of all services bought.[13] A reasonable interpretation of that is that many organizations have not yet streamlined their purchasing processes to include not only materials bought for production, but also various kinds of services that support other activities. A complementary reason may be that many services are considered so 'special' that purchasing specialists are not expected to be able to make a genuine contribution to the quality of the purchase and the sourcing process.

A critical reader of this sourcing maturity model could also question why one phase should be considered more advanced and sophisticated than another. A sourcing organization could do a very good job in terms of performance even though it is not operating at the highest possible level of sophistication. It could very well be the case that the more advanced ways of operating demand higher skills and thereby higher salaries among the sourcing staff. They could also require more expensive supporting technologies (ICT hardware and software, for example). Altogether, this could in specific cases (e.g. in small firms) turn out to be too high a price to pay in comparison with the potential improvements.

Still, these models do reflect judgements that are often expressed in today's business practice as well as textbooks when modern vs obsolete work modes are on the agenda. In fact they contribute to constructing a view on bad, good and excellent behaviour – and this model reflects a common understanding of today's good and bad purchasing practices.

Another important note of caution related to maturity models concerns the fact that there is not always a natural growth path from left to right; sometimes organizations may revert or 'fall back' one or several phases. The reasons for that may be external, in the case of economic recession when companies are looking for a 'quick buck'. Some North American car manufacturers reportedly went back to 'old-fashioned' sourcing behaviour with an extreme focus on price only, in the early 2000s when they were faced with heavy price competition in their customer markets. The reasons may also be internal, for example when a new purchasing director arrives. The point here is that there may be particular instances when external or internal factors require a particular, possibly 'less mature' orientation to bring sourcing strategy in line with overall competitive strategy. In addition, for some organizations, sourcing may just not be important enough and the organization as such not skilful enough to make it worth the cost of the change. The overall challenge is to try to reach the optimal situation between potential contributions and the costs of being able to exploit those.

Having discussed the different phases of thinking about and practising purchasing and supply management, and the broad paths of strategic change related to that, the following section focuses on what makes strategic change in sourcing so special, particularly in relation to the possible barriers to change.

2.4   Special features and barriers related to strategic change in sourcing

In our view, there are three features that provide somewhat special and challenging conditions for strategic change in purchasing and supply management. The first is the traditional, 'low-status' history of the function. The second emanates from the role of the buyer, who often gets and takes a position as 'controller' or 'policeman'. The third is the problem of measuring and demonstrating the results from purchasing and supply management.

It often happened that, in the early days, operational people from production moved into the firm's clerical units to apply their understanding of production-related issues and learn and apply some commercial practices. They were placed in a purchasing unit. Those professionals performed their job in isolation – at best in some cooperation with other purchasing specialists. This was in the era of 'buying', in terms of our earlier descriptions. Purchasing in manufacturing industries was for decades considered a low-status job. One comment reflecting this situation is the following quote from an IBM manager[14]:

> In the past when you could do nothing else at IBM we made you a buyer. When you couldn't design anything, when you couldn't build anything, when you couldn't carry anything, when you couldn't deliver anything – we put you into the purchasing organization.

Consider also the illustration in Figure 2.4, of a job test for teenagers, from a Swedish girls' magazine in the early 1990s.

At the same time, it should be recognized that people in sourcing, especially in retail firms, have always had a strong position in their organizations. In those industries, sourcing has always been acknowledged as a critical function. A typical retail firm has a purchasing ratio of close to 90%, as it normally does not add a large amount of value to the products it buys. Its value creation resides in the assortment of products being offered and the service attached to them.

With the increased purchasing ratios, improved status has also followed in other industries. This development, however, has in most cases been very gradual or slow. The low-status situation has made skilled people reluctant to take up purchasing assignments, which in itself has reinforced the negative image. Research has shown that traditionally, on average, purchasing employees of a certain

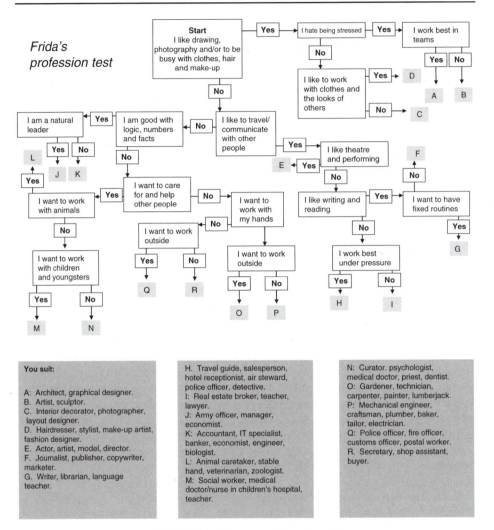

Frida's profession test

FIGURE 2.4 Who wants to be a buyer?

hierarchical position earned less than their counterparts in other functions, such as marketing. Even though this, to a large extent, is now history, and wage differences seem to be narrowing substantially in this respect, quite a lot of the image surrounding purchasing and supply management still seems to be affected by it.

The controlling role of purchasing emanates from the fact that the purchaser is in charge of the company wallet and will be held accountable for the expenditure. This means that he or she will have a strong focus on possibilities to save, or 'not to spend'. Every good new idea will have to be considered against the cost aspects. This somewhat negative role, in combination with the status aspect, has created certain perceptions of the competencies (e.g. educational level, international experience, project management skills etc.) of purchasing professionals as lagging behind other functions. This is probably also one reason for the special difficulty in creating strategic change in purchasing and supply management.

The third aspect is the difficulty of measurement. Prices of products bought are easy to measure and are being measured. But many other aspects of purchasing operations are difficult to measure. One such aspect is, for example, the avoidance of problems thanks to well-performed processes and procedures and/or skilful choices of suppliers. It is difficult to demonstrate the avoidance of costs, based on the avoidance or early elimination of upcoming problems. The ease of measuring prices becomes a liability in itself. It could very well be that low prices on the products bought create high costs in the processes that follow (quality control, recoveries etc). However, the things that can be measured more simply will prohibit investments in more difficult to measure, long-term improvements. Chapter 9 will discuss these issues in more detail.

Starting from these three special aspects of creating strategic change in relation to sourcing, one could identify four possible areas in which barriers to change could appear: within the sourcing department, in relation to other functional units inside the company, in relation to individual suppliers, and in relation to the overall supply market or network.[15] At this point we will be providing some basic considerations and illustrations; subsequent chapters will deal with these different barriers in greater detail.

Barriers within the sourcing department

One obstacle can be an initially unsuitable organizational design. The way of organizing a specialist department influences what work processes can be achieved and in what direction the unit might need to change. Other obstacles include processes and procedures, for example the budgeting system that also forces the sourcing unit into specific formats. Reporting systems and specific measures of performance, like price developments on products bought, may influence the work method in a certain direction that effectively can support as well as oppose a certain strategic focus. Other obstacles can be the current leadership; that is, an actual situation with a leader (or leaders) less suitable for the tasks at hand, or the occurrence of contradicting goals between actors within sourcing (for example between a central unit and an operational unit). Further obstacles can be the employees' competencies and attitudes. There could thus be many possible obstacles to change already inside the sourcing department as such.

Barriers in relation to other departments in the company

The type of obstacles that might exist within this category are usually a question of 'distance' to other units. They can be information and attitude distances, for example the often testified conflict in manufacturing companies between the sourcing department and the product development department. The product engineers often want to do the purchasing themselves and do not see any point in involving sourcing specialists. Likewise, there is often a conflict between purchasing and production. The sourcing specialists see their roles in a wider perspective than merely well-functioning production activities, whereas the production managers tend to consider sourcing as a buying function for the production process, no more and no less.

There are also similar conflicts in relation to senior management and the responsible financial controllers. The controller often wants to be able to measure the results of sourcing efforts. However, only certain tasks are easily measured. The risk is that the controller thus influences the purchaser to work with these kinds of tasks, when perhaps they actually should pay more attention to other matters.

This kind of obstacle can be the result of internal competition, but also of the sourcing managers' lack of experience when it comes to designing and carrying out the new tasks. A lack of competence creates bad experiences and thus leads to negative opinions and expectations, which creates 'negative spirals'.

Chapters 5, 11, 12 and 13 will deal both with barriers within the purchasing and supply department and with barriers in relations with other departments.

Barriers in relation to suppliers

To go from one work method to another between customer and supplier does in most cases require adjustments from both (or several) parties. If the supplier is to be able to give a different offer, for example a more complex problem solution, it takes another kind of collaboration with the customer. It may become a high-involvement relationship and include more people within the relationship, closer contacts, another content to the dialogue, another competence profile for the employees that are in contact with the customer, and so on.

As a consequence, the supplier can perceive the costs of change as much too high. It might also be that the supplier's technical, organizational and human resources do not fit with the method that the customer wishes to realize in the strategy development process. The insecurity about the effects of a change can be great; a different content in the relationship is hard to measure and value. The experiences that the parties have of each other from previous transactions can also have a great impact. If, for instance, a changed work method is based on the condition that the customer can provide accurate forecasts, and this has previously functioned badly, then there will be an obstacle to carry through the changes that the customer asks for. Furthermore, in this kind of question parties can have contradicting interests. One example can be when it comes to accepting an increased dependence on a certain customer or not.

Obstacles in relation to the overall supply network

If the form of collaboration with a certain supplier is changed in a substantial way, it may mean that increased energy and increased resources are invested in this particular collaboration. This can result in spreading effects to other (related) relations. Then, at least two things can happen: other suppliers can react negatively if they think that this entails that they themselves will receive a lower priority in the future. Alternatively, they may react positively if they think that the customer, through the 'investment', might learn things that later will benefit them as well.

The surrounding network or market system can have different structures and characteristics. The more 'network-oriented' a relation is, the more imbedded in a context of other connected relations it can be presumed to be. This means that a change can often come to influence more than one or two relations. To change existing relations can thus mean that many actors, activity patterns and resource constellations might need to be developed and adjusted to a new situation. This can imply very great obstacles to strategy development.

These are some of the special barriers to change, but obviously there are also several advantages. Among others, it could be argued that the function has such a multidimensional or cross-functional impact that there are plenty of opportunities and possibilities to demonstrate its importance.

2.5   Conclusion: The challenges for the purchasing and supply function

Strategic sourcing managers should be aware of the objectives and roles of their function and – preferably – also skilled in implementing change. The increasing degree of professionalism in the field is thus also reflected in the skills demanded from people. Today we see a much more systematic approach to analysing the competencies needed among purchasing staff, as discussed in more detail in Chapter 7. For example, it is increasingly common to recruit someone from the industry that they will buy from. Individual career plans are also becoming more common, as well as improvement programmes both for the function as such and for each individual (competence profiles, adapted capabilities in the teamed buying centre etc.). In general, there seems to be a strong awareness of the need for adequate and matching competencies on both sides of the business transaction.

The above discussion has provided several hints on what could be improved and what are considered 'good' or more sophisticated approaches to the present challenges. Obviously, many of the ultimate objectives can be described in terms of increased efficiency and effectiveness. Efficiency and effectiveness, however, can be very difficult to define in a specific case. In principle, it can be stated that efficiency demands that two important conditions must be met. The first condition is that the resources invested in the sourcing function shall (at least) generate the same value (positive amount) as they cost to carry out (negative amount). This condition can be expressed with a mathematical formula in this way:

$$\frac{(\Delta \ value_i)}{(\Delta \ cost_i)} > 1$$

This is the same as saying that the marginal revenue – that is, the revenue (value) of taking improvement measures within sourcing – shall be at a minimum as high as the marginal cost – that is, the cost of taking the measures. This is the main condition.

The second condition is useable in cases where the company has several interesting areas where action is needed to be decided on at the same time as the resources are limited. In this case, the condition is formulated as that the measure within sourcing must generate at least as much value as an alternative measure:

$$\frac{(\Delta \ value_i)}{(\Delta \ cost_i)} > \frac{(\Delta \ value_a)}{(\Delta \ cost_a)}$$

These two conditions can be seen as a foundation for a discussion about what returns the investments in sourcing might yield. This is, to use a technical term, the condition for an assessment of 'return on investment in sourcing or 'sourcing ROI'. Practically, it is often relatively easy to discuss what the investments within sourcing might cost (consultant fees, increased wages, ICT investments etc.). The problems in assessing the positive values are substantially more complex.

The challenge for purchasing and supply management is to be able to exploit the full potential of the function. In many cases it is quite obvious what measures would affect the operations of the firm positively. Still, it can be very difficult to make this happen. The challenge is, thus, not only to investigate and realize what should be done in the short-term and long-term perspective, but also how it could happen.

The rest of this book is very much concerned with the 'how' question. To a great extent, this 'how' question is mirrored in our above discussion of the barriers to change. Basically, we argue that strategic change is a complex venture that calls for several coordinated measures, even though the core of the initiative could rest on a specific measure. The development of sourcing can thus be initiated in different ways. The company can, for example:

- Start by changing the organization and management systems, e.g. start measuring other aspects than have been measured earlier or work towards clarifying important values for the future.
- Start by testing a new work method in a supplier relationship and then, if it is functioning adequately, spread the experiences. Another alternative of a similar kind can be to change the purchasing unit's composition, which might entail changes in the work process.
- The process can also be initiated with an educational or some other kind of competence development project, e.g. a work rotation programme.

There are consequently many possible ways, but they are not all equally fruitful in all situations. This is again a question of the context in which the change is initiated and how it is executed. The coming chapters will go into these various areas and methods of change in more detail, and discuss them in relation to various contexts. The chapters in Part III, Illustrations, should provide some particularly interesting discussions in this respect.

Notes and references

[1] Heinritz, S.F., Farrell, P.V. and Smith, C.L. (1986) *Purchasing: Principles and Applications*, Prentice Hall: Englewood Cliffs, NJ, p. 9.
[2] Dobler, D.W. and Burt, D.N. (1996) *Purchasing and Materials Management: Text and Cases*, McGraw Hill: New York; Van Weele, A.J. (2005) *Purchasing and Supply Chain Management – Analysis, Strategy, Planning and Practice*, 4th edn, Thomson Learning: London.
[3] Gadde, L.-E. and Håkansson, H. (1993) *Professional Purchasing*, Routledge: London, p. 13.
[4] Van Weele (2005) *opere citato*, Chapter 1.
[5] Wouters, M.J.F., Anderson, J.C. and Wynstra, F. (2005) 'The adoption of total cost of ownership for sourcing decisions – A structural equations analysis', *Accounting, Organizations and Society*, Vol. 30, No. 2, pp. 167–91.

6   Monczka, R., Trent, R. and Handfield, R. (2005) *Purchasing and Supply Chain Management*, 3rd edn, South-Western/Thomson Learning: Cincinnati, OH, Chapter 2.

7   Axelsson, B. and Håkansson, H. (1984) *Inköp för konkurrenskraft*, Liber: Malmö. See also Gadde, L.-E. and Håkansson, H. (2001) *Supply Network Strategies*, John Wiley & Sons Ltd: Chichester.

8   Van Echtelt, F.E.A. (2004) *New Product Development: Shifting Suppliers into Gear*, PhD thesis, Eindhoven Centre for Innovation Studies, Eindhoven University of Technology. Wynstra, F. (1998) *Purchasing Involvement in Product Development*, PhD thesis, Eindhoven Centre for Innovation Studies, Eindhoven University of Technology.

9   Axelsson, B. and Laage-Hellman, J. (1991) *Inköp – en ledningsfråga*, Verkstadsindustriernas Förlag: Stockholm.

10   Alternative maturity models or frameworks are presented by Keough, M. (1993) 'Buying your way to the top', *McKinsey Quarterly*, No. 3, pp. 41–62; Reck, R.F. and Long, B.G. (1988) 'Purchasing: A competitive weapon', *Journal of Purchasing and Materials Management*, Fall, pp. 2–8; Cavinato, J.L. (1991) 'Evolving procurement organizations: Logistics implications', *Journal of Business Logistics*, Vol. 13, No. 1, pp. 27–44; Freeman, V.T. and Cavinato, J.L. (1990) 'Fitting purchasing to the strategic firm: Frameworks, processes, and values', *Journal of Purchasing and Materials Management*, Winter, pp. 6–10; Chadwick, T. and Rajagopal, S. (1995) *Strategic Supply Management*, Butterworth Heinemann: Oxford; Monczka, R., Trent, R. and Handfield, R. (2005) *Purchasing and Supply Chain Management*, 3rd edn, South-Western College Publishing: Cincinnati, OH; Kraljic, P. (2002) 'Achieving e-PSCM excellence', Presentation at the NEVI 3rd National E-Procurement Conference.

11   Anderson, J.C. and Narus, J.A. (2003) *Business Market Management: Understanding, Creating, and Delivering Value*, 2nd edn, Prentice Hall: Upper Saddle River, NJ.

12   Frequently the Kraljic model or a version thereof: Kraljic, P. (1983) 'Purchasing must become supply management', *Harvard Business Review*, September–October, pp. 109–17. See also Van Weele (2005), *opere citato*, pp. 148–53; Gelderman, C.J. and Van Weele, A.J. (2002) 'Strategic direction through purchasing portfolio management: A case study', *Journal of Supply Chain Management*, Vol. 38, No. 2, pp. 30–37. Interestingly, the original, widely quoted Kraljic 2 × 2 matrix is not a portfolio model (although he also discusses 3 × 3 matrices regarding supplier vs buyer power positions), but a maturity grid distinguishing four different orientations towards the purchasing function depending on supply market complexity and the function's financial impact on company performance.

13   Fearon, H.E. and Bales, W.A. (1995) *Purchasing of Nontraditional Goods and Services*, Center for Advanced Purchasing Studies (CAPS): Tempe, AZ.

14   Gadde and Håkansson (2001) *opere citato*.

15   Axelsson and Laage-Hellman (1991) *opere citato*.

Chapter 3

UNDERSTANDING STRATEGIC CHANGE

Henrik Agndal, Björn Axelsson and Leif Melin

In order to develop sourcing capabilities and to be able to reap the benefits of potential improvements open to today's organizations, one cannot avoid addressing the process of strategic change. But what do we know about change processes as such? What do we know about contextual forces driving and counteracting change? What do we know about the specifics of change processes related to purchasing and supply management? The purpose of this chapter is therefore to introduce the field of strategic change, and to discuss how the body of knowledge in this field may contribute to the understanding of change in sourcing.

The chapter breaks down into eight parts. First, it addresses the mission and vision concepts and then turns to the issue of what strategy really is. Then, strategic change is defined and the idea that changes may vary in magnitude is introduced. Further, there are organizational and environmental influences on change that need to be understood and we continue by discussing the role of the individual in bringing about change. Having addressed change from a number of perspectives, the chapter then raises the issue of how change can be implemented (routes to change). Finally, we look at the possible role of consultants in change processes and implications for change in sourcing. This means that the chapter provides an overview of the body of knowledge of strategic change as presented in the literature, but also comments on strategic change from a purchasing point of view.

3.1   Mission and vision

A company's mission is basically its reason for existing. Generating money for its shareholders could be an important ingredient in a mission, but in a conceptual discussion this can be seen as more of a restriction for a firm. The mission as expressed in a mission statement outlines what the company considers its aims and role. For example, 'reduce and eliminate pain' could be the mission of a pharmaceutical firm.

Strategic change in purchasing and supply management cannot be put in motion without some reference to the mission of the firm. The intended changes, 'the right thing to do', should be aligned with the firm's mission.

The mission of the firm is strongly connected to goals and strategies. In order to do the right things in the right way, managers set goals, decide on strategies and make plans.[1] The vision expresses a future state. It differs from goals in the sense that goals should be well defined and preferably possible to measure.

Still, the vision should be challenging. If it is too narrow and precise, it ends up being a goal and, as such, acts in a limiting way. Visions should be inspiring and allow for several interpretations, but still point in a certain direction. Thereby, the vision helps to free energy and generates commitment and learning. The furniture retail firm Ikea has a vision: 'To create a better everyday life for many people'. This is a job that is never finished and always challenging, but at the same time gives direction.[2]

Thus, before entering into change processes in purchasing, it is advisable to recapitulate the mission and vision of the firm to make sure that the new ideas are in line with these overarching aspects of the firm's development. Basically there should be a clear connection between the vision (the desirable future orientation), the mission (what needs the company fulfils), the corporate strategy, the purchasing strategy and operative purchasing activities. The connection implies that all strategic purchasing activities should support the realization of the vision. Before looking at strategic change in a sourcing context, though, we need to look more closely at the concept of strategy.

3.2   What is strategy?

Early writings on strategic management focused primarily on developing terminology and tools intended to aid managers in formulating and implementing strategies. At this time, strategy was primarily an issue of planning – *rational* planning. Management, often in the form of the CEO, was seen as the formulator of strategy. Skilful management led to the successful implementation of strategy. Academics studying strategy were primarily concerned with performance outcomes of various types of strategies.[3]

Strategy as planning

At this time, strategy was largely equated with top management's outspoken plan for the firm's activities. There was a focus on the content of strategy, this content being formed by top management. This way of viewing strategy is closely related to how organizations were viewed at the time, with a strong focus on hierarchical, functionally organized systems. Top management decided on strategy and middle management transformed strategy into instructions. These instructions were conveyed to lower-level organizational members who performed their tasks accordingly.

While the normative tools and theories of strategic management became increasingly more sophisticated over time, until the 1980s the notion of strategy as a conscious plan of action was rarely brought into question. Some scholars subscribing to novel views of strategy formation, however, were increasingly arguing against the meaningfulness of such a narrow way of defining the term strategy. For example, Mintzberg and Waters[4] referred to strategy as the dominant pattern in the stream of decisions and actions of an organization. Strategy was thus seen by some scholars no longer as what firms' managers said they planned for their firms to do – or even what they said they currently did – but how the firms actually behaved.

There is a pertinent logic behind applying such a definition. If people are asked to define the concept of strategy, most are likely to equate it to a plan.[5] If the same people are asked to identify a strategy based on the behaviour of an individual or an organization, though, they will attempt to identify patterns in the behaviour of that individual or organization. If such a pattern can be identified, the conclusion might be that there is an underlying plan, regardless of whether this is actually the case. It is by the pattern in behaviour that strategy is understood, not by the underlying plan, which may not even exist.

Early writings on strategy largely considered strategy as being static. Strategy was formulated by top management. When it failed to yield the desired outcome, a new strategy was formulated by top management. Within this approach, the *content* of strategy was in focus, and researchers tried to find correlations between on the one hand the structure of organizations and strategy-forming bodies, and on the other hand the content of strategy. Less attention was placed on the *process* of strategy formation; that is, how the content of strategy was conceived. With an approach to strategy that focuses on patterns in organizational actions and decisions, however, greater interest in how strategies form rather than simply what they contain follows naturally.

Strategy as action

With a focus on strategy as firm behaviour – that is, actions – the notion that strategies can form in different ways arose. Several ways in which strategies come about can be identified (see Figure 3.1). First there are intended strategies that are also implemented, corresponding largely to the traditional understanding of strategy as a plan. These may be referred to as deliberate, realized strategies.

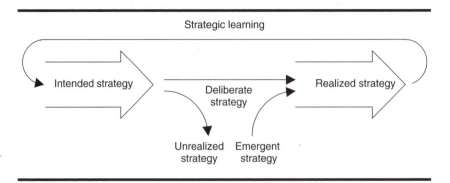

FIGURE 3.1   Types of strategy. Source: Adapted from Mintzberg, H. and Waters, J. (1985) 'Of strategies, deliberate and emergent', *Strategic Management Journal*, Vol. 6, pp. 257–72. © John Wiley & Sons Limited. Reproduced with permission.

Some of those strategies intended to be implemented, however, never come about. They may be referred to as unrealized strategies. There are also strategies that were never intended, but that nonetheless form over time. That is, patterns of actions may take shape without there being any outspoken efforts on behalf of management; some strategies just 'emerge'. With this view on strategy, clearly intent is not a prerequisite for strategy formation.

The typology of deliberate and emergent strategy, however, only provides a partial understanding of strategy formation. Observations of real-life strategy formation indicated that many strategy processes contained elements of both emergence and deliberation. A purely deliberate strategy would imply an unrealistic situation in which no adaptation to environmental conditions would be necessary and that no learning from past outcomes of strategy making need take place. A purely emergent strategy, on the other hand, would indicate an equally unrealistic situation where the firm exercises no control over its activities, simply responding to changes in internal and external conditions. Actual strategies, thus, are neither purely deliberate nor purely emergent in nature.

Generic types of strategy formation

Mintzberg and Waters further develop some of these notions into eight generic types of strategy formation[6]:

1. The *planned strategy* is where leaders articulate intentions, which are translated into action, the implementation process and its outcomes being checked through formal control systems. This is a deliberate strategy, relying on a stable environment.
2. The *entrepreneurial strategy*, dictated by the visions and interests of a strong leader, is a largely deliberate strategy, which permits adaptations to environmental changes and thus contains emergent aspects.
3. The *ideological strategy* is in place when visions and values are shared by organizational members and is also largely deliberate in nature.

4. The *umbrella strategy* entails that there is a broadly defined strategy in place, in regard to which individuals respond as far as constraints allow them to. This form of strategy clearly contains both emergent and deliberate elements and may even be described as deliberately emergent.
5. The *process strategy* is in place when leadership controls the process of strategy making rather than the content of strategy. Like the umbrella strategy, the process strategy contains both emergent and deliberate elements and may also be described as deliberately emergent.
6. The *unconnected strategy* means that different organizational units are free to devise their own strategy. On an organizational level strategy is clearly emergent, although it may be deliberate on an organizational subunit level.
7. The *consensus strategy* is emergent since it entails mutual adjustments between organizational actors as a consequence of the absence of a centrally directed strategy.
8. The *imposed strategy* is dictated by environmental conditions over which the firm and its actors have little control. This form of strategy is thus largely emergent in nature.

With this background in mind, it is obvious that strategy is a rather complex concept. Furthermore, the notions of deliberate and emergent strategies are clearly relevant in a purchasing context. The outcome of the strategic developments of the purchasing operations at IBM as described in Chapter 1 consists, most likely, of significant elements of both deliberate moves as well as emergent ones. Likewise, the eight generic types of strategies presented above may be applied in a purchasing context.

In purchasing the unconnected strategy – that is, when management pursues strategies without connecting them to other strategic developments going on in the firm – is possibly becoming less common. The underlying reason would be that there is growing awareness of the role and importance of purchasing operations. Along with that follows a natural striving to integrate purchasing developments with the rest of the company. The same argument could be used to suggest that imposed strategies may be more significant. Much of the developments in the purchasing field are triggered by outside developments, such as globalization, new technologies and so on. As far as the other strategies are concerned it is more difficult to speculate about possible tendencies in regard to the field of purchasing. We can only conclude that they all could apply.

The process of strategy

Strategy as planning can start with a top-down or bottom-up approach.

Top-down processes address what needs to be done in order to make sure that intended aims are reached. A basic question is first to define the point of departure: 'Where are we now?' This needs to be responded to on various relevant dimensions. If the strategy process (and content) relates to sourcing issues, it could be expressed as the contribution by purchasing to corporate net earnings and/or more specific figures such as the number of suppliers and the degree of participation in new product development.

The second issue entails formulating responses to the question: 'Where do we want to go?' This addresses important moves to make on an overall basis, which in subsequent steps can be specified in greater detail (e.g. changes in country structure in sourcing, number of suppliers, staffing issues etc.). After that follow various activities and, finally, follow-up and learning.

The bottom-up process can start with plans for each single supplier relationship. Planning includes setting targets as well as making activity plans. When this is all added up, a cumulative view of the intended purchasing strategy emerges. In practice, companies often utilize a combination of top-down and bottom-up approaches.

3.3   What is strategic change and how can it be defined?

If we accept that strategy is a pattern of organizational actions, strategic change is consequently a change in that pattern. To understand strategic change is thus to understand the process through which organizational behavioural patterns form. When defining strategies as emergent or deliberate, one actually refers to the process through which the strategy was arrived at. A continuum with purely deliberate and purely emergent change as theoretical end points provides a useful way of characterizing strategic change, especially when combined with a typology that also allows strategic changes to be characterized as more or less reactive or proactive in nature.

Proactivity can be defined as 'an active search for new strategic options and strategic steps taken in new directions, although neither the internal nor the external situation obviously requires new strategic actions'.[7] A reactive strategic change is consequently one that forms in response to conditions and changes in the internal and external context of the firm. A largely proactive and deliberate strategic change thus represents a consciously implemented change undertaken, without there being pressure for the firm to do so.

If something unpredictable happens in the firm's environment to which the firm must respond, management devising and implementing new strategic actions may still be seen as largely deliberate change, but also reactive in nature. Further, it is conceivable that as a response to a pressing external situation, firm behaviour adapts without any specific direction dictated by management, representing a change that is more emergent and reactive in nature.

A fourth type represents a largely emergent strategic change that is still characterized by a great deal of proactivity, observable for example when management seeks out opportunities without there being much in the way of conscious thought given to which opportunities should be exploited (see Figure 3.2).

To the two-dimensional typology in Figure 3.2 a third dimension can be added, namely that of degree of *magnitude* of strategic change. In addition to being proactive or reactive, strategic change can also be revolutionary in nature or take the form of continuous adaptation, generating a two-by-two table indicating four ideal type change situations (see Figure 3.3).[8] Situation 1, proactive and revolutionary change, corresponds to a major strategic change, the initiative for

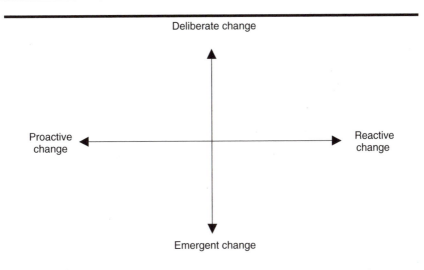

FIGURE 3.2 A matrix typology of strategic change. Source: Adapted from Melin, L. and Hellgren, M. (1994) 'Patterns of strategic processes: Two change typologies', in Thomas, H., O'Neal, D., White, R. and Hurst, D. (eds), *Building the Strategically-Responsive Organization*, Chichester: John Wiley & Sons, pp. 251–71. © John Wiley & Sons Limited. Reproduced with permission.

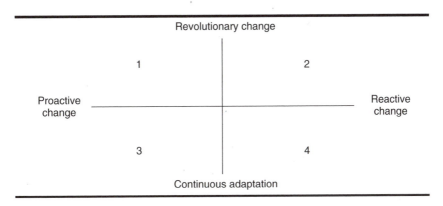

FIGURE 3.3 Four types of strategic change. Source: Adapted from Melin, L. and Hellgren, M. (1994) 'Patterns of strategic processes: Two change typologies', in Thomas, H., O'Neal, D., White, R. and Hurst, D. (eds), *Building the Strategically-Responsive Organization*, Chichester: John Wiley & Sons, pp. 251–71. © John Wiley & Sons Limited. Reproduced with permission.

which finds its origin in the organization without there being an obvious immediate need to undertake such a change. Situation 2 still entails a major strategic change being implemented, but occurs as a necessary reaction to an overt problem; that is, a typical turnaround. In situation 3 the company initiates and drives change without being pressured to do so, but undertakes change in small, continuous steps of successive adaptation. Situation 4 refers to a similar adaptive change process, but finds its origin in some organizational or environmental pressure for change.[9]

Different types of change have different implications and are more or less significant to the firm. There is no doubt that these classifications also apply to strategic
change in relation to sourcing. Some changes may be step by step, for example
applying a new quality assessment method. When applied over time they may
result in dramatic consequences. Other changes appear to be dramatic, for example
in situations of major turnaround of the entire firm, as in the Thomson case in
Chapter 13.

3.4   What organizational and environmental factors influence strategic change?

Above strategy is defined as a pattern of organizational actions. Strategic change
is defined as a change in the pattern of strategic actions. Patterns do not form
by themselves, however. There are a host of different influences on strategic
change. As implied above, they can be found both in the organization and in the
environment.

When the planning approach to strategy was increasingly put into question,
observations of actual strategy formation indicated that the influence of the firm's
environment was underestimated and that the abilities of managers both to plan
and to manage change were similarly overestimated.[10] Other factors not included
in early models of strategy formation concerned for example the internal climate of
the firm – its *culture* – and the importance of *power relations* among key actors. Yet
other researchers began regarding strategy as a result of how managers *interpreted*
their tasks and *environmental constraints*.

With the criticism of the 'planning' school of strategic management, several
alternative approaches to understanding strategy formation emerged. With the
introduction of theoretical frameworks such as contingency theory, population
ecology and institutional theory, the idea that strategy formation may be a reaction
to events more or less outside the firm's control took a firmer hold.

For example, contingency theorists argue that there is no *a priori* determinable
single best strategy for a firm. Rather, what is an appropriate strategy depends on
environmental conditions and changes in these. Strategy is seen as *adaptation* to
the environment; that is, strategy is *contingent* on the environment. To apply this
view thus entails considering the specific situation of the individual organization
faced with a change situation.

The population ecology approach to strategy employs thinking from biological
evolutionary theory to explain firm survival and growth as a function of fit with
the environment. Some organizations are 'selected' for survival.[11] The successful
organization is the one that can *change to fit* the 'ecological' structure.

Institutional theory looks at strategy as something that forms through a process
of adaptation to regulatory frameworks, *imitation* of successful competitors and
adoption of permeating professional norms.[12]

Within each of these perspectives a variety of studies have been conducted to
identify and explain environmental influences on strategy formation, influences
that act as pressures for change, triggers of change and barriers to change.

The organization, its products and services, its production facilities, its human resources, its competitive position in the marketplace, its needs and its opportunities also have impacts on strategy formation. That much was clear to the earliest strategy scholars.

An extensive review of strategic change literature concluded that studies can be defined as either being concerned with strategy making as a *rational* process, as a *learning* process, or as being concerned with managerial *cognitions*.[13] Those studies that regarded strategy making as a rational process focused on the impact on financial performance of organizational variables such as size, age, prior performance, prior strategy, top management characteristics and governance structures.

Those studies that focused on strategic change as a learning process stressed performance problems and changes in leadership, and the subsequent impact on a variety of managerial activities. Those studies that focused on the cognitive processes of managers were concerned with the impact of performance (problems), management characteristics and changes in perceptions about the organization.[14] A variety of organization-related triggers and drivers of change have thus been identified in past research.

Sometimes, organizational influences on strategy fail to lead to changes in strategy, however. Long periods of time may pass without any changes in strategy. There are thus apparently also forces *preventing* change. The concept of *deep structure* is used to describe 'the set of fundamental "choices" a system has made of (1) the basic parts into which its units will be organized and (2) the basic activity patterns that will maintain its existence'.[15]

Deep structures are resistant to change because past decisions rule out many options while simultaneously making other options more likely. Simply put, organizational and other systems tend towards stability because of their inherent *inertia* and their *history*. In organizational systems, obligations to stakeholders could be one example, while previously made investments and organizational culture are others. Of course, the environment also constrains strategic change. Organizations do not exist in isolation. The activities they can undertake are limited by what customers, suppliers, competitors and so on allow, but also by regulatory frameworks, financiers, economic climate and so on.

However, the environment is always perceived by the actors and these perceptions are dependent on each actor's subjective mind, where different cognitive structures lead to different interpretations. A purchasing manager may, for example, regard the actual supplier market as a dynamic set of resources that could be used in several ways to increase the competitive advantage of the firm, for example through collaboration in product development processes. Another purchasing manager may regard the very same supplier market as a production system that should deliver some specific components at the lowest price. These two subjective views lead to different conclusions about strategic purchasing actions. The environment is certainly out there in an objective sense, but it is the subjective way that this environment 'exists' in the mind of the actor that determines each strategic action.

In sum, there is a variety of organizational and environmental pressures for, triggers of and barriers to change, which can potentially have an impact on strategy formation. Of course, all these environmental pressures, triggers and barriers to change are also prevalent in relation to sourcing. It may, for example, be easier to get momentum in a major strategic change process if the company is in a crisis situation (as in our Thomson case in Chapter 13) than if that is not the case (like in the NCC case in Chapter 12). There could be environmental influences such as changing market conditions or technological developments that trigger changes in sourcing, and there may be organizational triggers such as changes in the overall corporate structure and organizational design. Characteristics of management also affect changes in purchasing, as do the deep structures discussed above. Many CEOs as well as CPOs testify to difficulties in making change come about due to cultural issues. These factors affect the way change processes run as well as their outcome.

This overview may be relevant as a basic framework in understanding change in purchasing. There are different points of departure in terms of context, and there are different likely outcomes due to differences in contexts as well as interpretations of the contexts at hand. There are, thus, reasons to consider the 'who' and 'how' to make change happen in various kinds of change contexts.

3.5   Who makes strategic change happen?

Several strands from the discussions above can now be gathered together. The notion that strategy can be more or less deliberate or emergent in nature has been introduced. There are also environmental and organizational factors that affect how strategies are formed.

Strategic change does not come about as a direct consequence of environmental and organizational conditions, though. Only through the actions of human beings do strategic changes – that is, changes in the patterns of actions of a firm – come about. The agent of strategic change has also often been in focus in the strategic management literature. However, 'in the rational model, the strategic management process is a linear and sequential process based on the formulation of a strategy (performed by the upper echelons), the diffusion of the strategy to the organisation and its environment, and, finally, implementation by the organisational actors'.[16]

Traditionally, top managers were considered as creators of strategy. With a view of strategy that stresses the process through which strategy forms and that recognizes a variety of influences on strategy formation, considering only the role of top management yields a very narrow picture of strategy formation.

Recently, the *strategizing* perspective has emerged as a reaction against traditional models of strategy formation. On a general level, the term is used to signify 'the continuous formation and transformation of strategic patterns', implying that strategy formation should not be seen as a process with natural starting and ending points.[17] Adopting a 'strategy formation in practice' approach, the strategizing perspective focuses primarily on the role of individuals in the development of strategy and recognizes that strategic patterns are formed and transformed in processes where individuals interact with each other.

The activities of individuals, in turn, are seen as directed by their understanding of the context in which the process of strategy formation takes place. One can thus talk of simultaneous, continuous and intertwined processes of acting and thinking in regard to strategy.[18]

Others have also put forward strategizing as an umbrella concept to facilitate greater understanding of strategy process formation and focus on the impact of the individuals' understanding of their own and the firm's situation. Strategizing is then seen as the way in which the organization interacts with its environment, emphasizing the role of individuals in this process. More specifically, 'strategizing describes the actions that arise in the interplay between actors when the organization fulfils its functions'.[19]

Far from regarding only the CEO or the top management team as the formers of strategy, this perspective thus recognizes that all individuals inside a firm may be involved in strategy formation, or strategizing. It also stresses the influence of external actors on strategy formation: 'strategizing thus describes the continuous, contextually embedded interplay occurring in organizations, outside organizations and between organizations'.[20]

Strategizing is thus a useful concept to describe how strategy processes – which may contain elements of emergence and deliberation, and which may be more or less revolutionary or incremental in nature – develop over time. In the strategizing perspective the focus is not only on those involved in formulating the firm's outspoken strategy, but also on those who implement strategy. This is coherent with an understanding of strategy as a firm's behavioural pattern, since that pattern forms through all individuals' actions, not only those undertaken by management.

In summary, how an organization behaves is a consequence of how different organizational members act, in turn a consequence of how they interpret the organizational and environmental context. Different organizational members are involved in strategy formation, though, not just top management. Sometimes top management is not even involved in forming new strategy.

3.6   How can change be implemented?

Above we noted that there are two types of realized strategies, those that were intended and those that were not indented. A central question for managers is how to turn intended strategies into realized strategies. Given (1) the notion that strategic change equals change in patterns of organizational actions; (2) that there are a number of potential pressures for change, triggers of change and barriers to change in the organization and the environment, and (3) that strategic change is brought about by individuals through an ongoing process where they interpret and act in regard to these pressures, triggers and barriers, how can intended change be implemented?   ·

A number of researchers have proposed different models concerning the implementation of change. Below three approaches are discussed that are especially relevant for the subsequent chapters of this book.[21]

Routes to change based on the scope of change

The context in which strategic change takes place is of great importance for all activities relating to change. Are there different types of change processes that yield different types of outcomes? What problems occur during such change processes? Which barriers have to be overcome? The framework presented in Figure 3.4 implies that there are four alternative routes to change.[22]

The first route entails initiatives from one party, the aim of which is to implement comprehensive change. This is referred to as 'top-down' change and corresponds to early notions of strategy formation.

The second case involves the 'snowball method'. One party may still initiate a project but in a more piecemeal-like and not necessarily top-down fashion; for example, removing the quality control of products bought from a certain supplier. This has an impact on the way the cooperation between buyer and supplier will have to change, and the quality control process be reorganized. This could, in turn, become a source of inspiration for change in other parts of the cooperation between the two parties, but also to other parties in the network. In this case, the overall process of change is much more emergent in nature rather than a matter of joint negotiations.

Changes can also be negotiated with the whole group of actors involved in the change ('negotiated change'), while the aim is still to implement comprehensive change. A variety of issues must be negotiated, such as who will contribute what and under what conditions as well as how to share risks and gains. This is referred to as 'systemic jointism'; that is, all those involved in the change move together in the same direction.

The fourth case, 'negotiating for change', entails the continuous negotiation of change, implemented piece by piece, involving the negotiation of a number of issues. This occurs when two or more parties, but not all relevant actors, negotiate for change. It might also be that they do not negotiate the total number of issues.

These four routes to change should, of course, be considered as generic ones. Little is said about contextual factors conditioning what approach would be a better

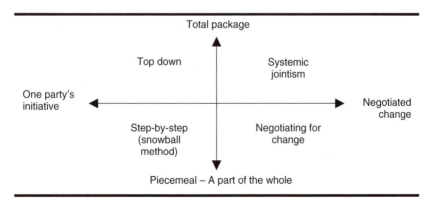

FIGURE 3.4   Types of managed change process. Source: Adapted from Storey, J. (1992) *Developments in the Management of Human Resources*, Oxford: Blackwell Business. Reproduced by permission of Blackwell Publishing Ltd.

choice given the circumstances surrounding the proposed change. What can be said is that the step-by-step approach is beneficial, in the sense that it starts with small changes that can act as inspiring benchmarks for the rest of the organization. Potentially, however, those who initiate the process may fail to win the support, confidence or cooperation of those concerned by the change. Negotiating for change can therefore be a better way, if the negotiating partners manage to come to an agreement and are powerful enough to ensure that negotiations result in a beneficial outcome.

The other two routes to change, the 'total packages', have strengths in the sense that they start as a comprehensive initiative, either by a managerial approach forcing its will onto the organization or by negotiating with all important stakeholders. They could also have severe disadvantages if they fail to make the affected actors on lower levels accept (and be motivated for) the change. The top-down process could at times be necessary, in which a leader or a leading coalition (see below) decides to force their will through, even though there might be resistance at lower levels. But it is not very controversial to suggest that the advantages of a bottom-up procedure often outweigh those of the top-down approach. An interesting challenge is to be able to build an effective bottom-up organization in cases when initial top-down initiatives are necessary.

How to create an effective bottom-up organization

There are two classical pathways to achieving an effective bottom-up organization, one that may be described as a discontinuous path, and one that may be described as a continuous one (see Figure 3.5).[23] In following these paths, there are four basic change processes involved (illustrated as circles in the model), including taskforce-driven change, widespread participation of organizational members, top-down turnaround and bottom-up initiatives.

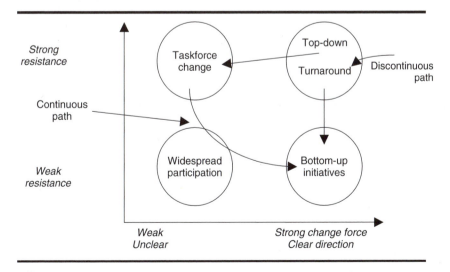

FIGURE 3.5 Classic change paths. Source: Adapted from Strebel, P. (2000) 'Pathways to bottom-up organizations', in Strebel, P., *Focused Energy*, John Wiley & Sons: Chichester, pp. 10–24. © John Wiley & Sons Limited. Reproduced with permission.

A discontinuous path starts with a taskforce setting the direction, presenting the rest of the organization with details to be implemented. In a sense, change management creates upheaval (i.e. top-down turnaround), during which those individuals opposing change are driven out of the organization in an attempt to induce bottom-up initiatives from the remaining organizational members. The central issue is thus that opportunities are created for as many as possible to participate in the change, otherwise widespread bottom-up initiatives are not likely to emerge. This alternative is appropriate when, at first, there is no clear direction for change, while at the same time there is strong resistance to change. The taskforce thus creates the direction for change, resistance to change being weakened as those opposing change are silenced or leave the organization, while those who remain actively participate in change.

This type of change can be described as discontinuous because, when seen from the perspective of the evolution of the organization, it is disruptive and takes place quite quickly. A drawback is that while the change is intended to generate bottom-up initiatives, it is still a top-down process where management may be tempted to take over if change does not proceed as quickly as hoped for. Thus, there is a risk that the intended bottom-up initiatives are again replaced by top-down directives.

A continuous path entails shifting from taskforce-induced change to bottom-up initiatives through widespread participation. Rather than presenting organizational members with the new 'rules', they are induced at the very beginning to take part in forming these 'rules' of change. While also taking its starting point in resistance to change and a weak direction for change, since more organizational members are involved in defining what change is to be undertaken, resistance weakens more quickly. Due to more widespread participation in defining what changes are to be undertaken and how to go about this, however, the direction of change remains unclear for a longer period of time, the process becomes less manageable, and its implementation takes longer (hence, it is continuous in terms of an organization's development). On the other hand, commitment to change is greater among organizational members and participation in bottom-up initiatives increases since the 'rules' of participation are looser than in the case of the discontinuous path.

Routes to creating and keeping momentum for change

The third view of strategic change referred to here has been developed by Kotter.[24] Basically, he has created an eight-step model applicable to a typical change situation, as illustrated in the model in Figure 3.6. Each of the eight steps is discussed in terms of what to do, goals with each step, and what not to do.

The first step entails *creating a sense of urgency* for change; that is, bringing about the perception that change is needed. For this to work, very tangible reasons for change should be stressed, supported by for example market research and studies of what competitors are doing. At this stage it is also crucial not to underestimate the forces that prevent change. For example, people often downplay changes in the environment that may negatively affect the organization or argue that such changes primarily have an impact on others. The goal is thus to create awareness regarding the need for change. While it is not necessary to do this among a wide group of people, it is important not to ignore those that might potentially oppose change.

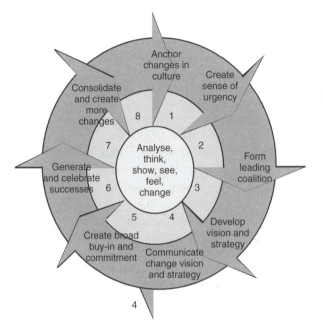

FIGURE 3.6   An eight-step change process. Source: Based on Kotter, J.P. (1996) *Leading Change*, Boston: Harvard Business School Press. Reprinted by permission of Harvard Business School Press. Copyright © 1996 by the Harvard Business School Publishing Corporation; all rights reserved.

The second step entails the formation of what is referred to as a *leading coalition*; that is, to form teams of people who are committed to change, people who are able to think and behave differently from what has been done in the past. When teams or leading coalitions are formed it is important to enrol not only individuals with experience and commitment to change, but also individuals who have a great deal of legitimacy in the eyes of co-workers. There is a high degree of risk that the coalition leading change will fail unless its members are able to trust each other. The creation of trust among coalition members is thus an integral part of the process of coalition formation.

In the third step of this change management process, *vision and strategy* are developed. Only at this stage is strategy formed. Doing so at an earlier stage, before a sense of urgency is created and before a coalition for change is formed, will seriously jeopardize the possibilities of implementing change at all. Since the aim of vision is to provide focus on the need for change and what type of change is required, the vision should be powerful, tangible, realistic and clearly communicable. The subsequent strategy should clearly set the direction concerning what has to be done to fulfil the vision, providing detailed action plans, budgets and a time frame.

It is naïve to assume, however, that the creation of strategy by itself will bring about change. The fourth step entails that both vision and strategy are *communicated* to those who take part in implementing it. When communicating goals and means, fears, opposition and lack of understanding regarding change must always be met, never avoided. Those affected by the change must also be made to feel that they are part of it and that they will benefit from it. If ambitions are perceived as unrealistic or unclear, though, it is likely that the intended change will never be realized. Strategy and vision should thus not be communicated until they are well developed.

In the fifth step, the creation of *buy-in* and *commitment* to strategy is in focus. The aim here is to motivate people to exhibit entrepreneurial behaviour and make them feel empowered and confident to take part in change. Assigning novel roles to organizational members, possibly breaking up old hierarchies and incentive structures, and ensuring that all parties have the information they need to take part in the change process are important components of this step. Simultaneously, it is vital not to ignore those who might obstruct change, regardless of their position in the organization.

Having laid the ground for organizational members participating in change in the previous steps, the sixth step of the change management process entails the *generation and celebration of success*. As the implementation of change progresses, feedback between organizational levels becomes crucial to developing two-way learning and removing obstacles such as bureaucracy. Performance relating to change should be measured and progress should be made clearly observable. Good performance should also be rewarded. It is important at this stage not to undertake too many change-related projects at once, since then the progress and success of each may not be as clear.

In the seventh step, *consolidating* and *creating more changes* are central. While consolidating earlier parts of the change, here it is important to maintain the sense of urgency created initially. Potential obstacles to future changes such as people falling back to old behaviours must also be carefully monitored.

In the eighth and final step, changes are not only consolidated but are also *anchored* in the organization's culture. While stories of past successes should be made part of the organization's identity and new organizational members should be made aware of the new visions and strategies, at the same time the organization should be vigilant against self-indulgent or complacent behaviours emerging.

This is a very straightforward model that captures much relevant practical experience. Many of the recommendations could be understood against the background of the previous discussion about strategy formation and change. The various points of departure for change, for example the resistance situation as referred to in the discussion by Strebel (Figure 3.5) and the various routes to change discussed by Storey and Sisson (Figure 3.4), as well as the kinds of change as discussed by Melin and Hellgren (Figures 3.2 and 3.3), could be very relevant complementary understandings of specific situations.

On the other hand, Kotter's framework could be criticized for being oversimplified and too rationalistic. The change process will rarely conform to such simple checklists, one could argue. This criticism is in line with the general criticism of rationalistic approaches above. Still, it provides a great deal of actionable guidance for managers involved in change processes.

3.7   Typical steps to strategic change in purchasing – the consultant's view

The approach developed by Kotter as well as most of the discussions above make little reference to changes in purchasing and supply management. We have interviewed two consultants experienced in strategic change related to purchasing, who present a more or less identical 'process map' for change. It can be described under five main headlines: (1) to define the current situation, (2) to indicate areas of change, (3) to decide on an overall change strategy, (4) to navigate the implementation process and (5) to follow up, correct and learn for future changes. This is a somewhat simplified version of Kotter's model, but anchored within the sourcing area.

Defining the situation

Defining the situation is primarily about two main issues, first to understand the challenge (i.e. what should be achieved) and second to understand the point of departure (what is the present state). It could also be seen the other way around, starting with a description of the present state and from there elaborating on the desired and possible future state.

Defining the point of departure could include a variety of issues. The two consultants have somewhat varying approaches and backgrounds. Consultant A works for a smaller consultancy firm specializing in (change management in) purchasing and supply management. Consultant B belongs to a much more diversified and bigger consultancy firm.

Box 3.1   Defining the situation

CONSULTANT A   To me the first step is to establish a dialogue with the stakeholders of the company. Those who asked me in of course, but also those who are involved as users of the services from purchasing, e.g. business area management, production, design, those responsible for quality etc. This way I get a feel for the levels of ambitions and also of the hopes and desires – and maybe the dedication to the change venture. I combine this with questions on experienced shortcomings in current performance.

My second step is to establish a comprehensive and reliable picture of the spending, i.e. carry out a spend analysis. I want to see what the company buys, how much, from which sources etc. With such an analysis, I can identify interesting patterns and point to possible future changes in the structure. My experience has given me a feeling for best practices in sourcing various commodities. Already here I get a feel for potential improvements.

The third step I normally take is to do an equally comprehensive investigation of the competencies in place. What's the experience and quality level of the purchasing staff, what basic infrastructure is in place, e.g. defined purchasing processes, clarity of responsibilities, expressed purchasing policy, awareness of purchasing strategy among the staff etc.? Through this step I get a feeling for the level of performance today and the potential for improvements among existing staff. I also get a basic understanding of today's practices.

The fourth step is to carry out an analysis of the situation, preferably by a SWOT analysis [Strengths, Weaknesses, Opportunities and Threats]. What have emerged as the strengths of this organization? Where are the weaknesses, in relation to a future desired state? What opportunities for improvement can we see and what are the likely potential gains involved? Are there any threats to this development? The latter could be both threats emanating from the spend analysis where, maybe, some markets have turned out to be inefficient or some suppliers are unwilling to change. There could be internal conflicts that may hinder the materialization of future ambitions etc. This is roughly the initial platform I prefer to build.

CONSULTANT B   Actually, we have a diagnostic instrument to measure purchasing maturity. We have some nine fields of study: staff, organizational design, communication, working methods in relation to suppliers, measurement structure etc. We pose several questions in each area to get a brief understanding of the level of the operation of the firm. These questions are addressed to a limited selection of people from within and outside purchasing. It is a very efficient method. In one day I will have plenty of material to be able to establish the level of the point of departure. The questions also cover 'should aspects', i.e. how the informants would like to see the purchasing operations working.

My second step is to come back to those who asked me in and present my analysis. We establish the point of departure and the expressed expectations of future states. Supported by my tool and my experience, I can briefly diagnose what it will mean in terms of developments and improvements to reach the desired levels. We could also discuss what is needed in order to get there and/or secondary goals; i.e. how far we can get given a lower budget. Generally, I want to spend quite a lot of time up front in projects to establish clear lines of communication, because what may be a small 'disconnection' can really grow as the project progresses.

The common features are evident. It is necessary to establish a fact-based view of the points of departure. It is also important to start working on the expectations. By involving several stakeholders and asking for their views on the present and desired states, they get involved in the process from the beginning. In this phase, a number of future opportunities as well as threats are already identified.

Indicating areas of change

The analysis of the present state and desired future states should be connected to the areas that need to be developed. It could be the design and implementation of new organizational design, including roles (decision structure, e.g. with commodity champions and commodity teams), processes and procedures. It could also include responses to identified needs for improved infrastructure such as ICT applications, the introduction of new management accounting principles or the need for competence developments among staff.

Box 3.2   Indicating areas of change

CONSULTANT A   We try to indicate visions of future behaviour and to indicate what will be different in actual behaviour as well as where the possible gains (and losses) are to be found. This is a way to build more explicit pictures of the future state we are heading for. Our experience is that it is more important at this stage to consider such 'pictures' than to start trying to be very accurate on potential savings and the like.

> CONSULTANT B   We try to think through where the biggest improvement potentials are and where they are easiest to harvest. Easy to harvest in combination with big gains is of course especially interesting. It normally has an impact on how we sequence our efforts.

Some form of initial analysis based on the introductory research thus appears to be a natural second step.

Thinking through the process of change – the implementation

The next step entails, in a smaller group (compare this with the leading coalition in Kotter's process), deciding on how best to approach the rest of the organization and other stakeholders.

Box 3.3   The implementation

> CONSULTANT A   This is a very critical aspect. One should be aware that once a process of this sort has been put into motion, everyone starts interpreting what is going on. Things you say and do that you may think are marginal could turn out to create severe barriers and mislead the energy of the process. I try to live according to the principle 'if anything can go wrong, it will'. We have to think of how we frame the reasons for the change in order to be interpreted in the ways intended. We have to decide on areas of priority, whether or not to go for a top-down or a bottom-up approach, who should symbolize the change etc.
>
> CONSULTANT B   We should be aware that even if we plan carefully in this step events that we haven't been able to calculate will occur. Therefore, one idea is to use this phase to get as well prepared as possible, to be better able to deal with the unexpected. Chance favours the prepared mind, as they used to say.

The planning efforts as well as the suitable routes for the change process depend on the type of change involved. If it is a minor change, maybe to introduce a new quality assessment system, the situation is very different from that of a major turnaround. If it is a situation with a very dedicated top management group and extensive crisis awareness, it is yet another situation that calls for adequate adaptations of the change strategy.

Navigating the implementation process

This phase could last for anything from a few weeks to several years, depending on the kind of change in question and what kind of process is being applied as well as how the process is run. This could be very complicated and in addition to all the steps decided on before include a lot of 'political' action. In our case in Chapter 12 (the NCC case) we can witness quite a lot of the kind of things that can move the process forwards as well as hindering it. Also the cases in Chapter 11 focusing on ways to resist change give thought-provoking insights.

Box 3.4   Navigating the implementation process

CONSULTANT A   To me this is the part when we leave science and move change processes into art. It is so important to be aware of and to be able to interpret small signs of activity that either will work in favour of the change or counteract it. It is important not only to actually perform, to get the new procedures, staff, organization or whatever it is in place. You need also to build coalitions of support, you need to use your networking skills. It could be networks inside the organization as well as outside. You need to think in terms of door openers, bridges to certain people and networks. You also need to think of timing: when to present certain ideas and when not to; framing: how to present what you want to see happen etc.

CONSULTANT B   It is very important to present early successes. Therefore one should early on try to develop some good business cases symbolizing the new work mode and indicating the potential benefits of it. When you have those in place, they should be communicated strongly and as accurately as possible. Avoid making too simplistic calculations. You need to be sure that what you say holds true.

It is evident that this phase could be very complex, and that many critical events that could prevent the change process are likely to occur. Communication skills in addition to the field of expertise (sourcing) are likely to be critical. Much of the success will frequently also be due to the 'political' skills of the key actors involved. We should also be aware that one should expect totally different patterns if the process is run as a top-down process with strong leadership, who may also be willing to show their dedication by exercising power, in comparison to a bottom-up process based on learning and self-motivated staff.

Learning and follow-up

The final phase is the learning and follow-up, but it should not only be left as the last task. Learning and follow-up is a continuous issue. A change team needs to be able to indicate the potential successes and failures. By tracking developments it is easier to communicate and build trust.

Box 3.5   Learning and follow-up

CONSULTANT B   Already quite early on, we need to be able to show that we are moving and that we – preferably – move as expected so we can communicate that we are on the right track. This could have to do with staffing issues (new staff are in place), supplier selection issues (that we have reduced the number of suppliers) or that we have moved some sources from high-cost countries to low-cost countries, if that's part of the change.

Of course, when the intended change process has been completed it could be a very valuable exercise also to conduct a thorough follow-up to learn for the future.

It seems evident that experience must be very important in order to run such complex change processes as discussed above. In some companies, such experience already exists, which could also for other reasons be appropriate to utilize. In other companies, such experience is lacking or, even if it does exist, it may not be relevant or appropriate to exploit it. This takes us to the overall issue of consultants and whether to use them or not.

3.8   Working with consultants or not

In struggling to improve purchasing and supply management practices, sourcing executives have often been frustrated by either lack of resources – time, money, skills – or by weak organizational links to critical corporate functions. Consultants provide both time and skills. If top management is unaware of the need to develop purchasing activities or unwilling, consultants typically have the ear of senior management. They can often help persuade top executives to invest in for example new resources (such as information technology, employees with new skill sets etc.).

We touched on the political aspects of change processes above. Consultants could be a way around this (compare a discussion towards the end of the NCC case in Chapter 12). Consultants can move through an organization, unfettered by corporate politics or by the myopic measures of job performance. This is something that often places purchasing professionals at odds with the greater goals of their companies. Professional advisers may well be utilized as leading agents of change.

What could consultants do?

Companies use consultants for a wide range of projects in the procurement and supply chain areas. Most typical engagements involve one or more of the following activities[25]:

- Straight cost reduction ('We spend €100, can you make it €50?').
- Strategic sourcing.
- Assessing or benchmarking existing supplier management or supply chain processes.
- Reengineering of supplier management or supply chain functions.
- Training, formal and informal.
- Outsourcing.
- Reorganization of the sourcing function following mergers and acquisitions.
- Developing and deploying software and IT systems (including electronic procurement, ERP systems and add-on software).

Consulting practices specializing in procurement and supply chain management (SCM) are loosely categorized according to four fundamental areas of activity: operational assessments or audits, strategy, implementation, and systems (that is, deployment of software – especially ERP and related software packages – and other information technology). Full-service consulting firms offer all four levels of activity – assessment, strategy, implementation and systems – but tend to have distinct strengths and weaknesses based on their historical roots.

Two general advantages of utilizing consultants have already been mentioned: that one immediately gets the experience on board and that they are outsiders to the internal politics. A third may be avoidance of myopia: there is a tendency that those close to the situation have an established view of the problems. The consultant can look at the situation with fresh eyes. There are some disadvantages too, one being that the learning from the experiences generated during the change process tends to stay with the consultant and may be difficult to transfer to the buyer. A second disadvantage has to do with uncertainty: it is difficult to know exactly how good the consultant is. The third negative aspect is the price: it is usually costly to employ consultants. A fourth possible disadvantage is the risk of mimetic behaviour, where the consultant may apply the same solution to any possible problem, following the current trend in strategy. However, the most important difficulty is perhaps not related to the consultant's field of speciality, but how to choose and interact with the supplier of consultancy services.

Working with consultants in a change process

Hiring a consultant to support in a process of strategic change is, of course, a complex service that is difficult to evaluate beforehand. The supplier's experiences of similar processes are key, as well as references that can witness to the consultant's prior performance. It should also be important to evaluate the team that will be involved from the supplier, the specific individuals as well as the composition of the team. Furthermore, the process, the various steps (toll-gates) and what kind of results as well as decisions to take in conjunction with the respective steps should be considered early on.

During the process it is a key aspect that the buyer and the supplier carry on a dialogue to fine-tune expectations and successively to correct actions. Other elements that need to be considered are the co-production aspects: could and should the buyer carry out some of the research by utilizing its own resources? How could the buyer facilitate the job of the consultant, for example by facilitating access to staff for interviews? How could as many as possible of the experiences generated also be harvested as a learning exercise for the buyer?

When the core of the service provision comes to an end, it is also important to decide about implementation issues. Should the consultant be responsible for that step as well or should it be something for the buyer to take care of, or should another consultant specializing in that activity take over? How long after the process is finished should the consultant be prepared to be mobilized for complementary activities?

Finally, it goes without saying that what has been discussed in this section is that consultants could be a good resource provided that competent and capable consultants are selected. Consultancy is a very complex service to purchase and the outcome of a change process with consultants involved is likely to be highly dependent on the specific supplier (consultant or consultancy firm) that has been chosen and how the buying firm interacts with it.

3.9   Returning to our general understanding of strategic change

In this chapter we have been dealing with both the process and the content of strategic change, with some predominance of process issues. However, the content side of strategic change is extremely important and the purchasing manager should always keep in mind two different aspects of strategic purchasing. On one hand, strategic purchasing issues are given by a translation of the overall strategic direction of the firm to the sourcing context, for example what are the strategic purchasing implications of a quality niche strategy compared with a typical cost leader strategy. On the other hand, the purchasing officers must themselves continuously follow the supplier market development in order to define new strategic challenges of the sourcing activities, but also for the strategic activities of the firm as a whole.

The most recent view on strategic change is the micro-strategy and strategizing perspective. This means an emphasis on the unfolding of strategy through the detailed processes and practices that constitute the day-to-day activities of organizational life and relate to strategic outcome.[26] As Henry Mintzberg puts it, 'Strategy in a sense is to move an organization forward... That is what strategy has to be about – not the neat abstractions of the executive suits, but the messy patterns of daily life.'[27] Strategizing emphasizes how daily activities shape the ongoing formation and transformation of strategic patterns of actions; that is, an activity-based view of strategy.[28]

This micro-strategizing perspective means a focus on the everyday activities of all practising 'strategists', to be found everywhere in the organization. In focus are the practices by which things happen and the actual, situated activities of different strategic actors. The social interaction between all relevant strategizing actors is the core of strategy processes, partly questioning the centrality of top managers for the actual strategic outcome, and rather exploring which actors may make a difference and contribute in the strategizing through their local actions with strategic implications. In this perspective, strategic change means introducing daily activities that break with the traditional, routinized and taken-for-granted ways of doing the purchasing and sourcing activities. This collective view of the strategist may be a powerful way to involve many in the strategic purchasing of the firm. The sensitivity to external changes implying threats and/or opportunities for future sourcing will certainly increase with several strategists in action.

3.10   Conclusion: strategic change in purchasing

This chapter has addressed the issues of strategy formation from a number of different perspectives, all of which are also relevant to consider in a purchasing context. To begin with it could be fruitful to be aware of some of the fundamental understandings of concepts such as strategy: as a plan, as a pattern of actions, as intended and as realized and so on. Further, the role of interpretation by the individuals involved as well as the power context are also parts of the general understanding. Secondly, we discussed what change is and could be and how it could be performed (e.g. continuous adaptation or revolutionary change), proactively or reactively and for example piecemeal versus the total package as well as a single-party initiative or negotiated change. The change process as such can also be prepared and analysed as a sequence of steps to take (Kotter), influenced by the specific context at hand, for example characterized by among others the above variables plus the resistance situation (Strebel). Altogether, this gives a basic roadmap that could help in identifying the specific venture and the more or less relevant routes to change.

This general understanding of change and the prerequisites for change is complemented by more practical experiences from driving change, departing from identified needs to change and develop sourcing activities. We focused on content (what it could consist of) *and* process, identifying some of the important things we know about such processes. There are several possible areas for change: organizational design, ways to cooperate with suppliers, changing and adapting the purchasing leadership, leveraging purchasing by means of improved ICT usage, competence development of purchasing staff and so on. Such areas will be dealt with in Chapters 4 through 10.

There are also numerous ways of running the change process as such, as a top-down or bottom-up process, exercising power or trying primarily to motivate and put people's inner drive in motion and so on. Such aspects will be dealt with, focusing on the role and reactions by the individual exposed to change, in Chapter 10. Practical experiences of causing and dealing with resistance are dealt with in Chapter 11, and complete specific cases of change management are discussed in Chapters 12, 13 and 14.

Notes and references

[1] Normann, R. (1975) *Skapande företagsledning* (Creative management), Aldus: Lund; Axelsson, B. (1996) *Kompetens för konkurrenskraft* (Competence for competitiveness), SNS: Stockholm.

[2] Normann (1975) *opere citato*.

[3] Rajagopalan, N. and Spreitzer, G. (1997) 'Toward a theory of strategic change: A multi-lens perspective and integrative framework', *Academy of Management Review*, Vol. 22, No. 1, pp. 48–79.

[4] Mintzberg, H. and Waters, J. (1983) 'The mind of the strategist,' in Srivastva, S. and associates, *The Executive Mind*, Jossey-Bass: San Fransisco: pp. 58–85; Mintzberg, H. and Waters, J. (1985) 'Of strategies, deliberate and emergent', *Strategic Management Journal*, Vol. 6, pp. 257–72.

[5] Mintzberg and Waters (1983) *opere citato*.

[6] Mintzberg and Waters (1985) *opera citato*.

[7] Melin, L. and Hellgren, M. (1994) 'Patterns of strategic processes: Two change typologies', in Thomas, H., O'Neal, D., White, R. and Hurst, D. (eds), *Building the Strategically-Responsive Organization*, John Wiley & Sons Ltd: Chichester, pp. 251–71.

[8] Melin and Hellgren (1994) *opere citato*.

[9] A similar distinction exists between changes in a system based on their *comprehensiveness*. 'Revolutionary change' is seen as all-encompassing, while there is 'piecemeal change' that is independent change in different, but several elements. The term 'focused change' is used to describe change that

may encompass different levels of a system (organization), but only one part of that system (organization), while 'isolated change' refers to change in one component of a system: Mintzberg, H. and Westley, F. (1992) 'Cycles of organizational change', *Strategic Management Journal*, Vol. 13, pp. 39–59.

[10] Mintzberg, H., Ahlstrand, B. and Lampel, J. (1998) *Strategy Safari. A Guided Tour through the Wilds of Strategic Management*, Free Press: New York.

[11] Hannan, M.T. and Freeman, J. (1977) 'The population ecology of organizations', *American Journal of Sociology*, Vol. 85, No. 5, pp. 929–64.

[12] Mintzberg *et al.* (1998) *opere citato*.

[13] Rajagopalan and Spreitzer (1997) *opere citato*.

[14] Rajagopalan and Spreitzer (1997) *opere citato* write that the 'distinction [between cognition and action] is important because cognitions provide the underlying logic for managerial actions'.

[15] Gersick, C. (1991) 'Revolutionary change theories: A multilevel exploration of the punctuated equilibrium paradigm', *Academy of Management Review*, Vol. 16, No. 1, pp. 10–36.

[16] Jess Hansen, A.M. (2002) *To Lead from a Distance: The Dynamic Interplay between Strategy and Strategizing – A Case Study of the Strategic Management Process*, ATV PhD serie 7.2002, Akademiet for Tekniske Videnskaber: Copenhagen pp. 22–3.

[17] Achtenhagen, L., Melin, L., Müllern, T. and Ericson, T. (2003) 'Leadership: The role of interactive strategizing' in Pettigrew, A., Whittington, R., Melin, L., Sánchez-Runde, C., van den Bosch, F., Ruigrok, W. and Numagami, T. (eds), *Innovative Forms of Organizing*, Sage: London, pp. 49–71.

[18] Melin, L., Ericson, T. and Müllern, T. (1999) 'Organizing is strategizing. Innovative forms of organizing means continuous strategizing', paper presented at the Nordfek Conference, August 19–21.

[19] Nygaard, C. and Hull Kristensen, P. (2002) 'Inledning – Strategen och Kontexten', in Nygaard, C. (ed.), *Strategizing: En kontextuell Organisationsteori*, Studentlitteratur: Lund, pp. 13–26.

[20] *Ibidem.*

[21] Storey, J. (1992) *Developments in the Management of Human Resources*, Blackwell Business: Oxford; Strebel, P. (2000) 'Pathways to bottom-up organizations', in Strebel, P., *Focused Energy*, John Wiley & Sons Ltd: Chichester, pp. 10–24; and Kotter, J.P. (1996) *Leading Change*, Harvard Business School Press: Boston, MA.

[22] Storey (1992) *opere citato*.

[23] Strebel (2000) *opere citato*.

[24] Kotter, J.P. and Cohen, D.S. (2003) *The Heart of Change: Real Life Stories of how People Change Their Organizations*, Harvard Business School Press: Boston, MA.

[25] Millen-Porter, A., Ciancarelli, A. and Van der Pool, L. (1998) 'Agents of change: Consultants make things happen', *Purchasing*, 5 November, www.purchasing.com.

[26] Johnson, G., Melin, L. and Whittington, R. (2003) 'Micro strategy and strategizing: Towards an activity-based view', *Journal of Management Studies*, Vol. 40, No. 1, pp. 3–22.

[27] Martin de Holan, P. and Mintzberg, H. (2004) 'Management as life's essence: 30 years of the nature of managerial work', *Strategic Organization*, Vol. 2, pp. 205–12.

[28] Johnson *et al.* (2003) *opere citato*.

Part II

AREAS AND INSTRUMENTS OF CHANGE

Chapter 4

DEVELOPING THE SUPPLY BASE BY CHANGING SUPPLIER RELATIONS

Anna Dubois and Finn Wynstra

In this chapter, we take a look at the 'external side' of strategic sourcing – supplier relations. After discussing changing perspectives on supplier relations, we analyse in some detail various dimensions of variety that there could be. Subsequently, we investigate alternative paths and patterns of change in relation to suppliers. This is followed by a case study of the purchasing behaviour of a manufacturer of fork-lift trucks over four decades. In that study we get to know how gradual changes develop step by step into patterns of strategic change. The next section deals with the possible ways of managing and/or coping with change in supplier relations, and the chapter ends with conclusions and implications.

4.1 Changing perspectives on supplier relations

Over the last two decades, there has been extensive discussion of the increasing importance of the purchasing function and the growing strategic orientation towards managing suppliers and the purchasing process (see Chapters 1 and 2). An important part of this is obviously reflected in how we perceive suppliers and the way they can contribute value to the firm.

TABLE 4.1   The classical vs the modern approach to purchasing and supply management

	Classical approach	*Modern approach*
Nature of function	Administrative	Strategic
Geographical scope	Local markets	Global markets
Number of suppliers	Many alternatives	One or two alternatives
Problem-solving style	Local solutions to problems	Coordinated solutions
Relationship posture	Competition	Collaboration
Time horizon	Short term	Long term
Quality targets	Acceptable quality levels	Zero defect
Logistics targets	Just in case	Just in time
Financial targets	Price focus	Total cost focus

Source: Adapted from Axelsson, B. and Laage-Hellman, J. (1991) *Inköp – en ledningsfråga*, Verkstadsindustriernas Förlag: Stockholm.

In Chapter 2, we have already described a series of stages or phases through which the orientation towards purchasing and supply management can go. In a kind of dichotomous analysis of these changes, many researchers and managers talk about an 'old' or 'classical' approach versus a 'new' or 'modern' approach to purchasing, as outlined in Table 4.1.

One of the most salient aspects in this comparison of a classical vs a modern approach regards the number of suppliers and the posture of these relationships. Allegedly, in the classical approach, value is being extracted from suppliers by creating competition between a substantial number of suppliers (per purchase category). The time horizon of these relationships is short, the focus is on price targets and the geographical scope of the relations is predominantly local. In contrast, in the modern approach, value is created through close collaboration with a limited number of suppliers that are engaged in long-term relationships with the customer. These suppliers come from a global market, and performance is focused on (reducing) total cost.

Consider the illustration in Box 4.1 for some reflections on the differences between the classical, competitive bidding-oriented approach, and the modern, collaboration-oriented approach.

Box 4.1   Relying on competition and independence vs cooperation and interdependence

The Swedish electrical contracting industry includes a great number of small firms, in addition to a few larger ones operating in several parts of the country. One of the many small ones, a company employing ten electricians, works regularly with the three large Swedish construction companies in the southwest part of the country. The tendering procedure maintained by these companies entails that the contracting firm typically produces ten tenders (approx. 40 hours are spent on each) in order to get one contract.

When considering the efficiency of this way of working, an obvious question would be: who pays for all the work spent on tenders that do not result in orders? Another related question is how good suppliers are being developed. The view of competition as a motivating factor, and the independence following as a consequence of staying 'unattached' to be able to play the market, has very strong roots.

The modern perspective on purchasing has therefore meant changing views on what drives efficiency. The rather simple idea that cooperation and interdependence, as both the cause and the effect of that cooperation, have the potential to yield more 'competitive advantage' to individual firms is thus neither straightforward to explain nor easy to translate into managerial action. The reason for the latter is that cooperation and interdependence are multidimensional concepts that cannot be applied in general, and hence purchasing strategies based on the modern way of thinking necessarily imply more analysis of specific situations and adjustments to specific conditions. In addition, they are more dynamic in the sense that specific interdependencies with suppliers may force the buying firm to adjust to changes that take place elsewhere.

Obviously, the characterization of a modern vs a classical approach is to some extent an overly simplistic representation of the changes that we have seen in the purchasing strategies of firms and other (e.g. nonprofit) organizations. However, it is striking how often this comparison is being used – by practitioners and researchers alike – to illustrate the main features of these changes. Apparently, there is an element of truth in it.

Still, although many things have changed for a lot of buying organizations during the past 20 years, there are different reasons for and specific characteristics of these changes. In addition, the extent and the consequences or effects of the changes undertaken are very different for different customers. Two aspects deserve particular mention here, as they affect the nature and extent of the changes in supplier relations: the type of industry involved and the purchase item under consideration.

In the first place, there are significant industry differences as regards the changes in the relationships with suppliers. It is impossible to provide a detailed assessment here of all the differences between the various sectors, but let us at least point out two extremes. On the one hand, we have mass-assembly industries like the automotive and electronics sector that have gone through extensive outsourcing programmes, and have increasingly focused on the reduction of the number of suppliers and intensifying the collaboration with the remaining ones. In these sectors, collaboration focuses not only on logistic optimization through initiatives such as just in time and just in sequence, but also on synchronizing quality assessment and control procedures, and on joint product development. Contracts for many parts of the automobile or mobile handset are concluded for the 'life of type'; that is, the period during which that specific final product is being sold on the market. For an illustration from the telecommunications industry, see Box 4.2.

Box 4.2   Main features of Nokia Mobile Phones' purchasing strategy

Nokia: Purchasing in the twenty-first century

- From traditional adversarial purchasing towards partnering and early supplier involvement.
- Strong participation in product development activities.
- Extended processes – supplier will participate in customer's processes.
- Supplier–customer–end-user chain will shorten.
- Fewer suppliers – larger assemblies will be purchased (system suppliers).
- Suppliers will have to be able to manage their own supplier base (network sourcing).
- Significance of short lead-times and flexibility will increase.
- Process teams will manage the business.
- Supplier relationship management will be as important a success factor as customer relationship management.

Source: Presentation Nokia Mobile Phones.

On the other hand, there are a number of sectors where this increased focus on partnering, collaboration and long-term commitment has not been that prevalent. Partly, examples may be found in industries where the existence of ample profit margins and the lack of substantial competition have prevented a more thorough and critical analysis of the potential of more closely managing purchasing and supply. Other examples may be found in sectors where the nature of the production process makes it more difficult to collaborate on a long-term basis. One notable example of this is the construction industry.[1] In comparison to many other sectors, the construction industry is still very much focused on short-term supply relationships, with an emphasis on price and on the efficiency of individual projects. One of the main reasons for this is that each construction project has a high degree of uniqueness, not only in terms of location but also in terms of the design, materials used and so on. In addition, the actual roles and distribution of tasks among the different contractors and suppliers may differ per project, which makes it difficult to agree on standard contracts and guidelines. For these reasons, and because of organizational structures where often the individual project managers still have a very strong role, long-term collaboration with suppliers is quite difficult and competitive bidding is much more prevalent. Chapter 11 presents an in-depth case study of change at a construction company, NCC, but there we will also see the significant problems that such an endeavour is facing – and, in this particular industry, this type of initiative is still rather the exception than the rule.[2] Similar industries with 'unit production' and low degrees of standardization of products and processes face largely similar problems.

The second aspect that affects the nature and extent of change in supplier relations regards the type of purchase item under consideration. One of the strongest notions in purchasing and supply management nowadays concerns the view that different types of purchase items need to be procured differently. Consequently, given the variety of its purchases, each firm will need a variety of relationships: not *just* arm's-length relations, not *just* collaborative relations, but *both*.

Obviously, this implies that in reality, when considering the 'modernization' of purchasing strategies, firms do not shift all of their supplier relations from one profile to the other, but that at most the overall *balance* of the relations will change. In other words, what arguably is happening is that customers choose collaborative relations more frequently than previously, rather than exclusively and instead of competitive 'relations'. To what extent this shift is taking place in each individual organization is dependent on a number of factors, such as the actual type of purchases being made. One related aspect that is being noted more recently as affecting the 'ideal' spread of relations in terms of collaboration vs competition is the customer firm's downstream market strategy. Firms that follow a cost-reduction, price-oriented strategy in the relations with their customers will – other things being equal – have more competition-oriented relations·with their suppliers than firms that follow a downstream strategy oriented towards innovation and product differentiation. Such observations are made, for example, in the automotive industry where premium brands such as BMW, Volvo and Jaguar are argued to have relatively closer relationships with suppliers than volume-oriented competitors such as Opel and Volkswagen. Interestingly, however, such a clear link between downstream market strategy and purchasing strategy may be obscured by the fact that an increasing number of firms are following dual strategies, combining a set of products focused on low-end, price-sensitive markets with products targeted towards the high-end segment. For example, some food and beverage producers combine the production of A brands with the provisioning of private labels for their retail customers. Consequently, these firms may need to combine price-oriented tactics with more innovation and collaboration-oriented tactics – for one and the same purchase category. Sometimes this may take the form of dual sourcing strategies for such categories, but in other instances it may be necessary to reconcile these goals in the same supplier relation, for instance when market structure and/or economies of scale dictate so.

The main conclusion from these observations is that to fully understand relationships with suppliers and the possibilities for change and improvement, we need to go beyond simple dichotomies of 'modern vs classic' or 'competition vs collaboration'. Supplier relationships are much more complicated and varied than that. In the next section a framework for analysis of this variety is presented and discussed.

4.2   A framework for analysing change in the variety of supplier relationships

Supplier relationships subject to a high degree of involvement are often referred to as close relationships or 'partnerships'. These relationships are also typically associated with high business volumes, long-term commitments and single sourcing arrangements. The reasons for this 'bundle' of relationship features can be found in some general trends that have characterized industrial markets during the last decades. First, increasing specialization has entailed growing interdependence among the operations of firms. In this regard, an important means for integrating their operations in order to manage these interdependencies has been to develop close cooperation with a set of important suppliers. The relationships with these suppliers have often been based on long-term commitments where both parties have made investments in adjustments that have been more or less specific to their counterpart. Hence, long-term commitment has been required for them to benefit from investments made in the relationship. Owing both to the commitment and the specificity of the adaptations, single sourcing has become the main 'rule' for these kinds of relationships. Thus there is a certain logic to the 'bundle' of relationship characteristics that are often described as 'the modern way of purchasing'.

However, to improve the understanding and analysis of the variety of ways in which firms 'design' their supplier relationships, there is a need for debundling the more or less established dichotomy of a traditional or classic vs a modern way of buying. A framework for analysis of different dimensions of relationships to nuance this simplified view has been suggested.[3] The framework distinguishes among four dimensions: the posture of the relationship (degree of involvement), the business volume with the supplier, the continuity of the relationship, and the sourcing policy (single or multiple sourcing). These four dimensions may also be helpful when trying to assess change patterns in supplier relationships.

Taking the posture of the relationship as a point of departure, this framework supports identification and analysis of different situations in which it would be useful to combine the features in different ways (see Table 4.2). For instance, there may be situations in which high involvement is necessary in relationships with a minor business volume. This may be an effective approach when the supplier has particular skills and capabilities that are critical to the buying firm's offerings or that represent great development potential. One example of this is Volvo Cars' relationship with Autoliv which, as a supplier of safety devices such as air-bags, is crucial for Volvo's position as a producer of safe cars. This requires high involvement in terms of close cooperation with the supplier to be in the forefront in developing new safety solutions. On the other hand, the business volume is, compared with other supplier relationships, still quite modest, although the value of safety components has increased over the years. In contrast, there may be a rationale in maintaining a low degree of involvement in relationships with a major business volume when standardized components with little (current) development potential are concerned. Salt supplies to chlorine production may be an example of this kind of situation. The degree of involvement may also differ in relation to the length of relationships. Short-term, highly intensive relationships and long-term relationships with a very low degree of involvement may both be sensible options in different situations: the first to solve specific problems and the latter when standardized items, not subject to any particular changes, are used for a long time.

TABLE 4.2   Degree of involvement in a relationship in relation to business volume, continuity and sourcing policy

Degree of involvement	Business volume		Continuity		Sourcing policy	
	High	*Low*	*Long*	*Short*	*Single*	*Multiple*
High						
Low						

Source: Adapted from Gadde, L.-E. and Snehota, I. (2000) 'Making the most of supplier relationships', *Industrial Marketing Management*, Vol. 29, pp. 305–16.

Although some relationships may remain positioned the same in relation to the four dimensions for a long time, others may be subject to change in one or several dimensions. For instance, a situation that requires close cooperation to develop a new technical solution may turn into a situation characterized by low involvement and increasing business volume once the product development is finished. Also, low-involvement relationships may develop in terms of involvement if, for instance, the buyer and supplier agree to jointly develop a customized version of a standard product.

When sourcing policies in combination with different postures are concerned there are no self-evident patterns, for several reasons. One of these concerns the rather 'theoretical' issue of *what* is considered subject to sourcing. That is, if for instance raw materials are considered as a product category by a buying firm, this category may be subject to multiple sourcing. If, however, a particular material within this broader category is considered, it may well be subject to single sourcing. Hence, putting boundaries around what should be subject to a sourcing policy in the first place is far from clear cut in most instances, and it may change over time. Furthermore, the 'business logic' in the connection between the degree of involvement and the sourcing policy may differ. An example of this, from a supplier's perspective, is presented in Box 4.3.

Box 4.3   Example of a firm that needed to rethink its view of customer relationships

A firm producing cutting equipment assumed that its most important customers, with whom it often cooperated to develop new technical solutions, would have a propensity to use the firm as a single source. Also, it assumed that its smaller and more distant customers would use the firm as one among several suppliers. However, a market study revealed that the opposite was true. The major customers generally considered it useful to be closely involved with several producers of cutting equipment. Two related reasons for their multiple sourcing policies were identified. First, the products were considered as very important for production and quality performance by the major customers, who, as a second reason, also perceived the suppliers to be leading the development in different application areas. And, since these customers wanted access to all these development areas, they felt a need to be closely involved with several leading suppliers. For the minor customers, which were often suppliers on the second or third tier in the same industry, cutting equipment was considered a commodity, and so they limited their purchases to one single source with whom little involvement was needed.

To conclude, the framework illustrates that single sourcing, long-term relationships, economic importance and a high degree of involvement do not necessarily go hand in hand. In various ways they can be combined with characteristics that usually are considered as belonging to a contrasting approach (multiple sourcing, short-term relationships and/or low involvement). There seem to be good reasons for a substantial variation in the combined positions among these dimensions. Consequently, change may also concern only one or two of these dimensions and not necessarily all of them, and although these changes of relationships are generally in the 'prescribed' direction, changes in other directions may clearly be motivated.

4.3   Paths and patterns of change

Having identified the various dimensions of variety in supplier relationships, it is now appropriate to turn to a more detailed analysis of the paths and patterns of changes that may occur. Chapter 3 has provided an extensive overview of different views on strategy and the different types of strategic change. Two distinctions that have been made are between the extent or magnitude of change – revolutionary change vs continuous adaptation – and the nature of the change – proactive vs reactive. Based on these distinctions, four situations are identified: revolutionary, proactive change; revolutionary, reactive change; continuous, proactive change; and continuous, reactive change.[4] Although it is arguably difficult to assign actual change patterns to just one of these four categories, a first characterization of these different paths may help to illustrate the variety and multidimensional nature of change in supplier relations.

Revolutionary, proactive change

In this situation, the proactive and revolutionary change corresponds to major turnarounds where the management of an organizational action is not preceded by a crisis. Such a change may, for example, be triggered by the recruitment of a new chief purchasing officer (CPO) or purchasing director – or an 'autonomous', proactive reconsideration of existing practices.

Box 4.4   Outsourcing IT services at ABN AMRO

On 16 December 2004, the ABN AMRO banking group announced a number of restructuring efforts to create increased group synergies. ABN AMRO, a prominent international bank headquartered in the Netherlands, mainly operates in three customer segments: consumer and commercial clients, wholesale clients, and private clients and asset management. The decisions accelerate and broaden the Group Shared Services (GSS) action tracks announced in August 2004.

GSS was established in 2004 to create value across the group through increased client satisfaction, higher operational efficiency, optimizing of operational risk and increased flexibility. It focuses on realizing synergies across the group through further consolidation and standardization. Regarding information technology (IT), GSS has analysed alternative delivery and sourcing scenarios: in-house consolidation, partial outsourcing, multivendor strategies and/or offshoring. This analysis shows that, for each scenario, this process will lead to a staff reduction over the next 18 months of approximately 1200 FTEs (full-time equivalents) out of a total of 5000 FTEs working across the group. Given the size of the operations of the bank in the Netherlands and the US, IT staff in these countries will be relatively more affected compared with those in other countries. Depending on the extent to which ABN AMRO will choose outsourcing as a solution for certain activities, it anticipates that an additional number of staff will be transferred to other employers in the future. The total costs regarding the GSS action tracks will be €870 million; the expected cost savings related to the GSS action tracks will increase from the earlier announced €500 million to at least €600 million per year as of 2007.

Source: ABN AMRO press release, December 2004.

With at least 25% of the workforce in IT being affected by these initiatives towards increased use of shared service centres and outsourcing/offshoring, surely this can be classified as a revolutionary change. At the same time, it can be primarily seen as a proactive change, since ABN AMRO did not seem to be in a crisis at the moment of the change: in November 2004, it expected to post 10% higher earnings in 2004 compared to 2003. This also prompted Dutch labour union officials to criticize the plans. Even though it may thus be classified as a proactive change, one could still argue that this initiative cannot be seen in isolation from similar efforts by other firms such as Shell and Philips, and the overall trend towards offshoring in the service industry.[5]

Revolutionary, reactive change

In contrast to the first situation, the change in this situation is a reaction to an overt problem. In Box 4.5, we provide the example of Dutch retailer Ahold's relations with building contractors.

Box 4.5   Ahold store development – open next week

In 1994, Ahold's Store Development department conducted an investigation into the opinions of various internal stakeholders regarding the perceived problems in the process of building and renovating stores. The conclusion was that people found the construction time too long, there was no clear project management, stocks were barely visible, the local shop manager had too little influence, and there was a large opportunity cost in terms of lost sales related to delays. The problem is significant as Ahold, in the Netherlands alone, renovates or builds 180 stores a year, investing roughly €120–130 million. The existing process of renovation was that, sequentially, each week or so a different section of the store was being refurbished. The problems signalled indicated that a minor adaptation to this process would not be significant.

Under the denominator 'Open Next Week', Ahold launched a programme in which stores would be (re)built in a maximum of 10 days, during which a complete store would be closed and fully renovated. By simplifying and standardizing the construction process, the construction time could be shortened, reducing not only the direct investment costs (target −20%) but the (enormous) opportunity costs of lost sales. Four specific new construction methods were being introduced: modular constructions (standardized shelves etc.); pre-fabrication;

pre-assembly (complete shelving systems including the product labels); collaboration and partnership with selected suppliers. In addition, the overall overhaul process is completely standardized by retail formula (Albert Heijn – food; Etos – pharmacy; Gall & Gall – liquor).

In fact, during the preparations – in total some five months before the actual construction period – Ahold built the complete inventory of each new store (shelves, cooling cabinets etc.) as a prototype in one of its three 'factories' around the Netherlands.

After a decade of implementing and refining this approach, the results are quite successful. There has never been a shop that has not opened within 10 days, and the investment cost reduction target of 20% (per square metre shop) has been achieved as well. Over time, a number of incremental changes have been made to the process, and currently new targets are being set. For example, the Albert Heijn stores want to move to 'Open This Week'. Also, some of the contractors have been changed during the years. One particularly significant challenge is to share knowledge and learning across the different shops, formulas and departments – especially in relation to new employees coming into the organization.

The experience from Ahold demonstrates that one particular problem in consolidating a certain strategic change is setting new and 'stretching' targets to let the change migrate into a sort of continuous adaptation. Below, we look at some examples of these more continuous, gradual changes.

Continuous, proactive change

In the third situation, the buying company actively drives, in small but continuous steps, the development of supplier relations in a certain direction.

Box 4.6   Systematic use of key performance indicators

A mechanical engineering company using several hundred parts suppliers changed its ways of measuring supplier performance. From having previously used about 40 performance measures that were seldom assessed and only used internally for infrequent decisions on supplier changes, two main key performance indicators (KPIs) were selected. One KPI focused on quality and the other on delivery performance. These were systematically monitored and once a month a list with the ten worst-performing suppliers on each KPI was distributed. These listed suppliers had to participate in a meeting at the buying company and together the buyer and suppliers analysed the situation and developed action plans. In parallel to this systematic procedure the requirements on the suppliers' performance were raised, for example lead times from order to delivery were reduced by 25%.

The obvious benefit of working systematically with a very limited number of performance measures, as illustrated in Box 4.6, is that the performance can be enhanced. This is owing to several factors. First is the attention given to low-performing suppliers, and to the costs involved in travel and meetings to solve the problems. Second, the joint analysis of problems surfacing when suppliers are not living up to standards sometimes results in identification of adjustment needs that concern both the buyer and a particular supplier. For instance, design changes may be needed in order to solve certain problems, or adjustments of the communication between the companies.

The systematic use of KPI in relation to suppliers also entails that suppliers that do not live up to the buying firm's expectations become aware of this and are thus not taken by surprise if, or when, they are replaced by other suppliers. In addition, since the KPIs for suppliers are directly related to the buying company's overall performance, the suppliers get a picture of how they contribute to the company's performance as a supplier. Finally, by dealing with two important performance dimensions across all supplier relationships in a standardized fashion, the interaction with individual suppliers can be focused on other, value-creating areas of the exchange with them.

Continuous, reactive change

In this final situation, the reactive way of moving step by step means that organizations adapt their operations in successive steps, in reaction to a perceived problem. Box 4.7 provides an example of how purchases of rock drills went through such a continuous, reactive change.

Box 4.7   Changing the relationship between Boliden and Sandvik

For quite some time, an open-pit mine at the firm Boliden in the north of Sweden had been buying considerable quantities of rock drills from supplier Sandvik. These drills were used as replaceable tools in drilling equipment operating in the pit to excavate rock for new supplies of metal ore. The relationship between the two firms, at that time, could be described as rather superficial; virtually no dialogue, for example on quality issues or new product development, was going on between the two. The drills were bought in large quantities as they often required replacement due to wear and breakdowns, and were paid for on a piece-price basis.

The responsible purchasing manager at that time was not satisfied with the quality performance of the drills, and decided that the most productive way of engaging the supplier in a more extensive dialogue was by changing the basis for compensation. After several discussions, Sandvik agreed to an incentive-based payment scheme, where the number of tonnes excavated per drill became an important parameter. Very soon, product engineers and quality managers from the supplier started to appear at the mine, requesting drill operators not to discard old, broken drills but to return them to Sandvik. Supplier representatives started to talk to the drill operators, soliciting information on various aspects such as the specific rock conditions in which most drill failures occurred and so on.

Gradually, the contacts between the supplier and the customer intensified, which subsequently led to a continuous stream of stepwise improvement initiatives.

One of the interesting aspects of the Sandvik–Boliden illustration concerns the fact that this change started from a relatively minor adjustment: changing the basis for compensation. Nevertheless, the ultimate consequences of this change were quite fundamental – at least within the context of this purchase category (drills).

Implications of different forms of change

Proactive change in supplier relations differs from more reactive change in the sense that the initiative lies to a greater extent with the buying firm. This creates its own particular problems, as we have seen in the case of ABN AMRO: some of the stakeholders, for example, may not be convinced of the urgency of the change. Proactive change, depending on its magnitude, therefore requires substantial efforts to create momentum and willingness of other actors to participate in the change. Obviously, the upside of this is that a buying firm that proactively changes particular aspects in its supplier relations can normally spend more time on planning the change programme and possibly also attract the attention of suppliers, especially if the change can be considered as 'leading edge'. For example, when several manufacturers in the electronics and automotive sector started introducing 'early supplier involvement' programmes in the early 1990s, they were able to attract the participation of suppliers partly because these felt this was a learning opportunity for them.

Reactive change, in particular when it is of a great magnitude, carries the challenge of creating a subsequent path of further improvements. Once the immediate cause of or reason for the change has disappeared in the background and the intended results have been realized, what are the next steps?

Putting change in its context

The distinctions among changes discussed in this section may not always appear as clear cut as depicted here. If individual changes are put in a long-term perspective, not many of them may seem revolutionary. Moreover, changes do not take place in isolation, and thus from some perspectives they may always be seen as reactions to other changes. Also, the time perspective can be considered as decisive of whether a change is considered revolutionary or part of a continuous process.

Think of the final example on rock drills. Depending on the importance of drills in the overall scheme of things, and possible repercussions that these changes have had in other purchase categories, the changes may or not may not be interpreted as a revolutionary change on the level of overall purchasing strategy.

The case study described in the next section illustrates a number of changes that may have seemed revolutionary to some of the parties involved at the time of the change, but that in the context of a 40-year period do not seem very dramatic. The case also illustrates stability as an important feature of the supply base of a company, and this stability may be seen as a 'platform' for change in other dimensions, such as technical development taking place within established supplier relationships. The latter concerns how changes are considered. If one is focusing on the suppliers, change may appear very different from when one is focusing on the technical solutions of the buying company. Although extensive changes may include change in both, some only affect either the supplier structure or the technical solutions.

4.4   Case study: Change and stability of the supply base in a long-term perspective

This section reports on a case study of the long-term buying behaviour of a manufacturing firm.[6] The background to the study was a perceived lack of long-term observations of buyer–supplier relationships. The aim of the study was twofold. The first was to describe the long-term development of the supplier base of a company. The second was to explore the reasons for changes in the supplier base, primarily by analysing why firms continue to buy from the same supplier and why they sometimes change suppliers. Before approaching the findings of the study, a brief description of the case company and the study is provided.

About the company and the study

The case study deals with the supplier base of a manufacturer of electrical forklift trucks. The company was founded in 1958, and since then it has grown substantially. In 2003 its turnover reached above SEK1500 million (€165 million). All development, procurement and manufacturing activities have, during the whole period, taken place at the same location in Sweden. The product range consists of a couple of basic models manufactured in a few thousand units a year. The most important in-house manufacturing activities are welding, painting and assembly. The extent to which these and other manufacturing activities are undertaken within the company varies for the different forklift models. One reason is that 'module' or 'system sourcing' has become increasingly applied, and thus the more recently developed models have fewer activities performed internally than the older ones. About 3500 different components of various sizes and values are purchased, and around 80% of these items are more or less customized for the firm.

The case study focused on which suppliers were used each year for ten different components. The components were originally selected to capture differences in technical complexity, customization/standardization, purchase volume and supplier market structure. All in all, they accounted for one third of the total purchase value at the time the study began (in the mid-1970s).

Change and continuity in the supplier base

The time series covered 39 years, and so for each component there were 38 possibilities for making some kind of change of suppliers. The study comprises ten components, making the total number of potential changes 380. Owing to

TABLE 4.3   Changes in the supplier base from one year to the next

Total number of potential changes	375	
No change at all – same supplier(s) remained	314	(84%)
Pure replacement – one supplier replaced by another	11	(3%)
One supplier added – the other(s) remained	17	(5%)
One supplier removed – the other(s) remained	20	(5%)
Other changes – more complicated patterns	13	(3%)
Total number of changes	*61*	*(16%)*

TABLE 4.4   Duration of the supplier relationships

Relationship duration in years	*Number of suppliers*
1–4	18
5–9	11
10–19	11
20–29	6
30–39	5
Total number of suppliers	51
Average duration (mean value)	11.4 years

missing data in the first years the complete data set consists of 375 observations. The changes are summarized in Table 4.3.

Table 4.3 illustrates the strong short-term stability of the supplier base of the company. In 84% of the observations no change at all occurred, meaning that exactly the same supplier(s) remained from one year to the next. In total 61 changes were observed, the majority of which concerned adding or removing suppliers. There was a slight variation observed among the different components in terms of continuity. The highest score for 'no change' was 92% and the lowest 74%.

The continuity of the supplier base is captured in Table 4.4, showing the duration of the relationships with the 51 suppliers that were used for the ten components over the period. Table 4.4 illustrates a variety among the relationships in terms of their continuity. Eleven suppliers were used for more than 20 years, and five for more than 30 years. On the other hand, some of the relationships were short in duration. Eighteen suppliers were used for four years or less. The average length of the 51 relationships was 11.4 years.

Reasons for making changes in the supplier base

According to Table 4.3, the buying firm made 61 changes in the supplier base during the period. The reasons for the changes were traced through interviews with informants from the forklift manufacturer. In particular, there was an interest in analysing the role of purchasing in these changes. On the basis of the interviews eight underlying causes were identified. Table 4.5 illustrates the distribution of the reasons for the changes of the supplier base.

TABLE 4.5   Reasons for change in the supplier base

Change reasons	Frequency (number of changes)
Price difference	20
Supplier performance	12
Supplier initiatives	7
Design and manufacturing	6
New models and variants	5
Customer requirements	5
Avoiding dependency	3
Consolidation	3

The objective of the case study was to shed some new light on the dynamics of the supplier base of a company. First, the study illustrated that the long-term development of the supplier base is characterized by a complex interplay between continuity and change in several dimensions. Some relationships have a short-term duration, while others are longlasting, even spanning the whole lifetime of the buying firm in this case study. The dynamics concern both new relationships and changes in ongoing ones. Furthermore, a change in the supplier base is not necessarily a sign of dynamic developments. In many cases these changes represent a rather simple switch from one supplier of a standardized component to another, with few dynamic effects. Secondly, the perceptions of the reasons for changes in the supplier base were analysed. The change patterns observed feature economic, technical and organizational causes. These were sometimes related to the buying company, while in other situations factors related to its suppliers or customers could be identified. For instance, a design change may have its origins in customer requirements or may be suggested by a supplier. The impact of such a change may, in turn, be different. Some design changes are made jointly by the buyer and one or several suppliers within the framework of existing relationships, while in other cases some suppliers may have to be replaced in order to cope, for instance, with new technologies.

The case study described above suggests that there may be several different drivers of change in supplier relationships and in the supplier base as a whole. Among the apparent sources of change are the buying firm and the individual suppliers. However, there are also other parties in the networks of the buying firm and its individual suppliers that may take the initiative to change. In the case study special requirements of the customers to the buying firm caused 5 of the 61 changes. For instance, some customers required a certain brand of some standardized components that resulted in adding suppliers to the supplier base. Furthermore, among the changes initiated by suppliers there were several changes that could be traced back to relationships between the suppliers and their other customers. In some of these cases the suppliers were asked to invest and focus on other products, which meant that they would not have the capacity and/or the right production equipment to continue their supplies to the case company. Hence, one way to categorize these changes would be to relate them to the customer and the supplier and to other parties in their respective networks, for example the suppliers' suppliers and their (other) customers.

Less than half of the observed changes in the case study were initiated directly by the purchasing function of the company. Changes initiated by the buying firm's customers and suppliers were almost as frequent as those emanating from the purchasing department. Furthermore, modifications of the product stemming from technical changes initiated by design and product development and requirements for new variants from marketing and sales proved to be important determinants of change. Together they accounted for one fifth of the total number of changes. Hence, based on this case study we may suggest that although the purchasing department is always the active party in implementing changes in the supplier base, its role in initiating and influencing change can display huge variations. Hence, mainstream textbooks may seem to overemphasize the role of purchasing and the purchasing department as a 'change agent'. This does not suggest that the purchasing function is of little importance to the performance of the company, but that its ability to pursue its own strategies is limited. An alternative view on the purchasing function, which may better describe its role, is to regard it as an interface between the operations of the buying company and the suppliers. We will return to this when discussing the changing role of the purchasing function in section 4.6. The next section focuses on the relation between supplier relationships and strategic change.

4.5   Managing and coping with change in supplier relations

Previous sections have pointed at some important aspects of change in supplier relationships. First of all, it has been suggested that the views on how suppliers may contribute to the performance of the buying firm has changed both concerning the extent and the nature of the impact. The variety of ways in which suppliers may contribute is closely connected to the way in which supplier relationships are dealt with. When strategic thinking in purchasing is concerned, the way in which a buying firm differentiates its behaviour towards different suppliers has long been on top of the agenda. Supplier portfolio analysis has been discussed, developed and applied extensively since Kraljic's article 'Purchasing must become supply management' was published in the *Harvard Business Review* in 1983.[7] In previous sections we have also emphasized the difficulties when it comes to the purchasing function's possibilities to pursue its own strategies in relation to suppliers, and provided examples of how changes may result from a number of reasons and be initiated by various internal and external actors.

Considering the field of strategy in general, as discussed in Chapter 3, the view of how the firm relates to its environment is obviously subject to debate. In addition, there are differing views as to whether strategies are to be considered as resulting from deliberate action or as emergent. If we start from these two aspects of strategizing and assume that (1) a firm to varying extents can have an impact on its environment, but also has to adjust to changes in it, and (2) strategizing includes elements of both deliberation and emergence, we may be in a good position to look into how supplier relationships may change in a process of strategizing. Hence, managing and coping with supplier relationships may be seen as the strategic role of purchasing from the buying firm's perspective.

Implications of the buying firm's strategizing for its supplier relationships

In Chapter 3, strategizing has been presented as a useful concept to describe how strategy processes – which may contain elements of emergence and deliberation in strategy formation, and which may be more or less revolutionary or incremental in nature – develop over time. Strategizing has been described as 'the way in which the organization interacts with its environment'.[8] Hence, for purchasing this interaction mostly concerns the suppliers, in addition to its interaction with other internal functions of the company. When interaction with suppliers is concerned purchasing represents the whole company; together with the marketing function, which primarily deals with the customers, these two functions are responsible for the majority of the interaction with the environment. Apparently, the nature of these buyer–supplier relationships is of great importance for the extent to which the firm may change at all. Internal change that can be executed in isolation, and thus without any effects for others, is naturally of very limited importance for the performance of the company. That is, strategic change always takes place through and in interaction with customers and suppliers. Also, very few extensive changes only affect one 'side' of the company; that is, either its supplier or customer relationships. For instance, changing some part of the technology of the company's product typically implies changes in the exchange with both customers and (some) suppliers. However, the extent to which the firm may influence its customers and suppliers may vary as a result of their positions vis-à-vis one another and their relationships with other firms.

Adding relationships to the view of the firm and its environment, so that relationships are considered as organizations that link the firm to its environment, may open up the opportunities and limits to strategizing for identification. Hence, there may be various potentials in developing relationships with buyers and suppliers in a long-term perspective, most of which are not known when the relational investments are made.

The purchasing function's role in strategizing

In section 2.2, three roles of purchasing were described: rationalization, development and structure. The relative emphasis on these three roles can be seen both as a cause and an effect in relation to how the firm interacts with its suppliers and thus how it utilizes the purchasing function for strategizing. The ways in which the roles are dealt with affects to what extent purchasing contributes to strategizing. Following the reasoning above, the strategic role of the purchasing function is determined by its ability to establish and develop relationships with suppliers that may contribute to the performance of the firm both in a short and in a longer time perspective. Hence, if rationalization is mostly achieved through short-term cost reduction efforts, the strategic position of the firm may not be affected to its advantage. The purchasing function's role to affect the supplier structure is, whether intended or not, always affecting the future possibilities of change.

Influencing and being influenced

A strategizing perspective on supplier relations leads to the identification of three paradoxes in managing and managing change in supplier relations, which all concern the balance of influencing and being influenced.[9]

The first paradox regards the fact that close supplier relationships are both essential for a firm's competitive success, and at the same time may restrict its ability to change.

A frequent discussion related to supplier collaborations concerns the risk of getting 'locked in', both commercially and/or technologically, into specific relations. The development of intensive, high-involvement relationships may narrow a firm's field of vision and its potential to develop alternative relationships. Close collaboration may be necessary to jointly develop and exploit new technologies, for example, but can at the same time harm the buying firm's flexibility to embark on competing technologies that are appearing in parallel.

It is therefore clear that there is a trade-off between the possibility to leverage existing relations and their resources and the flexibility to adapt to changes, but determining the preferred solution in a specific situation depends – in our view – very much on the perspective that firms and their decision makers have of their environment. If one agrees that an important part of an organization's resource base is located beyond its ownership boundary, and that relationships are critical in accessing these resources, networks of organizations may be seen as the 'natural form of organization'.[10] In such a situation, lock-in may not be seen as necessarily dysfunctional but as the inherent by-product of necessary close relationships.

If, on the other hand, one takes the idea of the self-centred, atomistic actor operating in a market of 'perfect competition' as the point of departure, close relationships may be seen as the exception to the rule, only to be applied if and when the benefits clearly outweigh the risks and when arm's-length relations are not effective.

In our opinion, managers could be much more explicit about these fundamental beliefs and perspectives, as this may help to clarify their preferences and behaviour – and, ultimately, possibly to change those where and when necessary.

The second paradox concerns the fact that supplier relationships may be used, on the one hand, by the buying firm to influence others (not only the supplier concerned, but also others) but, on the other hand, may be used by others to influence the buying firm.

One of the most frequent demonstrations of the first ways of influencing is ingredient branding, or the 'Intel Inside' phenomenon: leveraging supplier components/relations to convince final customers of the value of your final product. Alternatively, customers may indeed force such supplier relations on the manufacturer, which may be particularly cumbersome for manufacturers that are in relatively weak power positions versus such suppliers.

The third paradox is that the more successful a buying firm is in controlling its supplier network, the less innovative it becomes. Since most firms surely would like to control to a great extent their environments and thus their counterparts, it may seem strange to suggest that 'full' control is not what they should strive for. Control, however, has the downside of stifling creativity, renewal and innovation. The more 'open opportunities' suppliers have, the higher chances are that they may come up with new products, processes and procedures that may benefit the buying company. To quote an engineer of Philips Electronics, who was working on early supplier involvement together with purchasing representatives: 'Let's avoid trying to turn all suppliers into little Philipses!'

Being aware of these three paradoxes may be a helpful step in identifying particular opportunities for development of supplier relations. However, in these efforts it is important to notice that they are indeed paradoxes and thus are naturally combined effects as opposed to contradictions.

4.6   Changing the role of purchasing

This chapter focuses mainly on change in relation to suppliers. However, inter- and intra-organizational issues are difficult to separate, as how the firm works internally is closely related to how it may relate to its environment and vice versa. Moreover, the effects of a certain way of working towards external counterparts may be different depending on the firm's internal relations. In this section we focus on how the purchasing function may change its role as an interface between other vital internal functions, such as production, product development and marketing, and the firm's suppliers. Hence, when change of a purchasing function's role as an interface is concerned we may consider two different dimensions, one that describes how the purchasing function of a firm relates to other internal functions and one that describes how it relates to suppliers. Change in one of these dimensions will have different effects owing to the 'position' in the other.

The purchasing function's internal and external relations

In the internal dimension we identify three principal ways in terms of how the purchasing function is positioned in relation to other internal functions. First, it may be operating as an 'order-taking unit' that gets information on specifications, required volumes and delivery dates from for example the production function, and based on this carries out operational purchasing tasks as required. In contrast, the purchasing unit can be in a very strong position and thus more or less be dominating the conditions for the other internal functions. In these situations the purchasing function may include the firm's top management, which seems natural when the business operations of the company rest on what the purchasing function is able to buy. Third, the purchasing function may rely on interaction with the other internal functions, permitting them to influence each other in decision making regarding purchasing, production, logistics, marketing and so on.

The external dimension captures the way in which the firm deals with its suppliers. Here we rely on a modified version of the three generic forms of organizing: markets, hierarchies and networks.[11] First, the firm may purchase in a 'playing the market' fashion. In this way of working the firm relies on numerous available suppliers and on finding the 'best' one for each purchasing situation. Second, the firm may have organized some parts of its suppliers in supplier hierarchies, where *what is bought* and *from whom* are 'built into' the hierarchy even on several layers. These hierarchical relations are associated with exercising external control.[12] Hence, these situations may be described as 'order giving' in a given external structure. Third, the firm may interact with suppliers and perceive them as being part of a network in which not only the suppliers are considered relevant but also their relationships with various customers, suppliers and other counterparts.

Putting these two dimensions, and the three situations in each, into a matrix results in nine principal cases (see Figure 4.1).

The two dimensions have different features but are not independent. The framework suggests that the effects of external relations depend on how the firm works internally and vice versa. For instance, there is one situation in each dimension that is *interactive* in its nature: one focusing on internal and one on external interaction. Interaction permits adjustments of different kinds and the *direction* of these adjustments can thus be found in the dimension that permits interaction. Hence, the framework suggests that the way in which supplier relationships are working largely depends on the purchasing function's ability to include other internal functions in the interaction with suppliers.

The main unit of analysis for the proposed framework is the firm's purchasing function, but the model can also describe different purchasing situations and tasks

Internal dimension

		Purchasing conditions are decided by other internal functions	Purchasing dominates conditions	Purchasing interacts with other internal functions to set conditions
External dimension	Supplier market	1. The purchasing function finds the best offer based on internal purchasing requests	2. The purchasing function identifies the best offer on the market and other functions adjust to what is bought	3. The purchasing function decides what is to be purchased on the market in interaction with other internal functions
	Supplier hierarchy	4. The purchasing function administers purchases from given suppliers based on internal requests	5. The purchasing function buys from given suppliers and other functions adjust to these purchases	6. The purchasing function decides together with other functions what to order from given suppliers
	Supplier network	7. The purchasing function interacts with suppliers to fulfil internal demands	8. The purchasing function interacts with suppliers to develop the best buy to which other functions adjust	9. The purchasing function interacts with other internal functions and suppliers to decide the content of their exchange

FIGURE 4.1   Internal and external dimensions influencing the purchasing function's role.

within a firm. Increasing specialization typically entails an increasing variety of externally accessed resources. This implies that firms need to differentiate among purchasing situations in a number of ways and therefore a buying company may need to be involved in several different situations, as illustrated in Figure 4.1. Hence, how different parts of the overall purchasing function relate to different internal and external parties needs to be taken into account when organizing it, which is illustrated by the example in Box 4.8.[13]

Box 4.8   Reorganizing and changing the role of purchasing

For a long time, a firm producing various chemicals had maintained one central purchasing department responsible for all purchases. The stated mission for this department was to provide a service to the rest of the company. Production and sales were organized in different business units corresponding to different application areas for the chemicals. For all of the business units (BUs) the raw materials were considered of great importance in terms of price impact on profit and/or in terms of the quality of the end products. The raw materials used by the different BUs were mainly purchased from different suppliers and were based on different technologies. Hence, there were no synergies among the BUs' needs for these purchases.

For MRO (maintenance, repair and operations) including a wide variety of standardized products the situation was different, since the BUs' different production facilities required products that could be purchased from the same kinds of suppliers. These purchases were, however, difficult to coordinate since individuals within the different BUs wanted to decide what, and sometimes even from whom, to buy. Therefore, MRO purchases were made from a large number of suppliers (there were 10 000 in the supplier ledger) based on internal orders.

Two main problems were identified. First, the BUs wanted a closer connection to purchasing (or rather specific purchasers) for their raw material purchases in order to be able to develop important supplier relationships. Second, the indirect costs for MRO purchases (administration, materials handling, transportation etc.) had been found to be extensive. Indirect costs were assessed to SEK32 million (€3.5 million) on purchases worth SEK40 million (€4.4 million) annually.

Based on these problems the purchasing function was reorganized. Some purchasers were assigned to different BUs to concentrate on purchasing raw materials together with product and production engineers, while MRO purchases were kept as a central function. However, MRO purchases also became subject to extensive restructuring. The number of suppliers was found to be a main cost driver both directly, owing to the costs associated with dealing with the suppliers individually, and indirectly, since other cost drivers such as transactions, invoices and deliveries were related to it. A decision was taken to concentrate on just a few key suppliers providing, as distributors, wide ranges of products in different areas such as electrical components and tools, stationery and laboratory chemicals and equipment. Teams with representatives from the buying company and the key suppliers were set up and given cost reduction targets. These targets were approached by the teams developing joint routines that were different for different product areas, and that were based on adjustments to reduce the total cost of exchange.

The example illustrates how the purchasing function of a company was developed from having one central function corresponding to the first box in Figure 4.1, into two functions corresponding to boxes 9 and 5. For the raw material purchases, interaction with other internal functions, primarily product developers and production engineers and the suppliers, became the role of the BUs' purchasing functions. For the MRO supplies the previous freedom to decide what, and from what sources, to buy became limited for the internal users and the efforts to reduce the total costs of exchange were mainly a matter for the central purchasing function and the chosen key suppliers. Hence, the role of the purchasing function changed as well as its interfaces to internal and external parties.

Change in external and internal relations

The framework may be used to discuss change in the role of a firm's purchasing function as an interface between the firm and its suppliers. For instance, the current vogue for developing partnerships with suppliers has surely had different effects for different companies. To some firms the focus on developing partnerships with suppliers has meant a move from box 1, where the purchasing function plays the market, to box 7, where they try to develop supplier relationships and networks. However, if the purchasing function is tied to conditions set by other functions, as in box 7, the scope for interaction with suppliers is limited and therefore necessarily focused on what can be done by the suppliers in order to adjust to the firm's internal demands. A purchasing function in this situation may identify potentials in also making internal adjustments to be better able to take advantage of the suppliers' resources. As a result they may try to develop their ways of working into the situation described by box 9 in Figure 4.1, in which adjustments are made possible by external *and* internal interaction. If this is not perceived as a possible route, the purchasing function may have to adjust to the situation in such a way that certain problems, for example with complex technical specifications, are solved mainly by the supplier(s), instead of being subject to interaction between internal and external counterparts, for instance the firm's development engineers and the supplier's production staff. Apparently, this way of dealing with problem solving does not always result in efficient solutions for the buying firm.

In such situations as the ones described by box 9, the purchasing function typically gets another role in that it becomes a coordinating function between the firm's internal functions, such as production, R&D and product development, and some of the supplier's internal functions. Particularly in the automotive industry, 'cross-functional teams' including buyer and supplier representatives have been a means to achieve an organized way of interacting during product and production system development. In these situations, where technical interdependencies within some kind of end product, such as a car or a truck, stretch across the boundaries of several firms, the challenges become directed towards developing other boundaries or limits for interaction between the companies. In the automotive industry these challenges are often dealt with by 'modularization', where efforts are made to keep technical interdependence within modules while the interfaces between them are kept as clear cut as possible. This way of organizing interfaces thus implies directions for interaction; that is, with whom to interact and with whom *not* to interact.[14]

The firm's capacity to deal with a variety of relationships in different ways is arguably of huge importance for its performance. This variety, however, is subject to dynamic forces, in that the conditions for the relationships between the buying firm and its suppliers change over time. As a means for considering how to cope with internal and external change, the framework may be useful as a platform for discussions dealing with directions and limits for interaction. These decisions can be directly translated into how the purchasing function needs to be organized as an interface between different internal and external parties (see also Chapter 5).

If the purchasing function of the company is seen as an interface between the operations of the company and its suppliers, the strategic role of purchasing is to link these activities, rather than to promote specific purchasing strategies. Fulfilling this role in the most appropriate way requires purchasing to be a representative of suppliers as well as of the buying firm. Through being well informed about the needs of its own company and the skills and capabilities of different suppliers, purchasing may act as an agent of change and connect suppliers with the firm's internal functions, such as product design and manufacturing.

4.7   Conclusions

We started this chapter by stating that the previous description of a change from a 'classic' to a 'modern' type of purchasing behaviour may be to oversimplify the development of purchasing. However, many firms are struggling towards the ideals featuring the modern approach, while others develop their own mixes of relational features. Most firms consider it important to differentiate the purchasing behaviour towards different suppliers and the routes to develop the basis for this differentiation have become increasingly dynamic. We have given examples and provided possible rationales for some of these changes.

Owing to the increasing complexity characterizing the situations of buying firms, the advice regarding how to deal with change in supplier relationships cannot be uniform. However, on a general level most firms still seem to have untapped potentials by working with too many suppliers and dealing with too many of them in an arm's-length fashion.[15]

Overall, buying firms will be confronted with the need to simultaneously manage a portfolio of changes: from proactive, revolutionary changes to reactive, continuous changes. As such, this requires a delicate balancing act not only in terms of resources to manage these changes at any given point in time, but also in terms of planning for subsequent, consecutive changes. It may be increasingly true that change is the only constant, but there is still a need for pacing and coordinating various change efforts.

While focusing on change we have also pointed at the importance of recognizing stability as a necessary condition for change. Although these may concern different dimensions, for example supplier relationships and technology, they can be seen as prerequisites for each other.

As far as the role of the purchasing function is concerned, we have highlighted the importance of recognizing its interaction not only with external counterparts but also with other internal functions. Trying to establish supplier relationships without being able to interact with other internal functions is a difficult and potentially costly task.

To conclude, supplier relationships are becoming increasingly important to most firms owing to increasing specialization and technological complexity. However, there may be very different paths and patterns of changes in and of supplier relationships. These paths and patterns may also become increasingly complex because of the interdependence that characterizes the development of important supplier relationships. Therefore, a transition from a relational to a network focus may become the next challenge for many firms. Whereas this builds further on a development towards a reduction of the number of suppliers and towards developing closer relationships with a few of the remaining ones, it adds several dimensions, for example how to relate to the other counterparts of the suppliers and how to organize the interfaces with the suppliers and the internal functions of the buying firm.

Notes and references

1   Dubois, A. and Gadde, L.-E. (2000) 'Supply strategy and network effects – Purchasing behavior in the construction industry', *European Journal of Purchasing and Supply Management*, Vol. 6, No. 3/4, pp. 207–15. This particular issue of the journal was fully dedicated to purchasing and supply (chain) management in the construction industry. See also Cox, A. and Thompson, I. (1997) ' "Fit for purpose" contractual relations: Determining a theoretical framework for construction projects', *European Journal of Purchasing and Supply Management*, Vol. 3, No. 3, pp. 127–35.

2   See for a similar case study Holmen, E., Håkansson, H. and Pedersen, A.-C. (2003) 'Framing as a means to manage a supply network', *Journal of Customer Behaviour*, Vol. 2, No. 3, pp. 385–407.

3   Gadde, L.-E. and Snehota, I. (2000) 'Making the most of supplier relationships', *Industrial Marketing Management*, Vol. 29, pp. 305–16.

4   Melin, L. and Hellgren, M. (1994) 'Patterns of strategic processes: Two change typologies', in Thomas, H., O'Neal, D., White, R. and Hurst, D. (eds) *Building the Strategically-Responsive Organization*, John Wiley & Sons Ltd: Chichester, pp. 251–71.

5   Karmarkar, U. (2004) 'Will you survive the services revolution?', *Harvard Business Review*, June, pp. 1–8.

6   Dubois, A., Gadde, L.-E. and Mattsson, L.-G. (2003) 'Change and continuity in the supplier base: A case study of a manufacturing firm 1964–2002', *Journal of Customer Behaviour*, Vol. 2, No. 3, pp. 409–32.

7   Kraljic, P. (1983) 'Purchasing must become supply management', *Harvard Business Review*, September–October, pp. 109–17. See also Bensaou, M. (1999) 'Portfolios of buyer–supplier relationships', *Sloan Management Review*, Vol. 40, No. 4, pp. 35–44; Dubois, A. and Pedersen, A.-C. (2002) 'Why relationships do not fit into purchasing portfolio models', *European Journal of Purchasing and Supply Management*, Vol. 8, No. 1, pp. 35–42; Gelderman, C.J. and Van Weele, A.J. (2002) 'Strategic direction through purchasing portfolio management: A case study', *Journal of Supply Chain Management*, Vol. 38, No. 2, pp. 30–37.

8   Nygaard, C. and Hull Kristensen, P. (2002) 'Inledning – Strategen och Kontexten', in Nygaard, C. (ed.), *Strategizing: En kontextuell Organisationsteori*, Studentlitteratur: Lund, pp. 13–26.

9   Håkansson, H. and Ford, D. (2002) 'How should companies interact in business networks?', *Journal of Business Research*, Vol. 55, No. 2, pp. 133–9.

10   Piore, M. (1992) 'Fragments of a cognitive theory of technological change and organizational structure', in Nohria, N. and Eccles, R. (eds), *Networks and Organizations: Structure, Form and Action*, Harvard Business School Press: Boston, MA, pp. 430–44.

11   Thompson, G., Frances, J., Levacic, R. and Mitchell, J. (eds) (1991) *Markets, Hierarchies and Networks: The Coordination of Social Life*, Sage Publications: London.

12   Håkansson and Ford (2002) *opere citato*.

[13] Some parts of the example are further described in Dubois, A. (2003) 'Strategic cost management across boundaries of firms', *Industrial Marketing Management*, Vol. 32, No. 5, pp. 365–74.

[14] See von Corswant, F. (2003) *Organizing Interactive Product Development*, dissertation, Department of Operations Management and Work Organization, Chalmers University of Technology, Gothenburg (Sweden).

[15] Dyer, J.H. and Singh, H. (1998) 'The relational view: Cooperative strategy and sources of interorganizational competitive advantage', *Academy of Management Review*, Vol. 23, No. 4, pp. 660–79.

Chapter 5

ORGANIZING FOR STRATEGIC SOURCING

Frank Rozemeijer and Finn Wynstra

This chapter is about designing effective organizations for sourcing. Organizing and organizational design are key tasks of (sourcing) management. The strategic change process often departs from changes in organizational designs. It seems as if major changes in patterns of behaviour to a great extent are due to changes in organizational design, processes and procedures. If there are other points of departure, major change will often ultimately include changes in organizational issues. Through this chapter, we aim to equip sourcing leaders with the understanding of the general roadmap to organizational designs and the tools necessary to design organizations that are effective and efficient. The basic model we propose is that changes in performance will normally require changes in organizational design.

Before moving into the various designs and behaviours of a purchasing organization, let us first start by defining what an organization is. Organizations can be defined as *social entities* (people or groups of people) that are *goal-oriented*, deliberately *structured activity systems* with an identifiable *boundary*.[1] Often, organizations are perceived to be something about charts, job descriptions and related documents that define the extent and limitations of responsibility and authority of individuals. These belong to the 'necessary evils' of running a company.

Clearly, this is indeed one part of reality. An organization can be defined as the formal way in which a company has assigned duties, responsibilities and authority to employees to manage its activities, products, functions and markets to meet its objectives. However, there is more to say. Organizations can also be looked at as political arenas, where groups of people have conflicting interests and use power in order to realize their own goals.[2]

From a contingency point of view, there is no such thing as the one best organization. To determine the best organizational design, one should closely look at the internal context (e.g. strategy, core competence, processes, available technology, capabilities of people) and external context (e.g. market developments, government regulations, competition). Even then, more than one design alternative might be appropriate. Driven by shifting demands of customers, suppliers and employees, organizations tend to evolve over time (see Box 5.1). This also holds true for sourcing. Sourcing departments nowadays differ a great deal from what they were in the 1970s or 1980s, and they will, no doubt, be different in the future.

Box 5.1   Over time, organizations can become dysfunctional

A global chemicals company worked for several years in a decentralized manner in sourcing. Based on a survey in a major division, the corporate purchasing group of the company came to the conclusions that (1) information on suppliers and prices applied in one location was isolated from the rest of the company; (2) sharing best practices and transfer of knowledge was achieved informally, and at worst accidentally; and (3) leverage initiatives only concentrated on well-known or easily understood commodities rather than those really requiring attention. The conclusion of the corporate purchasing group was that the lack of a coordinated approach resulted in wasted effort, in reinventing wheels and in opportunities being missed completely. The message was clear: the current sourcing organization had become dysfunctional – a new organizational design, new structures and processes were needed.

Source: Rozemeijer, F.A. (1998) 'Corporate purchasing synergy: Structured optimization or a matter of opportunism?', *Conference Proceedings 7th International Annual IPSERA Conference*, London, pp. 441–52.

In the next section, we explore some of the organizational developments that we can trace in today's practice and the likely future trends that we can identify. We also discuss the ways in which these will influence the organization of sourcing in the future. After that we move on to looking at the basic roadmap of organizational designs.

5.1   Developments in organizing the sourcing function

Before the 1980s, concepts like purchasing portfolio management, total cost of ownership, supplier partnerships, early supplier involvement and cross-functional buying teams were not yet very well known and/or applied in practice. Since then, some major shifts have taken place, which are reflected in the statements made by general managers and purchasing managers of some large manufacturing companies (see Box 5.2).

Box 5.2   Major shifts in purchasing

The changing role of purchasing and supply management can best be illustrated by the statements recently made by some general managers of some large manufacturing companies:

- 'Purchasing in our organization is too important to leave it only to buyers.'
- 'Purchasing in our company is moving into the line... it is becoming more and more a line responsibility.'
- 'Going for sustainable cost savings in purchasing and supplier relationships requires cross-functional teamwork.'
- 'If there is anything more important than purchasing in our company, it is a well-kept secret.'

Source: Van Weele, A.J. and Rozemeijer, F.A. (1999) 'Getting organized for purchasing and supply management in the information age: Towards the virtual organization', Chapter 5.1 in Hahn, D. and Kaufmann, L. (eds), *Handbuch Industrielles Beschaffungs Management*, Gabler: Weisbaden, pp. 625–37.

These changes do not stand by themselves, but are related to more fundamental changes that are going on in the workplace. According to some, the workplace will shift in six important ways[3]:

- *From vertical to horizontal: the new organization.* The horizontal dimension – looking across territories to focus the effort of the organization on common goals to serve customers – will become more important than the vertical dimension based on the company's internal hierarchy. For sourcing, this means that the functional orientation will be replaced by a process orientation. Purchasing processes within organizations will increasingly be organized around cross-functional buying teams ('internal integration'). One step further in this concept is to have joint development or improvement teams (e.g. supplier councils) with key suppliers ('external integration').
- *From one place to many places: the new work setting.* Work is already no longer tied to one fixed physical place. Virtual offices will emerge and expand rapidly. Extensive computer networks will enable buyers and sourcing managers to communicate with people around the world as easily as they talk with someone in the next office. This reduces the need for buyers to have a separate department or desk. Buyers may log into their systems from homes, offices, hotels or supplier locations. Database management will become much more important for future buyers than archiving and paperwork, enabling them to free themselves from their physical workplace.
- *From fat to lean: the new staffing principle.* Bigger is not better any longer: smaller is more efficient, more flexible and more innovative. The desire for 'fat' organizations that relied on redundancy, encouraged overstaffing and could afford to waste people on nonessential tasks has been replaced by a preference for 'lean' organizations with focused efforts. Companies rely on external contractors for internal services. They expect existing staff to do more

work before they add more people to help them. For purchasing and supply management the consequences are significant. Through advanced systems support (i.e. e-procurement) the transactional work can be moved closer to the users and may be conducted by the users themselves. As a result, the size of the average sourcing department will decrease. Integrated systems will make sourcing processes more transparent. The pressure on buyers and purchasing managers to provide added value and professional support to internal users will also increase. Purchasing has to provide value, or otherwise it will disappear into the line organization.

- *From status and command rights to expertise and relationships: the new power source.* In flatter organizations that delegate responsibilities to an empowered workforce, formal authority derived from hierarchy is less important than professional expertise. Leadership of *ad hoc* teams carrying out specific projects is more important than fixed formal titles. The best source of power is having something to contribute in the interaction with customers, suppliers and/or specialists in other departments. Buyers should ensure that they have skills and ideas to offer, for example by tapping into the Internet and other interactive multimedia sources of information enabling the technical specialists to have the information that they want at their fingertips.

- *From position to performance: the new reward principle.* Compensation and pay have traditionally been based on principles such as the place of the job in a hierarchical grading system or seniority. In the future, fixed salaries determined by abstract organizational principles will be augmented by a variety of contingent forms of compensation (e.g. bonuses, commissions, profit sharing), which are related to actual contributions in meeting predefined individual or group goals and targets. Future buyer salaries will probably only partially consist of a fixed salary: they will be defined mostly by the extent to which buyers contribute to meeting individual goals and targets and meeting group targets (being set by cross-functional buying teams, supplier alignment teams and/or joint development teams).

- *From 'employment' to 'employability': the new security.* Large organizations can no longer guarantee lifetime employment and few people would believe such a promise anyway. If security no longer comes from being employed, it must come from being employable. But employability security (the knowledge that today's work will enhance the person's desirability for future opportunities) is a promise that can be made and kept. Employability security comes from the capability to accumulate human capital (skills and reputation) that can be invested in new business opportunities. In the future people will need portable career assets (skills, knowledge and experience) that can be applied anywhere. People will become, inside as well as outside organizations, more and more self-managed entrepreneurial units. We feel this is especially true for buyers who operate in markets where technologies, products and organizations are changing rapidly. Knowledge is only of temporary value. More valuable is the ability to learn and to know where to find the most relevant sources of information. Continuous training and education, job rotation, networking and gaining a wide experience will become the most valuable assets for the buyer of the future, which beyond doubt will pay off handsomely.

In some companies the workplace of the future, even in the field of purchasing and supply management, is already under construction (see the example of IBM in Chapter 1). The walls in sourcing are coming down and the bridges are going to be built: bridges consisting of up-to-date communication and information technologies and superior business and communication skills.

In line with the general developments described above, some of the key design features of future sourcing organizations are[4]:

- A global procurement board or council that oversees global activities.
- A chief procurement officer (CPO) who executes purchasing council decisions.
- Small professional procurement staff, acting as internal consultants and/or process managers who oversee strategic and tactical responsibilities.
- Procurement experts will be increasingly co-located with their internal customers and/or strategic suppliers to achieve greater understanding of requirements, planning and integration opportunities.
- A flat horizontal structure with teams responsible for sourcing strategy development that are aligned with the business strategies.
- A separation of strategic/tactical and operational supply management responsibilities:
  - *Strategic/tactical*: develop and manage alliances and other critical supply relationships, develop corporate-wide contracts, manage critical commodities, develop corporate-wide electronic systems.
  - *Transactional*: execute transactions with strategic suppliers, use e-systems to obtain standard or indirect items through catalogues, source items that are unique to the operating unit, generate and progress material releases, and manage accounts payable and material control.
- Procurement will only be to a very limited extent involved with day-to-day operations or transactions and new positions will be created to manage the operational purchasing activities.
- International purchasing offices (IPO) will become an important part of the organizational structure as companies shift towards global sourcing.
- Supplier councils will increasingly become part of the purchasing and supply management organization.

5.2 Basic organizational structures

The activities of organizations involving, say, more than two dozen people are grouped together to form departments. These departments integrate the specialized work and form a hierarchy of departments. Generally speaking, departments are usually structured in the following five ways[5]:

- Functional.
- Product.
- Customer or market segment.
- Geographical area.
- Process.

Functional structure

Most companies start by organizing around activities or functions. Companies of modest size usually adopt the functional structure where for example purchasing is one function, production, marketing and personnel are other possible distinguishable functions. The purchasing and supply activities and staff are grouped into one specialized unit. This structure provides several advantages. First, it gathers together all workers of one type (e.g. the purchasing people) and allows them to transfer ideas, knowledge and contacts among one another. Second, it allows for a greater level of specialization. Third, using the example of a single purchasing function, pooling the workers allows the company to present a single face to vendors and exercise buying leverage.

Thus, the functional structure permits more scale and specialization than other alternatives for companies of a certain size. Functional organizations promote standardization and reduce duplication. The functions adopt one system or one policy for everyone rather than having each department invent its own. Companies often revert to the functional structure to reduce the proliferation and duplication of systems, standards and policies that result from independent units not sharing or cooperating.

The functional structure is declining in popularity because in many industries speed is more important than scale and this structure is not good at coping with great variety in products and markets, speedy innovation and short product lifecycles. Also, this structure creates a barrier between different functions, inhibiting cross-functional processes such as new product development (see Box 5.1).

Product structure

In this structure departments (organizational units), consisting of all functions, are formed around product lines in order to compress the product development cycle. Product structures have some weaknesses. First, general managers all want autonomy, resulting in each product division reinventing the wheel, duplicating resources and generally missing opportunities for sharing. These features are the strength of the functional structure. Therefore, companies usually augment the product structure with lateral functional processes.

Secondly, there is the possibility of loss of economies of scale. Not all functions can be divided into product units without a scale loss. These functions are often kept centralized and shared. This has created hybrid structures that are mostly product but have a central shared function. A central purchasing or procurement function can become a central shared function.

This structure is still the structural choice of many manufacturing companies, allowing them to manage strategies of product diversification and rapid development. Negative side effects of the product structure may be compensated for by lateral processes, central functions, shared service centres and front-office/back-office models.

Market structure

The most rapidly increasing type of structure is that based on customers, markets or industries. Its popularity reflects its compatibility with the following trends in business:

- Buyers increasingly insist on dedicated units to serve their needs.
- High-volume, single-sourcing arrangements make it economical for suppliers to dedicate a unit to serve a customer.
- There is increased willingness to outsource noncritical activities to suppliers.
- Competitive advantage shifts to those companies with superior knowledge and information about customer buying behaviour.
- There is an increasing proportion of service businesses in operation today. Services usually focus on and organize around market segments.

Market structures have disadvantages that are similar to those of product structures. First, they have the tendency to duplicate activities and develop incompatible ICT systems. Secondly, they have difficulty sharing common products and services, which may go to several market segments.

Geographical structure

Geographical structures traditionally developed as companies expanded their offerings across territories. There was usually a need to be close to the customer and to minimize costs of travel and distribution. Sometimes industries needed to locate near their sources of supply. Today, the economics of location is important, but information technology is making it less important in certain industries. The role of geography in manufacturing industries is complex, with a relationship between the ratio of product value to transport costs, and attention to the minimum efficient scale of a factory. In service industries where the service is provided on site, geography continues to be a structural basis for many companies (e.g. McDonald's). In other service industries (e.g. consulting) geography is becoming less important. Service companies that provide information and knowledge processing are increasingly becoming location free because, with the new information technology, much service work can be moved anywhere.

If we look at purchasing from a geographical perspective, we can observe a great difference between *international purchasing* and *global sourcing*.[6] International purchasing is when buying is from suppliers outside the firm's home country (e.g. low-cost labour countries) and is primarily a reaction to increased worldwide competition. It often lacks coordination of requirements between worldwide business units. Global sourcing requires the integration of requirements between units, in order to identify common purchases, processes, technologies and suppliers that can benefit from a coordinated sourcing effort. It often involves the implementation of global commodity teams and global information system.

When evolving from local buying towards global sourcing, companies may pass through several stages. The starting point is of course domestic purchasing, after which one might begin with international purchasing done by a local buyer and based on a (specific) need. In the next stage, subsidiaries are used to do some of the buying and foreign buying becomes a part of the (local) procurement strategy. One step further is to establish an international procurement office (IPO) in a certain geographical area (e.g. Eastern Europe or Asia-Pacific) aimed at among other things soliciting quotes or proposals, negotiating supply contracts, expediting shipments, performing supplier visits and building up a qualified supply base in that area.

Finally, when companies start aligning and coordinating their designing, manufacturing and sourcing functions globally, they enter the global sourcing stage. In this stage global procurement requirements are globally coordinated and bought in that area of the world that provides the best value. Whether or not companies should be involved in global sourcing depends on the level of competitive pressure, customer sophistication, worldwide business activity ('global companies buy globally') and geographical dispersion of suppliers for specific purchase requirements.

Process structure

The newest organizational structure is the process structure. In general, a process structure is based on a complete flow of work, such as that of the order fulfilment process, new product development process or the purchase-to-pay process. The advocates of the process organization suggest that the people from each function who work on the process should be gathered into a process team and given end-to-end responsibility for the overall process. The process team reports to a process leader (process owner). The structure is thereby converted from a vertical functional structure to a horizontal process structure.

Apart from process teams, companies can also enhance cross-functional collaboration by co-locating personnel, for example by co-locating sourcing experts with their internal customers:

- Co-locating with operations will lead to better insight into supplier performance, into requirements in cost, quality, delivery and cycle time, and into capacity, material and service needs.
- Co-locating with engineering will improve insight into evolving product and process technology requirements and into material specifications and it will facilitate support of new product development teams.
- Co-locating with marketing will lead to improved insight into forecasting and demand planning requirements and early insight into new product ideas.

Though residing in the customer department, the sourcing experts will formally report to the sourcing organization.

The process structure has been offered as an alternative to the functional structure. There is much to recommend it:

- Arguably the greatest advantage over the functional structure is the end-to-end look at the whole process. When combined with new information technologies, there is considerable opportunity for redesign of an entire process, which may lead to cost reductions (e.g. reduced inventories, reduced working capital, faster receipt of cash) and cycle time reductions.

- A change in one function's piece of the process may make an enormous difference in the pieces of the other functions. By having one manager in charge of the whole process rather than individual managers for each function, the resistance to process change can be overcome.
- A process with end-to-end coverage also lends itself to measurement more easily than functions do (see Chapter 9). Each function is responsible for a piece of the process. A unit responsible for the entire process is responsible for a reasonably self-contained piece of work. The integrating unit can control most of the variables that influence the performance of the process. Hence, the unit can be held accountable.

When compared with the functional structure, the process structure can break down barriers and achieve significant savings. However, the structure should be adopted with care. It is currently fashionable, which means that the weaknesses associated with it get suppressed. For example, instead of functional focus there is the danger of process focus, which may create barriers between the new product development process group and the order fulfilment process group. Another problem could be the difficulties in building purchasing and supply management expertise.

When purchasing people are located close to the various processes – as one in a team of others – they may suffer from a lack of the everyday 'feeding' of purchasing talk and insights. Thereby they step-by-step lose the expertise of their profession. For managers involved in strategic development of purchasing and supply management, the pros and cons of these design alternatives should be important aspects in their frames of reference.

Linking organizational design to coordination needs

No matter what type of structure is chosen, some activities will require coordination across departments.[7] Most companies deal with a complex world. They have to do business with multiple customers, multiple partners and multiple suppliers. They have to compete with rivals in many areas of the world. They employ different skill specialities, using multiple technologies while producing a variety of products and services.

If a company creates an organization to maximize its effectiveness in dealing with one constituency – for example customers – it fragments its ability to deal with others – for example suppliers. All the dimensions not handled by the structure require coordination through lateral management processes. These other dimensions are increasing in number and importance. In addition to focusing on more powerful and knowledgeable customers and concentrating its R&D investments on its leading technologies and core competencies, a company must leverage its own buying power. Today, we can therefore witness how companies often create multidimensional organizations built around their basic structure (e.g. functional, geographical, product etc.).

What brings a group of functional departments, business units and/or purchasing groups to meaningful cooperation and exchanging information and knowledge? Basically, there are two answers to this question: because a central power forces them to cooperate with each other (*mandatory basis*), or because they want to cooperate (*voluntary basis*). Other factors explaining successful cooperation include because they trust each other, because they have common and/or congruent interests, because they are complementary to each other in reaching a 'stretched goal' that each independent business unit cannot reach itself, and because if the cooperation is successful it leads to personal success in terms of career opportunities or financial rewards.[8]

Capitalizing on potential synergies across business units and/or functional departments has two sides, a 'hard' side and a behavioural, 'soft' side. The former comprises making plans together; designing a structure that encourages communication and solves its own conflicts; a good information and communication system, ranging from electronic mail by way of working sessions in cross-connections to office parties; as well as corporate identity, expressed in a house style, a published mission statement, corporate advertising and so on. These are all components that can be 'arranged'. The behavioural side comprises what is usually termed the 'corporate culture' or 'management style'. A set of shared values and dominant beliefs provides an important key to implementation of synergetic cooperation because it is a powerful force for providing focus, motivation and norms (e.g. informal rules).

There are three main types of *lateral processes* to achieve coordination and integration across business units.[9] First, there is informal, voluntary coordination that occurs naturally and spontaneously (minimal or extensive). This could take various forms. One example could be that two or more units realize that they have some common sourcing needs and decide to share experiences and work. Another example that is part of the NCC story (Chapter 12) could be that a purchasing manager identifies someone providing interesting experience and knowledge and starts a kind of mentoring arrangement.

Secondly, one can have formal groups or teams (simple, multidimensional or hierarchical). Several such measures, such as international purchasing councils, are also described in the NCC case.

Finally, there are integrators (roles, managers or departments). A good example of an integrating role is that of the chief procurement officer (CPO), who is often responsible for the whole purchasing function in a company. This lateral process can be illustrated by the IBM case in Chapter 1.

Alternatively, one can identify – on a more detailed level – six basic coordinating *mechanisms*[10]:

1. *Direct mutual adjustment:* achieves coordination of work by the simple process of informal communication. The people who do the work interact with one another to coordinate. Mechanisms used to encourage mutual adjustment within and between units are referred to as liaison devices: liaison positions (jobs created to coordinate the work of two units directly without passing

through management channels), temporary taskforces and standing commit-tees, integrating managers with formal authority, and the matrix structure.

2. *Direct supervision:* in which one person coordinates by giving orders to others, tends to come into play after a certain number of people have to work together. Fifteen people cannot coordinate by mutual adjustment; they need a leader who, by virtue of instructions, coordinates their work. For example, this may be a corporate sourcing team leader, responsible for coordinating the work done by his or her team members.

Besides these first two mechanisms, coordination can also be achieved by *stan-dardization* – in effect automatically, by virtue of standards that predetermine what people do and so ensure that their work is coordinated. There are four forms of standardization:

3. *Standardization of work processes:* programming of the content of the work and procedures to be followed (e.g. the instructions in a purchasing handbook, but also the assembly instructions that come with many IKEA or similar products).
4. *Standardization of output of the work:* specification of the results of the work (e.g. a purchasing manager is told to achieve a savings target of 10% so that the corporation can meet its overall profitability target).
5. *Standardization of knowledge and skills* that serve as inputs to the work: here it is the worker rather than the work or the output that is standardized. Coordination is then achieved by virtue of various employees having learned what to expect from each other; each knows exactly what the other will do and can coordinate accordingly.
6. *Standardization of norms* that more generally guide the work: workers share a set of common beliefs and can achieve coordination based on these (e.g. if every member of a corporation shares a belief in the importance of improving quality, then all will work together to achieve this aim).

These coordinating mechanisms can be considered the most basic elements of structure, the glue that holds organizations together. They seem to fall into a rough order: as organizational work becomes more complicated, the favoured means of coordination seems to shift from mutual adjustment (the simplest mechanism) to direct supervision, then to standardization, preferably of work processes or norms, otherwise of outputs or of skills, finally reverting to mutual adjustment.

No organization can rely on a single one of those mechanisms; all will typically be found in every reasonably developed organization. However, many organizations do favour one mechanism over the others, at least at certain stages of their lives.[11] In other words, the mechanisms used are contingent with the organization of the corporation. Mechanisms used to realize synergy in advanced network organi-zations (e.g. decentralized self-organization) should be different from traditional large-scale organizations (e.g. centralized procedures and control). When applied in a network organization, centrally controlled mechanisms to realize synergy will result in very high complexity and coordination costs.[12]

Organizations that favour none of the mechanisms seem most prone to becoming politicized, simply because of the conflicts that naturally arise when people have to vie for influence in a relative vacuum of power.

The above are some of the most significant coordinating mechanisms that could be and are combined in various ways. Strategic change in purchasing and supply management normally implies the introduction of several new or differently framed mechanisms. To achieve behavioural changes and better performance, new or improved ways of coordinating activities are often significant. These general mechanisms provide some of the most important choices.

But there are several complementary aspects to organizational design and organizing than the general function or product orientation and the above mechanisms. One such topic is the level of centralization and decentralization.

5.3   Centralization versus decentralization

When sourcing practitioners describe their organization they often do so by indicating the level of centralization/decentralization. Also, textbooks (mostly written by academics) contain chapters on organizing the purchasing function in which centralization versus decentralization is the main issue. Only recently have textbooks increasingly paid attention to structures that are neither centralized nor decentralized, but something in between.[13] The growing popularity of these so-called hybrid structures is also reflected in the 1988 and 1995 studies by the Centre for Advanced Purchasing Studies (CAPS).[14]

In 1988, 61% of the respondents indicated that they had a hybrid structure, while in 1995 this increased to 68%. The hybrid structure should allow selective opportunities to capture the benefits of centralization and decentralization, while ideally mitigating the disadvantages. Arguably, two conflicting sets of pressures are driving the development towards hybrid structures.[15] Globalization, standardization and efficiency pressures are pushing towards greater centralization. Customization, differentiation and responsiveness pressures push towards greater decentralization. In other words, both decentralization and increased centralization are simultaneously shaping future purchasing strategy. Eventually, different types of coordination (or hybrid structures) might be the resulting mid-range positions.

We start, however, with describing the two ends of the continuum: centralized purchasing and decentralized purchasing.

Centralized purchasing

Centralized purchasing structures are characterized by all (or the majority of) purchases being managed by a central purchasing group. In this approach, the operating units are consulted but are not fully responsible for their own buying. Centralized purchasing provides the firm with a single, collective sourcing and buying power.

This model captures a large part of the potential corporate purchasing synergies, but there is little user control or responsiveness to local needs. Historically, the primary advantage of centralized purchasing has been to realize a favourable price due to accumulated volumes. Unfortunately, when firms pursued centralized purchasing, they not only centralized the sourcing of parts with suppliers, but also the actual ordering process.

Decentralized purchasing

Decentralization occurs when there are multiple purchasing departments within the organization and all (or the majority of) purchases are managed by individual business units. In this approach, each business unit has its own autonomous purchasing function. Cross-business unit coordination, if any, is voluntary, *ad hoc* and informal. There is no centralized coordination or development of policies other than what might appear through the financial or other operating policies of the firm. This organization places all responsibility for purchasing activities at the field locations, and it serves to minimize corporate overhead. A disadvantage of this model is that the local purchasing units lack managerial or operating strength to provide the group with the economies, synergies and buying power that are often found in companies with centralized groups.

One variation on the decentralized form consists of voluntary purchasing councils that are based at field locations. A council consists of local purchasing personnel with similar product and service needs. They meet voluntarily and coordinate a single source and acquisition (negotiation, contracting and ordering) as though they were one group. In many firms, however, voluntary purchasing councils often disband due to lack of leadership or top management support and commitment.

Apart from the decentralized and centralized purchasing structures, there are three hybrid structures that are described in the purchasing literature:

- Coordinated purchasing.
- Centre-led purchasing.
- Federal (local-led) purchasing.

Coordinated purchasing

This model consists of decentralized purchasing units reporting to a business unit manager combined with a group (or individual) at corporate headquarters. This group oversees matters and issues of concern for the entire firm, and it seeks opportunities for the firm as a whole, where individual plant site personnel may not have this macro view.

A typical example can be found in a company that decided to reduce its external spend through combining the spend of the different business units. It appointed a former business unit director as the group purchasing coordinator (GPC) for a period of two years and his job was to realize the potential synergies that existed across the company. A purchasing board, consisting of a delegation of the business unit directors together with the CEO and a consultant, identified a small number of spend categories where great opportunities existed to realize savings. Next, a small number of lead buyers/lead buying teams were formed and projects were initiated, all coordinated by the group purchasing coordinator and a small staff.

The advantage of this model is that the firm attains the central group scope as well as the authority in dealing with suppliers, but it does not carry the full overhead cost often found with fully centralized groups.

Recently, a number of 'new' purchasing structures have been introduced in literature and practice: centre-led action network (CLAN) and federal organization purchasing (FOP).[16] Centralized functions have often been associated with large, unresponsive and bureaucratic traits, while decentralized functions have been shown to exhibit low critical mass, low skill levels and poor communication across units. The advantages of centralized structures are often the disadvantages of decentralized structures, and vice versa. CLAN and FOP are considered to be ways of organizing the purchasing function that avoid both the rigidity of centralized structures and the fragmentation traits of decentralized structures. The main difference between the two is that CLAN is centre led ('the centre makes it happen') and FOP is locally led ('the centre supports and facilitates').

Centre-led action network (CLAN)

A CLAN structure consists of a network in which purchasing action (actual buying) takes place in fully empowered decentralized purchasing units, but purchasing accountability and functional excellence are led from the corporate centre.[17] This organizational form tries to draw benefits from creating a large critical mass, while maintaining flexibility and diversity. CLAN combines user control and responsiveness to local needs with the ability to capture corporate purchasing synergies by using formal cross-unit coordination and integrating mechanisms (e.g. corporate group). Apart from providing leadership to the purchasing function, the primary interest of the corporate centre is to make networking happen between the independent business units (networking of this scale fails if it is not driven). Each of the purchasing teams in the business units reports to its own business manager and board, and is able to handle all the supply market issues necessary for that business to operate. In a CLAN, coordinated action is achieved (when needed) by temporarily bringing together buyers from the relevant business units who then together devise and execute the purchasing strategy. Any full member of a purchasing team, whether from purchasing or other departments, is at the same time a member of the functional purchasing family. Prerequisites of CLAN success are belief in the need, active support and a champion of change at the top of the company, buyers enabled by best-practice policies and techniques, effective systems infrastructure, buyers able to perform, and receptive internal users wanting to collaborate.[18]

Federal organization of purchasing (FOP)

Applying a number of federal principles to the sourcing environment results in an additional structural form: the federal organization of purchasing (FOP).[19] The FOP consists of a small central core, flat in structure, supporting and coordinating a number of autonomous sourcing units. These units are interrelated in some way due to shared facilities or services. The power of the sourcing function resides equally with these units, instead of being delegated downwards by the centre.

The units have a reporting line to the business unit heads, not to the central core. There is only a professional relationship between the federal purchasing unit and the central core.[20]

The five federal principles underlying the FOP are:

- *Subsidiarity*: power resides in the business units, not with the central core. Decisions can be made quickly (without bureaucratic procedures) by people with expertise and knowledge of the local environment, who are accountable.
- *Interdependence*: management of the interrelationships between business units and in particular between purchasing units is important to sustain the FOP. If relationships are not developed and maintained, the FOP risks fragmentation. The purchasing units have to feel that they are gaining some sort of benefit from being a member of the FOP, otherwise they will break away from it.
- *Common law and language*: real-time data, information and intelligence are provided via a global IT system, a common source of information, in order that decision points can be identified. There is access to information on the breakdown of corporate spend by supplier, business group or classification of goods and services purchased, supplier information and appraisal systems, contract details, code of ethics and so on. Policies and procedures provide the common law and basic guidelines to procurement areas.
- *Separation of power*: central involvement is limited to the requirements identified by the business units. Power resides with the business units, the formulation of strategy is the responsibility of the units and the role of the centre is essentially one of monitoring purchasing best practice, coordination and the provision of resources when required.
- *Twin citizenship* (dual citizenship): FOP requires employees to be members of the local BU as well as the whole company. The success of the FOP is dependent on employees considering themselves as one common body, having a higher priority than the individual business units or their self-interest. This gives employees both a corporate identity and the ability to work in a smaller local group with its own unity. A strong local identity and purchasing skill base are fostered under strong leadership, which in turn ensures that local purchasing managers are able to express views on behalf of their purchasing units and act as their agent when involved with corporate purchasing matters.

These modern forms of designing and organizing purchasing activities are, thus, somewhat more complex than the straightforward centralization or decentralization model. New technologies (ICTs) from one category of enablers and changing skills among purchasing staff is another. The modern forms enable companies to find better designs for their operations. However, there are more aspects to develop in this sphere.

Choosing the level of (de)centralization

Because of their complexity and their potential effect on competitive advantage, organizational design decisions are often the responsibility of executive (purchasing) management. By choosing who decides and by designing the processes influencing how things are decided, the management (e.g. CPO) shapes every purchasing decision made in the unit/company. The management (e.g. CPO) becomes less of a decision maker and more of a decision shaper.[21]

In a way, this is a new and more sophisticated way of centralizing the activities. Still, what structure is most effective in specific situations needs to be explored. To find an answer to such a question, one should look for the factors that determine the effectiveness of a certain structure. Multiple variables are hypothesized to be influencing purchasing structures, including external business context, volume of strategic purchases, information technology and purchasing maturity.[22]

Some claim that corporate purchasing organizations should be congruent with the overall level of *corporate coherence* and the level of *maturity* of the sourcing function.[23] Corporate coherence describes the ability of a multiproduct, divisionalized corporation to generate and explore synergies of various types.[24] This ability is often measured in traditional management literature by the proxy concept of 'relatedness' in terms of products and/or underlying resources and capabilities, the underlying rationale being that such relatedness indicates the presence of economies of scope.

In the context of this chapter, corporate coherence is related to the extent to which the different parts of the corporation operate and are managed as one entity. Major differences across business units in management style, vision, strategy, culture and structure reflect a low corporate coherence. In this situation, when a company lacks a clear corporate strategy and an integrated corporate structure and shows a weak corporate culture, the integration of the purchasing function will be a significant challenge. It could also be that a firm has a strong corporate culture that is negative to coordinating efforts (compare the NCC case in Chapter 12) and because of this does not easily handle coordinating measures. In such a case, there is a general lack of coherence between different parts of the organization (the top level wants coordination, the operative levels want to avoid it). The basic feature is that of coherence. The less coherence, the more difficult it is to achieve the strategic change.

Purchasing maturity (see Chapter 2) is related (among other things) to the level of professionalism in the purchasing function as expressed in its role and position, its involvement in major corporate decisions, the involvement of top management in strategic purchasing decision making, cross-functional teamwork, the availability of purchasing information systems, the quality of the people involved in purchasing and the level of collaboration with suppliers. Research in the Netherlands has found that when the purchasing function is highly mature, companies will use a different and more advanced approach to manage corporate purchasing than where one is dealing with low purchasing maturity.[25]

In cases where both purchasing maturity and corporate coherence are low, decentralized purchasing is most likely to be found. In such a situation, central coordination efforts will be barely sustainable. In this situation, we expect little homogeneity in specifications across business units. However, there are opportunities to realize purchasing synergy through exchanging information on supply markets, suppliers and prices by using voluntary working groups.

In cases where both constructs are high, a centre-led structure has a good chance of success. In such a structure cross-functional/cross-business teams conduct

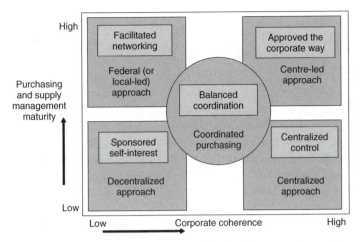

FIGURE 5.1 Matrix for selecting the appropriate organizational structure. Source: Rozemeijer, F.A. (2000) *Creating Corporate Advantage in Purchasing*, PhD thesis, ECIS/Technische Universiteit Eindhoven: Eindhoven.

coordination activities with the active support of the business units, while being strongly managed by a corporate purchasing staff.

If both parameters have a medium value, a hybrid structure, with both central purchasing and voluntary purchasing coordination activities, is most likely to be found. Federal (or local-led) purchasing consists of a small corporate purchasing staff supporting a number of autonomous, decentralized purchasing units in their voluntary efforts to exploit potential synergies.

The central purchasing model represents a situation in which most strategic commodities are contracted from a corporate purchasing department. The latter appears to be only feasible in organizations where purchasing at the operating company level is hardly developed and corporate coherence is high (see Figure 5.1).

5.4   Changing organizational designs

Corporate purchasing structures are not there on their own; rather, they are influenced and determined by changes in corporate strategies and structures. As these in most companies are subject to continuous change, the implication is that, as a result, purchasing structures have to change as well. Organizational change might be expected when mergers are going on (see Box 5.3). Some even claim that purchasing is the most important area to look for post-merger synergies. Often these potential synergies are used by management to legitimize the merger. Another important driver for organizational change is when a company appoints a (new) chief purchasing officer (see Box 5.4).

Box 5.3   Merger between HP and Compaq and its effect on purchasing

The merger between Hewlett-Packard and Compaq was a big challenge for purchasing management. It needed to integrate the purchasing operations of two large multinational companies into one single organization. This was not an easy task, as the merger involved a large number of purchasing professionals in many different locations around the world. Also, the two companies had different purchasing strategies and processes. However, the merger presented huge opportunities for synergies, by bundling the spend volumes of the two companies and having a more centralized corporate purchasing structure. Today, Hewlett-Packard has more buying power than ever before. Besides improving its buying power, the merger also presented an opportunity to leverage the purchasing expertise that existed in both organizations. One of Compaq's strengths was that its purchasing operation was centralized and the buyers were skilled in bundling spend volumes and leveraging purchases with suppliers. HP was more decentralized, but was more experienced at involving buyers in new product development to make sure that cost never got designed into a product.

Source: Carbone, J. (2004) 'Hewlett Packard wins for the 2nd time', *Purchasing*, 2 September.

Box 5.4   New CPO for Motorola

For most of its 75-year history, Motorola left purchasing up to its individual business groups although there were many components, materials and services that were common across different business units. Motorola was not capitalizing on opportunities to leverage its purchases and realize cost savings. In 2003, Motorola began its journey towards a more centralized purchasing structure under the leadership of Theresa Metty, who was appointed as chief procurement officer (CPO). Metty set an ambitious goal of reducing materials costs by $1 billion in three years and began implementing proven strategic purchasing initiatives, including leveraging company-wide purchases. Metty and her team also set up commodity teams, increased use of e-sourcing and established working with new product development teams to increase the use of standard parts and reuse components in multiple designs.

Source: Carbone, J. (2004) 'Motorola leverages its way to lower cost', *Purchasing*, 16 September.

Purchasing leaders should have the ability and a certain willingness to change their organizational structures if needed. A purchasing organization needs to be tailored to the specific business situation in order to be effective.[26] Sometimes this will result in purchasing organizations moving like a pendulum from centralized to decentralized to centralized to decentralized again. Chapters 11 through 14 discuss organizational change in more detail. Those chapters will illustrate that effective changes in purchasing organizations not only involve logic and rational behaviour, they are also a politically sensitive subject involving many different concerns and emotions.

5.5   Conclusion

This chapter has illustrated completely new workplaces compared to the sourcing organizations of a decade ago. The development towards strategic sourcing will create more instability within purchasing and supply organizations. First, movement of purchasing professionals between organizations often results in compensation discrepancies and new hires arrive with higher pay and benefits. Second, the need to elevate the level of purchasing professionals often results in 'buying' talent in the open market at a premium price. Third, new employees are increasingly demanding to work from home or remote sites, presenting communication, coordination and organizational challenges. Fourth, sourcing personnel will increasingly have dual reporting lines. Finally, professionals from other functional groups will increasingly accept assignments in procurement. These professionals often arrive from groups that historically pay more than procurement, creating pay differentials. When designing their organizations, sourcing leaders should pay attention to these potential social side effects of their new design.[27]

There is a great variety in approaches to materializing potential sourcing synergies. Approaches range from voluntary cooperation to formally managed cooperation. In this chapter we suggest a model indicating that the type of approach is related to the level of purchasing maturity and the level of corporate coherence. There is no standard recipe for success. The position taken in this chapter is that companies should choose among different alternatives based on how well they meet their specific situation, rather than on how fashionable they are. The insights presented in this chapter can be used as guidelines in deciding what is effective and what is not.

Notes and references

1   Daft, R.L. (1992) *Organization Theory and Design*, West: St Paul, MN.
2   Morgan, G. (1986) *Images of Organization*, Sage Publications: London.
3   Moss Kanter, R. (1995) 'Constructing the future', Northern Telecom Annual Report.
4   Monczka, R., Trent, R. and Handfield, R. (2005) *Purchasing and Supply Chain Management*, 3rd edn, South-Western College Publishing: Cincinnati, OH, Chapter 20.
5   This section is based for a large part on Galbraith, J.R. (1995) *Designing Organizations*, Jossey-Bass: San Francisco.
6   Monczka *et al.* (2005) *opere citato*, Chapter 10.
7   Galbraith (1995) *opere citato*.
8   Rozemeijer, F.A. (2000) *Creating Corporate Advantage in Purchasing*, PhD thesis, ECIS/Technische Universiteit Eindhoven, Eindhoven.
9   Galbraith (1995) *opere citato*.
10 Mintzberg, H. and Quinn, J.B. (1991) *The Strategy Process*, Prentice-Hall: Englewood Cliffs, NJ, p. 334.
11 *Ibidem.*
12 Rozemeijer (2000) *opere citato*.
13 Van Weele, A.J. (2005) *Purchasing and Supply Chain Management – Analysis, Strategy, Planning and Practice*, 4th edn, Thomson Learning: London.
14 Leenders, M.R. and Johnson, P.F. (2000) *Major Structural Changes in Supply Organizations*, Tempe, AZ: Center for Advanced Purchasing Studies; Leenders, M.R. and Johnson, P.F. (2002) *Major Changes in Supply Chain Responsibilities*, Tempe, AZ: Center for Advanced Purchasing Studies.
15 Faes, W. and Matthijssens, P. (1998) 'Managing purchasing co-ordination: How to build an effective intra-company relationship', *Proceedings 7th IPSERA Conference*, London, pp. 204–15.
16 Akbar, N. and Lamming, R. (1996) 'Federal organization of purchasing', *Proceedings 5th International IPSERA Conference*, Eindhoven University of Technology, Eindhoven; Cammish, R. and Keough, M. (1991) 'A strategic role for purchasing', *McKinsey Quarterly*, No. 3, pp. 22–39; Russil, R. (1997) *Purchasing Power: Your Suppliers, Your Profits*, Prentice Hall: London.

[17] Russil (1997) *opere citato*, p. 315.

[18] *Ibidem*, pp. 73–5.

[19] FOP can be regarded as a 'self-organizing network'.

[20] Akbar and Lamming (1996) *opere citato*.

[21] Galbraith (1995) *opere citato*.

[22] Corey, R. (1978) 'Should companies centralize procurement?', *Harvard Business Review*, November–December, pp. 102–10; Kraljic, P. (1983) 'Purchasing must become supply management', *Harvard Business Review*, September–October, pp. 109–17; Keough, M. (1993) 'Buying your way to the top', *McKinsey Quarterly*, no. 3, pp. 41–62; Birou, L.M., Fawcett, S.E. and Magnan, G.M. (1997) 'Integrating product life cycle and purchasing strategies', *International Journal of Purchasing and Materials*, Winter 1997, pp. 23–31; van Stekelenborg, R.H.A. (1997) *Information Technology for Purchasing*, PhD thesis, Eindhoven University of Technology, Faculty of Technology Management, Eindhoven.

[23] Rozemeijer (2000) *opere citato*.

[24] Teece, D.J., Rumelt, R.P., Dosi, G. and Winter, S.G. (1994) 'Understanding corporate coherence: Theory and evidence', *Journal of Economic Behaviour and Organization*, Vol. 23, pp. 1–30.

[25] Rozemeijer (2000) *opere citato*.

[26] Hughes, J., Ralf, M. and Michles, B. (1998) *Transform Your Supply Chain*, International Thomson Business Press: London.

[27] Monczka *et al.* (2005) *opere citato*, Chapter 10.

Chapter 6

LEADERSHIP AND VALUES FOR COMPETITIVE SOURCING

Ethel Brundin, Leif Melin and Björn Axelsson

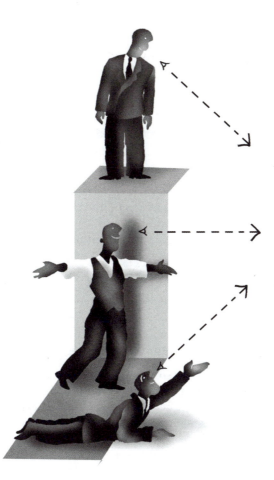

The creation of competitive advantage through successful sourcing activities requires good leadership from everyone involved in the purchasing function, certainly including the CPO (chief purchasing officer), other purchasing managers as well as top management. Most areas for change are interwoven. Changes of organizational design and use of ICT (information and communication technologies) will have consequences for leadership. Leadership in strategic sourcing is an important area of change in itself, but it cannot be dealt with as if there were no connections to organizational structures, ways to deal with suppliers, recruitment and development of human resources and so on. Still, as in all other chapters in this book dealing with areas of change, we will focus on one area.

In this chapter we thus take a close look at the role of leadership in the development of firms from a strategic sourcing perspective. In efforts to radically develop purchasing and supply management, it is quite common that one important starting point is the introduction of a new CPO. But in what ways can a new leader make a difference? A new leader alone does not make much difference. The effects will more likely be indirect through new processes that the new individual can put in motion.

We will consider leadership as closely related to the prevailing culture, and especially the dominant values, which means that the role of values in good leadership will be considered as well. That is one of the potential areas in which a new leader may contribute. But what is 'good' leadership – in general and especially in the purchasing area? How can leadership in general be looked at? What differences can leadership make in the processes of developing strategic sourcing capabilities?

In line with the overall perspective of this book on strategic change, this chapter will consider the strategic aspects of leadership in purchasing and supply. In strategy processes, the purchasing manager most often takes on a mediating and linking role between the top executives and lower levels of middle managers and employees. This intermediary role in the ongoing strategizing (step-by-step activities that gradually emerge as realized strategies; Chapter 3) does certainly not have to be passive. But in many business firms the management of strategy is still mainly unidirectional, following the hierarchical levels in a traditional top-down process. However, within more innovative organizations we could expect the strategic role of the CPO to be more proactive, not only actively translating strategic issues and directions from the top into purchasing, but also initiating new issues, meanings and momentum in the strategizing process.

In this chapter we will offer different views on leadership and make the reader reflect on (his or her) leadership in practice. We will provide a short overview of what leadership could be. To begin with we will highlight some important studies on what leaders and managers really do, after which we present a short version of the state of the art of leadership: what it is and what roles and styles of leadership are worth knowing about and reflecting on.

Even if some approaches overlap and are hard to distinguish from each other, we will provide an exposé including *rational approaches* such as the trait and skills approaches to leadership, style and situational approaches and leadership roles. This will be followed by views that are more *relation oriented* and emerging issues in leadership such as value-based leadership, including transformational leadership, visionary leadership and emotions.

Alongside our theoretical text we will draw some parallels to leadership with a focus on the purchasing leader. To provide some flesh and blood to the discussion we have interviewed three CPOs, one from an internationally operating manufacturing firm, one from a global retailing firm and one from a services firm with, primarily, domestic operations. The interview questions are presented in Appendix 6.1. The results from the interviews are intertwined with our discussion.

6.1 What leaders really do

To understand leadership it is worthwhile reflecting on the difference between management and leadership. One possible distinction is to regard leadership as dealing with the *interpersonal* aspects of a manager's job, where inspiration, imagination, influence and change are included in leadership, while planning and controlling represent the *administrative* part of a manager's job. Leadership involves motivating people, creating and having a vision that may mobilize people, communicating values and directions, and producing change to transform the status quo.[1] All these seem to be vital aspects in processes of strategic change within purchasing and supply management, where we argue that to be an assigned leader, in our case an assigned purchasing manager, involves both leadership and management.

As an introduction to the overview below of what leadership could be, we will present some interesting pictures of what managers/leaders really do. Mintzberg, in his famous study of managerial work, questions the dominant view at that time that managers primarily organize, coordinate, plan and control.[2] His early findings were that managerial work is inconsistent, scattered, contains many loose ends and does not at all comply with our picture that leaders are well organized and devote their time to structured tasks.

Mintzberg's contribution was an attempt to put managerial activities into a pattern of uniting activities. From his observations of executives at work, he found some similarities that formed three major managerial roles.[3]

First we have the *interpersonal roles* that arise directly from the formal authority of the role and involve some basic interpersonal relationships. The *figurehead* role means that every head of an organizational unit must spend some of his or her time engaging in ceremonial duties as an official representative of the organization. The *leader* role means both the direct leadership of, for example, hiring employees and the indirect exercise of the leader role in, for example, motivating and encouraging employees. The third interpersonal role is the *liaison* role, including all contacts the manager has outside the vertical chain of command and especially with people outside the organization.[4] This is all easily recognized by purchasing managers. Representing the purchasing function means exercising many liaison duties as well as inspiring staff and representing the firm and its employees.

The *informational role* is the second role with three subroles. First the manager is the *monitor*, including scanning the environment for information and receiving unsolicited information as a result of a network of personal contacts both outside and inside the organization. In his or her role as a *disseminator*, the manager passes important information to subordinates. Finally as the *spokesperson*, the manager sends information to people outside the organizational unit, including satisfying the influential people that control the unit with information. The purchasing manager receives a lot of information from various sources that needs to be disseminated and he or she appears as a spokesperson in relation to other units inside as well as outside the firm, not least suppliers. Purchasing policies including supplier policies need to be explained and defended, for example in policy documents, in conjunction with negotiations as well as overt activities such as 'supplier days', when representatives for significant suppliers are invited to an event at the buying firm.

The third role includes four *decisional roles*. As *entrepreneur*, 'the voluntary initiator of change', the manager adapts the unit to a changing environment.[5] The *disturbance handler* role includes managers responding to pressures more involuntarily. Every manager spends a lot of time responding to 'high-pressure disturbances'. As a *resource allocator*, the manager is responsible for who will get what, but is also authorizing decisions within the unit.

The fourth decisional role is the *negotiator*, including negotiations with top management, employees and suppliers. Again, we can easily connect these decisional roles to purchasing. CPOs and other purchasing managers are involved in everyday developments. They always have to deal with various kinds of disturbances, for example in relation to maverick buying and/or internal fights for resources, as well as fighting suppliers who are involved in attempts to control prices by cartels.

In relation to these three role sets (the interpersonal, the informational and the decisional, including their subroles), let us listen to two of the interviewed CPOs. They were asked the following question: 'Regarding yourself as a strategic leader of the sourcing/purchasing function, please describe this role of strategic leadership – what does this role mean and what is included in such a role?'

Box 6.1   The role of strategic leadership – two views

CPO, GLOBAL RETAIL FIRM: 'One important aspect of the role as CPO in comparison to e.g. production manager is that it is a boundary spanning role. I have responsibility for and I need to be able to carry on my dialogue with all the internal units, such as marketing, design and production. In addition to that I have directly or indirectly a great number of interfaces to suppliers and other external stakeholders. My job is very much about communication: knowing what kind of development we, from the point of departure of purchasing and supply, want and need and from that basis get involved in all these dialogues. In these contexts we need to listen to understand their respective points of view and explain ours.'

CPO, SERVICES FIRM: 'First of all I need to have full control over the company's expenditure: what we buy, in what ways and from whom. Secondly I have to constantly think of our structure, the design of various purchasing operations, decision forums etc. Thirdly, and most important, taking responsibility for the people in purchasing, making sure they have adequate qualifications for the job and relevant support in terms of support systems etc.'

The first example emphasizes various aspects of the interpersonal and informational roles. The second example leans more towards the decisional roles, even though aspects of the other role sets are mentioned too. This illustrates that these general aspects of leadership certainly apply to leadership in purchasing and supply management.

Kotter made a similar study to Mintzberg and came to the following description of what managers really do: they spend most of their time with others, not only their subordinates and bosses but also many outsiders, including people that might appear to be unimportant.[6] They are engaged in a lot of conversations and ask a lot of questions. But most conversations are short and disjointed – it is not unusual that a manager covers ten unrelated topics in a five-minute conversation, according to Kotter's observations. They rarely seem to make big decisions, nor give orders in a traditional sense, but they continuously attempt to influence others. Their working days seem to be quite unplanned and they often react to others' initiatives. Furthermore, managers spend time on establishing their agendas, made up by issues that address both long-term and short-term responsibilities. Several of the issues on the managers' agenda are not present in the formal plans of the corporation. Interestingly, issues on the agenda may focus both on the immediate future (1–30 days) and the long run (5–20 years), while formal plans are more likely to have three months to five years as the time frame. Managers obtain new information continuously through conversations with others.

In addition to agenda setting, Kotter found that the main activity of the manager is network building, where managers allocate both time and effort to develop a network of cooperative relationships with people who are important for the issues on their agenda, including subordinates, bosses and outsiders.

Stewart found the same evidence as Mintzberg that managerial work consists of a range of activities, but her conclusions ended up the other way around.[7] Referring to different aspects such as the pattern of relationships, the work pattern and the exposure, she holds that managerial roles differ in regards to *demands, constraints* and *choices*. Demands include expectations on the leader role. They can stem from people around the leader who have the authority to make these demands and/or be built into the formal/informal job description. Constraints can be either legal or company bound, such as legal restrictions, the technological level, the general knowledge or educational level in the company, support systems, the market situation and the like. Choices are up to the leader to make regarding for example strategic choices and goal setting. It is up to the leader if and how he or she chooses to expand the range of choices, and this role has some resemblance to the role of agenda setting.[8] Due to Stewart's thorough and in-depth methodological mix of observations, diaries and interviews, her work and material are still providing insightful possibilities to learn about managerial behaviour and a number of researchers bear witness to her academic heritage.[9]

It is quite obvious that the purchasing manager's reality fits with many of the roles identified by Mintzberg, Kotter and Stewart. Depending on where the purchasing manager is placed in the hierarchy and the specific nature of the organization, the environment and the specific person, the roles are more or less accentuated. However, it is a question for debate whether these roles are to be regarded as unifying or diversifying the leadership role of the purchasing manager.

6.2 What leadership could be

Defining leadership

The view of what leaders, including CPOs and other managers in purchasing and supply management, really do need not satisfy our agenda. It might be that they could or should do other things or the same things but in different ways and with new priorities. Therefore we move on to the question of what leadership could be and how leadership is defined.

Research endeavours have so far failed to agree on a consensus for a definition of leadership. Much normative advice exists on how leadership can be practised, even if the very core of leadership is not totally agreed. With this comes the difficulty of defining 'good' or 'effective' leadership. Leadership is probably one of the most forceful concepts that rhetorically appeals to most people but is hard to put into a general definition.

Yukl holds that the concept of 'leadership' has been transferred from an everyday use into the scientific agenda without being properly defined.[10] A provocative approach is therefore easily taken and some contend that leadership is a construct that does not at all reflect what an assigned leader or manager does in 'real life'.[11] Instead of posing the question 'What is leadership?' they pose the question 'Is there really leadership?' Some empirical evidence points in the direction that leadership in the general sense of being influential can be exercised by almost anyone and that leadership can be 'everything and nothing'.[12] Weick makes a thoughtful point in line with this when he exchanges the word 'leadership' with 'culture' and finds that they are indeed exchangeable.[13] Our interpretation of this is that leadership is very much dependent on and is a large part of the specific culture of an organization, at the same time as it is very much a matter of cultivating and affecting that culture. We will come back to that issue below.

We can take a more pragmatic approach in finding out what leadership could be. Yukl provides a set of leadership definitions made over the past 50 years, in which some common key features are distinguishable.[14] These are process, influence, a common goal and the involvement of followers. Leadership as a *process* is understood in different ways by different writers. Some see process as an influencing process, others as just any social process. Since leadership in this chapter is considered as an assigned role, the former meaning is applied here, although it may be disputable whether it is an interactive process or not.

Furthermore, the word 'process' suggests that leadership cannot be something that you turn on and off as it pleases you – as soon as you are appointed a leader you will be a leader around the clock. This has a range of implications that are not very often considered. For example, if you attend a party you would need to be aware of the fact that you in your position as a leader might be valued for this position at this party, rather than as a person just having a fun time.

Influence is a word with many and complex connotations – in fact it can be anything between a subtle influence that is hardly noticeable to a more coercively exercised type of power. In addition, influence can work in a one-way direction from the leader towards the followers and this power can be derived either from his or her position or his or her personal power[15] or it can be a jointly shared influence, such as empowerment. It also needs to be pointed out here that the leader influences or is influenced by others than immediate followers, such as customers, higher- or lower-ranked leaders, public sources and so on.

A *common goal* implies that it is the leader's task to make followers understand the goal – and avoid suboptimization. It can also be joint efforts between the leader and the followers.

Finally, *involvement of followers* mainly speaks for itself. It is impossible to be a leader without one or more followers – if they do not exist, the other connotations of process, influence and common goal would make no sense.

We will comply here with Yukl's latest definition that 'leadership is the process of influencing others to understand and agree about what needs to be done and how it can be done effectively, and the process of facilitating individual and collective efforts to accomplish the shared objectives'.[16] This definition pinpoints all the key features mentioned above.

A quick look back to the two quotes from our three interviewees ends up very close to this definition. The first CPO very much pinpointed the first part of the definition, the informing, information-seeking and influencing aspects. The second CPO put his focus on the latter part of the sentence, the facilitation of individual and collective efforts to accomplish shared goals. However, what this definition does not offer is to tell us what the goal is, what effective leadership is, whether leadership is emergent or assigned and how leadership should be practised.

For the purpose of this chapter we view leadership as a formal position and a specialized role. Furthermore, our definition suggests that rational as well as emotional processes are at work when leaders exercise leadership. We do not, in this chapter, have a readymade assumption about the outcome, which can be objectively measured or a matter of subjectivity,[17] nor what effective leadership is, since this is not within our scope. We will use the terms leader and manager interchangeably throughout the text. A final assumption, which hopefully goes without saying, is that leaders can be of either sex.

Next follows an overview of leadership, first from a more rational approach, followed by approaches from a more emotional point of departure.

6.3 Rational approaches

Rational approaches mainly include the idea that followers are to be directed by the leader, who knows best and is the responsible coordinator of the process towards the goal.[18] His or her role as the dominant player is thus not questioned as such. In order to connect to our sequence of questions emanating from what leaders really do and what leadership could be, we now turn to how leaders should be and what they should do.

Traits and skills approaches

Leadership texts in the early twentieth century took it for granted that some people are born to be leaders. The leadership characteristics were thus to be found in the person's personality and researchers tried to find out what traits were present among those born leaders and, thus, what is needed in order to become a leader.

Such characteristics were indeed found. Some pointed to factors such as leaders being taller, more intelligent, extrovert, self-confident, persistent and having integrity etc.[19] Often, reference is made to something called the 'big five personality traits': surgency, conscientiousness, agreeableness, adjustment and intellectance, each one of these including more specific traits.[20,21]

The main problem that has been pointed out is that the causality to company performance is missing. It has proven impossible to find, for example, top ten personality traits that have an impact on a company's results. Yet another intriguing setback is that the list of leadership traits increases with the number of studies made.[22]

For purchasing managers, this line of research may at first be of less importance in itself. Still, a short survey of ads for purchasing managers and/or specifications to headhunters when in search for CPOs shows that traits like persistency and integrity are often emphasized. In our case description in Chapter 12, we can notice that the CEO of NCC (a Nordic construction firm) was looking for an individual with the relevant conceptual understanding as well as persistency to carry out a major change venture. Later in that case study, the CEO emphasizes the need to be in possession of a certain toughness to be able to carry out the mission. This means that regardless of the scepticism above, we do tend to look at traits and skills as one important aspect of leadership in purchasing.

Later approaches in line with the rationalistic approach have taken the standpoint that personal characteristics presumably can be developed. The skills model of leadership is one such attempt and it includes technical, human and conceptual skills.[23]

Technical skills involve 'knowing the business'. Being a purchasing manager implies that it is important to be well up in purchasing procedures, understanding important concepts as well as organizational designs, to be able to evaluate and develop suppliers, carry out supply market analysis as well as influencing others and being strong in negotiation skills. These are but a few examples (compare Chapter 7, where various skill profiles needed at the various levels of purchasing maturity are discussed).

Human skills, the second of the three, mean that the purchasing manager is good at handling people; that is, being able to build relationships of trust and mutual commitment. This goes for relationships with team members as well as with representatives of other departments, with customers, colleagues from other companies and so on. Again, we can refer this to the introductory description of the CPO of the retail firm quoted before. It was emphasized how much his job as CPO was about communicating with people in all possible roles and personalities.

The *conceptual skills* relate to the managers' ability to build mental pictures of work processes and to relate parts to a coherent whole. In today's rather flat organizations, many purchasing managers, albeit maybe not CPOs, can be considered to fit hierarchically into a middle manager position and, as such, human and technical skills are considered a priority. In comparison, top managers (possibly including CPOs) need to be heavier on conceptual skills. When asked the same question as mentioned before (describe your role as a strategic leader) the third CPO interviewed answered as in Box 6.2.

Box 6.2   The role of strategic leadership – a third view

CPO, MANUFACTURING FIRM: 'One very strategic issue in my job is to be able to translate corporate goals and visions into the purchasing equivalents. Given the vision and basic business strategy of our company, to be the outstanding low-cost producer in our field in the world, what does it imply for purchasing management? One translation we have made to achieve the needed operational excellence in purchasing is that a lot of efforts need to go into coordination issues. We could demand our factories all over the world to just comply with this – and we do! But we also try to explain it, to get the people on board.

I have learnt that a good way to do this is have the message develop in dialogue with our staff. I'll give you one example. When I gathered our purchasing managers in some of the regions in France I started to ask them from where they buy some specific components, the suppliers, the countries of origin etc. Their point of departure was that everything was fine in their operations and that it could hardly be better. Step by step the whiteboard developed and we saw a picture of 30 – or so – suppliers for basically the same product emerge. It was then very easy to ask the intriguing question: Don't you think this could be done in better ways? After that we more easily entered into conceptually defining the role of purchasing in our firm and the issues of highest priority.'

The skills model can be elaborated in terms of individual attributes with competences including working experience and environmental factors in order to obtain an effective leadership outcome.[24] Individual attributes refer to general intelligence and intellectuality; a motivation to be a leader and to exert leadership and to take on this responsibility; and a personality of for example openness, stress management, tolerance of complex problems and curiosity.

Competencies are, according to this model, of three kinds: *problem-solving skills*, the ability to identify problems and solve them in new and creative ways; *social judgement skills*, the ability to understand individuals and their needs and the social system they are part of; and *knowledge*, the actual implementation of the two former skills.

For example, a purchasing manager is supposed to comprehend the variety of issues that occur in his or her everyday life and, combined with his or her knowledge about the team members, he or she should be able to integrate the two dimensions of problem solving and social judgement into a workable whole. This very much comes down to the abilities of a purchasing manager to understand well enough what requirements are needed, for instance for a commodity manager responsible for the supply of business travel services, and also be able to find the right person for the job and equip him or her with enough support and skills to be able to carry out the assignment.

Similar to the trait approach previously dealt with, the relationship between skills and outcome is not an established one.[25] Another critique of the traits as well as skills approaches is that research has been made from the self-evaluation of leaders themselves. Even if these two approaches seem to have a set of weaknesses, they have both become popular again, as, for instance, have traits in value-based leadership (see further on in this chapter). In addition, a range of leadership instruments has been developed during the years where the leader can be made aware of his or her personality traits and how those traits might affect followers. Getting such an understanding about oneself could rarely be wrong for managers in general and – not least – for purchasing managers.

As interesting, perhaps, as being a successful leader is what traits and skills contribute to failure. A meta-analysis suggests that the following traits and skills may predict whether a leader will be successful or not: a manager who is not emotionally stable, does not have integrity, does not develop technical, cognitive or interpersonal skills and is defensive, puts his or her leadership effectiveness at risk.[26] Needless to say, this sounds very reasonable for purchasing managers as well. These are specifications of how leaders should *not* be.

Psychodynamics and leadership

Viewing leadership as dysfunctional is the basis for the psychodynamic approach. The underlying assumption of this approach is that you will become a better leader if you know yourself better. Knowing yourself starts with knowledge about your psyche, upbringing and critical experiences in your life and how these affect your leadership. According to this perspective, all individuals go through different maturation stages[27] and 'getting stuck' or being exposed in one of these or living through specific, possibly traumatic, childhood experiences might lead to dysfunctional leadership.[28]

So, for instance, having an autocratic parent might lead to passive leadership; being forbidden to cry might lead to angry leadership reactions. The metaphor of 'struggling with the demon' is used to characterize the neurotic organization and its leaders as dramatic, suspicious, detached, depressive and compulsive.[29] Male leaders' mid-life crises and how these can result in dysfunctional emotional behaviour have also been in focus.[30] Again, as a leader of purchasing operations, it could hardly be wrong to reflect on such background factors and try to interpret whether or not and in what relevant ways such backgrounds may affect your leadership. The question to follow is what to try to keep and develop and what to try to omit and/or get rid of.

Leadership behaviour

Leadership behaviour as well as situational leadership emerged as a response to the critique of the trait and skill approaches dealt with above. What leaders do and how they behave became an issue in focus. Different leadership styles were labelled, the initial ones simplified as autocratic, democratic and laissez-faire styles of leadership. The *autocrat* is dominant and prioritizes results. The *democratic* leader is willing to involve followers but in the end exercises his or her right to make the decision. The *laissez-faire* leader avoids leading and being involved if possible.

The Ohio State and Michigan studies were path breaking in the 1950s since they broke away from the personality approach and their findings still have a major impact on how we view leadership today. Their results – independent of each other – pointed in the direction that leaders act in accordance with a relationship orientation and/or a production orientation. As a consequence of these results, the now classical managerial grid was developed, which encompasses five leadership styles[31]:

- A high concern for production/results combined with low concern for relationships/people ends up in *authority-compliance management*, with a leader that reminds one of the autocratic leader viewing people as tools to achieve results and is perceived by his or her followers as demanding, controlling and hard-driving.
- A high concern for relationships and low interest in results leads to *country-club management*, where the leader emphasizes a warm working climate and the social needs of the people he or she leads.
- A style that combines a high concern for people and a high concern for results is labelled *team management*, reminding one of the democratic leader who has a belief in involving followers, does not avoid conflicts and trust his or her people.
- A concern for neither people nor results is called *impoverished management* and ends up in a leader who avoids involvement with followers and is noncommitted, pretty much like the laissez-faire style.
- Finally, *middle-of-the-road management* is more of a compromising leadership style trying to combine a bit of both concerns, compromising in their balancing between concerns for followers and for results.

When asked the question 'When looking backwards one or two decades, what do you consider as the most striking differences between the purchasing managers (including CPOs) of today in contrast to those days?' the purchasing manager from the services firm (with previous experience of both the automotive and the construction industries) said the following.

Box 6.3   Purchasing leadership styles over time

CPO, SERVICES FIRM: 'The CPO and the general stereotype of a purchasing manager has changed dramatically. Previously it was very much the so-called 45-degree man [showing a person with a big stomach pointing in an angle 45 degrees out from the body]. That stereotype was a male, a loudly speaking and dominating person. Today's purchasing managers are – in general – more towards teamwork, open-minded, more communicative and willing to listen and to evaluate good suggestions etc.'

This comment indicates a move away from authority-compliance management towards, most of all, team management, implying a high concern for both people and results and a more democratic orientation.

Being normative in its approach, claiming that the team management style was 'the best' style, the managerial grid was criticized for not taking into account contextual factors. This was done, however, in the *situational leadership model*.[32] In this model, the two dimensions of directive behaviour and supportive behaviour are combined and the model suggests that the leader needs to take into account the maturity of the followers and the nature of the organization's needs. This evaluation decides what leadership style is appropriate for each situation.

If followers have low maturity – which implies for example low competence or newness in the job, no specific loyalty, motivation or reliability – the leader should use a directive style. High maturity of the follower indicates, on the other hand, a delegating style by the leader.

Although very normative in its approach, and in spite of the criticism that has been directed towards this model that it is one-dimensional (i.e. from the perspective of the leader only), it has proven to be a practical tool to many leaders over the years.

One of the first leadership models that *de facto* took into account that a two-way relationship exists between the leader and the followers was the path-goal theory. The theory builds on expectancy theory, suggesting that followers are motivated by their trust in being able to perform, that their work will lead to a wished-for result and that there is a fair enough payoff in exchange for their efforts. The leader is supposed to take into account the followers' needs and ease their way to reach the goals by defining goals, clarifying the path, removing obstacles and providing support.[33] The four different leadership styles concerned are, according to the theory, directive, supportive, participative and achievement-oriented behaviours. The *supportive* leadership style 'provides guidance and psychological structure'; the *directive* leadership style 'provides nurturance'; the *participative* leadership style 'provides involvement'; and the *achievement-oriented* leadership style 'provides challenges'.[34]

The basic idea of this model is that the leader should work with the different styles in accordance with the needs of the followers and the structure of the task at hand. So, for instance, if the task is repetitive and boring and the followers are not satisfied, then a supportive style would work. On the other hand, if work is complex and demands creativity to be solved, and the expectations are high among the followers, achievement-oriented leadership would work.

This path-goal idea seems easy to connect to our purchasing maturity matrix with the six stages from Chapter 2. It is likely that a purchasing organization operating on for example level 2 in comparison with level 5 or 6 will differ greatly concerning what kind of tasks to perform. Significant parts of the latter operations will be characterized by complexity and a need for creative solutions (business development upstream). The aforementioned will more likely be characterized by more repetitive operations. The kind of leadership style best fitted for each purpose could vary in line with the theory.

The path-goal theory has, however, not been free from criticism, mostly because it is considered too complex. On the other hand, the model is easy to relate to and pinpoints relevant issues, such as followers' work motivation[35] and the context-specific aspects of leadership styles.

Leadership roles

Mintzberg's study on managerial roles (referred to earlier in this chapter) has become a classical piece of work within leadership research but even so, it only offers descriptive accounts of managerial behaviour and offers no explanation to the 'why question'. Mintzberg seems to have been aware of this fact himself, since he concludes that "[a] synthesis of these findings paints an interesting picture, one as different from Fayol's classical view as a cubist abstract is from a Renaissance painting".[36] After 20 years of research he seems to be cynical, stating that: 'It is necessary to point out that managers, in fact, hardly ever "do" anything.'[37]

In contrast to Mintzberg's conclusion that managers end up doing practically nothing, others conclude that managers do a lot – especially those who are effective leaders.[38] This argumentation is critical to previous theories and models about leadership roles, since it argues that these do not take into account the full spectrum of being a leader. Leaders of today, including purchasing managers, are exposed to a range of networks, 'outside' as well as 'inside' pressure, a high speed of external changes as well as organizational changes, and therefore they need to respond to complexity and diversity. In short, this approach suggests that behavioural complexity, encompassing cognition as well as the ability 'to conceive and perform multiple and contradictory roles', is decisive for effective leadership.

Relying on a model of four dimensions – or polar opposites – that the proponents of this approach believe is in consistency with the complex reality that managers face today, eight different roles emerge, two roles in each quadrant.[39] The polar opposites are:

- On the horizontal level: internal focus vs external focus.
- On the vertical level: flexibility vs stability.

The following combinations give rise to particular roles:

- By combining an external focus with flexibility, the two roles of innovator and broker can be identified. These two roles relate to adaptation. The *innovator* is more prone to change and eases processes of change, whereas the *broker* is more focused on upholding legitimacy and political networking.
- The combination of an external focus with stability results in the producer role and the director role. These two roles deal with rational goal pursuit. The *producer* is task oriented and wants to achieve closure, whereas the *director* is involved in formulating goals, clarifying roles and setting standards for achievement.
- Combining an internal focus with stability ends up in the coordinator role and the monitor role. These two roles are both related to internal control and stability. The *coordinator* plans, controls and sees to it that structure is withheld.

The *monitor*, on the other hand, seeks information, spread this and stands for continuity.

- The interpolation of an internal focus with flexibility gives rise to the facilitator role and the mentor role. The *facilitator* and the *mentor* deal with human relations processes, where the former is interested in consensus or compromise solutions and the latter takes care of individual needs and supports individual development.

The basic idea is that leaders cannot – and should not – be placed in either one of the polar opposites nor in only one of the possible roles. On the contrary, the conclusion is that the more roles a manager is able to perform, the more effective is his or her leadership.

An empirically grounded study has illustrated that ineffective leaders perform just a few of these roles, whereas effective leaders are able to combine most of the roles depending on the exposure they face.[40] The effectiveness is measured by superiors as well as followers, which gives effectiveness a special meaning here, considering that most leadership research regarding roles is based on self-evaluations. Still, it is interesting to notice that the authors are able to give some kind of evidence for effectiveness in leadership.

These findings have a range of implications for purchasing leaders. So, for instance, the purchasing leader is supposed to face and deal with a complex reality where it is not enough to rely on one or a couple of leadership styles and roles alone. He or she has to encompass at times paradoxical internal and external challenges and demands and needs to be able to parry between different roles and also to perform a set of them at the same time. This conclusion could be a suitable moment for reflection by our three CPOs. When asked 'As a manager/CPO of purchasing what are your most important leadership tasks?', some of the responses were the following.

Box 6.4   Purchasing leadership tasks

CPO, SERVICES FIRM: 'Still, unfortunately, one very important task is to "sell purchasing" in the organization. The role and possible impact of a well-functioning, adequately staffed purchasing organization is still not fully understood. Related to this is, in my case, to fight for adequate amounts and qualities of resources. Connected to this is also the task of building skills and competence, including energy and empowerment of my staff.'

CPO, MANUFACTURING COMPANY: 'We have a very strong focus on coordination these days. We have bought so many operations through mergers and acquisitions and we need to be better able to exercise economies of scale. To me, then, the most important task for the coming years is to develop the infrastructure (IT systems etc.) to enable our people to be better off in those issues. But it takes a lot of efforts to sell this message to our purchasing and management staff all over the world. Also interacting with suppliers to explain to them what is going on is a demanding task in my leadership.'

CPO, RETAIL FIRM: 'The most important leadership task, in addition to being the link between various functions inside our firm and in outside contact with suppliers, is to make my staff fit for purpose. This has to do with motivating them and supporting with basic infrastructure including training. A specific task that occupies me a lot right now is our constant effort to try and break cartels in various supply markets. We have over the years learnt that there is quite a lot of such business practices going on and we spare no efforts to counteract it.'

These quotes show that purchasing managers fulfil, more or less, all the roles mentioned. However, the focus varies somewhat depending on the specific contexts of the various firms. The services firm is in a process of structuring and upgrading its purchasing operations. It needs, first of all, to get the necessary infrastructure in place. This has to do with staffing, developing processes and procedures as well as influencing the general attitude to purchasing. The manufacturing firm has a similar situation, even though its focus is on the international context of its operations. The retail firm has for quite a long time had most of its infrastructure in place and is focusing more on everyday efforts to exploit opportunities for improvement given its stable structure. These aspects suggest that the dimensions of an internal vs external focus as well as flexibility vs stability are valid.

So far, we have mainly taken into account different views on leadership that could all be referred to as 'rational'. However, structural changes, flatter organizations, innovative forms of organizing, demographic changes, globalization, life-long learning, increased competencies and new emerging values, among other things, have called for new demands on leaders that go beyond the above. The focus as reflected in management research (and practice) has turned more towards a two-way relationship between the leader and the followers. New catchwords have been put on the agenda that direct our opinion about leadership, such as its responsibility to provide meaningful work, emotional commitment and challenges, being visionary, ethical and inspirational. These views could still in a general sense be considered 'rational', as these orientations are still taken to purposefully achieve an improved outcome. Nevertheless, they differ from the definition of rational given above where rationality is looked at in a more narrow sense (decision oriented, clear ideas of ends and goals and so on).

To distinguish the two broad categories, we will discuss the coming ones under the label 'relationship-oriented' processes of leadership, which are also in line with our leadership definition. To once again return to our sequence of questions starting from what leaders really do, via what leadership could be and how and what leaders should be and perform, we now move on to the specific implications on leadership of various modern forms of organizing. In short, what can leaders achieve (more and in better ways) given these new contexts?

6.4 Emotional processes

Emotions

That emotions matter in leadership processes is a well-established argument today.[41] The communication of emotions matters greatly in all relationships where the manager is involved. One classic study among flight attendants gave us an emotional vocabulary, when it referred to 'emotional work' and 'emotional labour' as well as 'expression' and 'feeling rules' and 'emotional stamina'.[42]

Emotional work is the basic good manners to care about people and how they feel, whereas emotional labour is more related to our occupation as a leader. When we are a leader it is not as natural to sit down in the coffee lounge and express feelings about this and that, about colleagues and above all not about people we lead. With the profession also follows certain expression rules such as not expressing too much anger, sadness, worry and the like, especially not in front of followers, or to express joy at someone's success, even if this is not what is actually felt. At times of turbulence and uncertainty such as mergers or downsizing, the leader is supposed to show feelings of self-confidence or at least calmness. At a deeper level, leaders are at times supposed to follow certain feeling rules, indicating that it is appropriate to actually feel a certain emotion even if this is not the case. For instance, if a member of the team is grieving, the leader is expected to a certain extent to grieve as well. Emotional stamina is the exposure of feelings over a longer period of time – in accordance with expression and feeling rules – that are not in line with the leader's own and actually felt emotions:

> A young businessman said to a flight attendant, 'Why aren't you smiling?'
>
> She put her tray back on the food cart and said, 'I'll tell you what. You smile first, then I'll smile.'
>
> The businessman smiled at her.
>
> 'Good', she replied. 'Now, freeze and hold that for fifteen hours.'[43]

Emotional stability is the point of departure for the popular concept of emotional intelligence.[44] To be emotionally intelligent includes five major components. In short, these are:

- *Self-awareness*, the ability to know yourself, your strengths and weaknesses, and how your way of being influences other people.
- *Self-regulation*, which is mainly the ability to control one's temper and being able to think before you act.
- *Motivation*, so an emotionally intelligent leader is driven by a passion for his or her work much more than by a high salary or the status of being a leader.
- *Empathy* is the ability to shoulder other people's feelings. For instance, if there is a delicate situation, such as making people redundant, the emotionally intelligent leader is able to refer to the feelings and the particular situation to which this gives rise.
- *Social skills* are important since they involve networking abilities, not only with the immediate surroundings but with other departments, customers and, people who are strategically important for the department/organization. To maintain this network is equally important.

Emotional intelligence is a widely used concept today and a wide range of instruments exist in order for managers to evaluate their current emotional stability.

To be a middle manager, which a purchasing manager normally is, is often an exposed position. This brings up the emotional balancing act that middle managers often have to perform in change processes, when they need to keep continuity at the same time as they need to enthusiastically force change.[45] Any imbalance between emotional commitment to the change and attentiveness to the emotions of the team members will lead to either chaos or inertia. The implications for purchasing managers are obvious: there is a need to know how the team members react and act emotionally on change. Some people show high activity and among these it is a little easier to realize whether they are enthusiastic or angry, worried and so on. However, among those who show low activity it is more difficult to understand whether they are satisfied and calm about the change or whether they are discouraged.

Emerging research on emotions takes the two-way relationship into account in so far as the interpretation of leaders' emotions is decisive for their relevance and effect.[46] In practice, this means that if the leader yells it becomes the emotion of anger if it is interpreted as such by his or her team members. Once interpreted, these members consciously or unconsciously make a decision regarding what they make of the anger and act accordingly. Viewed in this way, emotions can work as either driving forces or restraining forces in the process of practising leadership.

Driving forces are created among organizational members and thus are the effect of emotions that give rise to an advancement or progress towards the group and/or organizational goal. *Restraining forces*, on the other hand, are the effect of emotions that restrain the progress of the process in the direction towards the goal. For example, if a leader is frustrated and shows his or her frustration, this communicates to the team members that something is wrong or is in the way to reaching the goals. From this, the team members can decide what to do about it – and if they act in order to solve the situation, the frustration works as a driving force.

The co-producing of emotions between the leader and the group members has power implications for the leader. By showing and expressing his or her emotions the leader is interpreted as offering a 'positive' role model, explicit in his or her communication, implying that the organizational members think it worthwhile to meet and act on his or her intentions. Emotions, in this sense, work as producers and reproducers of goodwill for the leader and give the leader 'power gain'.[47] The opposite will occur where emotions are not 'out in the open', and where the leader is not expressing or showing his or her honest emotions, ending up in an atmosphere of confusion, implying a hidden agenda, leading to 'power drain'.

This approach contends that there are no negative or positive emotions, only emotions working in a negative or positive direction.[48] This means that anger and frustration can work as driving forces whereas expressed confidence may work in the opposite direction if this is the emotion expressed but not actually felt. It also means that if the purchasing manager is able to express and display honest emotions, be they frustration, worry, concern, strain or satisfaction (just to mention a few), these can give him or her mutually created 'power'.

Emotions have also been proven to serve as constructors of *emotion sediments*, good-mood setters and bad-mood setters.[49] Emotion sediments build up from a range of situations or issues where earlier emotions have played a role and where emotions tend to 'build on' each other in one way or the other, and that eventually sediments the opinion about a person, an issue, a situation or a behaviour. If a purchasing manager has an argument with a team member and this is not settled, the aftermath will build the basis for the future and in the next encounter it is the very starting point in the discussion, even though it may be 'unemotional' in character. The possible sedimentation of emotions points out the importance of not leaving emotional issues aside. On the other hand, an encounter may be very pleasant in character and leave behind a basis for sedimentation of positive emotional vibrations that can be useful in future difficult situations.

Typically, good-mood setters and bad-mood setters are more evident at the end or the beginning of social encounters. Emotions as good-mood setters ease up the atmosphere and are aimed at giving relief in strained situations or with difficult issues. The latter is more often noticeable at the beginning of meetings where a bad mood, perhaps resulting from another situation, issue or encounter, influences the mood at the present meeting. Being aware of emotions as mood setters, the purchasing manager can purposely create a desired atmosphere.

All in all, new perspectives view emotions as natural, a source of energy, being part of a co-produced phenomenon and helpful in the leadership process in order to meet goals. Leaders could, thus, have a strong impact on the kind of emotions produced in a certain organization or in relation to specific contexts and issues. They could contribute to good and bad mood atmospheres. This conclusion forms the bridge to take us back to the previously introduced issue of leadership and culture.

Leadership and culture

We touched on the connection between leadership and culture, referring to Weick who found the two concepts to be interchangeable. It is somewhat debated whether or not culture could be managed, whether or not an organization is a culture or has a culture. We think that a leader, not least in purchasing, in similar ways as setting the atmosphere, could do a lot to influence the value system of his or her organization. Schein provides some good arguments for this.[50] He says that a leader influences the value system in several ways, especially the following ones:

- *Attention*: leaders communicate their priorities, values and orientation through the choice of issues they ask about and measure, commitments they make, praise and criticism. A lot of this takes place naturally as an ingredient in the leaders 'walking around'.
- *Reactions to crises*: crises are especially important as it then is a matter of 'electrified' situations when the potential for learning values is extra high.
- *Role behaviour*: leaders communicate values and expectations through their own behaviour. What they do is often more important than what they say. The leader who declares a certain policy but afterwards doesn't live according to it communicates that it isn't really that important.
- *Distribution of rewards*: the applied criteria, for example for salary increases or job positions, communicate what is valued by the management of the organization. Formal acknowledgements, ceremonies and informal praise communicate too. To fail to recognize behaviour and performance communicates indirectly that they are not important or not wanted.

- *Criteria for employment, selection and dismissal*: by recruiting the 'right' kind of personnel the leaders will influence the culture. The same goes for the appointment of certain individuals to specific positions and assignments.

In line with this reasoning, some argue that a core task for the leaders of an organization is to clarify and develop the company's culture by interpreting and creating meaning for the role of the organization.[51] According to this view, leadership consists basically of three issues:

- *Handling and activities*: to make things happen, for example to negotiate with suppliers and make sure that the logistics actually work (robust action).
- *Rhetoric*: to face staff and suppliers (and others) in a straight and open dialogue. It is about listening and communicating and thereby laying the ground for coherent and stable interpretations.
- *Identity building*: in dialogue processes to make clear what the organization is and should be and what its basic values are. This goes on at several levels in an organization; the company as such, the purchasing unit, the team and so on. It is always important to pay attention to issues such as who the company is, what it stands for, how it wants to be interpreted and understood.

This comment brings us to one more related stream of new thinking about leadership, which emphasizes vision, sense making and inspiration.

6.5   Vision, sense making and inspiration in leadership

Another classification of leadership is the division between charismatic leadership, inspirational leadership and transformational leadership.

Charismatic leadership describes in fact the characteristics of both the leader and the followers in a special situation of devoted adherence to one leader. The charismatic leader is often characterized by great self-confidence, dominance, sense of purpose and the ability to articulate goals and ideas to followers.

Inspirational leadership means that the followers are drawn to the goals and purposes of the corporate mission rather than the leader as such.

Transformational leadership includes both charismatic and inspirational leadership as well as intellectual stimulation and individual consideration. The transformational leadership style is often contrasted with the transactional leadership style, being at the opposite ends of a continuum.[52] Transactional leaders focus on setting goals, being explicit in what the leader expects from organizational members, control and feedback to keep everybody on track.[53] Furthermore, transactional leaders strive for standardization, formalization and efficiency. Transformational leaders inspire others through the vision to take risks and come up with creative ideas, reflecting the roles of the innovator, broker, facilitator and mentor (see above).

However, relating the two leadership styles to learning capacity, the combination of the two leadership styles (perhaps a 'mission impossible') should be the best from a learning perspective.[54] Transformational leaders foster learning in terms of exploration in a context of change, while transactional leaders motivate individuals to exploit current learning by concentrating on existing tasks.

To summarize, transformational leaders focus on managing change, emphasizing experimentation and risk taking, while transactional leaders focus on incremental change and continuity, emphasizing prior logic and incremental evolution of the status quo; that is, reinforcing and refining current routines. The most effective strategic leaders are those who can adapt their transformational and transactional behaviours to the proper situation, equally hospitable to both exploration and exploitation.[55] However, for strategic change to take place in the purchasing context of the firm, the transformational leadership style is a proven way to encourage organizational members to reassess current routines and challenge current assumptions and mental models.[56]

A short reflection here is that the various levels of purchasing maturity (compare the purchasing maturity model in Chapter 1) could lead us to distinguish various types of purchasing organizations and that maybe these new ideas about leadership may apply differently to the various situations. The lower levels (level 1 and 2 in the model) imply that purchasing is basically an *administrative (clerical) operation* inside the firm. The middle levels imply that the purchasing operations are similar to a *service operation*, giving service to the rest of the organization and consisting of service-oriented staff. Purchasing does have many of the typical attributes of a service organization.

The higher levels, levels 5 and 6, imply purchasing organizations that are more disposed to business development, redesigning business processes, developing supply markets and so on. Such organizations consist to a large extent of highly educated specialists and have more of the attributes that one would find in a typical so-called professional organization, or organization of professionals. Stereotypes of such organizations are consultancy firms, law firms and similar operations, where most individuals have a strong professional identity and are expected to be very strong in solving problems, conceptual understanding and the like.

The managerial process is likely to be very different in the three archetypes of organizations. It may for example be more relevant to have strict role descriptions, leaving little room for individual problem solving, in the administrative organization. In order to foster a services climate it is more likely that the service organization has more ingredients of empowerment (freedom to act and solve problems). The leadership should most likely emphasize key values to the firm and thereby facilitate relevant action. The professional organization, in turn, gives even more freedom to each individual to interpret and act and it is absolutely critical to intellectually equip and empower the staff. They are expected to interpret and understand the relevant decisions to take and activities to perform in very complex situations. Their own judgement is critical and therefore it is even more important that they are embraced with the cognitive thinking and understanding of the corporate value systems. In such organizations one would expect the prevailing atmosphere and the intellectual climate to be highly critical ingredients. In such contexts transformational leadership should, thus, be highly relevant.[57]

Close to these types of leadership is *visionary* leadership. A vision is an attractive and possible future position for the organization. It is a new direction towards the future, not a plan. Visionary leadership, which means 'to be in the future', includes involving 'everyone' in the formation of the vision; continuously communicating the vision; creating engagement and commitment to the vision; getting co-ownership from 'all' members of the organization (unit); rewarding important steps towards the realization of the vision; and being prepared to modify the vision – the vision is a moving target (because of a changing environment). These important aspects relate to the discussion on leadership and culture above.

In order to be able to make good judgements, each individual in an organization should be prepared. This has to do not only with knowing their respective fields of expertise, but also what is important in this specific context, including the specific organization he or she works for. Neither the task, the specific goal, nor the method of carrying out the assignment is a 'given'.[58] Still, the organization expects proper action and an excellent outcome. Awareness of the value system of that firm – and what that means for specific job assignments in specific situations – makes the individual better able to act in relevant ways. The same goes for the vision. Awareness about the vision makes it easier to take relevant decisions and judgements for present and future actions, not least in relation to issues of strategic change. This reasoning is equally relevant for leaders as it is for followers.

The importance of these kinds of aspects has also been underlined in a study of 'enduring' firms.[59] Collins and Porras studied firms that had survived for several decades and had, more or less, continuous success. They came to the conclusion that one of the common features of these firms was a very strong culture and a high identification with strongly felt meaningfulness about the mission of the firm among its employees.

In order to be successful in strategic change initiatives, the leader needs to understand the predominant culture of the organization and adapt a suitable style of change leadership to this cultural context. In modern forms of organizing – that is, with a more horizontal and process-oriented structure, where teamwork, projects and network represent the mode of integration and control (rather than the traditional hierarchical form) – the strategy process is characterized more as a collective effort/endeavour.

Such interactive strategizing certainly implies new roles of leadership: first being the strategist that is initiating and framing direction (e.g. through a visionary approach), but then being a strategist among many in the realization of a vision through the unfolding of new strategic actions and patterns. In the 1980s a study of successful leaders in different contexts focused on the importance of both management of attention – for example creating attention through attractive visions – and management of meaning – for example creating a sense of shared meaning through continuous communication.[60] This study added the importance of the management of trust, where trust (especially in relation to employees) also requires consistency and sustainability in the strategic direction.

This discussion emphasizes aspects of the infrastructure of companies that can be considered complementary to the ones previously discussed and reflected by our three CPOs. Let us again return to them to see if they cover some of these aspects. They were asked the following question: 'Could you give an example of an important (strategic) change regarding sourcing/purchasing that you/your company have decided on and implemented during the last five years? Tell us also what you found especially problematic in carrying out that task.'

Box 6.5   Leading strategic change

CPO, MANUFACTURING FIRM: 'My most important mission has been to make the international coordination of our purchasing operations come true. As already mentioned, it has been difficult to get immediate understanding and acceptance for these ideas. One thing that worked well, however, was to create local heroes. When someone in our organization had done something especially good I had them tell their story, I videotaped it and I used it to communicate all over the organization. These local people became good role models, easy to connect to and identify with. The attention to what was expected got clarified at the same time as everyone saw their chance to become exposed as a local hero. In this way I managed to communicate the meaning of our mission more effectively. Over the years, I have learnt that such small moves of individual recognition often have dramatic effects on motivation and identification with the firm and our mission. I have also started to put much more emphasis on the periodical (every six months) individual dialogue I have with my staff. I think that is a very powerful way to influence (and get influenced) on our key values.'

CPO, SERVICES FIRM: 'One of the toughest challenges has been to change the mood and the conceptual thinking about purchasing among my staff and the rest of the company. When I was in the automotive industry with a well-developed and professional purchasing operation it was like a self-playing piano. Everyone knew what to do, they took initiatives that generally were relevant, and the entire operation just went on and performed at a high level. The 'average mass' of people was so knowledgeable and prepared. I didn't understand it then, but when I have tried to develop our operations here I have realized what a difference it is when, like in this case, people aren't trimmed the same way. Everything is much heavier; initiatives that are taken prove often to be wrong or bad etc. The challenge is to change this organization towards the kind of coordination we had at my previous occupation.'

CPO, RETAIL FIRM: 'I consider the implementation of the sourcing strategy we developed, seven years ago, as one major change process. We developed the overall mission for the purchasing operation and expressed it in a few sentences. It was made operational in eight strategies dealing with key topics of our operation: total supply chain management including taking action in the supplier's own purchasing process, global sourcing should really mean global, explicit code of conduct and strong focus on targeting and measuring and so on. We developed the reasons for this and the consequences of it. This way we created a meaning and a vision for our operations. Maybe, and most important, it turned out to be much easier to communicate and interact with other parts of our company as well as suppliers. The targets gave us better opportunities to take charge. The other aspects gave energy and direction and promoted initiative taking among my staff.'

These examples illustrate quite clearly the role of these aspects from recent management thinking. Creation of meaningfulness, understanding the context and the mission, empowered staff and so on seem to be very much what it is about. This perspective (visionary, transformational leadership) has been taken one step further in the reciprocal model of leadership recently proposed.[61] In a study of leadership in innovative forms of organizing, the overall question was how new ideas are invented, developed, shared and destroyed in ongoing processes of 'sense making'. The traditional view is that leaders frame and give sense to organizational members, the followers, and that leaders have the skills that are required to manage meaning. The assumption is that the specific meaning that a leader is giving sense to is also accepted by organizational members.

However, recent research argues that meanings communicated by leaders are translated by the receivers; that is, their sense making implies a partly or totally new meaning of the communicated ideas. The consequence is that we need to replace the top-down, unidirectional view of sense giving from leaders with a view of more reciprocal sense-making processes, where leaders may frame visions but where the realization and modification of visions are the result of reciprocal sense giving and sense making, including bottom-up sense giving influencing the strategy process.[62]

6.6   Conclusions

The purchasing leader faces and deals with a complex reality where it is not enough to rely on one or a couple of leadership styles and roles alone. He or she has to encompass at times paradoxical internal and external challenges and demands and needs – or sets of dualities – to be able to parry between different roles and also to be able to perform a set of them at the same time.

We have given an overview of the development in thinking as portrayed in leadership research. This development has been reflected against some of the patterns displayed in purchasing management. Illustrations from interviews with three CPOs have also contributed to a translation of the general aspects to purchasing management contexts.

We can conclude that the various lines of thinking have something relevant to transmit to purchasing management. The rational models such as the traits and skills approaches and the psychodynamic approach give us a view on several characteristics of the leader and in what contexts they may fit. The discussion about leadership roles gives us a map by which we can orient ourselves to see what parts of the various roles we fulfil – and reflect on possible implications of various biases.

It may be that these aspects of leadership still do not provide the full picture. Given the development in today's organizations towards flatter organizations and new ways of organizing in terms of projects and networks, recent developments in leadership literature emphasize what has here been labelled 'relationship approaches', in which the emerging leadership is looked on as an interactive process between leaders and followers. The leadership process is not unidirectional. The new developments also pinpoint other, 'softer' aspects of leadership where emotions, creation of a 'climate' or a value system and a rewarding job environment play a crucial role. Still, it should be emphasized that the purchasing manager also quite frequently needs to take tough decisions such as hiring and firing suppliers, engage in challenging political battles internally and so on.

Purchasing is to a diminishing extent a unified unit, located in one room, dealing with purchasing issues only. It has, as have so many other functions, become an integrated part of the process-oriented company. It is, as are so many other modern organizations, characterized by teamwork, projects and being part of and acting in networks.

For such reasons we should take a serious interest also in the modern thinking about leadership as presented here. As has already been pointed out, the moves from a purchasing operation in line with levels 1 or 2, via 3 and 4, to 5 and 6 in the maturity model introduce quite a lot of changes in the purchasing operation. This has also got to do with the leadership aspects. We think that the more there is a development towards the higher levels of purchasing maturity, the more relevance there is for the modern thinking about leadership!

Appendix 6.1   Interview questions

1. Could you give examples of important strategic issues (i.e. issues that are important to work on/solve in order to stay competitive) in your sourcing/purchasing operations?
2. Regarding yourself as the strategic leader of the sourcing/purchasing function, please describe this role of strategic leadership (what does such a role mean, and what is included in such a role)?
3. Could you give an example of an important (strategic) change regarding sourcing/purchasing that you/your company have decided on and implemented during the last five years? Tell us also what you found especially problematic in carrying out that task.
4. As manager/CPO of purchasing, what are your most important leadership tasks?
5. When looking back one or two decades, what do you consider the most striking differences between the purchasing managers (including CPOs) of today in contrast to those days?

Notes and references

[1] DuBrin, A.J. (2004) *Leadership: Research Findings, Practice, and Skills*, 4th edn, Houghton Mifflin: Boston/New York; Kotter, J.P. (1990) *A Force for Change: How Leadership Differs from Management*, Free Press: New York.
[2] Mintzberg, H. (1973) *The Nature of Managerial Work*, Harper & Row: New York.
[3] Mintzberg's idea to observe executives probably derived from Sune Carlson's study in the early 1950s. One of Carlson's famous conclusions is that managers' behaviour is more like that of puppets than that of conductors of orchestras. Carlson, S. (1951) *Executive Behavior*, Strombergs: Stockholm.
[4] Mintzberg, H. (1990) 'The manager's job: Folklore and fact', *Harvard Business Review*, Vol. 68, No. 2, pp. 163–76.
[5] Mintzberg (1990) *opere citato*, p. 171.
[6] Kotter, J.P. (1999) 'What effective general managers really do', *Harvard Business Review*, Vol. 77, No. 2, March–April, pp. 145–55.

7   Stewart, R. (1967) *Managers and Their Jobs: A Study of the Similarities and Differences in the Ways Managers Spend Their Time*, 2nd edn, Macmillan: Basingstoke; Stewart, R. (1976) *Contrasts in Management: A Study of Different Types of Managers' Jobs: Their Demands and Choices*, McGraw-Hill: Maidenhead; Stewart, R. (1982) *Choices for the Manager: A Guide to Managerial Work and Behaviour*, McGraw-Hill: Maidenhead and Prentice Hall, Englewood Cliffs, NJ.

8   Kotter (1999) *opere citato*.

9   Such as Lowe, K.B. (2003) 'Demands, constraints, choices and discretion: An introduction to the work of Rosemary Stewart', *Leadership Quarterly*, Vol. 14, No. 2, pp. 193–7; Kroeck, K.G. (2003) 'Rosemary Stewart on management: Behavioral scribe, squire of theory, pragmatic scientist', *Leadership Quarterly*, Vol. 14, No. 2, pp. 204–16; Parry, K.W. (2003) 'Of complexity and distillation: Stewart's contribution to understanding what managers really do', *Leadership Quarterly*, Vol. 14, No. 2, pp. 216–21; Den Hartog, D.N. (2003) 'What indeed do managers do? Some reflections on Rosemary Stewart's work', *Leadership Quarterly*, Vol. 14, No. 2, pp. 221–9; Wahlgren, A. (2003) 'Choices, constraints, and demands: Stewart's model for understanding managerial work and behavior', *Leadership Quarterly*, Vol. 14, No. 2, pp. 229–34; Ammeter, T.P. (2003) 'Contributions of Rosemary Stewart's work to thought on the management of information systems', *Leadership Quarterly*, Vol. 14, No. 2, pp. 234–8.

10 Yukl, G. (2002) *Leadership in Organizations*, 5th edn, Prentice Hall: New York.

11 Alvesson and Sveningsson (2003), Bennis and Nanus (1985) and Kotter (1990) differentiate between leaders and managers. Leaders are prone to change and innovation and 'doing the right thing', whereas managers are prone to stability, order and efficiency and 'doing the thing right'. Here we will use the terms interchangeably since we believe that it takes both to be a leader/manager. In our daily talk we often use the word manager, including the characteristics that are assigned to leaders as well as managers by Bennis and Nanus and Kotter. Alvesson, M. and Sveningsson, S. (2003) 'The great disappearing act: Difficulties in doing "leadership"', *The Leadership Quarterly*, Vol. 14, pp. 359–81; Bennis, W. and Nanus, B. (1985) *Leaders: The Strategies for Taking Charge*, Harper & Row: New York.

12 Alvesson and Sveningsson (2003) *opere citato*, p. 375.

13 Weick, K.E. (1985) 'The significance of corporate culture', in Frost, P., Moore, L., Louis, M.R., Lundberg, C. and Martin, J. (eds), *Organizational Culture*, Sage: Beverly Hills, CA, pp. 381–90.

14 Hemphill, J.K. and Coons, A.E. (1957) 'Development of the leader behavior description questionnaire', in Stogdill, R.M. and Coons, A.E. (eds), *Leader Behavior: Its Description and Measurement*, Bureau of Business Research, Ohio State University: Columbus, OH, pp. 6–38; Burns, J.M. (1978) *Leadership*, Harper & Row: New York; Katz, D. and Kahn, R.L. (1978) *The Social Psychology of Organizations*, 2nd edn, John Wiley & Sons Ltd: New York; Rausch, C.F. and Behling, O. (1984) 'Functionalism: Basis for an alternate approach to the study of leadership', in Hunt, J.G., Hosking, D.M., Schriesheim, C.A. and Stewart, R. (eds), *Leaders and Managers: International Perspectives on Managerial Behavior and Leadership*, Pergamon Press: Elmsford, NY, pp. 45–62; House, R.J., Hanages, P.J., Ruiz-Quintanilla, S.A., Dorfman, P.W., Javidan, M., Dickson, M. and associates (1999) 'Cultural influences on leadership and organizations: Project GLOBE', in Mobley, W.H., Gessner, M.J. and Arnold, V. (eds), *Advances in Global Leadership*, JAI Press: Stamford, CA, pp. 171–233; and Yukl (2002) *opere citato*.

15 French, J. and Raven, B.H. (1959) 'The bases of social power', in Cartwright, D. (ed.), *Studies of Social Power*, Institute for Social Research: Ann Arbor, MI, pp. 150–67.

16 Yukl (2002) *opere citato*, p. 7.

17 *Ibidem*.

18 *Ibidem*.

19 Stogdill, R.M. (1948) 'Personal factors associated with leadership: A survey of the literature', *Journal of Psychology*, 25, pp. 35–71; Stogdill, R.M. (1974) *Handbook of Leadership: A Survey of the Literature*, Free Press: New York; Mann, R.D. (1959) 'A review of the relationship between personality and performance in small groups', *Psychological Bulletin*, Vol. 56, pp. 241–70; Lord, R.G., DeVader, C.L. and Alliger, G.M. (1986) 'A meta-analysis of the relation between personality traits and leadership: An application of validity generalization procedures', *Journal of Applied Psychology*, Vol. 71, pp. 402–10; Kirkpatrick, S.A. and Locke, E.A. (1991) 'Leadership: Do traits matter?', *Academy of Management Executive*, Vol. 5, No. 2, pp. 48–60.

20 Surgency = extroversion; energy and activity level; and need for power. Conscientiousness = dependability; personal integrity; and need for achievement. Agreeableness = cheerfulness and optimism; nurturance; and need for affiliation. Adjustment = emotional stability; self-esteem;

and self-control. Intellectance = curiosity and inquisitiveness; open-mindedness; and learning orientation.

[21] Digman, J.M. (1990) 'Personality structure: Emergence of the five-factor model', *Annual Review of Psychology*, Vol. 4, pp. 417–40; Hough, L.M. (1992) 'The "Big Five" personality variables – construct confusion: Description versus prediction', *Human Performance*, Vol. 5, pp. 139–55.

[22] Northouse, P.G. (2004) *Leadership: Theory and Practice*, 3rd edn, Sage Publications: Thousand Oaks, CA.

[23] Katz, R.L. (1955) 'Skills of an effective administrator', *Harvard Business Review*, Vol. 33, No. 1, pp. 33–42.

[24] Mumford, M.D., Zaccaro, S.J., Connelly, M.S. and Marks, M.A. (2000) 'Leadership skills: Conclusions and future directions', *Leadership Quarterly*, Vol. 11, pp. 155–70.

[25] Northouse (2004) *opere citato*.

[26] Yukl (2002) *opere citato*.

[27] These stages are family of origin, maturation/individuation, dependence, counter-dependence and independence.

[28] Northouse (2004) *opere citato*.

[29] Kets de Vries, M. (1994) 'The leadership mystique', *Academy of Management Executive*, Vol. 8, No. 3, pp. 73–92.

[30] Kets de Vries, M. (1999) 'Organizational sleepwalkers: Emotional distress at midlife', *Human Relations*, Vol. 52, No. 11, pp. 1377–401.

[31] Blake, R.R. and Mouton, J.S. (1964) *The Managerial Grid*, Gulf Publishing: Houston, TX; Blake, R.R. and Mouton, J.S. (1978) *The New Managerial Grid*, Gulf Publishing: Houston, TX; Blake, R.R. and Mouton, J.S. (1985) *The New Managerial Grid III*, Gulf Publishing: Houston, TX.

[32] Hersey, P., Blanchard, K.H. and Johnson, D.E. (1969/2001) *Management of Organizational Behaviour: Leading Human Resources*, 8th edn, Prentice Hall International: London; Blanchard, K.H. (1985) *SLII: A Situational Approach to Managing People*, Blanchard Training and Development: Escondido, CA; Blanchard, K., Zigarmi, P. and Zigarmi, D. (1985) *Leadership and the One Minute Manager: Increasing Effectiveness Through Situational Leadership*, William Morrow: New York.

[33] House, R.J. and Mitchell, T.R. (1974) 'Path-goal theory of leadership', *Contemporary Business*, Vol. 3, pp. 81–98.

[34] Northouse (2004) *opere citato*, p. 130.

[35] See also McClelland's need for achievement: McClelland, D.C. (1965) 'N-achievement and entrepreneurship: A longitudinal study', *Journal of Personality and Social Psychology*, Vol. I, pp. 389–92; McClelland, D.C. (1985) *Human Motivation*, Scott Foresman: Glenview, IL.

[36] Mintzberg, H. (1975) 'The manager's job: Folklore and fact', *Harvard Business Review*, Vol. 53, pp. 49–61.

[37] Mintzberg, H. (1994) 'Rounding out the manager's job', *Sloan Management Review*, Vol. 36, No. 1, pp. 11–26.

[38] Denison, D.R., Hooijberg, R. and Quinn, R.E. (1995) 'Paradox and performance: Toward a theory of behavioral complexity in managerial leadership', *Organization Science*, Vol. 6, No. 5, pp. 524–40.

[39] Quinn, R.E. and Rohrbaugh, J. (1983) 'A spatial model of effectiveness criteria: Towards a competing values approach to organizational analysis', *Management Science*, Vol. 29, No. 3, pp. 363–75.

[40] Denison *et al.* (1995) *opere citato*.

[41] Huy Q.N. (2002) 'Emotional balancing of organizational continuity and radical change: The contribution of middle managers', *Administrative Science Quarterly*, Vol. 47 (March), pp. 31–69; Brundin, E. (2002) *Emotions in Motion: The Strategic Leader in a Radical Change Process*, JIBS Dissertation Series No. 012, Jönköping International Business School: Jönköping; Fineman, S. (2003) *Understanding Emotion at Work*, Sage Publications: London.

[42] Hochschild, A.R. (1983) *The Managed Heart: Commercialization of Human Feeling*, University of California Press: Betheley, CA.

[43] Hochschild (1983) *opere citato*, p. 127.

[44] Goleman, D. (1995) *Emotional Intelligence*, Bantam Books: New York; Mayer, J.D., Ciarrochi, J. and Forgas, J.P. (2001) 'Emotional intelligence in everyday life: An introduction', in Ciarrochi, J., Forgas, J.O. and Mayer, J.D. (eds), *Emotional Intelligence in Everyday Life*, Psychology Press: Philadelphia, p. xiii.

[45] Huy (2002) *opere citato*.

[46] Brundin (2002) *opere citato*.

[47] *Ibidem.*

48 *Ibidem.*

49 *Ibidem.*

50 Schein, E. (1992) *Organizational Psychology*, 3rd edn, Prentice Hall: Englewood Cliffs, NJ.

51 Eccles, R.G. and Nohira, N. (1991) *Beyond the Hype – Rediscovering the Essesce of Management*, Harvard Business School Press, Boston, MA.

52 Burns (1978) *opere citato.*

53 Bass, B.M. and Avolio, B.J. (1993) 'Transformational leadership: A response to critiques', in Chemers, M.M. and Ayman, R. (eds), *Leadership Theory and Research: Perspectives and Directions*, Academic Press: New York, pp. 49–80.

54 Vera, D. and Crossan, M. (2004) 'Strategic leadership and organizational learning', *Academy of Management Review*, Vol. 29, No. 2, pp. 222–40.

55 March, J.G. (1991) 'Exploration and exploitation in organizational learning', *Organization Science*, Vol. 2, No. 1, pp. 71–87.

56 Vera and Crossan (2004) *opere citato*, pp. 228–35.

57 Axelsson, B. and Laage-Hellman, J. (1991) *Inköp – en ledningsfråga* (Purchasing – a leadership issue), Mekanförbundets Förlag: Stockholm.

58 Axelsson, B. (1996) *Kompetens för konkurrenskraft* (Competence for competitiveness), SNS: Stockholm.

59 Collins, J.C. and Porras, J.I. (1998) *Built to Last: Successful Habits of Visionary Companies*, 2nd edn, Random House: London.

60 Bennis and Nanus (1985) *opere citato.*

61 Achtenhagen, L., Melin, L., Müllern, T. and Ericson, T. (2003) 'Leadership: The role of interactive strategizing', in Pettigrew, A., Whittington, R., Melin, L., Sánchez-Runde, C., van den Bosch, F., Ruigrok, W. and Numagami, T. (eds), *Innovative Forms of Organizing*, Sage Publications: London, pp. 49–71.

62 Achtenhagen *et al.* (2003) *opere citato.*

Chapter 7

DEVELOPING AND MANAGING KNOWLEDGE AND COMPETENCIES

Björn Axelsson, Pieter Bouwmans, Frank Rozemeijer and Finn Wynstra

Knowledge and competencies are important sources of strategic change. Major improvements should be made possible by developing the skills and capabilities of the individual as well as improving the organizational systems for learning and knowledge management. Knowledge and competencies help people to carry out their job assignments, achieving a better understanding of relevant business processes, but also improving abilities to interact with colleagues and business partners.

Competence development is a critical ingredient in all processes of strategic change. Without it, the vision for the new direction may be less well understood and areas of change such as, for example, organizational design and utilization of ICT may be leveraged insufficiently.

On an aggregated level, the improved total knowledge base of the organization will be better fitted to act according to various business perspectives. It will also provide the firm with various abilities to learn, in dynamic processes, from its own practice and from the environment.

In this chapter, we first talk about the similarities and differences between knowledge, competencies and capabilities, and the different areas within those related to sourcing. After a discussion on assessing knowledge and competencies, separate sections deal with, respectively, knowledge management and competence and capability development. In the subsequent section, we outline a roadmap for sourcing related knowledge and competencies in relation to the various stages in sourcing maturity discussed in Chapter 2, and we conclude with some final observations.

7.1 Knowledge, competencies and capabilities

Over the last decade, purchasing has quickly developed from an operational towards a tactical/strategical profession. With this development, purchasing decision making has become more and more knowledge and competence driven.

In common speech, knowledge, competencies and capabilities are often used without further definition and sometimes also interchangeably. There are, however, good reasons to be more accurate on these concepts. There are also good reasons to distinguish among various kinds of knowledge, competencies and capabilities as well as a time perspective: knowledge, competencies and capabilities to deal with today's business and/or the business challenges of tomorrow.

Knowledge

If knowledge is nothing different from data or information, there would be nothing new or interesting about knowledge management. However, there is a great difference between information and knowledge. Without human intervention, knowledge cannot exist. Many organizations neglect this characteristic of knowledge, resulting in large systems in which nothing other than information is stored. A recent study conducted at several purchasing organizations of large Dutch companies showed that information is often regarded as knowledge.[1] Numerous IT systems have been implemented that should create a knowledge organization. However, there is more to knowledge management than simply implementing an advanced IT system.

We propose the following definitions of data, information and knowledge:

- *Data* is a symbolic representation of numbers, amounts, quantities and facts. Examples of data are 'it is 25 degrees' or 'the project costs €2 million'. Data is easy to save and reuse.

- *Information* arises when a person gives sense to gathered data. For example, 'the project costs €2 million, half a million more than budgeted' gives information about the realization of the project. Conclusions can be drawn based on information.
- *Knowledge* is the ability of a person to perform a task by connecting data (external sources) with their own information, experience and attitude. For example, it could consist of abilities to recognize and act on specific emergent risks for project budget overruns.

Knowledge is dynamic, since it is created in social interactions among individuals and organizations. It is also context specific, as it depends on a particular time and space. Furthermore, knowledge is humanistic, as it is essentially related to human action. Knowledge is of an active and subjective nature, represented by such terms as 'commitment' and 'belief' that are deeply rooted in individuals' value systems.[2]

Knowledge can be defined as a function of information, experience, skills and attitude: $K = f(I * ESA)$.[3] In addition, one can argue that knowledge derives from information in the same way as information derives from data. Data becomes information when it has been given sense. This is also true for knowledge. When information is given sense and used in executing a task, knowledge is created. To be able to give sense, existing knowledge is needed (see Figure 7.1).

Two different components of knowledge exist. There is an explicit component, which is transmittable in formal, systematic language (information), and an implicit (also called tacit) component, which is context specific and hard to formalize and communicate.

Not all knowledge that is available within an organization should be managed. Organizations should define what knowledge is necessary to stay competitive in the market today but also tomorrow. *Crucial knowledge* is sometimes defined as knowledge essential for the existence of the organization now but especially in the future.[4] Furthermore, knowledge can be classified into four categories:

- *Promising knowledge (A)*: knowledge that does not offer a contribution to the core business today, but will be very important tomorrow.
- *Key knowledge (B)*: knowledge that is used to realize business objectives.

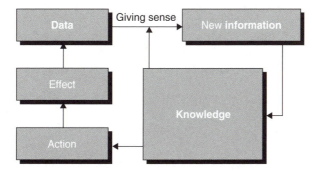

FIGURE 7.1   Data, information and knowledge.

- *Core knowledge (C)*: knowledge that is necessary to perform certain tasks. The knowledge has some value but will not help the organization to stay competitive.
- *Old knowledge (D)*: old knowledge has no value for the organization.

Knowledge is dynamic and what is innovative knowledge today will ultimately become the core knowledge of tomorrow. Thus, defending and growing a competitive position requires continuous learning and knowledge acquisition.[5] Some researchers have talked about the knowledge lifecycle, and argue that this lifecycle is becoming shorter and shorter.[6] To gain a market position with new knowledge is not difficult, but to keep that position is hard.

In section 7.4, we will discuss methods of managing and developing knowledge in more detail.

Competencies

The tasks of the purchasing function can be said to consist of a multidimensional mixture of demands, individuals and coordination mechanisms. They are actually situation specific. The resources and knowledge of the purchasing function include tools, such as software and so on, but the most important resources in the end are the employees.

The individual competencies, what they consist of, how they can be motivated and how they can be made to collaborate are based on this argument, genuine key factors for the function as such to realize the full potential of sourcing. The individual's competencies have to do with his or her ability to pursue defined activities. The individual is competent in relation to a certain task if he or she is able to carry out the necessary activities to fulfil the task at the quality level expected. This is made possible by certain sets of skills and knowledge.

These skills could be to know and be able to carry out supplier analysis as well as being skilled in certain languages, for example to the level necessary to carry out negotiations in that language. Knowledge covers topics related to supplier markets, products and technologies and so on, as well as knowledge of relevant theories of various kinds. A distinction could also be made between levels of knowledge: having a general orientation or being a knowledgeable expert. Another distinction has to do with the level and kind of education (the formal knowledge). Skills and knowledge in combination with motivation provide the basis for the individual's competence, which in itself could be graded into levels of various kinds, for example a novice, a senior, an expert and so on.

Capabilities

Capabilities refer most often to the abilities of a firm or an organization to fulfil its assignments. They are the combination of human resources, technologies, production equipment and organization as well as processes and procedures applied. The organizational unit could improve (or worsen) its capabilities through a variety of measures and combinations of efforts.

This means that there is no automatic connection between increases in competence among the human resources and increased capabilities on the organizational level. Normally one would expect increases in individuals' competencies to support the organizational capability, but one could also think of the opposite. Think for example of the purchasing professional who acquires increased knowledge through education, but due to organizational measures and/or technological constraints (still) has to carry out a very routine-based job, which he or she is no longer motivated to do. The individual's new level of knowledge and competence would, in such a case, be negative to the organizational capability.

The organizational capability is also interesting as it – at least for business firms – should be considered in light of the relative improvement of the firm versus its competitors. If relevant competitors improve their routines and human resources faster than the focal firm, the relative capabilities of that firm would *de facto* be lowered.

One very important aspect of capability development is organizational learning. This has to do with the organization's abilities (e.g. processes, individuals etc.) to learn both from experience and from other ways to generate new collective insights. The learning of the individual has many similarities with that of the organization. Organizations as such do not learn; organizational learning always needs to be performed by individuals. Yet the context of organizational and individual learning could still differ a lot. One illustration is when new behaviour is required. The individual has to learn a new pattern of activities (and/or 'unlearn' the old). The organization could learn a new pattern by exchanging the individual previously in charge of the function in question with someone else.

In section 7.5, we discuss methods of developing competencies and capabilities, both for the short and long term, in more detail.

7.2   Areas of sourcing knowledge and competencies

There are many ways to distinguish particular fields of knowledge and competencies, and the appropriateness of and choice of a specific distinction are quite context specific. In general, one could argue that the more mature or sophisticated an organization's purchasing strategy and philosophy, the more detailed the categorization of knowledge and competence areas should be. The same applies for the complexity and dynamics of the internal organization and the external environment: increasing complexity and dynamics call for a more detailed way of identifying, classifying and measuring knowledge and competencies.

Given the multitude of possible solutions, therefore, we only provide some illustrations here, with regard to the classification of both knowledge and competencies.

A recent study, based on the experiences of a number of Dutch firms, defines six knowledge domains for purchasing managers and buyers that firms need to monitor and develop.[7] The domains were validated using a survey among purchasing managers of large (global) Dutch companies. The following knowledge areas were distinguished: organizational, professional, supply market, supplier, customer and product knowledge. This could be considered one possible way to present the generic knowledge that relates to the profession of purchasing, but there are many alternatives. The various areas are explained in detail below.

- *Organizational knowledge.* To be able to perform in the best interests of the organization, it is essential to have knowledge of, for example, its business objectives and values. This supports the purchasing officer in taking relevant decisions and creates an awareness of the role of purchasing in the broader organizational picture.
- *Professional knowledge.* Purchasers require knowledge of important concepts and theories that are needed to realize business objectives. In recent years much research has been done in the area of purchasing and supply chain management. Many concepts, theories and tools have as a result been developed. The literature and case studies also indicate that purchasers need several skills to perform their tasks (e.g. negotiation skills). These skills differ from those needed by other members of the organization and are a prerequisite to operating effectively and efficiently.
- *Supply market knowledge.* Supply market knowledge could be defined as 'the systematic detection of changes occurring in the supply market and their subsequent interpretation as potential opportunities and threats to the customer market position'. Purchasers require knowledge about its firm's supply markets for a wide range of reasons: cost modelling, negotiation, ensuring continuity of supply, sourcing alternatives, strategic planning, accessing supplier innovation, procurement process improvement and reducing cost/adding value. A distinction can be made between knowledge on a macroeconomic (overall economy) and a mesoeconomic level (specific sectors).
- *Supplier knowledge.* Purchasers are expected to know the most about suppliers.[8] As an organization reaches a higher maturity level, knowledge of the relation with the supplier, performances and structures becomes more important. A distinction can be made between knowledge of the organization of the supplier (e.g. structure, processes) and the relation of the company with the supplier (e.g. past performances, current contracts). But it could also be essential to know about the supplier's R&D activities and ability to improve and develop. This is especially important when the supplier is considered a 'partner'.
- *Customer knowledge.* The purchaser's job is to purchase goods and services for his or her customers. These customers can be found within the organization (internal customers) and outside the firm (external customers). Purchasers are more and more involved in cross-functional teams in which the wants and needs of the customer become important. Purchasers need to

be able to identify the customer, to know their wants and needs and their expectations.

- *Product knowledge.* Finally, knowledge of the product is important to be able to participate in cross-functional teams and to be able to offer the customer the best product. Distinctions can be drawn between the goods and services bought and the end product (delivered to the external customer). The importance of knowledge of products bought seems obvious, as the task of purchasers is to buy products. Knowledge of the end products becomes relevant when interaction exists between the purchasers and suppliers and (internal) customers, for example in cross-functional project teams.

The results of our survey indicate that purchasing managers and practitioners acknowledge the growing importance of knowledge for their jobs. Customer knowledge was considered to be the most important knowledge domain, while product knowledge, in that specific study, scored as the least important among the above knowledge areas.

In terms of competencies, Philips Medical Systems (an operating unit of Philips Electronics) identifies the following areas:

- ICT capabilities.
- Cost management capabilities.
- Communication skills, such as the ability to speak the 'language' of other function.
- Relationship management capabilities.
- Change management skills.
- Long-term vision.

As stated above, we do not believe that there is just one way of classifying purchasing knowledge and competencies, but that does not mean that it should not be done. First of all, going beyond a mere mission statement of 'developing more and better knowledge and competencies', it provides guidance and support for a more differentiated and focused management effort. Secondly, even the process of *developing* such a classification is useful for most organizations, as it will inevitably lead to a discussion on what knowledge and competencies are or are not important to the organization.

7.3   Assessing knowledge and competencies

Although much has been written about knowledge management in general, only little is available specifically on knowledge management for purchasing and supply management. Still, many firms practise methods of developing knowledge among individuals involved in purchasing activities, as well as learning and capability development on an organizational level. Many companies have also defined relevant areas in which knowledge and skills are needed. One such company is Ericsson.

Box 7.1   Ericsson's definition of knowledge and competence areas

This is a description of practices in the late 1990s. Within the general Ericsson Competence Management (ECM) programme, the corporate-wide purchasing body had set up a specific competence profile for purchasers. The profile comprised eight dimensions:

1. Sourcing skills.
2. Project management.
3. Ericsson knowledge.
4. Information management (including IT).
5. Business operational understanding.
6. Business intelligence (= market knowledge).
7. Social skills.
8. Product knowledge.

Dimensions like Ericsson knowledge and social skills were common to all Ericsson companies and departments. But the sourcing skills dimension was specifically introduced by this unit. The dimensions were plotted in a spider graph, with five levels on each dimension, to illustrate desired and actual positions. This is illustrated in Figure 7.2.

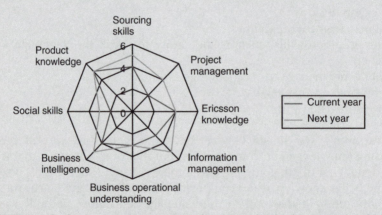

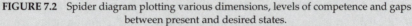

FIGURE 7.2   Spider diagram plotting various dimensions, levels of competence and gaps between present and desired states.

This was used both when analysing the individual and as a way to develop a weighted average of a team or a department. The actual position in the illustrated example shows no gaps on product knowledge, business intelligence and information management. Gaps do however exist in the areas of social skills, sourcing skills, project management, Ericsson knowledge and business operational understanding, although they are not bigger than one level.

This is a rather common tool to support ongoing improvements. The typical pattern is that the individual makes a self-evaluation and the subordinate of the individual makes his or her evaluation along the same dimensions. The two analyses are then the basis for identifying gaps and deciding on actions and mutual commitments to make improvements take place. In this way each individual will have his or her own improvement plan and those plans are (at best) in line with an overall desired development of the unit in question.

The desired improvement level is identified as the difference between actual and desired (by the manager or the organization because of present or future tasks).

Within Ericsson, this process was complemented by specific development programmes related to the specific competence areas. Someone had to be responsible for identifying ways to increase for example social skills. For each of the dimensions in the competence 'spider web', sourcing named one 'champion' who had as his or her responsibility to act as a kind of 'teacher' or coach in that dimension. This champion need not be a world champion him- or herself, but should rather be interested and act as a guide for people looking for courses and the like in that specific area. Champions can also help the human resources group to find and develop competence improvement activities in their area. Champions did not have a budget, nor did they have a responsibility that employees follow courses. Champions should have the following characteristics:

- Burning interest.
- Good sparring partner.
- Marketer.
- Accepted by the organization.
- Excellent social competence.
- Strong driving force.
- Serve as an example.
- Have a good network.
- Have the authority to carry out activities with external (i.e. not their own) resources.

Champions can or should even come from different groups. The purchasing director of OEM and Software, for example, was at one time the champion for business intelligence, and a person from Strategic Procurement was the champion for the area of sourcing skills. The then HRM manager himself was champion for Ericsson knowledge and social skills.

In the latter area, it is important to do something to help people to improve if necessary, for example in the recent case of a number of layoffs. Many companies merely conclude that some of their employees have insufficient social skills, but do nothing about it. Depending on the outcome of the development discussions, plans were drawn up on ways to improve the competence profile with the help of, for example, courses or job rotations (in fact most often short-term project assignments within other departments).

From this overview, it is evident that Ericsson had identified a number of areas for knowledge and competencies and a system to identify various levels. For the specific individual, this means that he or she will get to know the views that others holds about their competence. They will also be involved in a dialogue on how they can improve and in what areas the organization wants them to improve. Not all positions in a company demand the same profile.

In practice, it could be difficult to decide on the level of competence in each specific area. How this could be done is demonstrated by another example of how a multinational firm, utilizing a similar system as Ericsson, has tried to operationalize the various dimensions and levels. In Table 7.1, we have illustrated two levels for two attributes, independence and commercial competence.

TABLE 7.1   Translating attributes of purchasing competence into operational measures

Attribute	Elements	Level 2	Level 5
Independence	Organizing ability Project management Negotiation ability Problem solving	Acts according to given directives. Participates together with manager or experienced colleague (level 4 or 5) in projects, negotiations and problem solving.	Very independent, organizes his or her work completely by him- or herself and can work as support for new recruits. Develops his or her knowledge eagerly and actively shares this knowledge. Can manage complex projects.
Commercial competence	Financial questions Negotiations Cost development Tactics Strategy Purchasing policy	Common economic knowledge. Is informed about the cost development within his or her product area. Knows the purchasing policy. Certain knowledge about negotiation technique and strategy.	Extraordinary theoretical and practical competence. Very thoroughly informed about the cost development within his or her and related product areas. Also has good knowledge about the general conditions. Designs tactical and strategic plans in a global perspective for both his or her own purposes and an assortment of colleagues.

It is important when utilizing a system like this to be consistent in what kind of evaluations deserve what level of rating. If not, it is likely that one individual will be rated a 5 on a certain dimension while another will get a 3 – in spite of identical abilities.

A final illustration comes from a European telecommunications firm, which was facing a situation in which many of its new purchasing managers had no prior experience – and thus possibly also less or no knowledge and competencies – in the area of purchasing and supply management.

Box 7.2   Action learning in a telecommunications firm

A telecoms firm hired an external consultant for developing and executing an in-company training programme to cater for the collective training needs of its purchasing staff. The main reason for the firm to invest in this training programme was based on the fact that the majority of the newly appointed category managers within the new corporate purchasing organization had only recently started working in their newly designed jobs and faced a deficiency in actual purchasing knowledge and skills. Most of the category managers came from other disciplines than purchasing (e.g. marketing, sales etc.).

With the assistance of the consultant's Knowledge and Skills Assessment Tool, the firm was able first to assess the individual learning needs of the staff involved. The assessment tool (see also Appendix 7.1) is built in Microsoft Excel™ and consists of three main parts: (1) general information, (2) professional knowledge and (3) skills and behaviour. In the first part, respondents are asked to describe their general educational and professional background. In the second area, purchasing knowledge and experience are measured. Respondents are invited to indicate their level of knowledge and experience for a certain concept/tool or activity on a four-point scale, ranging from rookie level to expert level. The expert level is described as: 'I have full knowledge of the concept/activity and I am very experienced in successfully applying the concept/conducting the activity in practice.'

The third part of the assessment is aimed at measuring specific business skills and behaviour. Behaviours are underlying characteristics that lead to superior performance in an individual's job. They include qualities, skills, attributes and traits that help people to be successful. The assessment tool describes a large number of different behaviours along several scales. Respondents are invited to indicate for each behaviour what description best reflects their current level with regard to that specific behaviour. If a respondent has filled in the complete assessment, the Excel program accounts for the average scores.

This assessment made clear both combined learning needs for the staff as well as individual skill gaps for which individual training courses can be offered (for instance enrolment in national or international training courses). Based on this assessment and on discussions with the CPO and his staff, the consultant designed a comprehensive but powerful action learning programme for the category managers. The end result of the programme was to be that each category manager would be able to develop a sourcing strategy for his or her category, which could be presented as a category business case to top management for final approval.

The theoretical framework as well as the instruments used (e.g. diagnostic models, portfolio approaches, contract models etc.) were customized for this specific programme by the consultant, although in close collaboration with the client and aligned with its own sourcing manual. Change management issues like how to create commitment within the organization for these category sourcing plans was one of the main topics of this programme. Successfully implementing a category sourcing strategy in practice demands a lot of the interpersonal skills of the staff involved.

The action learning programme comprised three (two-day) workshops. Workshop I explored the analysis of the internal context (e.g. Who are my stakeholders?) and external context (What are the developments on the supply market?). Workshop II focused on the creative part of searching for (saving) opportunities and translating them into a sourcing strategy. Workshop III finally entered on the implementation of the category sourcing strategy and explained to the category managers how to secure the results. In each workshop, there was room for discussion with the CPO about all kinds of internal issues (e.g. practical issues like 'Who am I reporting to?', 'Who will be in my category team?'). Between the workshops, the category managers worked on their category sourcing plan, based on homework assignments and sometimes coached by the consultant. At the close of the action learning programme, the category managers went through all the necessary steps to develop and secure their category sourcing strategies.

7.4   Developing and managing knowledge

In the evolution of knowledge management, and thinking about knowledge management, several streams can be identified. The first stream focuses on exchanging knowledge objectively (explicit knowledge) using ICT solutions. The second stream emphasizes the importance of tacit knowledge: experiences, skills and attitude, knowledge that is not objectively transmittable. The final and currently most popular stream implies that the development and management of a knowledge-intensive organization determine the degree to which the goals of the organization can be equated to the personal goals of the knowledge worker.

As reflected in Figure 7.3, knowledge management may be defined as 'managing the operational processes in the knowledge value chain to increase the pleasure in and to get an optimal return on the production factor knowledge'. Managing these operational processes is influenced by and influences management at a strategic level. At this level, a continuous cyclical process should be created and managed that leads to developing, defining, communicating and evaluating of the mission, vision, goals and strategy of the organization (MVGS).

It is important that these elements serve the overall ambition of the employees of an organization. Eventually, knowledge management focuses on the availability of the right knowledge within an organization to execute the strategy: 'given what the firm believes it must do to compete, there are some things it must know and know how to do'.[9] At the strategic level, the decision is also taken to develop knowledge or competencies or to gather information for the long-term survival of the company.

At the operational level the knowledge processes in the value chain should be managed efficiently and effectively. Based on the mission, vision, goals and strategy, the knowledge gap – the knowledge that is not yet available within the organization – should be defined and the missing knowledge acquired or developed. Several sources exist for the acquisition of knowledge, for example competitors, suppliers and customers, consultants, universities, the Internet and other buying professionals. Next, the knowledge should be shared, applied and evaluated. Knowledge management is most urgent for those processes of the value chain that are the least productive.

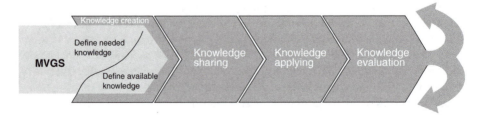

FIGURE 7.3   Knowledge value chain (MVGS = mission, vision, goals and strategy).
Source: Weggeman, M.C.D.P. (1997) *Kennismanagement, inrichting en besturing van kennisintensieve organisaties*, Scriptum: Schiedam.

Motives for knowledge management for purchasing and supply

Now that we have defined purchasing knowledge and discussed knowledge management, it seems relevant to mention the motives that managers and practitioners define to manage their purchasing and supply knowledge. Two main motives can be identified: to prevent the loss of existing knowledge and to increase the level of knowledge.

First of all, employees leave organizations for several reasons (e.g. other jobs, illness). If not managed well, the knowledge that is owned by the employee will leave the organization as well. Organizations have in the past spent much time and effort in developing and acquiring this knowledge again. Several years ago, a purchasing team that was involved in major projects split up, because no major projects were available at that time. Members of the team left the organization or were replaced within the organization. Currently many major projects have been started again. The expertise has left the organization and as a result this knowledge needs be rebuilt. This is considered time and cost consuming.

Secondly, purchasing managers and practitioners expect an increase in the total knowledge level by managing knowledge within their organization. This will lead to improvements of processes, savings and better means to compete. When two purchasers of different divisions are negotiating with the same supplier, knowledge can be shared about how to approach that specific supplier. Also, demand might be bundled in order to gain savings.

Barriers to and enablers for knowledge management

In developing and managing knowledge, many barriers and enablers can be identified that hinder the efficiency and effectiveness of the processes. Based on case studies and a survey among purchasing managers and practitioners, Box 7.3 lists several barriers that an organization could be faced with (see also Chapter 10).

Box 7.3   Barriers to knowledge management

1. *No clear definition of knowledge.* Purchasers and purchasing managers are not aware of what knowledge is and thus what and why knowledge should be shared.
2. *Purchasers are unaware of who owns what knowledge.* One reason why knowledge is not shared within organizations is simply that purchasers do not know each other or are not aware of the knowledge that a colleague owns.
3. *No incentive to share knowledge ('What's in it for me?').* Why should a purchaser share his or her knowledge? He or she already owns the knowledge and can apply it in daily practice. Sharing knowledge is assumed only to be time consuming and no incentives are in place to motivate the purchaser to share knowledge.
4. *Geographically dispersed.* Because departments and groups of large companies are often physically and geographically dispersed, purchasers argue that it is difficult to share knowledge.

5. *Systems are not available or user-friendly.* Purchasers argue that the available systems are not available, adequate or user-friendly.

6. *The content of systems is not up to date.* During the case studies many aspects concerning the content were mentioned. First of all, information is often not available in systems. Second, the information and knowledge are often not up to date, or are ambiguous.

7. *Purchasers do not have the skills to use the systems.* Some of the interviewees claim that they, or some of their colleagues, do not possess the skills to use the systems correctly. This concerns having the administrative skills as well as understanding what data should be entered in the systems and how.

8. *No time is available to share knowledge.* One often heard barrier during the case studies is time. Purchasers have no time available or do not take the time to share knowledge. Documenting their knowledge is often avoided because it is time consuming.

9. *Transparency is threatening.* Transparency in processes, contracts and supplier relations means that some flaws may be revealed. Purchasers are afraid to be punished or criticized for these flaws.

10. *Risk of becoming redundant.* When someone owns certain unique knowledge, he or she is important to the organization. If they share this knowledge purchasers are afraid of becoming redundant and therefore losing their jobs.

11. *Knowledge is regarded as power.* Knowledge gives an individual or a group a certain position in the organization. Individuals are respected for their unique knowledge and groups gain benefits that other groups within the organization cannot achieve.

12. *Lack of respect for colleagues and their knowledge.* One precondition of knowledge management is that colleagues respect each other and their knowledge. A lack of this respect results in less communication, interaction and openness and thus in less knowledge sharing.

13. *Knowledge is assumed to be unique.* Purchasers argue that projects in which they are involved are unique. Sharing knowledge concerning these projects would be useless.

14. *Knowledge is sensitive and confidential.* Purchasers have the perception that their knowledge is sensitive and confidential. Contracts and relation with suppliers, for example, may as a result not be shared.

Source: Bouwmans, P. (2002) *Purchasing Knowledge: Key to Purchasing Performance,* MSc thesis, Eindhoven University of Technology: Eindhoven.

From the list above, it appears that five barriers (i.e. 2, 3, 4, 6 and 8) are hindering the development and sharing of knowledge the most. Respondents in our study scored these five barriers below three on a five-point scale. Based on this information, it makes sense to

- Make very clear who owns what kind of knowledge in the organization.
- Create visible incentives to share knowledge.
- Facilitate intercountry communication by videoconferencing and/or travelling.

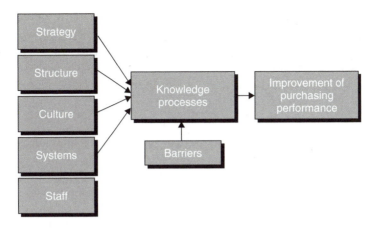

FIGURE 7.4   Organizational design variables for knowledge management.

- Keep the content of the information systems up to date.
- Make people aware that though it might cost time to share knowledge in the short term, it pays off in the long term.

Managing knowledge and competencies thus implies creating and managing the organization in such a way that these barriers will to a large extent be removed. Many organizations have over the years implemented systems and embedded processes and activities in order to improve purchasing performance and remove these barriers (Figure 7.4). The following describes several best practices and recommendations categorized along five organizational design variables that are currently used by sourcing organizations.

Strategy
The strategy should give the purchasing department the means to be an indispensable link of the organization. It should make employees aware of the fact that purchasing and supply is not an operational function, but that purchasing and supply departments serve as the knowledge and competence centre for the organization. Furthermore, in order to commit all employees, a value proposition should be made to communicate the added value of purchasing knowledge and competence management. Parallel to these processes, the purchasing department should define its knowledge gap and consequently its knowledge strategy and goals. These should eventually be translated into a mission that can easily be communicated to managers and practitioners.

Box 7.4   Strategy and knowledge management

> The purchasing organization of a large global electronics company had defined its strategic goals as focused on proving and increasing the added value of the department by developing new knowledge, creating international networks and standardizing purchasing processes.

Purchasers are despatched to the different parts of the organization to share their knowledge and exploit their competencies. They constantly emphasize the importance of purchasing throughout the organization by communicating new contracts and savings.

Structure

Although the position of purchasing and supply in organizations has improved over the years and has gained management attention, the added value is still questioned by the members of the organization. Sourcing departments should be organized around the knowledge and competencies of purchasers and should install several structures in which purchasers meet to get acquainted and share knowledge to solve the problems or benefit of synergetic opportunities. Furthermore, purchasing managers indicate that it is important to assign knowledge managers to create and share knowledge and to keep knowledge up to date. Finally, sourcing departments should make sure that they work with common work methods and one language throughout the organization.

Box 7.5   Structure and knowledge management

During the annual procurement seminar of a global financial services company, European purchasers gather to discuss certain topics in teams. The seminar ends with a presentation from each group presenting the findings to a panel consisting of internal customers, local, regional and global procurement management and experts. The panel chooses certain topics that need further attention. Purchasing communities are set up to further discuss the topic and to share knowledge between members of the organization.

A global oil company has set up a structure of meetings in which all stakeholders (purchasers, strategic suppliers, customers, contractors etc.) may share knowledge about topics concerning purchasing and supply (e.g. contract techniques).

The Dutch purchasing department of a global electronic company appoints, based on individual knowledge and competencies, purchasers to the divisions. To make sure that these purchasers are still able to communicate, a support centre has been set up that is responsible for implementing the purchasing processes and tools. Also, the intranet serves as a mean to share information and knowledge concerning the processes and developments in purchasing and to share contracts throughout the organization. A webmaster is assigned to keep the information and knowledge up to date.

Culture

Global companies have to deal with many different cultures as a result of geographical dispersion and different maturity levels, as discussed in Chapter 2. Purchasing departments are currently trying to create a culture in which knowledge is easily created, shared and used. This change needs management commitment and involves extensive discussions about the concept and added value of knowledge management and the need to create, share and use knowledge. Purchasers need to feel that they are recognized and rewarded and need to have and demonstrate respect for their colleagues.

Box 7.6   Culture and knowledge management

Because of the successful implementation of a large IT system in America, purchasers who were responsible for that implementation were asked to present their successes and failures for a large group of European purchasers. The American purchasers felt recognized for their achievement.

Some time ago, 25 members of a purchasing organization volunteered to take places in the call centre during a television programme for Unicef. Although they were very busy answering phone calls from people who wanted to donate, they also got to know each other better as people rather than just colleagues.

Systems

Although (ICT) technology facilitates processes and is a good means to gather and share information, sourcing managers should be aware that these systems can never be a substitute for face-to-face interaction. Furthermore, the success of the system depends on the commitment and priority of the user entering the data. If not managed well, the working methods and information will be ambiguous and not up to date. Many initiatives have already been taken by companies to remove the barriers mentioned above.

Box 7.7   Systems and knowledge management

To make sure that the implementation of e-business within a European airline is used and understood correctly, two people are assigned full-time to supporting the implementation of the tool. By answering questions and supporting the users, they ensure that the system is used in similar ways and the output can be understood throughout the purchasing organization.

The support centre of the Dutch purchasing department of a global electronic company has developed a supplier information system (SIS) that is now implemented throughout the world. The system only contains preferred suppliers of the company. The system is integrated into the firm's intranet and is accessible to all members of the company. The buyer who holds the contract is shown, including his or her contact details. He or she is also responsible for keeping the contract information up to date. One person from the support centre is responsible for updating the information in the system.

Some purchasing organizations have been developing procurement portals in which purchasers have to work to be able to fulfil their tasks. The systems are thus integrated into the primary processes.

Staff

The change in the role of purchasers asks for different knowledge and competences. Purchasers need to be top-performing professionals who are eager to learn by sharing and using knowledge. The willingness to learn should already be addressed in the assessment cycle.

7.5   Developing individual competencies and organizational capabilities

What we have argued so far is that, in practice, one has to concentrate on developing competencies and capabilities both on the individual and on the organizational level. Such development also has to be oriented to both the short- and long-term aspects of competence. Learning and improving for today's business and building strategic capability for the reorientation of the firm and for its long-term development are both needed.

Table 7.2 provides an overview of three main factors in competence and capability development: (1) sources of competence development; (2) methods for using these sources; and (3) result variables; that is, what the competence process will lead to. These are discussed one by one below.

Sources

Regarding competence development, we differentiate between three main sources: education, on-the-job learning and recruitment.

- *Education* consists of those activities that are organized to enable the employees, besides their normal tasks, to be educated in operationally directed positions. It can also concern more general knowledge building. These activities can be carried out internally, where the company's internal units also supply the education (e.g. corporate university, e-learning), or externally, where the service is purchased from independent suppliers. Pros and cons with an internal or external solution coincide with the general discussion about insourcing vs outsourcing earlier. When choosing external procurement of education, two main variants can be possible, a transaction- and a relationship-oriented method. Pros and cons of this have been discussed in Chapter 4.
- *On-the-job learning* is the learning that takes place in connection to the workplace and/or the tasks. It might be a question of knowledge transmitted in dialogue from one employee to another, which arises through visits to other internal units or work rotation within the company. Work rotation as a way of widening one's horizons and generating new experiences is usually proclaimed, not least in discussions with individuals within purchasing functions, as a very efficient way of achieving competence development. On-the-job learning can also take place in external relations in different ways. For example, the purchaser might be offered opportunities not only to visit the company's suppliers but also others, for instance the company's own customers, to further learn from these about the conditions for his or her own job. An important part of the company's

TABLE 7.2 Sources, techniques and methods for competence development

Sources and tools for competence development	Methods to use and important aspects of a systematic improvement process	Which entails (consist of) and builds (creates)	Which in the short and long run results in
Education 1. Internal 2. External purchases → Pedagogical techniques → Standard/ customized → Purchasing strategy (when purchasing)	*Value system* – Psychological contracts through for example development dialogue – Career, reward, management systems and leadership	Competence development (improved capability to realize the business idea)	Satisfied customers, good economic results today (internal/ external customers)
On-the-job learning 1. Internal 2. External in business relations and in other situations → Rotation, dialogue, priorities	*Organizational structure* – Responsibility, overview, feedback, freedom of action etc. for the individual – Integration and specialization through: a) Function vs flow orientation b) Team or not c) Specialist vs generalist knowledge		Developed ability for long-term survival and sustained competitive advantage (which among other things requires the capability for innovation at a corporate or unit level)
Recruitment 1. The labour market's (internal/external) conditions 2. The educational system in the society 3. Local and regional resources → Resource/need analyses → Recruitment politics and selection method → Environmental influencing	*Financial/key ratio management* – Measurement of human capital – Investment calculations – Balanced scorecard – Management by budgets – Other key ratios	Building of development competencies, strategic capability	

product and process development takes place within the business relations. These are in other words also an important source for development of the employees who work, or are offered opportunities to work, within them.

- *Recruitment* signifies the recruitment that takes place of fresh employees with different backgrounds and qualifications. How it works and supports the advancement of the operations depends among other things on how the education system and labour market's structure contributes to forming the potential and current employees' competence. Important techniques here have to do with, for example, the principles for recruitment.

Methods

The methods for supporting employees' competence development and building organizational capabilities can be divided into four main areas.

To support the development of employee competence through organizational design
Different archetypes for organizational structuring have been discussed relatively extensively in Chapter 5. The organizational structure in the specific company (and the specific sourcing function) also affects the working methods of the buyers and the direction of competence development. In the function-oriented organization they can, all other aspects unchanged, be expected to develop their profession as buyers – 'specialist knowledge purchasing' – in a positive way. They are placed in a 'sourcing culture'.

At the same time, there is a risk that they do not develop some parts of their knowledge as well, for example the understanding of and knowledge of the needs of the customers. This knowledge is probably more nurtured in the market- or process-oriented organizational structure, following the discussion in Chapter 5.

Whichever organization structure is found most suitable, there are some fundamental demands (a glimpse from the motivation theory) that, to a varying extent, need to be covered for the work to be motivating and developing.

There have been a number of studies on how work can influence employee satisfaction and motivation.[10] Through analyses of a large number of work tasks, these studies developed a fine division of different criteria of importance for work satisfaction and motivation. The fundamental question was: 'What does it take for work to be satisfying and motivating for the individual, at the same time as the organization gets a high-quality and efficient performance and a low absence and low staff turnover?'

The studies found that this could only be achieved if the individual could reach three critical psychological conditions. The first was that the work must be seen as *meaningful* and worth the effort or important. The second was that the individual had to feel *personally responsible* for the results of the work. Third, the individual had to be able to – that is, have the possibility to – *judge* in a credible way the result of his or her work him- or herself.

What should the tasks look like to make it possible to reach these conditions, and thus the desirable targets for both the individual and the organization? Meaningfulness requires that the work is characterized by:

- Demands on varying abilities (skill variety) – the capabilities and competencies of the individual must be challenged.
- Clearly identified task (task identity), to have the possibility of fulfilling a 'complete' work from start to finish with a clear result.

- Meaningful task (task significance), that the work is significant or has an identifiable influence on other people's lives.

To be personally responsible demands some form of autonomy; that is, that the work gives the individual some degree of freedom, independence and possibility to plan and decide how the work is to be carried out. To judge the results requires feedback, so that the individual in some way gets information about the effects of his or her work. All of these are also important foundations for the development of tasks within purchasing.

To support the development of employee competence using value systems

As can be learned from Table 7.2, there are several methods for actively sustaining and creating a value system for a company's purchasing function. Psychological contracts are among other ways formed in collaboration between manager and employee when expectations and commitments are regulated, for example in connection with a development dialogue. But the systems are also created through the career systems and the reward (and penalty) systems of the particular company. These elements are to a great extent directed towards focusing on the individual. The reasoning thus naturally leads to a discussion of the competence of single employees, how it can be mapped and developed and how employees can be motivated to be involved in this kind of competence development.

Competence development supported by 'competence careers'

On a general level, we have already touched on the subject of what is demanded in order for work to be motivating and the importance of the company's value system for employees' competence. An important element that can support the purchasing function's competence development in a very forceful way is a career path. Since there are natural limitations for how many can (and want to) become sourcing managers (line career), it might be especially important to develop complementary career paths in the form of specialist careers and more generally so-called competence careers.

This means that there are a number of levels, or platforms, to strive towards concerning the employees' specialist competencies. It might be the path from junior buyer via a couple of steps to senior buyer. In this way, the single employee always knows which level he or she is on in a number of dimensions. Thus he or she also knows within which levels improvements are mostly needed and can thus direct his or her own competence development towards these areas.

This is an interesting example of a – probably – efficient way of supporting and enforcing the competence development of employees and thus of the purchasing function and the entire company. By evaluating, for example in connection with development discussions, the position of the individual on such a 'competence ladder', deciding on new development targets and what activities are demanded (e.g. what sources should be used) for reaching those targets, an important tool for successively building the individual competencies in the purchasing function is created.

Supporting competence development through measurement and key ratios
Measurement is, as already mentioned, one way to enforce the realization of desired results. To measure the result of the purchasers, purchasing team, purchasing department and purchasing function's operation, for example in the form of the internal users' perceptions of the services they receive (customer satisfaction index), is an important way of supporting and directing the activities. When it comes to the development of employees and their competence, other measurements may also be important. One aspect is to work with some form of so-called human capital index. This can mean that personnel within the purchasing function are regularly questioned about their work situation; see Box 7.8 for an example from a construction company.

Box 7.8   The construction company's questions to create a map of human capital

Each year the construction company directs questions to its employees in order to keep track of the effects of annual improvements. Examples of some of the questions are:

- Whether the employees experience their competence as adequate for their tasks.
- Whether they have the proper possibilities to use their entire competence and to educate themselves.
- Whether they are given new and challenging tasks or alternatively that they themselves take the initiative.
- Whether they are satisfied with their situation and if they feel that they get the proper support from colleagues and company management.
- The number of days of education and/or other active competence development that they have received since the last measurement.

The result of these measurements is a way of seeing how the 'competence capital' is developing. This can then lay a foundation for prioritization of especially important efforts.

Another important element, in line with the thoughts on 'balanced scorecards' (Chapter 9), is to be able to create a measurable structure of competence. This would mean that what in certain companies is called a 'purchasing licence' is created. All employees who for example pass level three within all measured dimensions receive legitimacy to perform certain kinds of purchases.

Finally, the licence works as a way to create a perception of and a foundation for continued competence efforts. The more people within the sourcing function who have such a licence, the higher the total individual competencies within the business's operations will be. What is measured does not need to be totally correct. The importance is that it guides and that it contributes to a continuous development of the purchasers' competence.

We return to our example of Ericsson (see Box 7.1) to provide an example of a way to mix these tools and methods.

Box 7.9   The competence management process at Ericsson

The first step in the competence management process consists of an analysis phase, in which both future requirements and the present situation are analysed. Based on that, a gap analysis is conducted, and in the second phase the resulting competence gap leads to 'competence sourcing' activities. Usually, most competence management programmes fail to reach this second stage, as the first phase requires quite some time. The second phase, however, determines some 80% of the final success of any competence management (CM) process, while the first only accounts for 20%. One of the reasons why CM has been so successful is that the second phase has indeed been carried out.

The analysis of the present situation builds on several activities:

- Personal development discussions between employees and their direct superiors.
- Compass – self-assessments by every employee.
- TQM assessments.
- Competence profiles defined for each individual (see below).
- Management planning.

Management planning activities are carried out by Human Resources, and concern some 30 people of the 130 people in the sourcing organization. Activities include the evaluation of current managers of the different staff and product groups within the sourcing group, and monitoring of (young) 'stars' who may come to belong to the Top 400 of Ericsson managers corporate-wide.

The analysis of future requirements includes a review of:

- Customer and market needs.
- Technology.
- Products and services.
- Competitors.

This analysis results in a definition of required strategic and critical competences. In this exercise it is important to use your 'gut feeling' too and rely on broad scenarios: it is more about directions instead of places. However, it is rather difficult to have those responsible let go of the technical and concrete details (what switches will be used etc.). Ericsson has several scenario plans, tools and documents that give input for this analysis of future requirements:

- Desired position following year.
- Strategies for growth.
- Ericsson strategic plans.
- Best practice.
- Vision for five years ahead.

The second phase, sourcing of competence, includes activities – or sources – such as:

- Training programmes.
- On-the-job training.

- Recruitment.
- Organizational development.
- Cooperation with universities and the like.
- Partnerships with suppliers and other companies.
- Consultants.
- Acquisition of companies.
- Outsourcing.

Basic courses that are being offered and that most people have followed include entrepreneurship and negotiations. Additionally, three modules on sourcing skills are being offered. Module I has been followed by 70% of all personnel, and the other two by smaller groups. Only Module III is given by external trainers. The success of these sourcing activities also depends on the attractiveness of the activities being organized. Events include a department meeting every third week, where usually 40–70 of the 130 people in total turn up, where an Ericsson speaker is invited to talk, for instance, about a new product or some special project. These meetings take place on Friday afternoon, and explicitly have also a social aspect to them. Job rotations usually last only 1–2 weeks and are decided on an individual basis, there are no department or corporate-wide plans on that. For new recruitment, the goal is now to only hire academics (currently, 20% of all staff have an academic degree). New hires may include fresh graduates or people with purchasing experience from elsewhere. It is no disadvantage if they have no Ericsson experience, but a combination of a technical background and commercial interest usually forms a good profile. Sourcing competencies from supplier relations has also been explicitly acknowledged as an alternative, but in reality the true effects from that are not yet visible.

Short-term versus long-term results

The results of these sources and methods to develop competencies and capabilities (Table 7.2) are twofold. One is to be able to run today's business in an appropriate way. The other is to build a base of capabilities to be able to take on the challenges of tomorrow. The latter means basically the creation of what has been called dynamic capability.[11] It has, at times, been considered an 'insurance premium'.[12] Nobody knows exactly what is needed tomorrow. There is a great danger that the knowledge, competencies and capabilities developed will never be utilized or exploited. But there is also a great danger that the firm that only builds knowledge fitted for today's business will be unable to reorient when needed. Therefore the creation of some 'surplus' competencies acts as an insurance fee.

The kind of surplus most often discussed is the education of the human resources. The highly educated staff may not need all their cognitive understanding for running the business, but they will hopefully be in a better position to interpret coming challenges. Another aspect of surplus or 'excess' resources could be to devote time to and create genuine discussions during which conflicting views can be explored. Such activities have proven important for the long-term qualitative growth of organizations.[13]

7.6   Strategic change in sourcing and the role of knowledge, competencies and organizational capabilities

As represented in the purchasing development model (discussed in Chapter 2), purchasing departments are operating in different maturity stages in which different knowledge, competencies and organizational capabilities are required. Based on the knowledge domains identified in section 7.2, we have defined – in collaboration with various purchasing managers – a matrix in which the required knowledge per stage is defined. This is presented in Appendix 7.2.[14]

In the *transaction orientation* stage, purchasers only need understanding of the ethics, processes and procedures used by the organization. Furthermore, they require understanding of where and how to buy the goods and services according to the specification of the customer.

At the *commercial orientation* stage, the purchasers are proactive and negotiate with suppliers for lower prices. An increase in the need for concepts and theories about purchasing and supply management can be identified. To be able to negotiate, the purchaser furthermore needs more understanding about the product, but also about the supplier itself.

The *purchasing orientation* stage is characterized by cross-unit coordination and compliance with nationally negotiated contracts. Understanding of the structure and opportunities of the supply market and understanding the customer's wishes become important to be able to negotiate in the best interest of the organization.

In the *process orientation* stage the focus is on reducing total systems cost by the cooperation of supplier, purchaser and customer. Purchasers need to create knowledge and develop competencies to be able to build partnerships with the supplier, work in cross-functional teams and use the opportunities that IT offers. Also, the purchaser requires understanding of the macroeconomic level of the supply market.

The fifth stage, *supply chain orientation*, is characterized by extensive cooperation with supplier and customers. Purchasers need to have excellent purchasing competencies and have an excellent understanding of the organization, supplier and customer. In the final stage, *value chain orientation*, sourcing strategy is based on the recognition that delivering value to the end customer is most important for success.

Suppliers are consistently challenged to support their customer's product/market strategies and to actively participate in product/business development. Only few organizations, if any, are operating at this stage. Value chain integration goes to the core of a business itself; it is a whole new level of complexity and sophistication.[15]

The depth and nature of knowledge related to the maturity model

So far our discussion has centred around what kind of 'technical' knowledge could be needed to act according to each level of purchasing maturity. There

TABLE 7.3   Aspects of the work situation with an impact on
competencies

Assignment	The task	The method	The goal
Reproductive	Given	Given	Given
Method based	Given	Given	Not given
Goal based	Given	Given	Not given
Creative	Not given	Not given	Not given

is also another level worth consideration. That is the depth of knowledge and understanding. To approach this aspect a matrix on various aspects of work situations (task assignment) could be fruitful (Table 7.3).

The task, the method of performing that task and the goal of the task performance could either be given or not given. Depending on various combinations the task assignment therefore becomes a totally reproductive one (given, given, given), or a method-based, goal-based or creative one.

It is likely that there will be a great difference in what kind of competence (including knowledge) among individuals will be best fitted to carry out the various tasks. The totally reproductive tasks demand very little individual thinking and arguably a very limited conceptual understanding. It would score low on most knowledge dimensions above: organizational, professional, supply market and so on. The method-based assignment means that the purchasers should at least know the specific methods, processes and procedures that they are applying.

The goal-based task opens up more freedom for acting. The organization, team or individual has to meet defined goals but have freedom to choose and forge methods for achieving it. The creative task leaves even more room for 'forging' the activities. In this case the purchasing organization, team or individual acts to develop the business of the firm. The latter role should call for genuine understanding of concepts (conceptual thinking), in-depth understanding of the organization, the supply markets as well as the customers, in order to be able to see possibilities, to act on the right ones and in relevant ways.[16] There are great needs for genuine understanding of situations and contexts, in goal-based and creative task assignments, to make the relevant interpretations, decisions and actions.

It is also very likely that the various tasks are best supported by different kinds of leadership, as discussed towards the end of Chapter 6.

It is interesting to connect this discussion to the various maturity levels. As the more mature purchasing organizations act in more synchronized ways, one could argue that the job of the sourcing representative becomes more reproductive. If so, the most creative job assignments should be at levels 2 to 4 – but not at the later stages. On the other hand, one could also argue that at stages 5 and 6, the routine work is basically eliminated or automated. The remaining sourcing work, with more strategic issues, could be labelled 'upstream business development'.

7.7   Conclusions

Why should a sourcing manager be interested in knowledge and competence management? We could think of this question in relation to two situations: running the everyday business and the strategic change situation.

This chapter has shown that in order to perform effectively and efficiently as a buyer, more and more knowledge and competencies are required. The sourcing task becomes more knowledge intense. Through this, sourcing knowledge is becoming an important asset for companies. We have found two major motives. The first is the risk of knowledge leaving the organization. Experienced and senior purchasing managers may leave the company and will take their unique knowledge with them. This knowledge needs to be created again, which is often very costly and time consuming. Secondly, effective use of knowledge is expected to lead to an improvement of sourcing performance. By sharing ideas, experiences, best practices and failures, purchasing problems may be solved more quickly and nonexpected ways for improvement may become apparent. It is expected by sourcing professionals that the net benefit of knowledge management (increased value minus the extra costs of knowledge management) will increase performance.

In relation to strategic change, competence development is a normal requirement. This has to do with the changes needed to take advantage of ICT in better ways, to fulfil a new role given a new organizational design and so on. It is also necessary to better understand the visions of a new challenge, to understand the underlying logic (to create conceptual understanding). This could increase motivation and reduce resistance (see Chapters 10 and 11).

Sourcing managers increasingly realize that knowledge is important, but do not have a clear view on what purchasing knowledge is exactly. We defined knowledge as the ability of a person to perform a task by connecting data with their own information, experiences and attitude. Based on research, we have defined six purchasing knowledge domains: organization, profession, supply market, supplier, customer and product.

In this chapter we also described five organizational design variables (i.e. strategy, structure, culture, systems and staff) that can be identified as the most important enablers for managing sourcing knowledge. These variables determine to a large extent whether purchasing knowledge can be managed effectively and efficiently in a specific company. Major barriers to knowledge are experienced in the areas of systems and incentives.

The methods for supporting employees' competence development and building organizational capabilities can be divided into four main areas: organizational design, value systems, career management and performance measurement.

Notes and references

[1] Bouwmans, P. (2002) *Purchasing Knowledge: Key to Purchasing Performance*, MSc thesis, Eindhoven University of Technology: Eindhoven.

[2]   Bertrams, J. (1999) *De kennisdelende organisate*, Scriptum: Schiedam.

[3]   Zack, M.H. (1999) 'Developing a knowledge strategy', *California Management Review*, Vol. 41, No. 3, pp. 125–45; Weggeman, M.C.D.P. (1997) *Kennismanagement, inrichting en besturing van kennisintensieve organisaties*, Scriptum: Schiedam.

[4]   Bertrams (1999) *opere citato*.

[5]   Zack (1999) *opere citato*.

[6]   Bertrams (1999) *opere citato*.

[7]   Bouwmans (2002) *opere citato*.

[8]   Cavinato, J.L. and Kauffman, R.G. (2000) *The Purchasing Handbook: A Guide for Purchasing and Supply Professionals*, National Association of Purchasing Management, 6th edn, McGraw-Hill: New York.

[9]   Zack (1999) *opere citato*.

[10] Hackman, J.R. and Oldham, G.R. (1975) 'Development of the job diagnostic survey', *Journal of Applied Psychology*, Vol. 60, pp. 159–70.

[11] Teece, D.J., Pisano, G. and Shuen, A. (1997) 'Dynamic capabilities and strategic management', *Strategic Management Journal*, Vol. 18, No. 7, pp. 509–33.

[12] Kinch, N. (1996) 'Att leda lärande – från kompetensutveckling till utvecklingskompetens' (To lead learning – from competence development to development competence) in Hård af Segerstad, P. (ed.), *Idéer som styr*, IPF: Stockholm.

[13] Normann, R. (1975) *Skapande företagsledning* (Creative leadership), Aldus: Lund; Axelsson, B. (1996) *Kompetens för konkurrenskraft* (Competence for competetive advantage), SNS Förlag: Stockholm.

[14] Bouwmans (2002) *opere citato*.

[15] Monczka, R.M. (2002) 'Supply management: Where are we headed?', *Purchasing*, June 6.

[16] Axelsson (1996) *opere citato*.

[17] In 2004, Compendium was taken over by AlfaDelta and its name was changed to AlfaDelta Compendium. The original parts of the assessment tool are used with the company's permission.

Appendix 7.1   The knowledge and skills assessment tool

In order to be able to assess individual knowledge and skills, Compendium[17] (a Dutch consultancy firm specialized in purchasing) developed a knowledge and skills assessment tool. The assessment tool is built using Excel software and consists of three main parts:

- General information.
- Professional knowledge.
- Skills and behaviour.

In the first part, respondents are asked to describe their general educational and professional background (e.g. current job title, years of experience in purchasing, highest level of education etc.). In the second part, individual purchasing knowledge and experience are measured. Respondents are invited to indicate their level of knowledge and experience for a large number of concepts/tools and activities on a four-point scale. The scale ranges from 'rookie level' to 'expert level'. The expert level is described as: 'I have full knowledge of the concept/activity and I am very experienced in successfully applying the concept/conducting the activity in practice.' Some of the questions in the second part are illustrated in Figure 7.5.

The third part of the assessment is aimed at measuring specific business skills and behaviour. Behaviours are underlying characteristics that lead to superior performance in an individual's job. They include qualities, skills, attributes and traits that help people be successful. The assessment tool describes 20 different behaviours along several scales. Respondents are invited to indicate for each

PURCHASING KNOWLEDGE AND EXPERIENCE	Rookie level*	Basic level*	Senior level*	Expert level*
To what extent do you have knowledge of and experience with activities, tools and techniques related to the different phases of the sourcing process?				
a) Defining a specification (e.g. functional and technical specification)	☐	☐	☐	☐
b) Requesting a proposal and selecting a supplier (e.g. RFQ, prequalification)	☐	☐	☐	☐
c) Negotiating with suppliers (e.g negotiating strategies)	☐	☐	☐	☐
d) Commercial contracting (e.g. contract forms, contract management)	☐	☐	☐	☐
e) Ordering and expediting (e.g. purchase order, overdue list, chasing suppliers)	☐	☐	☐	☐
f) Evaluation (e.g. supplier rating)	☐	☐	☐	☐
To what extent are you able to find purchasing facts and analyse them?				
a) Evaluation of contracts and suppliers (e.g. # contracts, # suppliers)	☐	☐	☐	☐
b) Category volume/spend analysis (i.e. financial data analysis)	☐	☐	☐	☐
c) Conducting supply market analysis (e.g. price developments, network relationships)	☐	☐	☐	☐
d) Conducting supplier analysis (e.g. opportunities, developments)	☐	☐	☐	☐
To what extent are you familiar with the following sourcing strategies?				
a) Volume concentration (i.e. bundling volumes and negotiate frame contract)	☐	☐	☐	☐
b) Global sourcing (e.g. broaden competitive supply base geographically)	☐	☐	☐	☐
c) Supply base optimalization (i.e. reduction # suppliers)	☐	☐	☐	☐
d) Early supplier involvement (i.e. involve suppliers early in new product development)	☐	☐	☐	☐
e) Supplier development (i.e. supporting suppliers with performance improvement)	☐	☐	☐	☐
f) Competitive bidding (i.e. tendering)	☐	☐	☐	☐
g) Partnership (i.e. close cooperation with suppliers on cost, quality and logistics)	☐	☐	☐	☐
h) Systems contracting (i.e. reducing administrative complexity for routine products)	☐	☐	☐	☐
i) Standardization and/or harmonization of specifications	☐	☐	☐	☐

*Rookie level: Concept/activity is new for me and I have no experience in applying the concept/conducting the activity in practice.
Basic level: I have basic knowledge of the concept/activity and some experience in applying the concept/conducting the activity in practice on a small scale.
Senior level: I have almost full knowledge of the concept/activity and I am experienced in applying the concept/conducting the activity in practice.
Expert level: I have full knowledge of the concept/activity and I am very experienced in successfully applying the concept/conducting the activity in practice.

FIGURE 7.5   Measuring individual purchasing knowledge and experience.

BUSINESS SKILLS AND BEHAVIOUR

This assessment explains and details 20 different behaviours: qualities and characteristics that are linked to successful performance in a wide range of roles across the business, also Purchasing and Supply Management. The success of xyz Purchasing will rely on what is achieved through critical success factors, business plans and personal targets and also how it is achieved through our values and behaviours.

Behaviours are underlying characteristics that lead to superior performance in an individual's job. They include qualities, skills, attributes and traits that help people to be successful. Behaviours go beyond the traditional focus on academic qualifications, technical skills and experience, providing a framework for assessing and developing deeper-seated personal skills. They are observable and measurable. Behaviours are also capable of being changed and developed in people rather than being fixed and immovable.

This assessment helps to give a common language and consistent framework across xyz Purchasing for using behaviours in all aspects of people management – recruiting, training, developing and appraising performance of our employees.

Behaviours will provide us with a common language for managing people, a consistent framework for human resource management and a powerful tool in improving the focus and clarity of all employees towards our goals and mission.

On the following pages 20 different behaviours are described along scales. Please indicate for each behaviour what description of the behaviour best reflects your current level with regard to that specific behaviour. Select only one!

FIGURE 7.6   Measuring specific business skills and behaviour.

1 Adaptability: Willingness to accept changes and ability to maintain effective in changing environment

a) **Rather unwilling to change.**

b) **Willing to change.** Understands and accepts the need to change the way things are done and maintains effectiveness in variety of work situations.

c) **Adapts priorities.** Changes own priorities in light of new information or changes in the business environment; reviews and re-orders 'to-do' lists. Works effectively in an uncertain environment of shifting priorities. Accepts changes to own job and responsibilities.

d) **Adapts own goals.** Changes own goals, plans and/or projects to fit with changes in the business. Works effectively in complex, ambiguous, rapidly changing environments.

e) **Adapts business goals.** Makes short- or medium-term changes to business goals for own area of the business in order to address specific changes.

f) *Adapts business strategies.* Makes significant changes to xyz's strategy to meet new challenges

☐ ☐ ☐ ☐ ☐ ☐

2 Analytical Thinking: The ability to tackle issues and problems in a logical, step-by-step way

a) **The employee doesn't show this behaviour.**

b) **Handles familiar problems.** Uses common sense to understand an issue or problem. Thinks through problems in a logical way. Solves common, familiar, routine problems effectively. Makes straightforward calculations.

c) **Breaks problems down.** Breaks problems down into component parts. Considers issues from a range of different angles. Uses several different analytical techniques to dissect a problem. Processes a volume of information and data to reach a sound understanding of the issues at hand.

d) **Sees trends.** Sees causal links and 'chains of events' that lie behind an issue. Recognizes trends, patterns or ambiguity in data and information. Spots flaws and weaknesses in arguments put forward. Carries out analysis of interrelated problems and issues. Analyses problems from a wide range of different perspectives.

e) **Conducts complex analysis.** Identifies key issues even when critical information is ambiguous. Develops flow charts, maps and visual tools to help understand the connections between different aspects of a problem. Systematically breaks down multi-dimensional problems. Interprets trends, patterns or ambiguity in complex information.

f) **Conducts extremely complex analysis.** Analyse is abstract problems in challenging, uncharted areas. Tests out hypothesis using modelling techniques. Identifies and analyses a wide range of solutions to the given problem, knowing the pros and cons of each solution.

☐ ☐ ☐ ☐ ☐ ☐

FIGURE 7.6 *(continued)*

behaviour what description best reflects their current level with regard to that specific behaviour. Figure 7.6 illustrates what the tool looks like for two behaviours.

If a respondent has filled in the complete assessment, the Excel program automatically calculates the average scores. By comparing the outcome of the assessment with a standard functional profile, the consultant is able to provide the individual with detailed advice on where he or she should improve knowledge and/or skills. The outcome can also serve as input for developing a tailor-made action learning programme (see the example in Chapter 6).

Appendix 7.2 Knowledge, skills and competencies for different sourcing maturity stages

	Transaction orientation	Commercial orientation	Purchasing orientation
Organization A = Strategy B = Structure C = Culture D = Systems E = Staff	C Purchasing ethics E Processes and procedures	A Goals of organization, approaches to performance measurement, financial strength and stability B Structure of organization D Internet E Competencies and skills	A Mission, vision and strategy of organization and purchasing department B Structure of purchasing department C History of organization, communication, human resource policies D Intranet, document management E Who is who, past functions of people
Profession F = Strategic cost management G = Strategic sourcing H = Supply chain management I = Skills	G Make or buy H Enterprise resource planning, material requirement planning, capacity requirements planning I Ability to work in teams, customer focus, computer literacy, creativity	F Contract management, pareto analysis, price analysis G Competitive bidding, supply market research, project management H Approved supplier list, supplier quality assurance, auction negotiation, purchasing intelligence, decision support systems I Interpersonal communication, ability to make decisions, analytical skills, negotiation, influencing and persuasion, understanding business conditions, conflict resolution, leadership, managing internal customers, organization/time management/tact in dealing with others	F Cost analysis, break-even analysis, spend classification, value analysis G Commodity strategies, global sourcing, environmental management, financial risk analysis, portfolio analysis, supply base management H Vendor rating, intranet I Managing change, strategic thinking, problem solving, structuring supplier relationships
Supply Market J = Mesoeconomic level K = Macroeconomic level			J Supply-and-demand analysis, utilization rate, order situation and sales, inventories, market structure, globalization, industry concept of competition, market concept of competition, available suppliers, important trends, experiences with certain market, reputation of the market
Supplier L = Internal knowledge M = External knowledge	M Address, website, offered products, price level	L Relationship of supplier with organization, person within organization responsible for supplier, contracts available with supplier M Reputation, structure, size, financial situation, major competitors, relationship of supplier with other suppliers, general conditions	L Current projects with suppliers M History, problems experienced by supplier, news announced by supplier, performance history of supplier
Customer N = Internal customer O = External customer		N Who is the customer, expectations of purchasing department	N Spend analysis, forecast, goods and services the customer needs, judgement of customer about performance of purchasing department
Product P = Purchased product Q = End product		P Alternative goods/services, quality, package, installation instructions, safety functions, guarantees Q Minimum safety requirements, minimum standards	P Class, different types of product, applications, aftersales services, customer services, maintenance requirements

FIGURE 7.7 Knowledge, skills and competencies for different sourcing maturity stages.

	Process orientation	Supply chain orientation	Value chain orientation
Organization A = Strategy B = Structure C = Culture D = Systems E = Staff	A Environmental issues, current and projected collaborative relationships B Governance structure C Shared values	A Supply chain strategy B Network organizations C Collaborative culture D E-based tools across the supply chain	A Value chain strategy D E-based tools across the value chain
Profession F = Strategic cost management G = Strategic sourcing H = Supply chain management I = Skills	G Insourcing/outsourcing, performance-based partnerships, cross-functional teams, leadbuyership	F Strategic cost management across the supply chain, cost engineering, TCO, target costing H Benchmarking, supplier development, JIT-II, EDI, CPFR, VMI, ESI, E2E-connection	F Strategic cost management across the value chain, total value of ownership, value engineering G Value-based sourcing
Supply Market J = Mesoeconomic level K = Macroeconomic level	K Business cycle and economic growth, development of industrial production, average utilization rate in industry, price development, interest rate, development of wages, productivity of development, political climate	J Advanced supply market analysis, future technology Development	J Future business development, value chain mapping M Future technology roadmaps
Supplier L = Internal knowledge M = External knowledge	L Past projects with supplier M Processes at supplier, innovative power of supplier, business reasons for changes, cost-price structure	L Suppliers of supplier, customers' supplier M Supplier satisfaction surve	M Core competencies of the suppliers
Customer N = Internal customer O = External customer	N Pooling of demand O Person responsible for external customer	O Who is the external customer, goods and services customer needs, expected demand	O Total customer satisfaction, co-creation
Product P = Purchased product Q = End product	P Core benefit of good or service, features Q Necessary components that should be bought	P New features/technologies or options Q Application of end product	Q New product/market combinations, growth

FIGURE 7.7 (continued).

Chapter 8

CHANGE THROUGH LEVERAGING INFORMATION AND COMMUNICATIONS TECHNOLOGY

Jens Hultman and Björn Axelsson

As already noted in the first chapters of this book, strategic change in purchasing and supply management frequently seems to have its point of departure in the introduction and improvements of information and communications technology (ICT). The dramatic changes at IBM illustrated in Chapter 1 give us one such example. The current chapter will show that leveraging ICT is not only related to the initiation of change but can also be the very point of departure for a change process on its own. Even if the trigger to change is something else, ICT is still, more or less always, an important ingredient in current sourcing improvement processes.

In this chapter we take a closer look at the many different ways in which ICT can contribute to strategic change within purchasing and supply management. The aim is to provide an overview of a number of ways in which the exploitation of ICT enables changes in sourcing activities and behaviour as well as in business opportunities. We look at both some specific ICT applications and at the changes that their implementation implies. The chapter covers three main aspects of ICT and change. First, it seems a necessity to start with a discussion of the general promise of ICT and its generic effects. Second, the chapter outlines a discussion on how these general effects can translate into ICT in sourcing activities. The chapter concludes with a discussion on the strategic aspects of ICT implementation. The lesson is that ICT exploitation is not just about buying in new ways, but essentially about improvement and behavioural change.

8.1   On the promise of information and communications technology

ICT was definitely a dominant driving force in the economy during the second half of the twentieth century. Ever since the innovation of the semiconductor in Silicon Valley in the 1960s, ICT has been discussed as something that will influence, and to a great extent already has influenced, the way business firms conduct marketing and purchasing activities.[1] Since then, many innovations have come and gone. Some have been short-lived and some have been more persistent. The focus on the exploitation of new technology seemed to reach new heights with the broad commercialization of the Internet ten years ago. The impact of the Internet, both in theory and practice, has been significant, but it has been a bumpy ride. Many decisions on ICT exploitation are affected by the many lessons learnt during the Internet hype. However, in many ways practitioners seem to have been more pragmatic than many scholars. In addition to the impact that new ICT had on research in many different disciplines, well-established textbooks were also rewritten and reoriented under the assumption that new ICT required a complete rethinking of a company's marketing strategy and the transaction and communication models on which it built its business.[2]

Today, authors of textbooks and articles discussing the exploitation of, for example, Internet-based applications seem to give at least two contradicting views of the potential of the technology. One is to see it as something that completely alters the way business is done. Others present a somewhat contrasting, or moderating, view of the role of ICT and how firms should deal with it and exploit it. These arguments basically say that although ICT will have a dramatic impact on many businesses and will demand new requirements from many managers, the basic rules of the business will not be altered. This means that ICT is still very important, but in a different way. In a recent and thought-provoking article, this view is stressed by the claim that 'IT doesn't matter'.[3] The point made is that ICT is becoming so taken for granted in our day-to-day business processes that it does not form a base for the creation of competitive advantages as it perhaps did a decade ago. This would for instance mean that any firm that has not yet put extensive efforts into bringing much of the technology in place should have this as its top priority in a strategic change process. For example, a PC industry player without an integrated system with direct linkages between component production and the fast-moving market is unlikely to manage to keep up with the industry's competition. In this industry, many aspects of the Dell Direct system have been widely benchmarked by other players. Thus, it could be argued that today, an integrated system like the celebrated Dell Direct system is more an infrastructural prerequisite than a basis for competitive advantage. This was not the case a few years ago.

Box 8.1   Two testimonials on the impact of ICT

During the second half of the twentieth century, ICT was one of the driving forces. Many are those who have expressed the enormous impact that ICT has had or will have on business activities. Here are two examples.

The paradigm shift encompasses fundamental change in just about everything regarding the technology itself and its application to business. The old paradigm began in the 1950s. The late 1980s and the 1990s are a transition period to the new paradigm. Organizations that do not make this transition will fail. They will become irrelevant or cease to exist.[4]

Electronic commerce is no longer an alternative, it is an imperative. The only choice open is whether to start quickly or slowly. Many companies are still struggling with the most basic problem: what is the best e-commerce model? Unfortunately, there is no simple answer for this question.[5]

The two views on the impact of technology presented in Box 8.1 both point to the important role of ICT, either as a way to create a competitive advantage or to avoid a potential disadvantage. In purchasing, it could perhaps also be possible to talk about ICT as an infrastructural prerequisite. At least, it seems reasonable to assume that no one interested in purchasing and supply chain development, including strategic change, should avoid bringing ICT into the picture. One specific reason for the spurred exploitation and broad diffusion of information technology after the commercialization of the Internet is that Web-based applications, to a great extent, have scale and cost advantages that their forerunners lacked. Just a few years ago, the opportunity to do business electronically was a privilege that only large business firms could make use of. Business systems such as, for instance, EDI (electronic data interchange) or ERP (enterprise resource planning) systems were too costly or too complex for many small firms to handle. Nowadays, the way small businesses can do business has undergone some interesting changes. The development of new, less expensive technology and user-friendly technical applications is one reason for this change.

The underlying cause for the impact of ICT is that, at a much lower cost than a few years ago, businesses can obtain increased reach, transparency and richness in inter- and intraorganizational flows of data through the exploitation of ICT. The gains in efficiency and decreased costs of information, communication, distribution and transactions are highly relevant also for purchasing and supply management. The promise of ICT, as we interpret it, is that its exploitation opens up four main opportunities or generic effects:

- ICT enables efficiency in flows of information, distribution and transactions and, hence, ICT is freeing up resources for more strategic tasks.
- ICT enables enhanced quality of decision making as firms can gather and get access to more accurate and timely data.
- ICT enables stability and coherence through increased overview as information becomes available for processing and analysis.

- ICT enables new infrastructures in which behaviour can be built in, such as the introduction of a new supplier. An ICT-based infrastructure where only the explicitly chosen suppliers are available will enable compliance and reduce maverick behaviour among the people involved.

8.2   Sourcing development with the use of ICT

During practically the same time as the development of ICT as a viable tool for creating enhanced efficiency in purchasing activities, the role of purchasing, both within the firm and within the supply chain, has changed quite substantially. This change process was described in the first chapter of this book as the gradual development from purchasing to supply management. It is most interesting to see how the developments have been parallel and are most certainly, to a large extent, intertwined. Indeed, the shift of purchasing from being mainly a clerical function to becoming a strategic and managerial issue has called for an increased need for enhanced coordination and communication. In addition, as we can see many examples of today, increased abilities to communicate and to coordinate activities enabled by ICT are also likely to have opened up new ways for exploiting sourcing. It is thought-provoking to look at ICT as a tool to manage behaviour – and to compare it with other tools for that same purpose, as in the case of the Portuguese East-India Corporation in Box 8.2. The step from what we call ICT and what the East-India Corporation had then is not a large one. What we see, for instance in the reduced amount of maverick buying in the IBM illustration from Chapter 1, is that by utilizing ICT and a disciplined staff, companies can make the periphery work in synchronized ways, very similar to the Portuguese East-India Corporation.

Box 8.2   Making the periphery work in coherent ways

The Portuguese developed new instruments for navigation, which enabled the switch of potential dangers to advantages. In various models, grids and tables they collected representations of stars and their positions in relation to the sun and so on. In short, they built a portable and manipulable system (to be compared with modern Global Positioning Systems). In such ways the leaders of that time, in that business, could make the periphery work for themselves. To be able to benefit from this control there was also a need for stronger discipline among the staff that was employed and worked on the ships. They were requested to follow designed routes in line with instructions from back home. The Portuguese could dominate the world instead of becoming dominated by it.

Source: Edenius, M. (2000) 'IT och vårt behov av kontroll – Vad har Birgersson och Pasteur gemeinsamt?' (IT and our need for control – what do Birgersson and Pasteur have in common?), *Human IT*, April.

Through a review of prevalent research on sourcing and ICT, several interesting examples of how information technology has enabled efficiency and effectiveness in a business-to-business context can be found. Let us mention two such important examples that have spurred a great deal of thought. The first example is the development of the SABRE system in the airline industry.

The computer reservation system SABRE was implemented in 1967 by American Airlines and IBM to support communications between the airline industry and the travel industry and generated much attention both from academics and practitioners during the 1980s.[6] The idea was to cut transaction costs and to facilitate interfirm coordination and data entry (see Box 8.3). One perhaps could also argue that SABRE was an early example of a customer relationship management system (CRM), where information about customer preferences was stored and processed so that it could be acted on (an early version of a frequent flyer bonus system). This is, however, another story.

Box 8.3   Knowing the airline passenger at American Airlines

For instance, say you are one of American's most frequent flyers. As your morning flight takes off from Dallas-Fort Worth International Airport, the SABRE system transmits to an on-board computer in the cockpit a message that you are sitting in Seat 2B (you were previously upgraded to this first-class seat by SABRE). The American Airlines stewardess brings you a Bloody Mary, compliments of the captain (SABRE knows that you prefer this drink before 11:00 A.M., and a gin martini on the rocks, very dry, after lunchtime). SABRE has scheduled your connection in Atlanta, so that you have a convenient thirty minutes before your continuing flight to New York. Yes, SABRE looks after you. One can see from this example how information, and the new communication technology that controls this information, can be an important weapon for competitive advantage.

Source: Rogers, E.M. (1995) *Diffusion of Innovations*, 4th edn, Free Press: New York.

The second example is the now closed-down project COVISINT. Created by some of the largest players in the automotive industry (e.g. Ford, DaimlerChrysler, General Motors and others), COVISINT was meant to be a US-based online e-business exchange for OEMs (original equipment manufacturers) and automotive component suppliers. The project ultimately failed, but during the time that COVISINT was a reality in the automotive industry, it created quite a few concerns among supplier managers in that industry.[7] COVISINT was established to serve the automotive industry with a platform for electronic procurement. Through the presence of products and prices and through applications enabling price comparisons and electronic auctions, suppliers in the automotive industry were exposed to competition that had not been so evident before. The problem that COVISINT experienced was that it could not lure enough suppliers. Certainly, this was a serious problem since marketplaces like COVISINT are dependent on large volumes as their business model is built on charging traders per transaction. Even though the high-flying project COVISINT failed, it is likely that we will see similar attempts to set up large buyer-oriented marketplaces in the near future.

In the coming section, we outline different ways to exploit ICT-based applications along the following dimensions: *coordination, communication* and, as in the case of COVISINT, *competition*. This delineation refers back to Chapter 4, where a discussion on transactional and relational buying was outlined. As we want to emphasize the already mentioned aspect of ICT as an enabler of coherent (and institutionalized) behaviour, which largely is about coordination, we have decided to explore that aspect of coordination in a separate section. The communicative applications intend to support or substitute for face-to-face communication. The coordinative applications aim to support the collection and provision of information regarding supply. Competition-oriented applications aim to create markets and market transparency. Altogether these applications connect almost all the sources for strategic change dealt with in this section of the book. This relates to changes in organizational structures and performance measurement, as changes within such fields are largely enabled by ICT. It relates to competence development and learning in similar ways and it is a possible tool in developing specific supplier relationships, and so on.

ICT and competition

The changes in the competitive structure that recent ICT applications have created are quite challenging (sometimes threatening and sometimes attractive and beneficial) in their nature. The commercialization of the Internet and the broad diffusion of electronic marketplaces created expectations that ICT would rapidly affect competition and create much more commonplace transparency. This was seen as a threat to prices and brands from a marketing (compare purchasing) perspective.[8] The effects were outlined as shown in Box 8.4. Even though this general view on market transparency has been challenged, the concept of market transparency implies associations to both threats and opportunities.

Box 8.4   The opportunity and threat of market transparency

The vast sea of information about prices, competitors and features that is readily available on the Internet helps buyers 'see through' the costs of product and services. For some, that's bad news. For others, it's a great opportunity:

- ICT exploitation creates a market transparency that severely impedes the seller's ability to obtain high margins.
- ICT exploitation creates a market transparency that basically will turn all products and services into commodities.
- ICT exploitation creates a market transparency that weakens the general view on loyalty to brands.

Source: Sinha, I. (2000) 'Cost transparency: The net's real threat to prices and brands', *Harvard Business Review*, Vol. 78, Mar–Apr, pp. 43–50.

When reviewing research on ICT and enhanced competition, it seems as if there are two general ways of exploiting ICT to boost competition, or competitive advantage. Let us first look at the possibility of exploiting ICT applications to enable fierce competition and commoditization.

Here, two good examples enabled by ICT applications are electronic auctions and open marketplaces, where costs of comparison are low and transparency in terms of prices is generally high. Electronic auctions have attracted quite a lot of attention during the last few years, even though the expectations have broadly not been met yet. One example of a company that has decided to really explore the potential of electronic auctions is presented in Box 8.5. A few of the circumstances that make electronic auctions applicable can be mentioned. First, volume is important to make auctions worthwhile. Second, it is important that it is possible to clearly specify demand. Third, the cost of switching suppliers seems to be vital for applicability.

For procurement purposes, the reverse (downward) auction is the most relevant. These are auctions where buyers invite sellers to bid and the lowest bidder gets the deal. Even though reverse auctions are perhaps not as common as was expected a few years ago in the heyday of the Internet era, quite a lot of firms are assessing whether electronic auctions are applicable to their business environment or not. This assessment is even more important in the light of recent studies showing that the implementation of auctions can be harmful, as it is argued that buyers initiating e-auctions risk destroying previously established relationships and that a lack of trust could emerge in the long run.[9]

Box 8.5   The potential of e-auctions

The electronics firm has some test periods during which a wide variety of commodities in various regions globally have been subject to tests with e-auctions. The results so far:

- 15–20% average savings. Total volume contracted €200 million, total savings €32.5 million.
- Negotiations that would take 2–3 weeks were completed in 1 hour.
- 30% of the total spend was assessed to be suitable for e-auctions.

Source: Information presented by a representative from the company of an application provider workshop, 2004.

E-procurement systems that aim at enhancing competition can take various forms. Pioneering scholarly work on e-procurement with the aim of classifying and structuring different types of procurement applications states that there is a danger of simplification of the e-procurement phenomenon when treated as a general application of ICT. Instead, there are several different types of applications existing in practice. When addressing open marketplaces for procurement, a classification between what firms buy (i.e. either operating inputs or manufacturing inputs) and how firms buy (i.e. either on a spot basis or through systematic sourcing based on long-term contracts) can be made. For sourcing purposes, a distinction between open (neutral) and buyer-oriented (biased) marketplaces can be made here. In conclusion, we would like to elevate three interesting and currently applied applications that enhance sourcing efficiency and competition:

- *Open marketplaces*: electronic commerce applications that are neutral and often run by a third party. Open marketplaces are often applied for spot purchasing behaviour.
- *E-procurement marketplaces*: electronic commerce applications that are buyer oriented. They enable the buying firm to conduct systematic electronic sourcing through inviting sellers to their own solution.
- *Electronic auctions*: applications that support electronic bidding and enable dynamic pricing. In the buyer-initiated (reverse) auction sellers are invited and – normally – the lowest bidder gets the deal.

The above discussion pointing at the new opportunities for competition (and collaboration) is interesting to explore in a process of strategic change. They provide means to vitalize the supply markets and to improve commercial conditions.

ICT and communication

The other way is to exploit ICT to boost competition by implementing applications that enforce relationships as a competitive advantage. In the coming pages we will look at ICT that enables communication and coordination. In industrial marketing and purchasing in general, business relationships are argued to be rather stable and long term. This is due to the level of adaptation and mutual dependency as well as the efficiency and effectiveness gains made possible through learning in long-term relations. This view is strengthened by the fact that initially transactional and competitively oriented efforts like the developments of the automotive marketplace COVISINT have shifted towards the adoption of more and more relationship-oriented attempts, when it comes to what applications they provide.

We can thus see that a transactional as well as a relational approach to purchasing and supply management could benefit from the application of ICT. The basic issue is what fits best when and in what ways. Regarding the enhanced ability for communication and reach, the promise of ICT can be summarized with the view that firms can overcome the tradeoff between reach (how many and how far it is possible to reach with a message) and richness (how much information that message can contain) from which traditional communications suffer.

Another benefit of using ICT applications is that communication can be conducted either synchronously or asynchronously. Telephone-based and personal communication, in comparison, needs to be synchronous; that is, the two or more individuals involved in communication need to be available at the same time. One main ICT-based communication tool that has spread immensely during the last years and that is often forgotten or taken for granted is e-mail. In a recent study on present and future usage of communication tools among industrial firms in the UK, it was found that in 2002 the telephone was still the most frequently used communication tool, but that e-mail had a strong, and growing, position.[10]

In our own work, we have noted that, quite paradoxically, an increased level of ICT exploitation can lead to problems in communication. In these cases, the increasing number of communication tools (e.g. e-mail, telephone, fax, extranet) has led to a situation where a need to collect the communication on a single platform has become urgent. In some cases, new means of communication disturbed the former functional channelling of information through a key account manager. Mail quotes from customers were sent directly to the in-house sales department, to product experts and to tool construction engineers. Meeting minutes were distributed, through direct access to extranet functions, to a large number of actors in the relationship. Contacts were taken aside from the traditional channels of communication. In these cases, instead of having a situation where all information was channelled through the key actors, the situation has come to the point where no one has a reasonably complete overview of the on-going activities in the relationship.

Recent studies by the Swedish Industrial Research and Development Corporation (IVF) report an increasing interest, especially by firms in the automotive industry, in ICT applications that support collaborative efforts and distributed engineering across firm boundaries.[11] The reason for the increased interest of the automotive industry in enabling cross-organizational collaboration in product development is clear from these recent facts from the Scandinavian Automotive Suppliers industry network shown in Box 8.6.

Box 8.6   Increased interest in collaboration in product development

Scandinavian Automotive Suppliers' summary of incentives for the increased interest in collaborative efforts in the industry:

- To spread risk in production and product development, R&D expenditure is subsequently pushed upstream. In addition, an increasing share of the production of the components needed in manufacturing is outsourced to suppliers. This implies that some aspects of the product development process need to be conducted across firm borders.
- To cope with increasing pressure from competition and diminishing margins, the industry moves production to low-wage countries. This implies that coordination of activities (including product development, since much production is made on platforms and in modules) needs to be enabled both within firm boundaries across continents and across firm borders and continents.
- To cut costs in product development, the industry seeks to increase the amount of digitalization of product development. This implies that an increased amount of data (both in terms of number and size of files) needs to be transferred across firm borders.

Source: Information presented at a seminar on Product Data Management arranged by Swedish Automotive Suppliers, Göteborg, 12 May 2004.

To facilitate the increasing need to communicate product data, the industry has recently come together in an agreement to standardize product data and product development communication under the umbrella SASIG (Strategic Automotive product data Standards Industry Group). This will enable automotive OEMs and suppliers in the US, Europe and Japan to communicate smoothly.

There are several different types of systems offered by several actors (one of the big ones seems to be Quickplace by Lotus Notes), ranging from very specific to very general in terms of what tasks the platform is supposed to support. Common features are that they can be easily maintained once the system is set up, and that they can be accessed through the Internet by their users. In addition, most collaborative platforms contain functions that enable document handling and filing and functions that enable notification and planning.

An additional problem that seems to have resulted from the 'reach opportunity' is the increasing information flow by which firms tend to be threatened. This problem can, to some extent, be handled by intelligent agents. Intelligent agents are software applications that perform routine tasks, for example search and filter information and perform automatic communication, based on the defined requirements and authorization that they are given by the user. There seem to be two different forms of intelligent agents: electronic commerce agents that negotiate and perform transactions and information agents that help users cope with and gather and sort information.[12] Just as with other ICT applications, the increased capacity turns them into applications that enable an increased quality in decision making through providing the users with accurate, sorted and timely data.

Before concluding this section, we would like to describe three interesting and currently implemented applications that enhance sourcing efficiency and communication:

- *Collaborative platforms*: applications that support post- and pre-purchase communication – often on an extranet – and thus enable both asynchronous and synchronous communication, the collection of communication threads to one single platform.
- *Collaborative product development systems*: applications that support spatially distributed communication in product development projects. These enable both synchronous and asynchronous communication and have specific functions – for example built-in viewers for CAD/CAM – that are designed for enhanced efficiency in product development.
- *Intelligent agents*: applications that search and filter information and perform automatic communicative tasks based on requirements and authorization that they are given by the user. They enable both negotiations and transactions (electronic commerce agents) and automatic information retrieval (information agents).

The selection of communication tools and the illustrations of opportunities as well as problems discussed has served the purpose of pointing at the potential for improvements based on enabled communication, and thus the trigger and enabler of strategic change that ICT provides.

ICT and coordination

There are several ICT applications that enhance coordination. The applications that perhaps many think of when it comes to coordination are ERP (enterprise resource planning) systems. ERP systems are widely diffused and used among both large and small industrial firms. The scholars that studied the SABRE system in the 1980s found that there was a need, and a potential benefit, in overcoming double feeding in the different systems that were used when making airline reservations. Twenty years later, creating seamless connections across firm boundaries is still something that many IT managers aim for. The principal idea is that the need for coordination of the chains of activities, both within and between firms, increases as the demand for efficiency increases. The major objective with an ERP system is to enable the integration and control of resources across departments and functions in order to obtain coordination of transactions. The focus is mostly to coordinate functions within a firm, even though later developments show efforts to coordinate and control flows across firm boundaries.

There are several problems with this. One problem is that there is no standard language into which data inserted into ERP software can be translated. Each system tends to have its own file system. Even though there is one big actor in the ERP software business, SAP, its software is often too costly and too complex for a small firm to handle, which means that some form of translation is often needed when coordination between two or more firms is aimed for. In a supply chain perspective, the chain often also stretches out to smaller firms. If the first generations of ERP systems mainly focus on internal coordination and materials planning, giving a snapshot picture of the current situation, the later generations of ERP systems have a distinct, and natural, focus on a whole chain as they support planning and decision making.

There are other specific applications supporting coordination across firm boundaries that have been labelled SCM (supply chain management) systems. The logic behind stretching the focus from a within-firm perspective or a between-two-firms perspective is that firms hereby obtain the ability to change and adapt their sourcing activities to an ever-changing environment. The key lies in viewing their supply from a chain perspective. A chain perspective can be applied to communication flows as well as physical flows through the supply chain. In a study of the role of the Internet in supply chain management reporting findings from a survey study covering a broad range of industries, it was found that the most popular SCM application enabled by Web technologies was transport management.[13] Supply managers were enabled to control arrival times and identify potential delays through tracking services. An example of how a firm has managed to coordinate quality control and support activities across firm borders is the global quality tracking system (GQTS) that GM has developed. For Saab Automobile in Trollhättan in Sweden, being connected with GQTS means that there is an immediate link between Saab and suppliers like Lear Corporation when there is a problem in production quality. Through GQTS, a message from Trollhättan to Detroit gives the supplier notification of a problem within 30 minutes.[14]

We would like to end this section by putting forward the following three interesting and currently implemented applications that enhance sourcing efficiency through improved coordination:

- *Inventory-level control systems*: applications that support coordination between the order and the level of inventory. When the inventory levels reach a designated level, a new order is automatically triggered.
- *Systems avoiding double feeding*: applications that support coordination between planning systems through transmitting and, if necessary, translating the information across firm boundaries.
- *Tracking systems*: applications that support coordination between production, order and inventory movements. They enable both internal and authorized external actors to follow inventory movements across specific check points from order, shipping and delivery to final destination.

Similar to the case of competition and information above, all these coordination efforts enabled by ICT solutions point to significant improvement potentials and thus important triggers and enablers for strategic change in purchasing and supply management.

8.3   ICT and strategic change

Before labelling change emanating from the exploitation of ICT as strategic, we need to give meaning to the word *strategic*. In the former sections, it was stated that there are some generic and advantageous effects that firms can make use of in leveraging ICT. Firm activities that actively strive towards these benefits, summarized as 'the promise of information and communications technology', can be labelled strategic in the sense that they intentionally strive towards the goals of obtaining, for example, cost savings and increased reach through implementing ICT. They intend to harvest the benefits embedded in the promise of ICT. However, ICT is not just about buying, introducing and exploiting the new technology.

Strategic change could also be considered change that is relatively important and irreversible. Decisions on rejection or adoption of technologies are decisions that can profoundly affect a company's ability to develop and fulfil offerings for many years. If the suppliers of Ford Motor Company decide to turn down the offer of e-procurement that they get, the decision will certainly imply a great deal of risk. In fact, in many cases it would probably mean that they would go out of business. Over the last few years, quite some attention has been paid to the pressure that large automotive players have put on their suppliers, using their relative strength, size and importance. For example, Box 8.7 shows an example of the rhetoric used in the Swedish Automotive Industry, as reported in the Swedish popular technology press in 2001.

Box 8.7   Demand from Volvo Cars regarding e-commerce capabilities

> Volvo Cars *demands* that suppliers make a bid for e-commerce via the Internet. This is a message that is communicated to all the suppliers of the Ford Motor Company. 'The suppliers that do not *learn and apply* the opportunities for rationalization that e-commerce enables will be left behind and risk being *out of business,*' says Lars Bolminger, purchasing manager at Volvo Cars.

Source: Andersson, G. (2001) 'Volvo kräver e-handel av leverantörerna' (Volvo demands e-commerce from its suppliers), *Ny Teknik*, 10 October, (www.nyteknik.se).

ICT is thus also strategic from the point of view of investment (or noninvestment). Historically, many firms have made serious and irreversible mistakes regarding ICT systems. There are a number of 'special' reasons why investments in technology can go awry. Some of these are related to network externalities, bandwagon effects and lock-in effects. Regarding external pressures for change, as illustrated by the quote from Volvo Cars, several researchers have acknowledged the importance of network effects and the adoption of new technology – also an aspect of strategic change. One important concept in that context is *network externalities*. Network externalities come into action when the value of a network increases with the number of actors (e.g. users of a technology) that are part of the network. Positive network externalities give rise to positive feedback.[15] For example, when you buy a fax machine, the value of fax machine technology is increased for you and for others, since you can now send faxes to me and others and receive faxes from me and others.

A similar phenomenon to the network externalities effect is the *bandwagon effect*.[16] This effect focuses on processes where organizations are triggered to adopt an innovation because of the pressure created by the number of organizations that have already adopted the innovation. A good example is the case of diffusion and standardization rivalry between two similar but incompatible formats for home video-recorder technologies that was launched in the 1970s. Even though the BETAMAX system introduced by Sony was introduced to the home video market first, the competing system VHS, first introduced by JVC, succeeded due to bandwagon effects. The bandwagon effect is similar to the description of the importance of a 'critical mass' put forward by advocates of the concepts of 'dominant design'[17] and 'path dependence'.[18] The concepts of dominant design and path dependence both describe, with a slightly different approach, how technology decisions can lead to *lock-in effects*. Perhaps the most striking example of technology and behavioural lock-in is the QWERTY design of the computer keyboards that most people use every day.[19] The case of QWERTY is often used to exemplify how decisions made through history in an industry affect the present by decision lock-in, via for example significant investments in the industry standard. Similar examples can be found in the automotive industry, the integrated circuit industry and the personal computer industry.

Much of the reason for technology lock-in effects is due to the fact that ICT systems should not be treated in isolation from the organizational system in which they are used. To make ICT implementation work, it needs to fit into the rest of the organizational system(s). We have, for example, in our own research come across cases where for decades firms have let separate systems develop in isolated islands. The marketing department has developed its own customer database or CRM system. The purchasing department has its own procurement system. The main operations, including manufacturing, have their ERP systems and/or supply management systems. The HRM department has an intranet supporting corporate communication.

As the ability to link one system with another (e.g. a customer database with an e-commerce system) through an extranet or other customer-centric application grows, problems occur with the inability to integrate. Due to the significant investments that might have been made in these systems, (sometimes very deep) lock-in conflicts occur. Many firms have experienced these problems, although not many would admit it.

In addition, the idea of the embeddedness of information technology brings us to the growing awareness that ICT alone cannot revolutionize organizations. Much of the literature from the heyday of the Internet age and the new economy shows a striking lack in human aspects of ICT implementation. The technical side of implementation pushed aside the fact that strategic considerations need to include developments in other dimensions, such as the organizational side of implementation, seriously taking organizational structures and people into consideration. The bias on the technology dimension and the inherent promise of information technology has probably by itself created inertia in ICT project management processes. In several studies, the problems with ICT implementation have been highlighted. For example, the failure rate of CRM implementation has been reported to be as high as 75%.

Evaluating specific ICT applications for sourcing development

When making a primary evaluation of ICT applications and the potential of exploiting them in sourcing activities, the general applicability in terms of what solution is suitable for which type of product or supplier could be useful. One way to do this is to apply the Kraljic matrix (see section 4.5) in order to show that different sourcing applications are suitable for different types of products, as shown in Figure 8.1.

For each type of product in the matrix, an appropriate ICT solution is suggested. For routine products, applications that support smooth and efficient commodity procurement are suggested. If possible, to ensure a broad range of offers, a solution where several suppliers are invited should be searched for. For these purposes, a third-party marketplace might be an option. For bottleneck products, for which the strategy is to secure supply, supplier-specific e-solutions might be appropriate. For strategic products, a solution that demands a long-term commitment and that supports stability and efficiency for a high-involvement relationship might be necessary to implement. For leverage products, where the supply risk is low

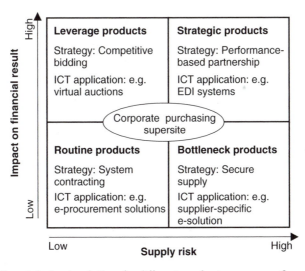

FIGURE 8.1 Different electronic solutions for different purchasing purposes. Source: Adapted from Van Weele, A.J. (2005) *Purchasing and Supply Chain Management*, 4th edn, Thomson Learning: London, p. 176.

but the financial impact is high, a solution that enables dynamic pricing to obtain competitive bidding might be appropriate.

To use the matrix also signals that different solutions demand different levels of involvement and integration. Hence, high-involvement applications such as EDI systems are suggested for sourcing strategic products where the strategy is to attain partnering with the supplying part and where the horizon is long term and the approach is systematic sourcing.

In the centre of the model above, a platform to support several purchasing purposes is outlined and labelled 'corporate purchasing supersite'. In our own work, we have found that the application that resembles this supersolution vision best is the effort of Ford Motor Company (FMC) and its eVEREST program, FMC's global purchasing e-business attempt to improve efficiency and effectiveness in sourcing and standardizing procurement processes between *all* FMC regions and brands and *all* suppliers, *all* over the world. This enormous effort is well on its way and thousands of suppliers and purchasing officers within the FMC organization are implementing this system. We have, so far, found that these efforts of FMC and its subsidiaries, such as Volvo Car Corporation, seem to create room for additional emphasis on negotiations and relational efforts with strategic suppliers. To accomplish this, sourcing specialists are distinguishing strategic products from routine products. For routine and commodity-like products, a strict transactional focus is attained and enforced by exploitation of competitive and transparency-enabling applications. For the purchasing staff at FMC and its subsidiaries, the benefits are obvious. All sourcing activities on one platform facilitate efficiency and enhanced control. Within FMC, the expectations of cost savings are enormous. For the suppliers, the benefits are less clear and the expectations a little more blurred.

8.4   ICT and institutionalized behaviour

As previously mentioned in this chapter, strategic change is very much about learning and adopting new behaviour. This is also valid when change is initiated through ICT exploitation. Organizing firm activities is largely about finding ways to make people behave according to certain patterns. From this perspective, understanding the power of ICT is basically about mapping practice (how processes are to be carried out) enabled by ICT. We divide processes into sets of activities and view how ICT can support the execution of these activities. In doing so, ICT enables the centre of an organization to make the periphery work according to its intentions (maybe also the reverse, depending on who is in charge of the tool), as illustrated by the case study of the Portuguese East-India Corporation in Box 8.2. Viewed in this way, ICT can be used as a tool to institutionalize new behaviour. When the new pattern of behaviour has become self-evident, something taken for granted, it can be labelled as institutionalized.[20] From a strategic change perspective, this may very well be the most important aspect of ICT. The creation of institutionalized behaviour answers to the need for, and inherent promise of, stability, coherence and efficiency that ICT can enable.

We have so far mainly addressed ICT and how it can institutionalize new behaviour. There is, however, another side to change and ICT as well. Most firms have a range of ineffective but institutionalized routines that, in order to increase the firm's efficiency and effectiveness, need to be managed. Such routines can be extremely challenging to deal with, since over time they seem to get built into firm structures. Thus, in addition to viewing ICT as a way to institutionalize, we would like to conclude that ICT can also be used as a means to *de-institutionalize* behaviour. For many firms, the purpose of exploiting ICT is to deal with such problems.

For example, in the model presented in Figure 8.2, mapping business relationships into post- and pre-purchase behaviour can open up a discussion on how ICT can support flows of information from a supply or purchasing perspective. Imagine

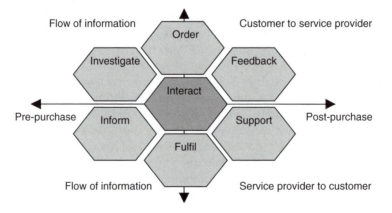

FIGURE 8.2   Mapping a business relationship from an order process view. Source: Adapted from Ford, D., Berthon, P., Brown, S., Gadde, L-E., Håkansson, H., Naudé, P., Ritter, T. and Snehota, I. (2002) *The Business Marketing Course: Managing in Complex Networks*, John Wiley & Sons: Chichester, p. 197. © John Wiley & Sons Limited. Reproduced with permission.

all the institutionalized activities that take place in day-to-day business activities and the potential of creating cost efficiency or automation of just a few of these. To understand ICT we thus need to explore how ICT supports us in mapping various phenomena and the ways in which the very mapping is done. For example, one can argue that ICT strengthens our abilities to make the periphery work for us, as in the case of the Portuguese East-India Corporation.[21] ICT makes it possible to move information fast and it maps phenomena in a compact and easily managed format. ICT is like a powerful energy enforcing the intellect and the body at the same time.

Supported by ICT, we can literally sit and boost competition or cooperation with spatially distanced actors. As in the case of the Portuguese East-India Corporation, supported by ICT systems we manage activities occurring far away from us. We manage processes at the same time as we can keep them at a distance. It is also clear that ICT in itself can build in dimensions that will foster disciplined behaviour. The conclusion is that every one of us, supported by ICT, could be his or her own 'manager' – regardless of whether it is a matter of a country, an army, a navy, a business system or a simple e-mail contact! Then it remains to be seen whether we all manage to get the pieces we move on the map also to move in real life, for example if we can discipline behaviour and make the periphery work for us.

There are important lessons to learn from this. By mapping day-to-day practice, management could provide directives for behaviour and design adequate behaviours and processes. Yet it also takes disciplined behaviour by staff all over the organization, the periphery, to move in the desired direction. The disciplined behaviour comes from defined work roles supported by 'carrots and sticks'. There are, of course, also several dangers in strongly forcing the organization to certain behaviours. It could make the organization and its staff less flexible: what does not fit into the designed ICT system is not possible to do and changing the design could take a long time and so on. Furthermore, the map may not be the best one; it could even be counterproductive. But when dealing with strategic change, the aspect of ICT, as discussed here, is a very central one.

8.5   Conclusion: ICT to enable developed sourcing capabilities

When using ICT to enable developed sourcing capabilities, there may be many managerial issues to consider over time. Some of these issues have a clear-cut answer, others do not. Some managerial questions are intriguingly loaded with both benefits and drawbacks – we can address them as balancing acts or managerial dilemmas. A number of these can be identified. We would like to conclude this chapter with a discussion that highlights three balancing acts regarding how ICT can enable developed sourcing capabilities.

Balance between making/buying the ICT capabilities

When entering ICT ventures, managers need to ask themselves: should we make or buy our IT applications? For many firms, large or small, there are problems associated with keeping IT development and support in-house and questions about what would happen if IT development were outsourced. As we see it, there is a need to manage a balance. For some firms the development of their own tailored systems is a possibility and for others it is not. For firms that, for various reasons, need specific or specialized applications, it can be necessary to search for capabilities outside the firm. In addition, the need for outside support can develop over time as applications become more complicated.

Balance between push and pull in implementation of ICT

The second balancing act that we wish to raise refers to what systems, applications and business models will be accepted/adopted by the suppliers and in what applications firms should invest in developing ICT support. Should firms move into ICT development in one giant leap or take a more careful, step-wise approach to ICT exploitation? What is it that determines the development pattern and pace? Are firms supposed to push their ICT development forward even if their business partners are not as ICT mature as one might wish, or are the suppliers or customers pushing the development? What is it that determines the speed of development in terms of ICT? Are our suppliers ready for a complete online relationship or should we balance the ICT exploitation? For what kind of relationships and events are ICT-enabled communication applications applicable? Questions on push and pull also bring forward considerations of to what extent ICT implementation should be customer/supplier centric, in the sense that firms should either adopt a push or pull strategy regarding the development of sourcing capabilities with the help of ICT tools. For many, the speed that some innovations have as they perform activities makes us believe that the speed of their diffusion will be the same. This is often not the case.

Balance between relational and transactional efforts

Finally, we would like to mention the balancing act between relational and transactional purchasing orientation. This issue has been raised in many different parts of this book, and seems to be central also in the discussion on ICT support. Even if there are such a plethora of opportunities associated with ICT exploitation, different applications, as we have shown, imply different things in terms of change. For example, applications like electronic reverse auctions can be a signal of a reorientation from a relational to a more transactional orientation. From a managerial perspective, the question to what extent ICT should be utilized to support a transactional or a relational orientation to business relationships can be brought up. As we see it, this balancing act and the others raised here are important strategic issues related to ICT exploitation.

Notes and references

[1] See for example the seminal article by Gordon Moore in which he observed the exponential growth in the number of transistors per integrated circuit (Moore's Law): Moore, G. (1965) 'Cramming more components onto integrated circuits', *Electronics*, Vol. 38, No. 8, pp. 114–17.

[2] See for example the preface of Kotler, P. (2003) *Marketing Management*, 11th edn, Prentice Hall: Upper Saddle River, NJ.

[3] Carr, N.G. (2003) 'IT doesn't matter', *Harvard Business Review*, Vol. 81, May, pp. 41–9.

[4] Tapscott, D. and Caston, A. (1993) *Paradigm Shift: The New Promise of Information Technology*, McGraw-Hill: New York.

[5] Wen, J.H., Chen, H-G. and Hwang, H-G. (2001) 'E-commerce web site design: Strategies and models', *Information Management and Computer Security*, Vol. 9, No. 1, pp. 5–12.

[6] Malone, T.W., Yates, J. and Benjamin, R.I. (1987) 'Electronic markets and electronic hierarchies', *Communications of the ACM*, Vol. 30, No. 6, pp. 484–97.

[7] *Information Week* (2000) '*Covisint's rough road*', August 7, pp. 42–50.

[8] Sinha, I. (2000) 'Cost transparency: The net's real threat to prices and brands', *Harvard Business Review*, Vol. 78, March–April, pp. 43–50.

[9] Smeltzer, L.R. and Carr, A. (2003) 'Electronic reverse auctions – Promises, risks and conditions for success', *Industrial Marketing Management*, Vol. 32, No. 6, pp. 481–8.

[10] Leek, S., Turnbull, P. and Naude, P. (2002) 'How is information technology affecting business relationships? Results from a UK survey', *Industrial Marketing Management*, Vol. 32, No. 2, pp. 119–26.

[11] Pramås, M., Ström, M. and Johansson, L. (2002) 'Gränsöverskridande produktutveckling med hjälp av Internet' (Collaborative product development supported by Internet technologies), Report no. 3006, IVF: Göteborg.

[12] State-of-the-art work on electronic agents can be found in the works of Pattie Maes, for example Maes, P. (1994) 'Agents that reduce work and information overload', *Communications of the ACM*, Vol. 37, No. 7, pp. 31–40; Maes, P., Guttman, R.H. and Moukas, A.G. (1999) 'Agents that buy and sell', *Communications of the ACM*, Vol. 42, No. 3, pp. 81–90.

[13] Information presented by a representative from Saab Automobile at a seminar for automotive suppliers in Eskilstuna, August 24 2004.

[14] Lancioni, R.A., Smith, M.F. and Oliva, T.A. (2000) 'The role of the internet in supply chain management', *Industrial Marketing Management*, Vol. 29, No. 1, pp. 45–56.

[15] Shapiro, C. and Varian, H.R. (1999) *Information Rules: A Strategic Guide to the Network Economy*, Harvard Business School Press: Boston, MA.

[16] Abrahamson, E. and Rosenkopf, L. (1993) 'Institutional and competitive bandwagons – using mathematical modelling as a tool to explore innovation diffusion', *Academy of Management Review*, Vol. 18, No. 3, pp. 487–517.

[17] Utterback, J.M. (1994) *Mastering the Dynamics of Innovation: How Companies Can Seize Opportunities in the Face of Technological Change*, Harvard Business School Press: Boston, MA.

[18] Rosenberg, N. (1994) *Exploring the Black Box: Technology, Economics and History*, Cambridge University Press: Cambridge.

[19] A conventional keyboard has the keys Q-W-E-R-T-Y as the top-left keys, hence the name QWERTY. An extensive description of the history and economics of QWERTY can be found in David, P.A. (1985) 'Clio and the economics of QWERTY', *American Economic Review*, Vol. 75, No. 2, pp. 332–7.

[20] Powell, W.W. and DiMaggio, P.J. (1991) 'Introduction', in Powell, W.W. and DiMaggio, P.J. (eds), *The New Institutionalism in Organizational Analysis*, University of Chicago Press: Chicago, pp. 1–38.

[21] Cooper, R. (1991) 'Formal organization as representation: Remote control, displacement and abbreviation', in Reed, M. and Hughet, M. (eds), *Rethinking Organization*, Sage: London, pp. 254–72.

Chapter 9

SUPPORTING CHANGE THROUGH PERFORMANCE MEASUREMENT

Björn Axelsson, Finn Wynstra and Frank Rozemeijer

'What gets measured, gets done' is a frequently repeated saying. Experts on strategic change emphasize the importance of goal setting and follow-up. In this chapter, we address this important aspect of strategic change and relate it to sourcing. The aspect of performance measurement, including review and reward, is a crucial one when considering strategic change in purchasing and supply management.

There is no self-evident answer as to what should be measured. Managers want to know whether a good job is performed well within the sourcing organization. But how could one trace and know that? Managers want to know whether there is progress in the change efforts. But how could one know that there really is progress being made? How could one know that a specific change initiative is developing in the desired way? What should be measured, how and why?

There is a general awareness that some measures could also be counterproductive. Measures could stimulate a nondesirable behaviour and consequently become a barrier to the desired change. Fortunately, some important new developments in the management accounting field are taking place, which maybe could help overcome some of these difficulties.

9.1   Measurement, change and motivation

Measurement is often used to follow up on performance. It has a control dimension: to monitor what has been done and achieved. The applied measurement systems could be more or less helpful and supportive, as is illustrated in Box 9.1. That same illustration also says a lot about the need for skilled people who design the systems as well as those who feed them and use them.

Box 9.1   Formula One racing and performance measurement

Over the last decades, Formula One motor racing has developed into one of the most competitive and expensive sports in the world. The participating teams (e.g. Ferrari, BMW-Williams, Toyota, Jordan) are spending lots of resources on finding ways to become a few hundredths of a second faster on the racing track. Performance measurement is extremely important in this sport.

In the 1950s, no contact was possible between driver and pit crew during the race, only afterwards. Often drivers drove around the racing track for hours without knowing their position, lap times or the condition of their car. Mercedes was the first team to introduce a so-called pit-to-car strategy, where the pit crew informed the drivers during the race with a number of cryptic hand movements about their position and other relevant information. In the 1960s, different teams started communicating with drivers during the race by using signs with information about position, lap times and pit stop strategy. Also, they started to communicate with the driver during the pit stop about the condition of the car. However, due to the great noise in the pit lane they could barely hear each other.

To solve this problem, in the 1970s Lotus introduced headphones to communicate with drivers during pit stops. This allowed them to exchange more information on racing strategy with the driver. In the 1980s Ayrton Senna, the former world champion, was one of the first drivers to use an intercom in his car. That enabled him to discuss performance and strategy with the pit crew during the race. He could ask questions like: What positions are my main competitors in? Can I come in for a set of new tyres?

In the 1990s, a new technology was introduced: two-way telemetrics. This technology enabled teams to send and receive data to and from the car during the race. Data engineers in the pit received technical data about the performance of the car during the race and they could modify the settings of, for example, the motor management system during the race. If the data indicated that the car became more unstable during braking, they could advise the driver to slow down a little on the corners.

Today, even more advanced sensor technology is used that should help the teams understand how race cars perform. The average race car is equipped with about 120 different sensors that continuously measure about 4500 variables (e.g. oil temperature, erosion of the motor, speed, fuel consumption etc.). Each lap on the racing track, the car sends 8MB of technical data to the pit crew. Engineers and pit crew members can use this accurate data, along with input from the driver, to modify the race car for better performance. However, due to new regulations, modification is no longer allowed during the race.

What can we learn from this case? First, it nicely illustrates that measurement is strongly related to increasing performance. Secondly, data gathering and interpreting should be done by professionals and not by the 'drivers'. Finally, performance measurement and communication are closely related to each other. The data becomes meaningful only when communicated to people who can do something with it (driver and/or engineer).

Measurements also have a function to draw attention to the figures and – on the next level – to the underlying causes of them. In addition, the measurements have a motivational function, both in relation to everyday operations and to specific change projects.

The obvious starting point for the manager (or anyone) who wants to change is to reflect on motivational issues. There seem to be a number of well-known conditions that have turned out to be rather stable over the past decades.

The first important aspect is that the change agent or the particular unit in focus for development perceives that a change is meaningful. The change and those affected need to be motivated, as there are always efforts connected with change processes. If the perceived meaningfulness is in place, positive energy is built up. This will in turn lead to action, which creates development. This will in its turn provide evidence that there are possibilities to influence the course of events (see Figure 9.1).

If the activities performed are measured and evaluated, the employee/unit gets feedback. The feedback will – if it goes well or the attempt is appreciated – give

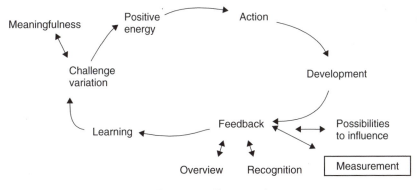

FIGURE 9.1   Change cycle.

recognition, otherwise merely attention. Feedback also provides overview and the possibility for learning. The loop can then continue for several turns as new challenges are composed. This is a simple model that holds plenty of common sense and can give certain guidance in connection with the initiation and realization of different kinds of change processes.

Given such a cycle, what is measured needs to qualify according to for example the following criteria[1]:

- *Valid* so that it measures the activities and events that are relevant.
- *Robust*, i.e. sufficiently stable to accommodate irregularities in order to enable comparisons over time.
- *Precise*, i.e. detailed enough to give the 'right' precision and be suitable as a basis for decisions.
- *Integrated* so that it captures the most important components for the process at hand.
- *Reasonable scale* to enable managers to distinguish 'better than', 'worse than' etc.
- *Economical* so that the costs of utilizing and capturing data are lower than the positive benefits from it.
- *Compatible*, so that the measures are comparable and exchangeable with other information within the organization.
- *Actionable*, so that the measures are understandable and help in pointing out further directions of action.
- *Behaviourally sound*, so that it does not stimulate counterproductive activities and efforts to circumvent the intended orientation of the activities.

These are some of the general demands put on measurement, and it may be a useful exercise to compare suggested measures with this list.

9.2   The rational planning model as a basis for goal setting

A typical goal-driven process looks very much like the sometimes criticized rational planning model (see Chapters 3 and 6), the point of departure for which is an analysis of a desired future state or position. It could be in a short-term perspective like one month, a quarter or similar and ranging to one year, three years and even five years and longer. Notice that the impressive development at IBM, described in Chapter 1, took seven years until the present performance had been reached.

The criticism of the rational planning model takes, among others, its point of departure from the fact that companies frequently express one desired goal and define the activities needed to reach it. Then, in practice, they tend to behave differently, as discussed in Chapter 3 on strategic change.

The typical steps in a rational planning process are the following ones[2]:

- *What have we done?* This means taking a view backwards, to see what has happened in the company as such as well in the purchasing and supply function. This provides some input into the identity of the firm and the respective functional units. Who are we and how have we become what we are? It should also give some hints on what is possible to achieve in the future: what kind of experiences do we have?

- *Where are we now?* This means that the firm and the purchasing and supply function tries to define its present state. It could among others be to clarify the role of sourcing in supporting the goals and visions of the firm as such, to consider the staffing and present work methods, to define the expenditure on various kinds of goods and services as well as suppliers, to define the present supply markets and so on. Such an analysis should make it possible for the firm to position itself, for example in the maturity model from Chapter 2.

- *Where do we want to go?* Based on a dialogue with, among others, corporate management and the most important internal users of the services provided by purchasing and supply, this step should result in some kind of goal setting. It could be aspects such as supporting the firm's ambitions to lower its leadtimes in relation to its customers. It could be to support, in the best ways possible, a process of lowering total costs for the products produced. It could also be to become an active partner in corporate product development. Or it could be to move from level 2 to level 4 on the purchasing maturity model (Chapter 2). Preferably, these ambitions should also be translated to measurable goals to facilitate the follow-up process.

- *How will we get there?* One important step here is to develop some kind of framework (or frameworks) that translates the goals and visions into measures to take. It could relate to ways of operating the purchasing business, for example going for more of a relationship than a transactional approach in relation to suppliers and supply markets (Chapter 4). It could thereby be a matter of reducing or decreasing the number of suppliers used in specific supply markets. Changes in internal interaction patterns and ways to interact with internal units within purchasing, as well as in relation to other functional units, could also be part of this step. Likewise, it could include identified needs for investments in new technology, new staff and so on.

- *How do we get it done?* This step takes it down to the activity level. Who should do what? When? Who is responsible for what? How do we make sure that we move in the right direction?

These steps actually relate to many of the other chapters of the book. An answer to the 'how' could, for instance, be changes in organizational structure (Chapter 5), capability building programmes (Chapter 7) or investments in ICT (Chapter 8). The purpose of the discussion here is to look more closely into the ways of following up, especially measuring the possible progress in purchasing and supply management operations.

9.3 The traditional measures applied to purchasing and supply management

One could make an overview of what is usually called the 'traditional' measurements of purchasing and supply management, as presented in Figure 9.2.

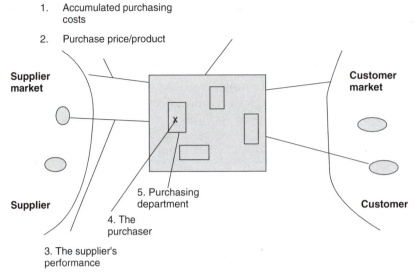

1. Accumulated purchasing costs

2. Purchase price/product

Supplier market

Customer market

Supplier

5. Purchasing department

4. The purchaser

Customer

3. The supplier's performance

FIGURE 9.2   Traditional measurement areas for sourcing activities. Source: Adapted from Axelsson, B., Laage-Hellman, J. and Nilsson, U. (2001) 'Modern management accounting for modern purchasing', *European Journal of Purchasing and Supply Management*, Vol. 8, No. 1, pp. 53–62. Copyright 2001, with permission from Elsevier.

We present and discuss these areas one by one in the following:

- Area 1, *accumulated costs for purchased goods and services* in relation to some kind of reference point such as in relation to last year, market index, intended goals and so on, has always been of interest to measure. It provides answers to questions related to the total spend in purchasing.
- Area 2, follow-up on *prices for individual goods and services* bought. Similar relations (to indices and so on) as above are applicable.
- Area 3, measuring the *performance of suppliers*. Traditionally three measures dominate: price development, quality rejects and delivery performance. But many more measures are possible. The three measures are used both in *a priori* evaluation of suppliers and as scorecards indicating the everyday operational development.
- Area 4, the *performance of the individual purchaser* (or team). Frequently used measures are indicators like the number of business deals done, the price development within the specific individual's (or team's) area of responsibility and so on.
- Area 5, the *performance and costs of the sourcing department*. This basically serves the purpose of comparing the costs of performing the sourcing job with the contributions. The latter are often captured in measures like price development, number of suppliers handled and so on. Also in this case several other performance indicators are possible.

These traditional measures still have a very strong position as a general follow-up on performance on a monthly, quarterly or yearly basis. Supported by ICT, it has become easier to capture data and also to make fast estimations and comparisons.

Thereby the steps from measurement to analysis and to action can be shortened. Their strong popularity is underlined by a recent field study, as presented in Box 9.2.

Box 9.2   Top ten of the most popular purchasing performance measurements in the US (2003)

1. Purchased item cost reduction.
2. Delivery on time.
3. Conformance to quality requirements.
4. Delivery time requirements achieved.
5. Cost measures.
6. Inventory.
7. Delivery performance overall.
8. Reduced inventory.
9. Return on investment.
10. Profit.

Source: Carter, P.L. (2003) 'Strategic measurement systems for purchasing and supply', *Proceedings of the 9th IFPMM Summerschool on Advanced Purchasing Research*, August 6–11, Salzburg.

For specific change initiatives this kind of measure could be very relevant, for example if the change aims at lowering prices on all or some specific goods and services bought. The underlying initiatives could include standardization of products used, aggregation of total volumes bought and directing the entire spend towards a limited number of suppliers, alternatively going for new sources.

In spite of their popularity, these traditional measures have been widely criticized.

9.4   The shortcomings of the traditional measures

In much of the modern view of purchasing and supply management, the traditional measures have been found to be counterproductive. If we refer to the purchasing maturity matrix again, the more sophisticated ways of operating seem to have, among others, the following three characteristics:

- An approach oriented towards *lowering total cost* as well as *contributing to the value-added* of the buying firm, not only by lower prices but also supporting differentiation efforts. This means that there is not just an interest in low price on the goods and services bought, but also in other costs (and possible value-added components) related to the purchasing and supply activities. It could refer to costs of quality as a consequence of poor quality, or costs of controlling quality, administrative costs related to how the purchases are done and so on.
- *One or two sources* for each function bought instead of many. This means a move from 'playing the market' towards a more long-term work mode. In the

latter case, the firm works together with one or two chosen suppliers during a longer time period: sometimes without having (extensive) possibilities to move to an alternative source. How can one be sure that the price paid is reasonable, in such a situation? The connection between price and value becomes much more complex.

- *Integrated problem solving* – not just in relation to external actors like suppliers involved, but also internally in cross-functional processes. The biggest potential to increase efficiency and effectiveness probably resides in the interface between several functions, for example in the interplay between purchasing specialists, construction engineers and business developers.

In light of this, most of the traditional measures will not provide value when confronted with the criteria for measurement presented above. They are relevant to support the less sophisticated ways of operating, but in relation to maturity levels 5 and 6 (maybe also 4) they could often hinder the desired way of operating the business. Referring again to the study from Box 9.2, we can see how this is reflected in the same sample of CPOs when asked about future measurements (Box 9.3).

Box 9.3   Most popular future performance measurements

1. Total cost throughout the supply chain.
2. Supply chain information availability.
3. Total cost measures.
4. Activity-based costing measures.
5. Total supply chain inventory levels.
6. Electronic commerce/EDI penetration.
7. Target costing requirements achieved.
8. Return on total supply chain assets employed.

Source: Carter, P.L. (2003) 'Strategic measurement systems for purchasing and supply', *Proceedings of the 9th IFPMM Summerschool on Advanced Purchasing Research*, August 6–11, Salzburg.

Most companies recognize the increasing importance of measuring total supply chain performance in contrast with measuring individual company performance. However, the appropriate models and metrics still need to be developed. This has been defined as a serious barrier, not least because of the strength of measurements. What gets measured gets done, but if what is measured are the things you do not want to be done, this is a serious shortcoming that could turn seriously intentioned initiatives into failures.

9.5   The promise of modern management accounting principles

Modern management accounting has, in general ways, addressed the problems indicated above. Much of that general development should be applicable to

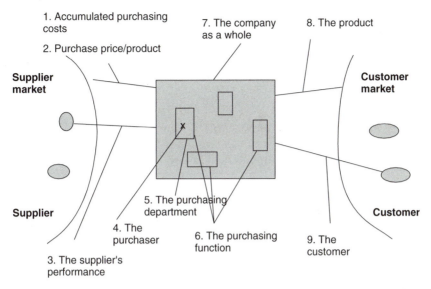

FIGURE 9.3 Additional measurement areas for sourcing activities. Source: Adapted from Axelsson, B., Laage-Hellman, J. and Nilsson, U. (2001) 'Modern management accounting for modern purchasing', *European Journal of Purchasing and Supply Management*, Vol. 8, No. 1, pp. 53–62. Copyright 2001, with permission from Elsevier.

purchasing and supply management. Those possibilities will be discussed below. Let us first present a picture showing the measurement areas that could be of interest; this overview is presented as an extension of Figure 9.2 (see Figure 9.3).

The most important development during recent years is an increased interest in measures related to the following areas:

- Area 6, the *sourcing function as a whole*. The purchasing specialists are just a part of all internal actors involved in the sourcing function (see Chapter 5). More integrated work modes call for adapted measurements. Desired insights into the real total costs of the operations and the values achieved call for new measures.
- Area 7, *sourcing as a function in relation to the company as a whole*. An interesting measure is purchasing's contribution to corporate value-added or to corporate profits. This is of course difficult to develop unequivocal measures of, but the more integrated the work modes and the more investments into sourcing, the greater the need for some kind of measurement and follow-up also on that aspect. Some very simple indicators could be total number of suppliers and/or total amount of the supplies that are bought in accordance with negotiated frame agreements. If the frame agreements in question are developed, based on certain theories of desired behaviour, these could be interesting indicators of progress (or the reverse). (In the case study of NCC in Chapter 12, this measure was very much in focus.)
- Area 8, *sourcing as a ratio of the specific product sold to customers*. How much is the own, internally produced value-added and how much is the contribution by outside sources? What impact does purchasing have on the success of each specific product?

- Area 9, *sourcing as a part of what it costs to handle a specific customer.* Most customers buy more than one product from a given supplier. The customers increasingly operate in line with a key account management approach. The same goes for suppliers. In such situations, the totality of what the one company buys from the other and what the supplier sells to the specific customer is in focus.

The desired new areas of measurement as well as new measurements in themselves find strong support in a number of modern management accounting techniques. Five of these will briefly be commented on below.

Balanced scorecards

The use of balanced scorecards is a method for measuring and targeting factors that are judged to create development power for the future. Based on one or a number of theories on what will create long-term success, management decides on what are the important indicators subject to follow-up. It could for example be the share of the staff with an academic background. The theory could indicate that people with such a background, on average, will be better fitted to understand complex business concepts and to better match the suppliers' competencies in relevant dimensions.

Open book accounting

The use of open books or cost tables means that customers and suppliers work with increased visibility of each party's cost structures. Production and other activities are jointly analysed and priced and alternative cost structures (activities) are discussed.[3]

Total cost of ownership (TCO)

TCO is about trying to identify all cost aspects of a product with related services that are exchanged between customer and supplier. These cost effects for the purchasing company could be ordering costs, stock-keeping costs, inspection costs, maintenance and so on. The accumulated effects over a product's lifetime are as completely as possible translated into financial figures. In this way the picture of the bought (and sold) products' total costs and values is built up. More about this method follows below.

While such an extensive analysis of the cost and performance of purchase items is appealing, there is substantial evidence, however, that purchase decisions are still often based on price.[4] The analysis of cost and performance differences of alternative offerings often faces problems such as lack of availability and the complexity of cost data.[5] One explanation for this is that many indirect costs associated with sourcing decisions can only be identified and reduced through collaboration with suppliers, which may take considerable effort and time.[6]

Activity-based costing (ABC)

ABC means that the costs to which a certain product or function leads are analysed and measured based on the activities performed and resources utilized. The costs of operating purchasing as well as other functions are connected to the relevant cost drivers. In this way efforts in time spent on supply market analysis, supplier assessments and so on become parts of the specified costs per product; the precision in the measurements becomes higher. This way, ABC could be an important tool for increased precision and provide an assembled picture of the effects of strategic efforts. ABC is often used as a method for calculating TCO.

Value analysis and target cost management

Given the fact that many cost and performance factors of products are locked in during new product development (NPD), this would be an obvious area for firms to invest time and effort for analysing the cost and performance of purchased parts.[7] Several tools and processes have been suggested for this type of analysis.

In *value analysis*, the attributes of products are assessed in terms of their functionality or performance, the costs associated with providing those attributes are calculated, and lower-cost alternatives are identified.[8] While value analysis may be applied to both existing and new products, value *engineering* regards the application of such analyses specifically in the context of new product development. Functional cost analysis (FCA) is derived from value analysis/value engineering (VA/VE) and focuses on costing the 'function' that products offer to customers.[9]

Target cost management (TCM) or target costing is a similar management accounting tool, aiming for optimal tradeoffs between cost, functionality and quality. However, this process starts from the objective of a *target cost*: a set amount of costs for a product (or, at lower levels, a part, component and so on) for which an optimal combination of quality and functionality should be achieved.[10] After setting the target costs, techniques like VA/VE, FCA, quality function deployment (QFD) and design for manufacture and assembly can be used to manage the tradeoffs.[11]

In essence, all of these NPD accounting methods may be applied to all kinds of parts and products, not necessarily only purchased products. However, as outsourcing of production and NPD tasks grows, they are increasingly often being applied to purchased items. The methods are widely used in the automotive and electronics industries; examples that, typically, are positioned on levels 4–6 in the maturity matrix (Chapter 2).

These five developments in management accounting can all be important building blocks in overcoming the shortcomings of the traditional measures and enabling the development of new ones. In a discussion of strategic change and movements towards more sophisticated ways of operating the sourcing function (stages 4, 5 and 6), new measurement techniques could play a significant role.

We think that two of these are more important in such situations than the others: the balanced scorecard and total cost of ownership. Therefore, they will be dealt with in more detail.

9.6 Balanced scorecards

Originally the balanced scorecard (BSC) developed by Kaplan and Norton pointed to four areas that should be subject to measurement: financials, customers, processes and learning and growth.[12] There were no specific measures of the purchasing and supply management activities, even though it was argued that these were part of the process or productivity measures.

The balanced scorecard model was developed as a reaction to the traditional measurement orientation towards historical events. Measuring turnover, profits and financial statements only reflects history. It would be more challenging to try to develop key indicators for future outcomes. The four areas identified served as a basis for the development of such indicators.

Within the purchasing and supply function itself, there have been several efforts to find relevant measures of future success. One is related to the education level of the staff of specialized purchasing managers. It could also be measurements of the satisfaction level of the internal customers, the users of the service supplied from purchasing. Another is to measure the number of frame agreements of a certain profile.[13] A third could be the number of suppliers. All these measures are based on some kind of theory that developments for good and bad of these figures would have an impact on future purchasing performance.

One important aspect of balanced scorecards is their fit with the overall competitive strategy of the firm. If for example the business strategy of the firm is cost leadership, which calls for operational excellence, the measures of most aspects of a BSC would be different from the situation with the business strategy being customer intimacy or product leadership (innovation). Relevant criteria for indicating good performance vis-à-vis customers could, in cost leadership, be their perception of price, in customer intimacy it could be customer value and in product leadership customer value plus speed of innovation. Similarly, relevant criteria for operations could be productivity for the cost leader strategy, return on R&D expenditure for the product leader and on-time delivery for customer intimacy.

Specific BSC measures for purchasing should, analogous to this, vary depending on the corporate business strategy as well as the theories of what will, in the future, create successful contributions from purchasing and supply management. These theories or frameworks could refer to areas such as people in purchasing, processes applied in supply chain management, relationships with internal customers as well as the structure of relationships with suppliers.

A recent study identified a number of barriers in the development and usage of balanced scorecards specifically in the area of purchasing and supply management (Box 9.4).

Box 9.4   Barriers in developing and implementing balanced scorecards in purchasing and supply management

Barriers during initiation and set-up

- Lack of commitment.
- Adverse support from consultants.
- Lack of top management support.
- Insufficient alignment.
- Lack of purchasing vision and strategy.
- Difficulties identifying strategic objectives and cause–effect relationships.
- Lack of completeness.

Barriers during roll-out and ongoing use

- Insufficient communication.
- Lack of sustainability.
- Lack of availability of performance data.
- Missing BSC reviews and reporting.
- Missing link between ownership and reward system.

Source: Wagner, S.M. and Kaufmann, L. (2004) 'Overcoming the main barriers in initiating and using Purchasing-BSCs', *Journal of Purchasing and Supply Management*, Vol. 10, No. 6.

A specific version of a balanced scorecard is the diagnostic toolbox developed in relation to the purchasing maturity model.

Purchasing maturity assessment tool

In order to be able to assess the level of purchasing maturity for its clients, Compendium (a Dutch consultancy firm specializing in purchasing) developed a purchasing maturity assessment tool based on Microsoft Excel™ software.[14] The underlying model is more or less comparable with the maturity model as described in Chapter 2. This model also consists of six stages, each describing a different level of purchasing maturity. The content of each stage is based on (academic) research and lessons learned from a large number of client projects.[15]

The assessment tool consists of seven different dimensions used to evaluate the different purchasing aspects of the company and especially of the purchasing organization. The dimensions used are the following ones:

- Strategy.
- Structure/organizational alignment.
- Sourcing.
- Supplier management.
- Steering and supervision.

Process	Phase 1 Transaction Orientation	Phase 2 Commercial Orientation	Phase 3 Purchasing Co-ordination	Phase 4 Process Orientation	Phase 5 Supply Chain Orientation	Phase 6 Value Chain Orientation
I. Purchasing Strategy						
a) What is the main message of your MD or CEO?	Keep the factory running; don't upset the business & ensure availability. Buy what is asked for!	Product related savings to bottom line; follow industry best practice & invest in better purchasing.	Idem phase 2 + operational improvement, and create synergy on corporate level & ensure more power on supply markets.	Idem phase 3 + purchasing is strategic function and should support the overall business objectives; purchasing is aligned to other business functions & strategies.	Purchasing source of competitive advantage. Supply chains and suppliers contribute to business success. Set breakthrough goals to stretch performance.	Purchasing & SCM source of competitive advantage. Value chains and suppliers contribute substantially to business success. Set breakthrough goals to stretch performance.
b) What is the bottom line of your purchasing strategy?	Buy what is asked for. Serve the factory. Ensure efficient ordering process & ensure availability.	Buy at the lowest price. Realize savings for limited % of total spend through competitive bidding.	Savings through synergy & lifecycle cost improvement. Bundling resources & volumes. Professionalize the purchasing function.	Buy at lowest total cost. Reduce TCO, cycle time and capital employed through cooperation with suppliers. Optimize the purchasing process through cross functional integration. Aim for product standardization.	Source at the world's leading suppliers. Supply chain optimization & continuous performance improvement; JIT (process performance).	Source at the world's technology leaders and aim at total customer satisfaction through efficient & effective value chains (e.g. value engineering).
c) Mainly operational/tactical/ strategic?	Operational planning	Operational/tactical planning	Tactical planning	Tactical/strategic– documented strategies	Strategic–formalized strategic supply chain planning	Strategic–purchasing strategy integral part of business strategy

FIGURE 9.4 Purchasing maturity assessment tool.

- Systems.
- Staff and skills.

In each dimension, there are five to nine questions describing the likely scenarios per stage of the maturity model. In total, there are 41 questions to be answered in order to get the overall score. Some of the questions of the strategy dimension can be found in Figure 9.4.

The consultant and/or purchasing manager will analyse the sourcing operations of the company and have it classified along these dimensions by ticking the answer that most fits with the current state of affairs. Once all questions are answered in this way, the Excel tool will automatically calculate the overall maturity score and the average scores per dimension. This forms the end result of the 'as is' analysis.

The next step is to determine the 'to be' situation on the same dimensions. This works the same as determining the 'as is' situation, only the questions are now answered from the perspective of what the sourcing function should look like three years from now, given the developments on customer and supply markets, corporate strategy, financial performance and so on. After all questions are answered, the tool automatically calculates the overall scores of both the 'as is' and 'to be' situations, and these are automatically illustrated by a maturity wheel diagram (see Figure 9.5).

This maturity wheel can be used as a basis for designing a purchasing development programme. It clearly identifies on what dimensions improvements need to be made in the coming three years. Based on this information, improvement actions can be defined and an action plan can be made. By performing an annual assessment, the tool can be used to keep track of the development programme. If no progress is being made in terms of purchasing maturity, corrective measures can be taken.

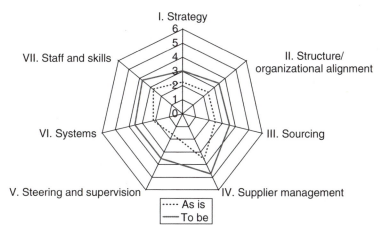

FIGURE 9.5   The maturity wheel diagram.

This tool is in line with the ideas from the balanced scorecard. It is a matter of developing a suitable framework and identifying what will drive future success, measure, follow-up and making necessary adaptations. This model could, however, be more detailed than a typical scorecard. In practice, therefore, it may be wise to differentiate between a corporate scorecard in which a very limited number of key indicators covering the purchasing and supply management area are present, and a more detailed scorecard covering the specific function, which could be useful to better track the development there. These areas are the cornerstones for reaching the desirable position in usually two or three years, and reassessment should be done constantly to evaluate progress.

9.7   Total cost of ownership

Considering total cost of ownership (TCO) instead of an exclusive focus on price is one of the most important aspects in strategic purchasing and supply management. However, it has proven to be quite hard to implement TCO systems for purchasing processes in practice. What could companies and specifically purchasing managers do to give total cost of ownership its appropriate place in the purchasing process?[16]

In a TCO approach the cost components are often divided into pre-transaction costs, transaction costs and post-transaction costs.[17] Figure 9.6 shows the most important cost components for each of these three categories. In general, all costs that are incurred by the purchasing company due to the influence of the purchase or use of an offering, including doing business with a certain supplier, need to be taken into account in TCO calculations.

The most important applications of TCO are in relation to:

- Outsourcing decisions.
- Supplier selection processes.

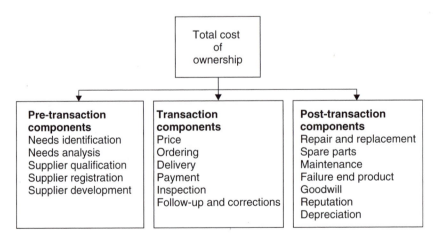

FIGURE 9.6   TCO components. Source: Adapted from Ellram, L.M. (1993) 'Total cost of ownership: Elements and implementation', *International Journal of Purchasing and Materials Management*, Vol. 29, No. 4, pp. 3–10. Reproduced by permission of Blackwell Publishing Ltd.

- Evaluating the performance of (current) suppliers.
- Structuring important (purchase) process changes.

Different levels of considering TCO in the purchasing decision making process can be identified:

1. *Just price:* as long as the product satisfies minimum requirements/specifications.
2. *Intuitively:* aspects other than price that differ between offerings are traded off against price differences, without objective information about for example quality.
3. *Informal:* similar to the previous level, but with objective information.
4. *Ad hoc:* the impact of differences in performance is calculated on a monetary basis occasionally and is project based.
5. *Formal:* a process has been laid down with a lot of available information and clear rules on when and how to apply TCO calculations.
6. *Monitoring:* similar to the previous level, but also including regular feedback concerning the TCO of the different purchasing items.

In general, most organizations appear to be on levels 2–4, which implies that there are possibilities for improvement. TCO looks very convincing as a way to come to an 'all-inclusive' cost estimate. As such it should be highly relevant in addressing the shortcomings of the traditional measurements as discussed above, but there are some important considerations to take into account.

Some considerations when applying TCO analysis

A common complaint about TCO is that calculations can easily become very sizeable and complex. That is why different methods are in operation. Roughly speaking, two alternatives exist: a monetary-based method and a value-based method.[18]

The best-known method is the monetary-based one, which allocates the costs of purchasing an offering (good or service) to the different cost components based on true costs. This is often done with management accounting methods such as activity-based costing. The monetary-based method is time consuming, but also precise and relatively easy to interpret. Based on such a detailed analysis, it is possible to derive a formula for future calculations, using the most decisive cost drivers (activities) and their accompanying costs. Such formulas could then be used to calculate the TCO of similar purchasing items (similar in the sense of comparable pre-transaction, transaction and post-transaction costs). This way, not every purchase needs to be analysed in detail and thereby much of the heavy work of operating such a system is overcome.

The value-based method combines monetary with qualitative performance information, which is harder to express in monetary terms. On the basis of nonmonetary, historical information, for instance vendor-rating scores of several suppliers, a total cost factor is calculated (see Box 9.5).

Box 9.5   Value based method of TCO calculation

Example: Electromotor, for application in the production process

Costs of nonavailability (hour)		€125	
Costs for energy use per hour (kWh)		€0.11	

	Brand A	Brand B	Max. score
Quality (lifespan, availability)	45	40	50
After-sales service	20	15	25
Delivery time, reliability of delivery	22	20	25
Total vendor rating score	87	75	100
Total cost factor	1.13	1.25	
[(100 − score)/100]+1			
Purchase price (€)	1250	870	
Lifespan (hour)	4000	3500	
TCO per hour	€0.35	€0.31	
[purchase price × total cost factor/lifespan]			

The value-based method is only suitable for a relative comparison between two or more alternatives. The absolute outcomes do not necessarily approach the true costs. After all, a supplier that scores 100% in the value-based method has a TCO that is the same as the purchase price. In practice, this will only hold true in extreme cases.

It should be clear that both the monetary-based method and the value-based method have their own strengths and weaknesses. Depending on the situation, as well as on the level of the purchasing company and the specific purchasing decision, one of the two methods will be more suitable. Box 9.6 summarizes the main tradeoffs for the choice between the two methods.

Box 9.6   Comparison of TCO calculation methods

Strengths	Weaknesses
Monetary-based method	
Number of factors/complexity can be adjusted to situation (flexible)	Time consuming
	Not useful for straight rebuys
Useful in identifying cost drivers	Not cost effective for small expenditures
Monetary formula-based method	
Easy to apply after initial development	Development of formulas time consuming
Effective for straight rebuys	Formulas require periodical adjustment
Value-based method	
Suitable for more qualitative aspects	Development time consuming

| Easy to use for straight rebuys | (Possible) subjectivity in determining weights |
| Uses the relative importance of existing performance criteria to determine weights | |

Source: Ellram, L.M. (1993) 'Total cost of ownership: Elements and interpretation', *International Journal of Purchasing and Materials Management*, Vol. 29, No. 4, pp 3–10.

When to use TCO analysis

It should be clear that TCO is neither suitable nor necessary as a supplier selection and appraisal method for all types of purchases. The monetary-based method is, as mentioned before, most suitable for financially important purchases. Deciding to carry out a TCO calculation is obviously also a tradeoff between benefits and sacrifices. As expected, TCO is applied most often for A items, placed in the upper half of the purchasing portfolio.

Besides that, TCO is also an often-used tool for the purchase of products that incur high indirect costs. For example, one could think of low-value consumables, which cause a lot of administrative costs, or machines and IT hardware demanding a lot of maintenance. In a more integrated sourcing operation with more customized solutions, for example in the form of augmented services, this is likely to become a more common case.

It is noteworthy that TCO is not used that much for purely product-related purchases like components and semimanufactured goods. One of the reasons is likely to be the larger inherent complexity; the TCO of a specific semi-manufactured product might be hard to calculate if this is used in different end products, and even in different ways.

Conditions for a successful and sustainable implementation of TCO methods

It proves to be very hard to implement TCO methods structurally and explicitly in the purchasing process. A few basic conditions appear to exist that could support such an implementation.[19]

Initial success, review and reward

Initial successes with TCO calculation are very important in creating commitment for such a review and reward system. These successes are in general important to make people believe in an effective use of TCO.

The review and reward system in place appears to be important as well. Research done with Dutch purchase and maintenance managers has shown that a number of factors affect managers' preference for expensive (in terms of purchase price) but more higher-value products (in terms of cost savings).[20] As might be expected, managers subject to a system rewarding price savings have a preference for lower-cost (in terms of purchase price) offerings, and managers subject to a system prioritizing TCO savings have a preference for higher-priced, higher-value offerings.

That said, it is noticeable that only a few companies explicitly review and reward based on TCO reduction.[21] In Europe, purchasers are (still) rarely discretionarily rewarded based on specific performance, in contrast to for example the US. If a discretionary reward exists, this is often based on a generic parameter such as profitability. The problem is that these kinds of general incentives are not that effective:

> In our bonus programme ... there is a company profitability part, a business unit profitability part, and there are specific personal targets. And we see that the personal targets are much more appetite-whetting than the profitability targets. (Director Purchasing Services, European chemical company)

This demonstrates that it is not only important to develop and utilize relevant methods of measuring the 'real' outcome of the business as such. Changes in such performance measures also call for changes in review and reward systems.

Quality of experience with TCO calculations

Before the first successes are achieved and review and reward systems are implemented based on TCO indicators, it is a prerequisite for the TCO calculations to be deemed to be relevant and sufficient. Furthermore, one needs to gain experience in setting up these calculations. An important factor in the quality of TCO calculations is the adequacy of the information used. Only if the information is adequate will people really use TCO calculations, for instance in reviewing and/or selecting an offering. Adequacy can be mainly related to two factors: availability and reliability.

An important way to increase the quality of TCO calculations is gradually to build up experience. As those calculations for different purchase items are executed more often, the calculations usually get more complete and reliable. Furthermore, creating the calculations becomes easier, which will reduce the costs of applying a TCO calculation.

Management support and sourcing maturity

Subsequently, management support is required to build up experience, not merely support from the purchasing and supply function, but also from general management. It is interesting that it seems that general management will only support an initiative aimed at TCO implementation if the company's purchasing function is ready for this; the purchasing function needs to have developed into a strategic and cross-functional-oriented process.[22] General management thus clearly has a role in supporting TCO initiatives, but will only do this if the sourcing function is sufficiently positioned for this.

In summary, one can argue that implementing a more TCO-oriented sourcing process is a matter of purposively guiding and supporting the creation of knowledge and experience, in combination with offering adequate (monetary and nonmonetary) incentives.

9.8 The quest for nuanced and differentiated measurements

It is evident that not all purchasing organizations should operate in the same way. Likewise, it is clear that not all goods and services should be bought according to the same principles. There is always a need for contingent approaches. This is also something that one should bear in mind when designing measurement systems and specific measures.

Furthermore, not all stakeholders in a firm need the same information. The latter is clearly illustrated in a recent study presented in Box 9.7, which argues that purchasing managers should differentiate in their communication about purchasing performance. The CEO is interested in different indicators than the CPO.

Box 9.7 Measurements adapted to various stakeholders

Measurement needs of the CEO (in ranked order)

1. Quality of purchased items.
2. Key supplier problems that could affect supply.
3. Supplier delivery performance.
4. Internal customer satisfaction.
5. Purchase inventory dollars.
6. Purchase cost savings.

Highest-rated measurements by CPO (in ranked order)

1. Price negotiations resulting in cost savings.
2. Use of leverage through combining volumes.
3. Past delivery performance.
4. Monitoring of delivery performance.
5. Quality and continuous improvement of supplier.
6. Department budget vs actual expenditures.

Source: Fearon, H.E. and Bales, B. (1997) *Measures of Purchasing Effectiveness*, Focus Study, Center for Advanced Purchasing Studies: Tempe, AZ.

The measurements should, as mentioned, also be adapted to the specific commodities bought. In this context, the purchasing portfolio can be used as a point of departure to discuss what kinds of key indicators and accounting techniques should be best fitted to the respective purchasing situation.[23]

For *routine products*, one can think of two purchasing approaches. One is to work according to a short-term, 'spot-market' approach. The other is to try to build the basis for a systems approach to such goods and services. This is to reduce handling costs and processing time; the selected suppliers provide a complete system ('one-stop shopping').

Suitable performance measurement approaches for the first alternative are to make comparisons against price indices, historical prices and so on (in line with areas 1 and 2 in Figure 9.2). The second alternative becomes more complex, but is definitely a situation fitted for some kind of TCO analysis.

Leverage products could be bought from several sources and are costly. A change in price could have significant effects on total expenditure. For such products, competitive bidding is often a recommended way of operating the business.

For such products several measurements could be relevant. One is to make a detailed breakdown of the components and activities that are inherent in the product. Such analysis could be used to set new targets based on 'should-cost' approaches. Of course, other market-based comparisons are also possible.

Strategic products represent high values but also high risks. Often suggested ways to handle such supply markets are to go for a partnership approach to enable a continuous development dialogue and to make sure that the supplier really understands the important aspect of today's and future business. Suitable techniques could be to model the total cost also across supply chains in line with the total cost of ownership and target costing principles described above.

Critical products represent low values but high risks. Also in such situations partnership strategies are appealing. Suitable accounting techniques include total cost of ownership and target costing, not least with a focus on lifecycle analysis.

The measurements mentioned could be complemented by other chosen indicators reflecting theories of progression, as discussed in relation to the balanced scorecard and the various areas of measurement as presented in Figures 9.2 and 9.3. In practice, many companies seem to work with brief indicators of performance, something that has been labelled 'catch-all' variables. The reasoning is for example that the suppliers that are able to deliver on short leadtimes are generally very capable. Therefore, the simple measure captures a broader range of capabilities.

9.9   Best practices

A recent study in the US investigates a number of companies in various industries to identify today's best practice when it comes to measurement of purchasing progress and performance.[24] According to these findings, purchasing performance measures must be:

1.   Aligned vertically with corporate goals and horizontally with SBU and other functional units.
     - Poor = No clear links between purchasing and corporate goals.
     - Good = Purchasing measures and targets are directly linked with other functional units, e.g. engineering, marketing etc.
2.   Comprehensive, reflecting both quantitative and qualitative measures.
     - Poor = No or few purchasing measures are reported.
     - Good = Multiple purchasing measures exist and reflect all critical quantitative and qualitative objectives of the firm.

3. Dynamic, with stretch goals.
   - Poor = No targets/goals are set.
   - Good = Targets/goals are set, reflecting commodity-specific opportunities and incorporating improvement relative to prior year.
4. Transparent and broadly communicated objectives and mandate.
   - Poor = Goals for purchasing are not communicated with the broader organization.
   - Good = Critical measures are transparent so that all individuals who can effect (and be affected by) change can make good decisions.
5. Tied to performance-based compensation.
   - Poor = Measures are not reviewed and used.
   - Good = Incentive compensation is tied to critical performance measures.
6. Backed up with an appropriate level of organizational resources.
   - Poor = No resources are devoted to developing performance measures.
   - Good = Resources are made available to develop measures, benchmark, set targets and report. Savings are measured relative to clearly defined, valid cost baselines.
7. Backed up with appropriate systems support.
   - Poor = Systems do not support tracking of performance metrics.
   - Good = Systems are capable of reporting on most key performance metrics.
8. Championed by strong leadership.
   - Poor = Leadership dedicates no time to the performance measurement process.
   - Good = Cost reductions are tracked and tied to financials at a purchased category level.

These are some general aspects of good ('world-class') and poor performance as far as measurements of general everyday activities are concerned. We think, however, that the same criteria for good management accounting practices should also apply in relation to strategic change.

9.10   Conclusion

In this chapter, we have addressed yet another important area of purchasing management and strategic change. Performance indicators play a significant role because of their visibility. It is therefore important that they are carefully selected, utilized and interpreted.

We have seen that there are a number of important criteria that should be met and that there are numerous possible measurements as well as many possible areas in which measurements could be done. With the increased information possibilities, it may be tempting to measure as much as possible, but that is not very wise. In practice, it is therefore important to select a limited number of indicators that could be altered and adjusted, and used over some time in order to make it possible to detect patterns of progress.

Strategic sourcing directors, CEOs and management groups in general should pay due attention to this aspect of the development of the purchasing and supply management function. No or too few measurements will not fully leverage the possibilities of using performance measurement in the drive for strategic change. Wrong measurements will be a strong force taking the organization in the wrong direction. Only a reasonable mixture based on an understanding of the specific business, the visions of it and relevant frameworks of how to get there will make this force a constructive one.

Notes and references

1 Axelsson, B. (2004) 'Inköp – en komplex funktion som kräver anpassad styrning', in Samuelsson, L. (ed.); *Controller handboken*, Svenskt Näringsliv Förlag: Stockholm, Chapter 19.

2 Kotter, J.P. (1996) *Leading Change*, Harvard Business School Press: Boston; Anderson, J.C. and Narus, J.A. (2003) *Business Market Management: Understanding, Creating, and Delivering Value*, 2nd edn, Prentice Hall: Upper Saddle River, NJ.

3 Nilsson, U. (2004) *Product Costing in Interorganizational Relationships*, PhD thesis, JIBS Dissertation series, No. 19, Jönkoping International Business School, Jönkoping.

4 Lehmann, D.R. and O'Shaughnessy, J. (1974) 'Difference in attribute importance for different industrial products', *Journal of Marketing*, Vol. 38, April, pp. 36–42; Håkansson, H. and Wootz, B. (1975) 'Supplier selection in an international environment – An experimental study', *Journal of Marketing Research*, Vol. 12, February, pp. 46–51; Lehmann, D.R. and O'Shaughnessy, J. (1982) 'Decision criteria used in buying different categories of products', *Journal of Purchasing and Materials Management*, Vol. 18, No. 1, pp. 9–14; Anderson, J.C., Thomson, J.B.L. and Wynstra, F. (2000) 'Combining price and value to make purchase decisions in business markets', *International Journal of Research in Marketing*, Vol. 17, pp. 307–29; Monczka, R. and Morgan, J. (2000) 'Competitive supply strategies for the 21st century', *Purchasing*, 13 January, pp. 48–59.

5 Ellram, L.M. and Siferd, S.P. (1998) 'Total cost of ownership: A key concept in strategic cost management decisions', *Journal of Business Logistics*, Vol. 19, No. 1, pp. 55–84; Plank, R.E. and Ferrin, B.G. (2002) 'How manufacturers value purchase offerings: An exploratory study', *Industrial Marketing Management*, Vol. 31, pp. 457–65; Wouters, M.J.F., Anderson, J.C. and Wynstra, F. (2005) 'The adoption of total cost of ownership for sourcing decisions – A structural equations analysis', *Accounting, Organizations & Society*, Vol. 30, No. 2, pp. 167–91.

6 Dubois, A. (2003) 'Strategic cost management across boundaries of firms', *Industrial Marketing Management*, Vol. 32, No. 5, pp. 365–74.

7 Berliner, C. and Brimson, J.A. (1988) *Cost Management for Today's Advanced Manufacturing*, Harvard Business School Press: Boston, MA; Cooper, R. and Slagmulder, R. (1997) *Target Costing and Value Engineering*, Productivity Press: Portland, OR; Davila, A. and Wouters, M. (2004) 'Designing cost-competitive technology products through cost management', *Accounting Horizons*, Vol. 18, No. 1, pp. 13–26.

8 Miles, L.D. (1961) *Techniques of Value Analysis and Engineering*, McGraw-Hill: New York; Cooper and Slagmulder (1997) *opere citato*; Morgan, J. (2003) 'Value analysis makes a comeback', *Purchasing*, Vol. 132, No. 18 (20 November), pp. 41–4.

9 Yoshikawa, T., Innes, J. and Mitchell, F. (1995) 'A Japanese case study of functional cost analysis', *Management Accounting Research*, Vol. 6, pp. 415–32.

10 Kato, Y. (1993) 'Target costing support systems: Lessons from leading Japanese companies', *Management Accounting Research*, Vol. 4, No. 1, pp. 33–47; Tani, R. (1995) 'Interactive control in target cost management', *Management Accounting Research*, Vol. 6, No. 4, pp. 399–414; Tani, T., Okano, H., Shimizu, N., Iwabuchi, Y., Fukuda, J. and Cooray, S. (1994) 'Target cost management in Japanese companies: Current state of the art', *Management Accounting Research*, Vol. 5, No. 1, pp. 67–81; Ellram, L.M. (2000) 'Purchasing and supply management's participation in the target costing process', *Journal of Supply Chain Management*, Vol. 3, No. 2, pp. 39–51.

11 Cooper, R. and Slagmulder, R. (1999) 'Develop profitable new products with target costing', *Sloan Management Review*, Vol. 40, No. 4, pp. 23–33; Dekker, H. and Smidt, P. (2003) 'A survey of the adoption and use of target costing in Dutch firms', *International Journal of Production Economics*, Vol. 84, pp. 293–305.

12 Kaplan, R.S. and Norton, D.P. (1992) 'The balanced scorecard – Measures that drive performance', *Harvard Business Review*, Vol. 70, No. 1 (January–February), pp. 71–9; Kaplan, R.S. and Norton, D.P.

(1996a) 'Using the balanced scorecard as a strategic management system', *Harvard Business Review*, Vol. 74, No. 1 (January–February), pp. 75–85; Kaplan, R.S. and Norton, D.P. (1996b) *The Balanced Scorecard – Translating Strategy into Action*, Harvard Business School Press: Boston, MA; Kaplan, R.S. and Norton, D.P. (2000) *The Strategy Focused Organization – How Balanced Scorecard Companies Thrive in the New Business Environment*, Harvard Business School Press: Boston, MA.

[13] Telgen, J. (2004) 'Inkoopcontrol, compliance en de Telgen box', in Santema, S. (ed.), *Inkoop voorbij 2004: een spiegel voor de toekomst*, NEVI: Zoetermeer, pp. 141–50.

[14] In 2004, Compendium was taken over by AlfaDelta and the name was changed to AlfaDeltaCompendium. The original parts of the assessment tool are used with its permission.

[15] Among others, Rozemeijer, F.A. (2000) *Creating Corporate Advantage in Purchasing*, PhD thesis, ECIS/Technische Universiteit Eindhoven: Eindhoven; Van Weele, A.J. (2005) *Purchasing and Supply Chain Management – Analysis, Strategy, Planning and Practice*, 4th edn, Thomson Learning: London; Monczka, R., Trent, R. and Handfield, R. (2005) *Purchasing and Supply Chain Management*, 3rd edn, South-Western/Thomson Learning: Cincinnati, OH.

[16] This section is largely based on Wynstra, F. and Hurkens, K. (2004) 'Total cost and total value of ownership', in Essig, M. (ed.), *Perspektiven des Supply Management: Konzepte und Anwendungen*, Heidelberg: Springer, pp. 463–82; Wynstra, F., Hurkens, K. and Van der Valk, W. (2004) 'Total cost en total value of ownership', in Santema, S. (ed.), *Inkoop voorbij 2004*, NEVI: Zoetermeer, pp. 77–92.

[17] Ellram, L.M. (1993) 'Total cost of ownership: Elements and implementation', *International Journal of Purchasing and Materials Management*, Vol. 29, No. 4, pp. 3–10.

[18] Ellram, L.M. (1995) 'Total cost of ownership: An analysis approach for purchasing', *International Journal of Physical Distribution and Logistics Management*, Vol. 25, No. 8, pp. 4–23.

[19] *Ibidem*.

[20] Anderson, J.C. and Wynstra, F. (2004) '*Purchasing higher-value, higher-price offerings in business markets*', internal working paper, Kellogg School of Management: Evarston, IL.

[21] Wouters *et al.* (2005) *opere citato*.

[22] *Ibidem*.

[23] Ellram, L.M. (1996) 'A structured method for applying purchasing cost management tools', *International Journal of Purchasing and Materials Management*, Vol. 32, No. 1, pp. 11–20.

[24] Carter, P. (2003) *Managing for Bottom Line Impact: Purchasing and Supply Strategic Performance Measurement*, Collaborative McKinsey and CAPS Research study, presented during the IFPMM Summer School in Salzburg.

Chapter 10

COPING WITH INDIVIDUALS' RESISTANCE TO CHANGE

Marc Reunis, Sicco Santema and Frank Rozemeijer

Probably every purchasing manager is familiar with the employee who just won't change. Sometimes it is easy to understand why: the employee might fear losing his or her job, not want to learn new skills or not look forward to join a new team. On most other occasions employee resistance is more difficult to understand. This chapter deals with the effects of individual behaviour on strategic change processes and how change leaders can anticipate or react to this. The importance of individual behaviour in such processes was already briefly mentioned in Chapter 2. Individual purchasers or buyers can play an active role in realizing change, a passive role or even actively resist change. The latter will be even more strongly demonstrated in Chapter 11 and – to some extent – in Chapter 12. A better understanding of possible individual reactions to a change initiative, and the underlying reasons, may help the change leader to better manage the process. The purpose of this chapter is therefore to explore the effect of individual behaviour on the process of strategic change and to derive some lessons for managing individual behaviour. The different concepts that are introduced in this chapter will be illustrated by the TradeRanger case. This case describes how a number of companies in the oil and chemicals industry developed and implemented an e-procurement tool.

10.1   Concepts of individual behaviour

How people react to change initiatives depends on their individual perspective. Depending on the functional role and position they have in the organization, they will have a different perspective on the world around them. For example, people working in purchasing will probably have a different perspective than people working in marketing or research and development. The influence of a change initiative on future job performance predicts to a large extent the individual reaction. For example, if a corporate ICT change initiative will lead to increased information accuracy for a buyer, it is more likely to yield compliance from that buyer. The key question is: what's in it for me? (see also Box 10.1).

Box 10.1   TradeRanger case – the importance of the individual perspective

Back in 2000, a group of companies from the oil and chemical industry decided to initiate a vertical Web portal connecting buyers and suppliers to streamline operational procurement processes. The Web portal was called TradeRanger. A considerable amount of organizational change was required by both buying and supplying parties to implement this Web portal. For example, legacy systems needed to be linked to the portal, processes needed to be redesigned and headcount needed to be reduced.

Within one of the participating oil companies, the early stages of the change process were accompanied by a great deal of uncertainty. In this case, the attitudes and behaviour of the various stakeholders differed considerably according to individual perspectives. Examples include data analysts who had some reservations about the amount of additional work in data alignment, data cleansing and standardization. While the analysts and IT personnel were worrying about more or tedious work, the operational purchasers were anxious about the lack of work and becoming redundant. The purchasing managers had a more positive attitude, as they envisioned the savings potential and increased process control. However, their colleagues in the business did not see the need for such a 'purchasing' project. Tactical purchasers were more concerned with the consequences for their responsibilities (e.g. effects on the supply base and the effort required to get suppliers on board). Overall, they were quite positive and willing to adapt, as they recognized the potential benefits for their own job performance. Finally, the project team had a strong focus on 'pushing' spend through the system, even when it was clearly not beneficial. Spend coverage was set as a key performance indicator for this project. In short, each stakeholder had their own biased perspective on the project and consequently showed different attitudes and behaviour.

The TradeRanger case shows how different individual perspectives can result in different reactions to a change initiative. An important aspect is the degree of freedom that the individual experiences in the change process. Individuals like to change but do not want to be changed. A certain behavioural change can vary from entirely voluntary to completely mandatory:

- Spontaneous or emergent change is based on the initiatives of individuals who want to change their personal situation. A supportive environment in which learning and personal development is stimulated can lead to these individual initiatives.

• Individuals can also be forced to change. In this situation they must decide to conform or not. Individuals make their own rational and irrational tradeoff before they decide on their course of action. This also includes the possibility for an individual to show behaviour that deviates from the desired direction.

For the remainder of this chapter we consider the situation where a change initiative starts with a goal that is formulated by the change leader. We adopt a managerial perspective of an individual change leader trying to realize change through influencing the behaviour of others.

The question of why people behave as they do and how this behaviour can be influenced is one of the central questions in the field of psychology. A *behaviourist* and a *cognitive* approach can be identified. Behaviourism aims at describing and explaining individual behaviour without any reference to mental events or to internal psychological processes. Behaviour is what you see and what actually happens in reality. On the other hand, cognitive theories primarily focus on the recognition of mental events and psychological processes. We argue that individual behavioural change implies a cognitive process. This process encompasses individual filtering of external input (e.g. an announcement to change the purchasing process made by the change leader). In order to develop effective interventions for a change leader, it is therefore important to address the underlying mental mechanisms that determine how the external input is filtered. In the next paragraphs, the cognitive approach is further explained by using the theory of reasoned action and the theory of planned behaviour.

10.2 A framework for behaviour

The theory of reasoned action (TRA) is an important contribution to the understanding of cognitive mechanisms.[1] This theory builds on the premise that humans are rational beings who process available information and based on that determine their behaviour. In short, TRA claims that individual behaviour is a function of the intention to perform a specific behaviour. In turn, the intention is determined by a person's attitude and the normative pressure as perceived by that person. All other variables are regarded as 'external' and only have their influence through attitudes and social norms. TRA is a valuable model for explaining individual behaviour, though its applicability is limited because of its underlying assumptions. The greatest limitation stems from the assumption that behaviour is under volitional control. The theory only applies to behaviour that results from a conscious thought process using the information at hand. Irrational decision making, habits or any other behaviour that is not consciously considered cannot be explained by TRA.

To overcome this limitation, the theory of planned behaviour (TPB) was developed.[2] This theory added the concept of perceived behavioural control (i.e. people's perceptions of their ability to perform a given task) to the TRA. Perceived behavioural control is determined by all factors that may facilitate or impede the behaviour performance. To the extent that it is an accurate reflection

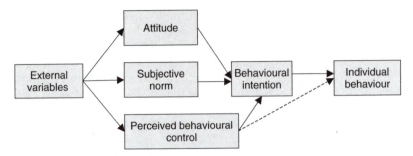

FIGURE 10.1   Theory of planned behaviour (TPB).

of actual behavioural control, this can, together with intention, be used to predict individual behaviour. The TPB model is shown in Figure 10.1.

Based on the TRA and TPB, scholars have developed more specific explanatory models for individual behaviour. For example, a model aimed at explaining the acceptance and adoption of various ICT tools (e.g. adaptive structuration theory, technology acceptance model, e-procurement adoption model, unified theory of technology acceptance and use).[3]

The TPB model is very suitable for the general discussion of individual behaviour in change processes, especially in situations where the change is not initiated by the individual, but by 'external variables' (e.g. a change leader). The TPB model can be used to explain how individuals will react to these external variables, how they influence the 'behavioural intention' and eventually the 'actual behaviour'. Below, we will discuss the four variables that according to this model determine the behavioural intention: attitude, subjective norm, perceived behavioural control and external variables. Each of the variables will be illustrated using the TradeRanger case.

Attitude

Attitude refers to an evaluative system of objects, people or events, reflecting a certain feeling. Attitudes include cognitive components (e.g. opinion or belief) and affective components (e.g. an emotional statement). An attitude is based on personal predispositions and a set of values and beliefs. Attitudes are focused towards a specific domain or application. For a specific situation like a change initiative in purchasing, individuals create an attitude based on their personal perception of the situation. Perception is the process of organizing and interpreting the sensory impressions in order to give meaning to the environment. Attitude is recognized as an important determinant of individual behaviour (see Box 10.2).

People tend to strive towards consistency between their behaviour and their attitude, even in retrospect. If a behavioural intention fails to materialize, the directed attitude will be diminished. For example, if a person does not attain a certain position, he or she reacts as if the job was not attractive anyway. This striving for consistency between two or more conflicting attitudes or between behaviour and attitude is often referred to as cognitive dissonance. The degree of importance, influence and reward determines the degree to which the dissonance is reduced.

Box 10.2   Attitude in the TradeRanger case

In the TradeRanger case, individual attitudes also explain a large part of the actual behaviour. For example, the operational purchasers whose jobs were jeopardized by the implementation of the Web portal showed quite passive behaviour. Their attitude was relatively indifferent towards the change and they reluctantly accepted the outplacement schemes of their company. This lack of spirit was quite a contrast with certain members of the project team, who showed great enthusiasm. They put in an extra effort supporting and convincing other stakeholders to realize the change objective, especially by addressing barriers and acute issues. They showed more energy than would be expected solely based on their personal situation.

Another example of a situation with limited explanatory power for behaviour was the case of superusers. These individuals were specifically trained in using detailed functionalities of the previous ERP system. Their job would become much easier with the new system, thus a positive attitude and behaviour could have been expected. However, the new system included their specific expertise and consequently was a threat to their expert power. Their attitude was therefore hardly positive at all. Concluding from these examples, it seems that attitude formation is the result of a highly personal interpretation of the situation at hand.

Subjective norm

The social context has an influence on individual behaviour. People look towards each other to determine what appropriate behaviour is. This is especially true in an organizational setting where individuals have to work with each other. People tend to copy the behaviour of their direct colleagues. In the TPB, these social influences are captured in the 'subjective norm'. This variable refers to the social pressure to engage (or not to engage) in a certain behaviour as perceived by a person. Here, normative beliefs of referents and motivation to comply play a role (see Box 10.3).

Box 10.3   Subjective norms in the TradeRanger case

Social influences played a role in the TradeRanger case. For example, peer pressure was notable between the members of the project team. A true sense of competition emerged between project members concerning the supplier adoption and the increasing of spend through the system. Peer pressure was also prevalent in other working groups. Joint attitude formation occurred through gossip, close interaction and influential opinion leaders. In the case, the negative peer persuasion seemed stronger than positive efforts to create buy-in of user groups. More general effects of the social norm were noticeable in the effects of the increased control. The system made all orders and actions visible to the organization and process control increased through automated approval schemes. This had a 'Big Brother' effect on the purchasers involved. They did not appreciate the fact that their boss was able to look at every turn and move they made. Overall, the case showed that social context and subjective norm had a substantial influence on individual behaviour.

Social influences are incurred from the social context, which is a subjective norm by nature. The composition of the social context comprises the direct working environment and the organizational context of a purchasing individual. The most salient referent does not necessarily have to be a formal work-related connection – that is, superior – but could be informal contacts. The latter can be just as – or even more – persuasive.

An important stream in behavioural science is directed towards the influence of the social networks on individual behaviour. Determinants of individual behaviour related to social networks include:

- Network position (i.e. embeddedness or connectiveness).
- Interactions in the network (i.e. all kinds of communication and persuasion strategies).
- Characteristics of the network (i.e. size, composition, cohesiveness and power distribution).

The specific individual may, thus, be connected to surrounding networks of social contacts. He or she could have a more or less central or marginal position and varying power positions. Such positions influence the behavioural intentions. In communication theory applied to marketing, this is utilized by the marketer and the technique is to identify opinion leaders and try to convince them in order to have them convince others in the next phase. In change processes, not least in relation to purchasing, various network connections and positions as well as opinion leaders may play crucial roles. It could be worth considering where to put the most energy in order to achieve the most influence.

Perceived behavioural control

Perceived behavioural control refers to people's perceptions of their ability to perform a given behaviour. This ability depends on personal capabilities and environmental restrictions (see Box 10.4). The individual's intellectual and physical capacities limit their ability to perform specific tasks. Naturally, not all intellectual and physical abilities are relevant for a specific behaviour, but only a subset that is related to a specific task. Training and education can increase the task-specific abilities.

Some subjective factors that influence the perception of control are:

- Personal attributes (e.g. personal locus of control, perceived scope of influence or the personal level of confidence).

- Changing tasks and responsibilities (can cause some reservations about the perceived behavioural control).
- Uncertainty (complicates the individual assessment of perceived behaviour control).
- A large degree of ambiguity in the change process can lead to increased hesitation, due to the uncertain required behavioural control.

Box 10.4   Perceived behavioural control in the TradeRanger case

In the TradeRanger case, perceived behavioural control also played a role. One of the objectives was to change the purchasing job profile towards one group of more tactical and another of more strategic orientation. This resulted in anxiousness among some purchasers due to the uncertainty of being able to perform the more strategic tasks. A small group was enthusiastic to further develop themselves, while the majority showed some reluctance or proved to be unable to make the change. In these instances, the behavioural control was internally limited.

Examples of external factors limiting the behavioural control were also prevalent in this case. For instance, when the first user group started getting their initial experience with actually using the new system, they found that the ease of use and the usefulness surpassed their expectations. This led to overenthusiasm. They expressed the need for using the system in a wider application domain – that is, for more suppliers and commodity groups – and they also wanted more functionalities. The system development and roll-out were still in progress and both the organizational processes, systems and suppliers were unable to fulfil their needs at that point. Here, the behavioural control was externally limited.

External variables

The external variables determine the three intermediate variables of the TPB model: attitude, subjective norm and perceived behavioural control. Behaviour and behavioural change are submitted to and affected by the direct and indirect influence of the organizational context. A special category of indirect behavioural influence is the corporate culture or, in other words, a company-specific set of standards of acceptable and nonacceptable behaviour. Many authors have stressed the importance of culture in organizational change. The receptiveness of an individual towards a change initiative could be the direct result of the organization's 'climate' for change. One should be aware of the fact that subcultures might exist and that they can deviate from the dominant organizational culture. The people working in the purchasing function as a subgroup could have specific cultural stimuli or impediments. Thus, a company is rarely one culture, it consists of several: professional groups, teams, business areas and so on. A general awareness of this could help the change leader be prepared for relevant interpretations and actions.

The organizational context also imposes other constraints on the individual abilities. For example, several prerequisites might be necessary to conduct certain behaviour. In the case of strategic change, a budget requirement and the mandate of top management are likely to play a role. Other constraining factors can be found in the regulatory, administrative or hierarchical systems of the organization. Furthermore, in Chapter 8 we emphasized the role of ICT to enable, govern and restrict individuals' behaviour. In general, rules and resources can both confine and facilitate the individual ability to perform certain behaviour. Besides formal sources of control, people can cultivate other sources of power, like expert or referent power, which can be utilized to enable certain behaviour.

Managerial implications

The TPB can act as a frame of reference for the change leader to derive possible interventions to change individual behaviour. The TPB provides a means of predicting and explaining individual behaviour by modelling the behavioural mechanisms that take place within the mind of an individual. Interventions should be directed towards the key variables influencing the cognitive mechanisms (e.g. attitude, subjective norm, perceived behavioural control and external variables). However, these elements are not easily calculated. Therefore, the mere awareness of them will support more relevant interpretations and will probably contribute to more adequate actions.

10.3   Managing individual behaviour

In this section, we adopt a managerial perspective towards changing individual behaviour in the purchasing function. Managerial action as performed by the change leader is regarded as an external variable in the TPB.

Interventions aimed at people's attitude

In order to successfully change people's attitude, interventions of the change leader should be aimed at the underlying beliefs of the people involved. Interventions should focus on:

- *Cognitive dissonance.* The implications of the cognitive dissonance theory for managing change are apparent: it provides the means to influence and predict the propensity of attitude and behavioural change.
- *Motivation theory.* Motivation theory is directed towards establishing, influencing and aligning individual motivation and change goals. It provides a foundation for many current managerial practices and is a powerful change tool. Motivation is the willingness to exert an effort towards a goal, because the effort has the ability to satisfy an individual need. The individual need is an internalized state that makes certain outcomes attractive and causes a stimulation or drive to achieve these outcomes. This drive can lead to a specific attitude. The focus on individual needs can be applied by:
  - *Goal setting.* There is little dispute in research about realistic and challenging goals leading towards motivation.

- *Reinforcement.* This has a high predictive power for work-related performance factors. Negative reinforcement or punishment is effective in the short term, while positive reinforcement (i.e. bonus and rewards) can yield more enduring changes in behaviour. The NCC case (in Chapter 12) will provide an illustration, for example of how much and how fast the obedience to frame agreements increased when that became a part of business area managers' bonuses.
- *Expectation management.* Expectancy theory shows that people act depending on the attractiveness of the expected outcome to the individual. Modern motivation theory tends to pinpoint the individuals' ability to develop themselves as a motivation factor.[4] If the work or change process in question can support or build expectations in line with the individual's visions in realizing his or her 'life project', it is likely to support positive attitudes towards the proposed change.

Interventions aimed at the subjective norm

Interventions affecting the subjective norm also provide measures to change individual behaviour. Interventions should focus on what referents are salient in a given situation and changing the perceptions of normative beliefs or the motivation to comply with these beliefs. Singling out employees as opinion leaders or acting as a role model are possibilities to influence a subjective norm. However, part of the subjective norm remains out of reach for the change leader. For example, it is very difficult for the change leader to influence the spreading across the organization of his or her change message. Each individual is likely to interpret, assimilate and forward a biased view of this change message. In addition, a subversive message can simultaneously be spread, resulting in a group deviating from the change objective or showing open resistance.

Interventions aimed at perceived behavioural control

Interventions directed towards increasing individual perceived behavioural control can provide the prerequisites for behavioural change. Two strategies can be applied:

- Constraining factors (e.g. budget, regulations and systems) can be lifted.
- Capabilities and competencies can be developed to raise the behavioural control, for example through training and education. Specific training for purchasing can focus on developing the necessary competencies for a purchasing professional (e.g. negotiation or analytical skills).

Managerial implications

Specific efforts and dedicated resources directed towards positive attitude formation and the social processes strongly determine if the project leads to a smooth and efficient change process. A clear change strategy enables a better execution of projects in terms of time and costs and is easier to translate into specific objectives. The clarity also ensures a better understanding and limited anxiety on an individual level, thereby leading towards a higher individual buy-in (see Box 10.5).

Box 10.5   Managing individual behaviour in the TradeRanger case

In the TradeRanger case, efforts at managing individual behaviour were especially prevalent in the phase of creation of buy-in. Besides the preparatory set-up of the change organization, with a multifunction, high-level steering committee and project team, directed approaches were also initiated to create buy-in. A specific method related to attitude formation and the subjective norm was to organize special design sessions attended by the internal key people responsible for a certain account and several representatives of the supplier. Together a customized process was designed on how the new marketplace could be used, with respect to the order flow, degree of digitalization and, most importantly, the responsibilities. These design sessions had an iterative character and lasted until the first transaction was successfully performed. The – sometimes difficult – social process of creating consensus resulted in a balance of the various individual interests. At the end of the session an action list for all parties was agreed on in a 'go live plan'. The result of this approach was a raising of the collective attitude: a high level of commitment of the individual stakeholders, and consequently a relatively high degree of effective activity after these design sessions. Support for the project team in realizing the commitments encouraged the perceived behavioural control, as well as sufficient budgetary space.

We have discussed a general mechanism of individual behaviour and ways to intervene in the underlying variables. The outcome, however, is not guaranteed. A change initiative might be confronted with varying degrees of opposition. This can range from some initial hesitation or procrastination to open and blatant resistance or even sabotage. In realizing change it is important to address these types of resistance effectively. Understanding, identifying and dealing with individual resistance are discussed in the next paragraphs.

10.4   Individual resistance

A managerial influence on individual behaviour implies a situation of subjected change. Through interventions, change leaders stimulate people to change their behaviour in a certain way so that it fits with a given change objective. Not every set of interventions directly leads towards the desired behaviour. On the contrary, a whole spectrum of reactions ranging from active participation to subversive resistance or even sabotage might be the result. In reality, individuals naturally defend the status quo if they feel that their security or status is threatened. They have their own agenda, which can deviate from the agenda of the change leader. Resistance is therefore an inevitable response to any major change initiative. It makes up an important part of managing change, since the occurrence is widespread and the effect on the overall project success can be quite substantial. Nearly every change leader will have encountered situations where resistance caused delay, complication or even failure of the project, even when the change project was well prepared and, in the end, beneficial for the company. Understanding, recognizing and addressing resistance are therefore important parts of managing change.

Understanding resistance

Resistance can be viewed from three different perspectives:

- Resistance as behaviour (e.g. an undesirable act or action).
- Resistance as an emotion (e.g. a certain feeling, like aggression or frustration).
- Resistance as a belief (e.g. a cognitive resistance resulting from unreadiness or reluctance to change). This implies that not the new situation itself but the path towards this new situation causes distress. Emotional resistance could be the result.

Each of these three conceptualizations of resistance focuses on a part of the experience that an individual has in response to change. The elements are intertwined, for instance both the cognitive and emotional part can precede the behavioural resistance.

Resistance can be defined as any conduct that serves to maintain the status quo in the face of pressure to alter it. This definition implies that not all resistance is a direct and open confrontation, but that there are gradations of resistance. Also, not all resistance is a conscious effort to obstruct change. Some types of resistance are less harmful and can be inherent to dealing with humans. Individual interpretation, assimilation, personal bias and reaction mechanisms like procrastination, indecisiveness, doubts or human error are examples of natural impediments in human change processes. The degree to which resistance can influence the progress of a project depends on the type of resistance. The following classification criteria can be used for resistance:

- Direct vs diffuse.
- Visible/open vs invisible/closed.
- Rational vs irrational/emotional.
- Influential vs noninfluential.
- Conscious vs subconscious.
- Active vs passive.

The most severe form of resistance is a conscious, active and influential form, where a direct confrontation is pursued with the intent to inflict damage to the project (i.e. sabotage). This can be either visible or invisible and based on both rational and irrational grounds. This radical form of resistance is likely to be an escalation of more moderate types of resistance that are not effectively addressed. Some such resistance elements are also described and indicated in Chapter 11 and in the NCC case in Chapter 12.

Recognizing resistance

In order to cope with resistance, one first has to recognize it. It is important for the change leader to identify the symptoms as early as possible. There are many different symptoms of resistance that might occur. To be able to recognize the basic symptoms of resistance, the following list might be useful[5]:

- *Creating false commitment or paying 'lip service'.* This is the case when an interest or commitment is expressed and not acted on. This includes agreeing verbally but not following through.
- *Mobilizing an informal network.* This means that negative gossip is spread, projected risks are amplified and initial failures are leaked to outsiders. Besides exaggeration, stigmatizing or ridiculing can also take place. Subversive gossip does not have to be limited to the change objective but can also take on a personal form, for instance by discrediting the change leader. Also, the advantages or process can be openly questioned.
- *Increasing complexity of the change.* By causing delays at every possible time, significant harm can be inflicted on a change project. For example, the 'prolonged argument', where discussion is continued about every possible explicit and implicit assumption to delay a decision process. Other examples include hammering on increased detail and the accuracy of a 'business case', introducing the need for a 'governance model', asking for second opinions or benchmarking studies.
- *Stimulating in the wrong direction.* People can purposefully interpret the change direction in a different way and actively support a deviated path. Also, energy can be applied to peripheral areas of a change project where the likelihood of success or the contribution is limited.
- *Creating scarcity.* By priority setting, the time invested in a change project can be limited. For instance, urgent matters concerning a client can always get a higher priority, especially at crucial moments in a change project. In addition, other organizational resources can be limited, like management time, financial resources, information, personnel, space or production capacity.

Box 10.6 Resistance in the TradeRanger case

After a long period of development and pilot testing, in April 2002 the first successful purchasing transaction was made through the TradeRanger system. Immediately, the main focus shifted towards scaling up the use of the system (i.e. increasing the number of suppliers and catalogues in the system, raising the utilization level of the operational buyer or people responsible for calling of orders). This shift of focus led to several types of resistance. Due to practical reasons, not everybody could be included in the design session, as mentioned in Box 10.5. This resulted in some operational buyers feeling that their valuable input was not used or was even being ignored. These buyers kept holding on to their usual way of working and simply refused to use the new system. The development and pilot testing phase did not help: 'What's the rush now, they have been developing and testing for years and suddenly they are in a hurry.' Any failure from the system was picked up by the buyers as proof that the old way of working was much better, which they used as a justification for their passiveness. Milder variants of resistance also occurred, like using the system ineffectively by still calling the supplier when an order was placed using the new system, or making an ERP order as well as registering it on the system. Less harmful were the cynical remarks and initial reluctance, where people finally, grudgingly, complied with the new way of working.

Picking up symptoms of resistance as early as possible is important. However, a note of caution must be made here. The notion that anyone who questions the need for change has an attitude problem is not true. Change leaders often perceive resistance negatively, and employees who resist are viewed as being disobedient and obstacles for the organization to overcome in order to achieve the new goals. However, in certain instances, employee resistance may play a positive and useful role in organizational change. Insightful and well-intended debate, criticism or disagreement does not necessarily equate to negative resistance, but rather may be intended to produce a better understanding as well as additional options and solutions. Initial symptoms should therefore not be misinterpreted by the change leader.

10.5   Managing individual resistance

Managing individual resistance starts with preventing resistance occurring through continuous attention to the underlying causes of resistance.[6] However, when resistance does occur, attention should be shifted towards preventing escalation or mitigating the effect. In both situations the change leader should address the causes of resistance rather than the symptoms.

Causes of resistance

There are many reasons why individuals might resist change. Since the early 1950s many researchers have attempted to identify and classify the causes of resistance. Some primary causes of resistance include:

- Lack of clarity and ambiguity in the nature of the change.
- Forces deterring individuals from changing.
- Degree of pressure.
- Interference with personal interests and/or interests of established institutions.
- Having to learn something new.

In many cases, people do not disagree with the benefits of the change initiative, but rather they fear the unknown and doubt their ability to adapt to the new situation. Also, people might fear that they will not be able to develop the skills

TABLE 10.1   Categorization of resistance factors

Category	Resistance factor	Link to TPB element
Psychological or emotional	Fear of the unknown	Attitude
	Low tolerance	Attitude
	Lack of management attention	Subjective norm
	Lack of trust in others	Subjective norm
	Need for security	Attitude
	Wish for 'status quo'	Attitude
Social	Ward off outsiders	Subjective norm
	Group solidarity and mutual dependence	Subjective norm
	Clash with current value system	Subjective norm
Cultural	Lack of motivation for innovation	Attitude
	Working culture not open to change	Subjective norm
	Different cultural backgrounds	Subjective norm
	Type of change does not fit with the organizational culture	Subjective norm
Organizational	Threat to the existing power/relationships	Subjective norm
	Change conditions (available resources)	Perceived behavioural control
	Perception of the change conditions and change experience	All
	Lack of skills	Perceived behavioural control

Source: Adapted from Cozijnsen, A.J. and Vrakking, W.J. (1992) *Organizational Diagnosis and Organizational Change* (in Dutch), Samson: Alphen aan de Rijn.

and behaviours required in the new work setting. In some cases, people feel mistreated and want to 'get even' to restore a perceived injustice.

More causes for resistance can be identified. A concise listing can provide a basis for understanding the concept. A quite common and prevalent categorization of causes of resistance is based on the sources of barriers to the desired behaviour. The following categories can be distinguished: psychological or emotional, social, cultural and organizational. Table 10.1 shows several examples of causes of resistance in each of these categories. They are also linked to the variables of the theory of planned behaviour.

To prevent resistance, the causes have to be diagnosed. The change leader should understand the state of mind of the people who are involved in the change project. The most salient factors that relate to a person's state of mind are facts, beliefs, feelings and values. Specific measures for preventing or addressing these causes of resistance can be derived from the TPB model:

- Attitude measures (e.g. provide clarity about the process, provide security, provide a fit with the status quo and use motivation techniques).
- Social norm measures (e.g. increase management attention, increase group dependence, communicate a clear value system/norm, create competition and joint design sessions).
- Perceived behavioural control measures (e.g. increase available resources, facilitate organizational support, helpdesk, manuals and development programmes for skills).

In some situations, the causes of resistance develop from a relatively harmless type to a more damaging type. This depends on the ability of the change leader to recognize these causes at an early stage and cope with them. Specific actions can be taken to counter resistance and prevent escalation. Again, the TPB model can be used to derive actions:

- Attitude measures (e.g. persuasive communication, negotiation, more coercive methods).
- Social norm measures (e.g. stimulating peer pressure, broad communication, competition).
- Perceived behavioural control measures (e.g. quick feedback of results, performance measurement and transparency).
- Measures related to (the effects of) the external environment (e.g. benchmarking and setting examples).

Box 10.7   Managing resistance in the TradeRanger case

For the specific task of creating buy-in and managing resistance, change management functions were established. These functions were responsible for the communication plan, acquiring feedback, demonstrating, training and organizing the design sessions. Besides measures of internal marketing, stimulation and facilitation of the required change, specific measures were developed to address the resistance of end-users to using the TradeRanger system. First of all, suppliers were included in the process of raising usage levels, by only accepting orders through the marketplace. At a later stage more of these controlling measures were introduced (e.g. performance reporting tools).

Although these measures effectively addressed the symptoms of resistance, the underlying causes were pretty much ignored. At a certain point the overflow of feedback culminated in a conflict in which project team and operational buyers were blaming each other for various faults. Also, the project team was accused of having too narrow a focus on increasing the spend coverage of the system, and the appointed change managers were leaving their locations too soon. The resulting counterproductive energy had to be addressed by the change leaders and a different approach towards creating buy-in was adopted. The change leaders showed a more personal approach and became more service oriented. Issues were split into 'need-to-haves' and 'nice-to-haves' and more time was scheduled to discuss issues with operational buyers and secure their input. This resulted in a more cooperative approach from the operational buyers and the roll-out continued more smoothly.

10.6   Discussion of underlying principles of individual behaviour

Using the TPB model to understand individual behaviour has its limitations. Although it is a straightforward way of deriving managerial actions, it does not model the dynamic nature of behaviour. In addition, it also neglects the underlying psychological principles that govern individual thought and action. In the discussion about resistance, we have briefly touched on these aspects and they will be further explored in this section.

The dynamic nature of behaviour

The TPB is a static model. In reality, however, behaviour has a dynamic nature, with constant feedback loops and historical influence playing important roles. The historical influence on behaviour can be a result of previous experiences directly or indirectly related to the change. A general wariness or agitation can be the result of previous negative experience with a comparable change initiative. In the short term, direct feedback of a certain act is an important determinant of new action in the same or in a different domain. The change of behaviour as a result of feedback or experience is the core concept of learning.

Underlying psychological principles governing individual thought and behaviour

The TPB assumes rational behaviour. However, behaviour cannot be solely explained by rational reasoning and also includes irrational components. Emotional, cognitive and unconscious mechanisms can strongly interfere with rational behaviour and, at times, cause totally opposite behaviour than one would logically expect. The principles underlying the irrational part of behaviour are difficult to grasp. However, since they take up an important part of everyday behaviour, they should always be kept in mind.

People can be in exactly the same situation, yet perceive and process it differently. The way in which a situation affects individual attitude is subjected to *individual filtering*. Perceiving and interpreting the environment can be burdensome and individuals have therefore developed techniques to make perceptions and predictions rapidly and provide the basis for their behaviour. They use shortcuts and only a selection of the possible inputs based on interest, background, experience and attitudes. These selective perceptions are not foolproof and can result in some flaws, like judging on a single characteristic (halo effect), overemphasizing a previous encounter (contrast effect), one's own characteristics attributed to another (projection), generalization and stereotyping. Also, mental models of reality might be simplified in order to extract essential features without capturing the full complexity of a situation. This is called bounded rationality, which was briefly introduced in Chapter 3.

The selective perception is based on an individual's *frame of reference*. This frame of reference is built up from a repertoire of tacit knowledge that is used to impose structure on, and impart meaning to, otherwise ambiguous social and situational information to facilitate understanding.[7] These highly individual cognitive structures serve as implicit guidelines to behaviour. Many authors have further developed the notion of frames of reference and used terms like cognitive maps, frames, interpretive schemes, mental models, paradigms or scripts.

Several *individual characteristics* play a role in shaping perception and influencing the individual filtering process. First of all, an obvious and widely recognized set of influences is related to biographical characteristics such as age, gender and marital status. Secondly, personality traits are relevant. At the basis of these traits lies personality, which is a difficult concept describing the way an individual interacts with their environment. Personality is determined by heredity, cultural environment and situational factors. It is very difficult to identify and isolate personality traits. However, to provide some explanatory power or means of classification, clusters are used like the widely applied Myers-Briggs Type Indicator (MBTI) with the following dimensions: extraversion, agreeableness, conscientiousness, emotional stability and openness to experience.

On a more fundamental level, personality has been studied extensively in psychology. The Freudian approach towards personality builds on the notion that it is shaped as the human mind learns to cope with raw impulses and desires. In the process of maturation these are banished to the unconscious, thus creating a reservoir of repressed impulses and painful memories that can threaten to erupt at any time. An adult person deals with this reservoir in a variety of ways (i.e. *defence mechanisms*). Some of these defence mechanisms, which provide explanatory power to the irrational part of human behaviour, are shown in Table 10.2.

The discussion of dynamics and irrationality is an addition to the mechanistic approach of the TPB. It does not dismiss the TPB, but can add to our understanding of why certain behaviour occurs or not. It can be used to further enhance managerial practice.

Managerial implications

The dynamic nature of behaviour has some important implications for managing change. It provides the justification for utilizing learning mechanisms to develop behaviour over time. In addition, it recognizes the importance of previous experience and history. Change leaders should be well aware of the influence of experience on individual behaviour.

Also, the irrational part of behaviour, with the influence of individual filtering, frames of reference, individual characteristics and defence mechanisms, has to be

TABLE 10.2   Classification of Freudian and neo-Freudian defence mechanisms

Defence	Brief explanation
Repression	'Pushing down' unwanted impulses and ideas into the unconscious
Denial	Refusal to acknowledge an impulse-evoking fact, feeling or memory
Displacement	Shifting impulses aroused by one person or situation to a safer target
Fixation	Rigid commitment to a particular attitude or behaviour
Projection	Attribution of one's own feelings and impulses to others
Introjections	Internalizing aspects of the external world in one's psyche
Rationalization	Creation of elaborate schemes of justification that disguise underlying motives or intentions
Reaction formation	Converting an attitude or feeling into its opposite
Regression	Adoption of behaviour patterns found satisfying in childhood in order to reduce present demands on one's ego
Sublimation	Channelling basic impulses into socially acceptable forms
Idealization	Playing up the good aspects of a situation to protect oneself from the bad
Splitting	Isolating different elements of experience, often to protect the good from the bad

Source: Adapted from Morgan, G. (1986) *Images of Organization*, Sage: Thousand Oaks, CA. Reprinted by permission of Sage Publications, Inc.

kept in mind. The discussion of (ir)rationality in this paragraph underlines the notion that the personality of the individuals and the specific situational context have a great influence on individual behaviour. To illustrate what this means, we will discuss the typical behaviour of different purchasing roles.

10.7   Individual behaviour in different purchasing roles

A great deal of knowledge on the way in which different people behave in different situations has been generated from behaviourism research. For the purpose of this book the typical behaviour of a few distinct roles is dealt with. These roles are often involved in various types of change in the purchasing function. The following roles are discussed: operational, tactical and strategic purchaser, and (middle) management.

Operational purchaser

In general, operational purchasers tend to have the following behavioural characteristics:

- The majority perform an administrative function and have a lower level of education. This might contribute to a passive nature: they do not want to be bothered with high-level process design and conceptual models, but just want to fulfil job expectations.
- They can be quite sceptical of anything that comes from the top and prescribes what to do.
- In a role change, some operational purchasers are willing to develop themselves towards more value-added functions; however, they might be limited by their own capabilities. If a change implies decreased control and limited freedom (e.g. in choosing suppliers) it is not appreciated.
- The operational purchasers tend to be reasonably susceptible to the opinion of peers and the 'gossip' factor therefore plays an important role. Enthusiastic first movers can thus be utilized effectively to convince the other operational purchasers in a nonthreatening way to be 'one of them'. Hierarchical pressure has also been proved effective.

Tactical purchaser

In general, tactical purchasers tend to have the following behavioural characteristics:

- An important concern for the tactical purchaser is the supply base for a specific commodity group. Therefore, the tactical purchaser is very anxious about possible changes in the relationship with the suppliers.
- Certain aspects of the job can be highly appreciated and add to job motivation (e.g. the fun of negotiation, personal contact with suppliers or closing deals).

When these are affected, this could result in resistance. The personality of the tactical purchaser might be one that is focused on this particular way of working (e.g. a real negotiator, focused on getting every penny out of the deal, or a trader, with a feeling for timing and the supply market).

- They might feel that they 'own' certain relationships with suppliers and will have difficulty letting them go. This is especially applicable when the supplier provides the tactical purchaser with few perks or if they have a long professional relationship with the supplier.

Strategic purchaser

In general, strategic purchasers tend to have the following behavioural characteristics:

- The strategic purchaser has a concern for how the purchasing function can be designed and operated to serve the company and its goals. In general, the strategic purchasers tend to be among the first people in the organization to be convinced about change efforts, for example electronic support and automation of the purchasing function.
- Personal 'ownership' of a project and a personal vision are very important for people's own performance and the way other roles can be motivated. Striking a balance between business and purchasing goals includes organizational politics. Strategic purchasers feel comfortable with dealing with cross-functional interaction.
- Often many purchasing initiatives will take place in the purchasing function at the same time and periodical activities, like renegotiating contracts, sourcing projects or preparing performance reporting, can take up a lot of capacity. The evaluation of certain e-ordering initiatives does not stand by itself, and the strategic purchaser naturally relates it to other initiatives and existing change programmes.

(Middle) management

In general, (middle) managers tend to have the following behavioural characteristics:

- They like quantifiable benefits, business plans, risks and investments. Compared to the other roles, managers tend to be risk averse, be sceptical about business cases and have a limited interest in business support functions (like purchasing).
- Middle managers tend to have local concerns, be highly sceptical about general approaches and are difficult to convince of the purchasing function. Other concerns, outside the border of the purchasing function and organization, are also included in an attitude to change, for instance, the importance of keeping everything quiet in the organization, other reorganizations or other external influences. Management has a much more external focus than all the other roles.

- The disposition towards purchasing and the position of purchasing in the organization influences the perceived importance by management. The management priority among initiatives, (hidden) agendas and commitment also plays a role in a priority-setting project. Even when top managers are convinced, they will have to free up resources and management time. An initiative overflow can take place, when many good ideas for the organization suffer from limited attention and resources.

Employees in different functions, roles and situations perform different tasks, each having specific role-related behaviour. These specific behavioural characteristics provide additional insight for managing individual change in different roles. Interventions derived from the TPB model can be refined for the specifics of a certain role and thus become more effective for the individual involved.

10.8   The change leader as an individual

We noticed above that among other things, resistance from those subject to change isn't always negative. Resistance could be based on a different analysis and highly relevant to take into consideration. In many change processes the change leader is not prepared to apply such open-minded views. The change leader has thought through all the 'why', 'what', 'how' and by 'whom' in the change process, preferably together with other members of the leading coalition (compare the discussion from Kotter in Chapter 3). There is a tendency for resistance to be interpreted as something negative: it disturbs the nicely designed route of change.

It is important for change leaders that they too could be analysed and understood and interpreted by the same models as the 'followers' (compare the discussion of leaders and followers in Chapter 6). Ultimately this means that their individual behaviour is a result of behavioural intentions, which in turn are related to attitude, subjective norms and perceived behavioural control. Furthermore, there is an influence of external factors such as the triggers to change from outside the change agent.

Basically, the change leader could benefit from carrying out some kind of analysis, or at least reflect on what factors could have influenced him or her. If so, questions like 'Why do I consider this a destructive resistance instead of an effort to make me better informed?' could lead to secondary thoughts like 'Well, I am so much influenced, without being aware of it, by the way we used to do it at my previous job. Maybe this is genuinely different after all.' The same principle goes for all aspects of a change process. In the NCC case in Chapter 12, some differences in perceptions, some biases of interpretations based on different frames of references and some actions based on other rationalities are described.

Many change leaders rarely pause to contemplate; often they are more inclined to move on with the change process than to reflect deeply on their own behaviour. However, in order to become more effective in complex change processes, it might be wise to do so. Executive coaching can be a way to slow down these change leaders and let them gain awareness and become aware of the effects of their words and behaviour on their employees.[8] Executive coaching consists of highly personal one-on-one question-and-answer sessions between coach and manager, usually lasting several months. If done properly, executive coaching can help change leaders to reduce their destructive behaviours and become more effective in aligning individuals to collective goals.

10.9   Conclusion

In this chapter, the role of individual behaviour in change processes has been dealt with. The importance of this perspective is substantial, since individuals' behavioural change is necessary to effect changes in the purchasing function. Based on this simple notion, the individual perspective is relevant in practically any change domain and provides the key to realizing a change objective. Therefore, not surprisingly, the individual plays an important role in nearly every other chapter in this book.

This chapter has clarified some of the concepts underpinning individual behaviour and has shown managerial guidelines to achieve behavioural change. First of all, an approach is introduced based on a rational cognitive behavioural mechanism: the theory of planned behaviour (TPB). Based on this model, interventions have been identified to influence attitude, subjective norm, perceived behavioural control and (effects of) external variables.

We have shown that dealing with resistance is an important aspect of managing individual behaviour. Symptoms and causes of resistance have been identified and discussed. The main advice for a change leader is not just to identify symptoms, but to address the underlying causes using the TPB variables (attitude, subjective norm, perceived behavioural control and effects of external variables).

The mechanistic approach to managing behaviour based on TPB has its limitations. The dynamic nature and irrational part of behaviour provide additional valuable insights into individual behaviour and are therefore crucial to keep in mind when shaping behaviour.

Finally, it has been recognized that behaviour is dependent on individual and situational context. General behavioural characteristics are described for roles that are typically involved in strategic change in the purchasing function: operational, tactical, strategic purchasers and (middle) management.

In short, to foster strategic change in the purchasing function, change leaders have to understand individual behaviour as an instrument in strategic change. Interventions to invoke individual behavioural change can be derived from behavioural theories, but should be applied with knowledge of causes of resistance, individual personality and the specific context.

Notes and references

[1] Fishbein, M. and Ajzen, I. (1975) *Belief, Attitude, Intention, and Behaviour: An Introduction to Theory and Research*, Addison-Wesley: Reading, MA.
[2] Ajzen, I. (1991) 'The theory of planned behaviour', *Organizational Behavior and Human Decision Processes*, Vol. 50, pp. 179–211.

[3] Some authors that contributed to specific models for the ICT domain are Bhattacharjee, A. (2001) 'Understanding information system continuance: An expectation confirmation model', *MIS Quarterly*, Vol. 25 (No. 3), pp. 351–70; Davis, F.D. (1989) 'Perceived usefulness, perceived ease of use, and user acceptance of information technology', *MIS Quarterly*, Vol. 13 (No. 3), pp. 319–40; Davis, F.D., Bagozzi, R.P. and Warshaw, P.R. (1989) 'User acceptance of computer technology: A comparison of two theoretical models', *Management Science*, Vol. 35, pp. 982–1003; DeSanctis, G. and Poole, M.S. (1994) 'Capturing the complexity in advanced technology use: Adaptive structuration theory', *Organization Science*, Vol. 5 (No. 2), pp. 121–47; Goodhue, D.L. and Thompson, R.L. (1995) 'Task-technology fit and individual performance', *MIS Quarterly*, Vol. 19 (No. 2), pp. 213–36; Oliver, R.L. (1980) 'A cognitive model for the antecedents and consequences of satisfaction', *Journal of Consumer Marketing*, Vol. 17, pp. 460–69; Reunis, M.R.B., Van Raaij, E.M. and Santema, S.C. (2004) 'Design of an e-procurement adoption model', *Proceedings of the 13th IPSERA conference*, Catania, Italy; Venkatesh, V., Morris, M.G., Davis, G.B. and Davis, F.D. (2003) 'User acceptance of information technology: Toward a unified view', *MIS Quarterly*, Vol. 27 (No. 3), pp. 425–78.

[4] Eccles, R.G. and Nohira, N. (1991) *Beyond the Hype: Rediscovering the Essence of Management*, Harvard Business School Press: Boston, MA.

[5] Harris, L.C. (2000) 'Sabotaging market-oriented culture change: An exploration of resistance justifications and approaches', *Journal of Marketing Theory and Practice*, Vol. 10 (No. 3), pp. 58–74.

[6] An interesting article on overcoming individual resistance is Kegan, R. and Lahey, L.L. (2001) 'The real reason people won't change', *Harvard Business Review*, November, pp. 85–92.

[7] Gioia, D.A. and Poole, P.P. (1984) 'Scripts in organizational behaviour', *Academy of Management Review*, Vol. 9, pp. 449–59.

[8] Based on Sherman, S. and Freass, A. (2004) 'The wild west of executive coaching', *Harvard Business Review*, November, pp. 82–90.

Part III

ILLUSTRATIONS

Chapter 11

THE REALITY OF ORGANIZING FOR PURCHASING SYNERGIES

Arjan van Weele[1]

Few purchasing managers will deny that the way purchasing processes are embedded in their organization determines the extent to which they can achieve purchasing excellence. The organizational structure with regards to purchasing partially determines the scope of purchasing as a function, and the contribution that it can make to improving the competitive position of the company. We are gradually seeing purchasing managers reporting higher up in the organization. A few progressive companies have even, as we have seen in the IBM case described in Chapter 1, appointed a corporate purchasing officer (CPO), who is sometimes already part of the general management or the board of directors. In many companies, however, the purchasing department still has a long way to go in terms of professionalization. Purchasing structures are subject to continual change. This is certainly true for multinational companies made up of many divisions and with many subsidiaries.[2] Here, the question is how the general management can achieve synergy among its business units without harming their autonomy too much.

Looking back at the past few decades, we can see that the question of how purchasing should be organized at a corporate level has been answered in different ways: periods of centralization have alternated with periods of decentralization. Where at the beginning of the 1990s the accent was on creating autonomy and individual responsibility and slashing corporate bureaucracy, we now see a trend where large corporations are desperately trying to reduce costs in the field of purchasing by combining forces. Modern information technology allows tactical purchasing processes (including sourcing, supplier selection, contract management and contract use) to be coordinated across subsidiaries, so that the operational purchasing processes (placing orders, monitoring deliveries and making accounts payable) can be decentralized. This is why most corporations these days do not choose to fully centralize the purchasing department or to fully decentralize it; they prefer to choose a hybrid organizational form that combines the advantages of both options. As described in Chapter 5, various types of coordination appear to be possible within the hybrid organizational model. The continual evolution of organizational forms within purchasing is not isolated, but can be explained by the changes in company strategies and related organizational changes within companies. In the early 1960s, Chandler maintained that the structure followed the strategy of the company (his famous utterance at the time was 'structure follows strategy').[3] As this chapter will show, we believe this claim to be particularly applicable to purchasing.

This chapter covers the driving factors and principles behind the development of purchasing, and particularly those behind the organizational development of purchasing. We start from the premise that organizational development in terms of purchasing is more similar to a hiking trip, with many obstacles and obstructions on the way, than to a consciously chosen, rational and smoothly running process. This idea is based on the many observations that we have made ourselves in the field, but also on the discussions that we have had with colleagues and top managers on the subject. Our experiences show that knowledge and a good eye for the political, often unspoken, social processes are essential for purchasing managers if they want to succeed in implementing effective organizational designs for purchasing.

The evolution of purchasing as a company function is illustrated through in-depth case studies of two large companies, Corus and NAM. Corus is a large European steel manufacturer, whereas NAM is a Dutch (natural) gas company. We look at the irrationality and emotional processes that can hide behind organizational processes related to purchasing. We investigated this subject using a small-scale research experiment. The results of this research allowed us to give some tips and suggestions. We finish with a summary and some conclusions.

11.1   Organizing purchasing within an international steel company: The Corus case study

Corus is an international company working in the field of the production, sale and distribution of steel and aluminium.[4] In 2003, its revenue amounted to about £8 billion, resulting from 17.8 million tonnes of steel deliveries, which were made from the UK (62% of production capacity), the Netherlands (34%) and USA (4%). The steel market is characterized by large professional consumers who source their steel from various manufacturers. About 27% of turnover was made within the UK, 52% within Europe and 10% in other countries. Most important customer markets are the construction industry (39%), automotive industry (16%) and packaging (15%). Over the past few years the steel market has been characterized by large overcapacity, which has given rise to a number of mergers and takeovers. As a result, the market concentration has increased over the last few years. The steel market is a tough market with strong price competition, which, until recently (2004), has led to continually falling revenues. With one thing and another, cost reduction has become a topical issue.

Due to its limited size, Royal Hoogovens, the independent Dutch steelmaker, was looking for a partner. Royal Hoogovens decided to merge with the British Steel Corporation (BSC) in 1989. As we will see, the developments within the company did not leave the purchasing function unscathed. In the last 15 years the purchasing organization has been subject to various reorganizations. This process is described in the following paragraphs. The discussion mainly concerns general and technical purchasing; the purchasing of raw materials, transport and energy is not included.

The 1970s and 1980s

During the 1970s, the purchasing function within Royal Hoogovens had its own directorate divided into three segments: transport, raw materials and energy and general purchasing. The third segment included the purchasing of maintenance and investments, purchasing of general goods and services, and purchasing of production materials. It had a functional organizational model.

By the early 1980s, the company was not able to react quickly enough to external developments, and a step was made towards forming business and service units. The so-called supporting activities, including general purchasing, were accommodated within these service units. The service units had to offer their services at a cost to the business units. Purchasing, at that time, was still centralized, but was more responsible for the quality and costs of its services than in the past. As one of the service units, General Purchasing had to write a business plan indicating how it would improve its services and organization, and how it would work together with its internal customers. Activities that were not regarded as key activities, including facility services, were contracted out.

The 1990s

The trend of contracting out work to suppliers continued into the 1990s. In general, the external orientation of the company increased. Royal Hoogovens realized that the strong internal orientation of the company had limitations, and that an 'outside looking in' approach could lead to surprising revelations. Benchmarking meant that a number of processes were not carried out in conformance with the market. This was a reason to consider contracting out these activities.

Compared to other companies (partly in the light of the World-Class Purchasing Benchmarking Initiative of Michigan State University) it seemed that the purchasing organization of Royal Hoogovens had a lot of improvement potential; it seemed to work with too large a number of suppliers. Shortly after this report was published, a number of MBA students from IMD in Lausanne were asked to make a critical analysis of the role and position of purchasing for the MRO (maintenance, repair and operational) spend within the company. At that time, a combination of circumstances put purchasing more in the limelight. Gradually the board of directors recognized the need for further development of the purchasing function.

In 1999, the international consultancy firm AT Kearney was called in to investigate the subject and to come up with recommendations for improving the purchasing organization, processes and results. Its 'House of Procurement' was used as a model to analyse purchasing and for the future development of the purchasing function (see Figure 11.1). The consultants set to work on the laborious task of implementing the recommendations from the different elements of this purchasing model. The idea of implementing everything in one go, in a project-oriented manner, appeared to be not very successful, however. The identified paths towards improvement proved to be more complicated than expected; the plans of the consultants met a great deal of unexpected internal resistance.

The period from 2000 onwards

Early in 1998, the board of directors at Royal Hoogovens, supported by McKinsey consultants, started a reorientation plan for the future. The conclusion from McKinsey was that Royal Hoogovens was too small a player to survive on its own in the international steel market and that expansion was essential. However, Royal Hoogovens apparently lacked the money needed for this expansion. McKinsey was explicit about the contributions that were to be made by purchasing: by bundling packages and aiming for synergy, significant savings could be generated that would lead to less working capital. As a result, the company needed less borrowing from banks (at high costs). Purchasing, therefore, was given top priority. This advice resulted in the setting up of reengineering schemes that needed to deliver 'speedy', 'substantial' and 'sustainable' purchasing results.

Royal Hoogovens needed to look for a partner. It found one in the British Steel Corporation (BSC), with whom it merged in 1999 (although it actually felt like Royal Hoogovens had been taken over by BSC). This decision was taken when the reengineering schemes with regard to purchasing were in full flow. The merger led almost immediately to a much reduced interest in the undertaken and ongoing purchasing initiatives. There was no harmonization with similar initiatives on the BSC side. When the dust from the merger had settled, in late 2000, the purchasing initiatives were started up again.

At Corus (the merged organization), discussions were started with the purchasing managers to harmonize the strategy across the purchasing segments throughout the company.[5] The organization was set up according to the 'hub and satellite' principle. In this way, the purchasing initiatives were spread across the whole

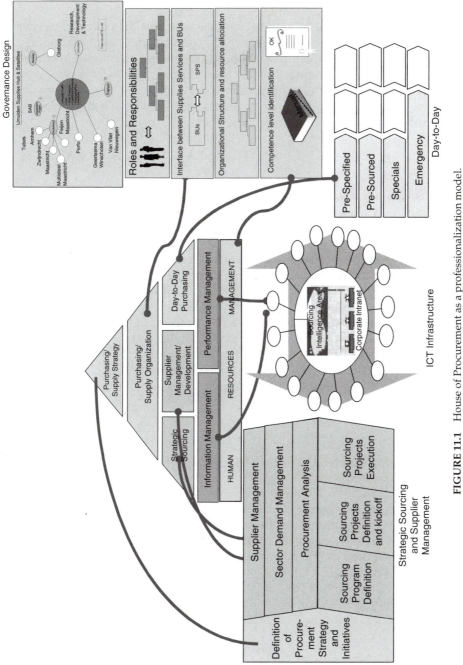

FIGURE 11.1 House of Procurement as a professionalization model. Reproduced by permission of AT Kearney.

company. This model was based on the idea of making use of the knowledge that was present in every division and operating company, and quickly realizing volume bundling. The whole process was managed by a director of supplies and transport who was based in London.

In 2003, a new CEO started at Corus. His view was that the company needed 'step changes' in various places. Again, various consultancy firms were involved in starting up the improvement processes. A substantial contribution was once again expected from purchasing. The CEO this time seemed to be in favour of a more centralized approach, and propagated (forcefully) the idea of increasing the number of Corus-wide purchasing contracts. He also wanted a more intensive exchange of best practices between business units.

Reflection

The Corus case study shows that purchasing was subjected to many changes almost continually from the early 1980s onwards. In all cases these changes were the results of changes in the company environment and the company structure. Purchasing had a strong following role here. The effectiveness of the changes largely depended on the constancy of the management. If top management lost interest, this influenced the progress of the purchasing initiatives. Numerous consultants steered the purchasing organization in different directions. Modern organization and purchasing models were propagated without thinking much about how they were affected by the specific company context. The intended, strategic changes always turned out to be more complex and take more time than expected. This reduced the momentum. The attention that the merger required from the management certainly had a negative effect on the time that was spent on the carefully planned purchasing initiatives. The improvement possibilities identified were realized, but the implementation took much more time than originally planned.

11.2   Organizing purchasing within gas and oil production: NAM case study

NAM is a Dutch company that extracts oil and natural gas. It was founded in 1947 by Shell and Esso to exploit the massive gas and (to a lesser extent) oil reserves that were found in the Netherlands. Although Shell and Esso are shareholders, the company processes and its internal management structure are fully linked to Shell. Annually, NAM delivers 50 billion m^3 of gas, which comes from the northern part of the country (Groningen; 27 billion m^3), the North Sea (11 billion m^3) and the rest of the country (12.5 billion m^3).[6] Currently NAM supplies about 75% of the annual gas requirements of the Netherlands.

Period until 1998

With a purchasing expenditure in the region of €1 billion, NAM is a large player in its supply markets. In its purchasing operations, NAM has traditionally differentiated between contracting and procurement. Until 1998 contracting, aimed at the purchasing of services, reported to the financial director. As NAM had different business units (BUs) there was a contracting department within each of these BUs. We could say that there was a decentralized organization with widely differing levels of professionalism. Procurement, set up for the acquisition of all (technical) materials, spare parts and installations, was part of technical services until that time. Contracting and procurement and logistics were separate worlds. By the end of the 1990s this was looked on by NAM's management increasingly as a deficiency. They felt they were missing out on opportunities to make use of better commercial possibilities. The provision of purchasing services to internal customers was felt to be unsatisfactory.

The period 1998–2001

In this period contracting and procurement (CP) were integrated into one function. Within the decentralized BU structure, centralization of CP was seen as one step too far. The CP units were therefore integrated into the BUs. This organizational change was used to harmonize the CP processes and systems among the business units at the same time. To improve its customer focus, it was decided that each CP unit would carry out a periodic, centrally coordinated customer satisfaction survey. Based on the results of this, each CP unit had to enter into a specific service contract with its BUs, where the service activities were agreed on and timetabled. The quality of the services supplied was monitored using simple KPIs (key performance indicators). Based on the evaluations, it was decided that each CP unit would improve its competence management and the training of its employees.

The period 2001–2003

During this period it was decided to merge the service units within the whole of NAM. This involved bringing all decentralized CP units to a central level. This was inspired by the fact that NAM could significantly benefit from a reduction of the number of purchasing employees (the advice was to reduce the number of purchasing employees from 95 to 56.5 full-time equivalents). Centralization of human resources related to purchasing at the same time offered the chance to improve the grip on the quality of the CP processes; furthermore, it made the bundling of different contracts easier. A concerted, corporate CP organization would allow for a united front to NAM's supply markets ('one single point of contact to the supplier'). The principle was sustained that CP should make a service-level agreement with internal customers every year.

The CP organization had barely recovered from this major organizational change when the management decided in favour of a merger of its central CP orga-nization with that of Shell Expro in Lowestoft, UK. They decided that the merged CP organization should once again be centrally controlled from Assen. To keep close to the internal customers, however, they worked from two separate locations.

Future

A further centralization of CP is expected. The CP activities will be merged with those of Shell Expro in Aberdeen, Shell EP in Norway and Shell International EP in The Hague. This new, centrally managed organization will operate from four different locations: Assen, Aberdeen, Stavanger and Rijswijk. Its task will be to standardize the CP processes, implement centrally led contract management and harmonize its purchasing information systems. The goal is to present CP to the market as a single body, named Shell EP Europe, and to achieve a flexible use of the further reduced CP staff. This will, of course, be done in such a way that the decentralized operations are maximally supported.

Reflection

Looking back, what are the most important lessons for NAM? Initially, the process of organizational change with respect to contracting and procurement was clearly outlined (see Figure 11.2). NAM's purchasing management thought that they would need three years to go through the various steps, from setting up a team to put the process in motion to finally proving the added value of CP. At the start of 1997, NAM's purchasing management had the idea that the whole process would follow a number of clearly marked steps. Five years later, it appeared that the original route map was by no means followed. Many delays and deviations occurred that were not foreseen. In its effort to create greater (shareholder) value, NAM's management's focus was on reducing materials costs and purchasing headcounts. The strong centralization of some of the staff departments could not have been predicted; this meant that the original reorganization plans with respect to contracting and procurement had to be significantly adapted. The application of e-procurement solutions were also not predicted in the original design. Another

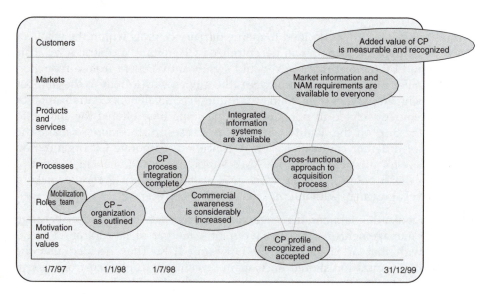

FIGURE 11.2   Reorganization route for NAM contracting and procurement.

major issue at the time of the reorganization plans was 'improving safety at work'. Because a lot of the operational work was contracted out, CP was able to guarantee the safety aspect by advanced contract management, and its working methods received respect in the broad layers of management. The result was that NAM's purchasing professionals were gradually taken more seriously by the management and the BUs. All in all, CP had reached a higher plane. This is something that the original plans were aiming for, but that was actually realized through a different route.

Looking back at the change process, we can see that when contracting and procurement are not the most strategic processes within a company, reorganization processes related to purchasing are significantly influenced by later, unpredicted events with a higher priority. These events can significantly disturb the original, well-prepared reorganization plans. In the NAM case the goal remained intact; only the route to the goal had to react to the changes that were not predicted at the start of the process. The focus of contracting and procurement on the safety issue also contributed to the recognition of the purchasing function. If purchasing management had kept to the original plans, however legitimate, this would have been disastrous. It is therefore extremely important in this type of reorganization process that the purchasing and change managers have the required flexibility with regards to the way they want to achieve their goals. In hindsight, this flexibility was crucial for gaining recognition from senior management.

We expect the changes with regards to contracting and procurement within NAM and Shell to continue. Internationalization and globalization will undoubtedly have their influence on future organizational purchasing structures and processes. There is already the question of how global category management will be introduced within Shell. It is unlikely that the current plans will be followed to the letter.

11.3   Creating purchasing synergy at corporate level: The balancing issue

When creating purchasing synergy at the corporate level, it is difficult to find the optimal structure. Based on the previous cases we might wonder whether such an optimum really exists. It is obviously better to assume that the actual structure will always move around a certain required optimum. Considering the fact that purchasing managers are dealing with a continuously moving field, they can better prepare themselves for a permanently changing purchasing organization. Within this movement, discussions are mainly about the question of how to find the right balance between centralization and decentralization. The organization of purchasing structures is in this sense more like a trek across rugged terrain than a journey with clearly defined phases and stages. The case studies above clearly show that the following insights are helpful when making such a trek:

- Do you have a clear goal to be reached with the professionalization and restructuring of purchasing that can act as a beacon for the trek?
- Which best practices for the reorganization process in question can be derived from other similar situations? Which of these can be used in our company?
- To what extent are the best practices time and situation specific?

- How important is purchasing compared to other company processes? What would any changes in the other company processes mean to the purchasing change plan in question?
- Who or what can help during the realization of the organizational changes, and who or what can hinder them?
- What contingency plans are needed if external circumstances change unexpectedly?
- Who or what determines the speed and the route taken?

With regards to the goal of organizational change, it is useful to determine beforehand whether the changes are fixed or not; that is, whether they are subject to change. Based on practical experience we recommend that, once determined, the goal should be kept in mind and not changed. Best practices, laid down in various organizational and process models, can give you something to work with. However, it is important not to regard these as the ultimate truth: over time you will notice that the value of these models is time- and situation-specific. Best practices will need to be changed regularly. After all, the important thing is that you have a good idea of what is driving the organizational changes; that is, which factors, and in particular which stakeholders, are crucial to keep the process going or to hinder the process of organizational change. In the following section we will show how insight into the 'soft side' of organizations can deliver hard insights.

Changes inside purchasing organizations

It is not easy to balance the fields of tension between centralized and decentralized purchasing. How do you compare the advantages of decentralization, greater involvement and autonomy, with the centralized advantages of bundling purchasing power and economies of scale? The answer to this question depends on the environment of the company, its governance structure, its culture and its management style.

The continually changing environment puts corporate purchasing structures, and with them the relationships between managers, under pressure. This makes the realization of purchasing synergy more difficult. To achieve results here, you need a good eye for the tensions that can occur between managers, employees and departments, and the political and power struggles that are almost always involved; these often go unsaid, but are felt strongly by the actors involved. In our opinion this makes it impossible to blindly implement organizational and process models. Changes in corporate strategies and structures are fluid due to changes in internal power regimes and positions within the internal company hierarchy.

To gain some insight into the political and power processes that can occur in relation to the question of centralized or decentralized purchasing, we carried out an experiment during a management conference. After sketching the structure of a (fictional) company (see Box 11.1), the participants, all purchasing managers, were asked how they could use their role to support or frustrate the given plans to create corporate purchasing synergy. We distinguished between two different roles: (1) the (cooperative) purchasing manager and (2) the (malicious) BU manager. The results of this experiment are described below.

Box 11.1   Creating corporate purchasing synergy: Dairy firm case study

You are part of a company with different, reasonably autonomous subsidiaries. Until now the business units, Dairy Firm BV, have not collaborated much in the area of purchasing. The subsidiaries (BUs) are situated in several countries, including the Netherlands, Germany, France, the UK and Spain. The company wants to expand, but external funding is very expensive. The board of directors feels that purchasing should be given priority. The board decides to establish so-called lead buyer teams that will have to make corporate contracts for common, strategic raw materials, packaging materials and components; the corporate agreements that will result from this exercise are to be used in the future by all business units. Each team is given clear targets, not only for the purchasing savings it needs to realize, but also with regard to the reduction of overheads and limitation of working capital. The money saved in this way can then be used for the necessary expansion of the company.

The discussion that follows this decision is carried out among the following two parties:

- *Business unit managers.* These managers have their own thoughts on corporate management's ideas. The advantages of the proposed purchasing coordination are mainly coming from the corporate management. The business unit managers themselves will not see many of the advantages. They are not very inclined to follow up on the corporate management's requests for cooperation. But they can't say that openly, of course. The BU manager tries to avoid losing his autonomy to select his own vendors and negotiate. What behaviour or which actions will help this BU manager to keep the situation as it is?
- *Purchasing managers.* The purchasing managers have generally been won over by the corporate management initiative. Finally they are getting their long-awaited recognition from the upper management. They see numerous possibilities for savings. As BU purchasing manager you want to put as much energy as possible into achieving collaboration between the business units. What behaviour or which actions can help you to realize the desired purchasing synergy?

The BU manager

When in the role of the BU manager, the participants seemed to be particularly creative in thinking up actions to ensure that the plans would not be implemented. In the discussion participants appeared very creative in coming up with ideas to frustrate corporate intervention. For instance, they suggested making the purchasers accountable for any mistake they had ever made and bringing their expertise into doubt under the motto 'They just do the ordering'. Another idea was to literally bury the BU purchasing managers with operational work to prevent them spending time on corporate projects. Many synergy projects in fact involve preparing corporate contracts. Frustration is guaranteed if you make sure that the preparation of this sort of contract is based on outdated specifications. When the contract is to be closed with the supplier, you should, as BU manager, turn up with the up-to-date specifications. This means that the whole job needs to be done again! This method of working is guaranteed to lead to frustration within the purchasing or lead buyer team in question, which of course does not include the best people from the BUs.

To derail synergy processes, it is essential that the BU manager receives regular reports. The planned meetings to discuss the issues with the purchasing managers should then be cancelled at the last moment. It will then take a few weeks before the BU manager involved can find any space in his diary. It is also important that the BU manager is conspicuous by his absence whenever important decisions need to be taken. He will then declare that he doesn't feel bound by the central contract because he didn't have any say in its realization due to a lack of time or something more important cropping up at the last moment. Another method that appears to be effective in practice is boycotting purchasing coordination initiatives by letting important information leak to the existing suppliers beforehand. An even better idea is to quickly make long-term contracts with these suppliers, which prevents new suppliers entering into a new contract. In all cases the differences between the BUs are magnified by emphasizing the very specific requirements and needs of the BU itself.

Table 11.1 gives an idea of the many examples of subversive behaviour that the purchasing managers involved were able to name in their role as malicious BU manager. All these examples would lead to the gradual undermining of well-intended corporate initiatives. After a while this would lead to doubt among higher management about the effectiveness of central purchasing initiatives. It is probably better to leave the purchasing entirely to BUs, they will think.

In essence, the behaviour of a malicious BU manager can be summed up as the following. They do everything possible to prevent decision making or, at least, to postpone it. The idea is to ensure that the proposed initiatives make no headway. The BU managers involved can do this with impunity and can make sure that it is difficult to confront them about their behaviour and attitude towards the corporate initiatives. They continually show goodwill, mainly verbally, although their actual behaviour shows anything but goodwill. The essence of their attitude is that they do not want to take any responsibility for, or give any active support to, the purchasing coordination initiatives that have been agreed. It is clear that in this sort of situation it will be impossible for a CPO or any lead buyer team to carry out the well-prepared corporate purchasing initiatives and plans.

The purchasing manager

The main problem that purchasing managers are confronted with when carrying out corporate purchasing initiatives is the fact that they are often given a great deal of responsibility (the board of directors gives them targets with regard to the realization of purchasing savings), but in their position they only have very limited powers to actually get the cooperation of the parts of the organization involved in these initiatives. This is why purchasing managers often end up frustrated and with the idea that they are 'flogging a dead horse'. It is very important that purchasing managers realize what a difficult position they are in.

TABLE 11.1   Examples of resistance behaviour by the BU managers and the effective behaviour of purchasing managers to create corporate purchasing synergy.

BU managers	Purchasing managers
• Quickly arranging a long-term contract with an existing supplier. • Holding a 'trial' with the alternative product from the new supplier; then purposely letting the trial fail. • Pointing to P&L accountability and stating that the choice of suppliers requires its approval. • 'Saying one thing and doing another' in numerous agreements. • Overcomplicating issues. • Methodologizing. • Continually asking for written justification of proposed supplier choices. • Questioning the method of working. • Sudden, unannounced absences at crucial moments in the process. • Questioning the expertise of the purchaser. • Making endless analyses. • Then announcing that the BU manager has missed lots of points and that the purchasing team would be better to start again. • Purposely leaking all information to the existing supplier. • Indicating the consequences of changing suppliers to customer contacts: 'This choice is going to lose us customers.' • Letting the purchaser slave away on outdated specifications, and then changing the specifications continually. • Magnifying all differences. • Pointing to the difference in standards between the BUs: 'We can never align the specs.' • Which contracts/purchasing terms are we going to use from which BU?	• Looking for momentum within the organization: finding a corporate theme or initiative to latch onto (e.g. NAM example 'Safety'). • Securing covering for your back: looking for management support. • Looking before you leap. • Weekly reporting indicating progress status. • Actively involving BUs in decision making, making the BU manager owner of the process. • Purchaser must know what he or she is talking about. • Factual knowledge. • Market knowledge. • Achieving credit by BU managers through short-term successes. • Effective troubleshooting. • Realizing concrete savings. • Communicating lots of issues to the CEO/CFO. • Making the finance director your ally. • Bringing in good examples from outside. • Communicating decisions, ideas and plans along the line. • Involving the users from the very start. • While collaborating with other BU managers, beginning and improving the process. • Communicating effectively with BU manager and BU purchasers. A communication plan is essential. • Making good time and keeping up momentum. • Feeding decision makers with information about competitors, new methods. • Setting up a monitoring system; making use of current contracts! • Letting the BU manager be accountable to be CEO for his contribution to corporate synergy.

Essence of the possible BU manager's 'resistance behaviour'

- Taking all measures to avoid decision making or at least to postpone it; drawing out discussions endlessly, insisting on consensus.
- Working with impunity, so that no one can be held responsible.
- Having an eye for precision.
- Purposely not wanting to take responsibility.

Essence of effective behaviour of a purchasing manager

- Making sure that the energy lies with the line management, letting them take responsibility for purchasing.
- Recognizing supporters quickly and getting them on your side.
- Pushing on where others give up.

The solution revolves around the recognition that realizing targets related to corporate purchasing initiatives is primarily a line management responsibility. This means that the purchasing manager primarily has a leading and supporting role. Projects aimed at achieving purchasing savings should be presented to the line management beforehand in the form of a persuasive business case. The CPO should ensure that all the measures from line management are coordinated and regularly harmonized. Under these terms, the CEO and CFO can manage the whole process. The CEO and CPO should together also ensure that the team has sufficiently qualified members and that they operate according to previously established and agreed procedures and templates (for example with regard to the sourcing methodology to be followed, and sourcing plans to be prepared for the often cross-functional teams).

To summarize, the purchaser must ensure that the energy remains with the line management and let them take responsibility for corporate purchasing initiatives. It is also crucial that the purchaser recognizes his or her supporters and opponents at an early stage.

What is remarkable in the experiment is that the participants (all experienced purchasing managers and directors) had no problem answering the questions. They answered questions from the point of view of the (negative) business unit manager with the greatest of ease. They had numerous, colourful examples of subversive, undermining behaviour against well-thought-out corporate initiatives; these could have filled an article all by themselves. It was perfectly clear to us that such behaviour is common in the companies involved. We think it is essential that top managers and purchasing representatives develop a good eye for this and are aware of it. Otherwise their well-meant plans and actions will never achieve the desired objectives.

Organizing for excellence

The Corus and NAM case studies reflect the many changes to which purchasing structures in large companies are subject. We conclude that changes in purchasing structures are also determined by changes in the *company* structure. Our research experiment illustrates the way in which effective changes within purchasing organizations can be frustrated, depending on the script that the stakeholders involved are working to (in this case limited to BU managers and purchasing managers). The hypothesis that we want to formulate with regard to organizational changes in purchasing is that effective change in purchasing requires a combination of (1) bringing in the right concept and models offered from the purchasing theory (see House of Procurement) and (2) being able to give an effective meaning to the change management principles. In our opinion, the 'best' solution has little to do with logic alone. See Chapter 3 for a detailed discussion on strategic change.

11.4   Reflection on organizational changes in corporate purchasing structures

We have clearly seen that effective changes in corporate purchasing structures do not only involve logic and rational behaviour. Both the case studies at Corus and NAM and the research experiment show that organizational changes in purchasing are a politically sensitive subject involving many different concerns and emotions. An effective approach to change allows for logic and emotions to interact. In his or her role as intelligent change leader, the purchasing manager can certainly make use of the following ideas to determine an effective approach to change.

In complex change situations there is a so-called multiple reality. Issues involving change, particularly when combined with reorganizations, are perceived and interpreted differently by each employee and manager. Before starting such a process, but also during it, the CPO would be wise to regularly validate and check the expectations of the most important stakeholders involved against his or her own expectations (see also Chapter 10). This means that he or she should pose the following questions regularly to the BU managers involved: do the expected outcomes of the corporate procurement initiatives coincide with their expectations? Do they feel they sufficiently benefit from these initiatives? In order to be able to engage in this type of discussions, top managers would be wise to recruit experienced line managers for this sort of senior purchasing job.

In practice, it seems to be very difficult to create purchasing synergy at a corporate level in situations where there are absolutely no other collaborations at that level. If your organization is managed in a relatively decentralized way, from a rational point of view it would be a good idea to develop synergy in purchasing, but there is no way that it would succeed. This idea is in line with the insights presented in Chapter 5, where it was argued that the optimal purchasing structure is determined by two types of variables: purchasing maturity and corporate coherence.[7] Many managers and consultants fail to see this distinction, whereby purchasing structures are chosen based on rational considerations even though it is obvious beforehand that these cannot work in the given corporate context. Corporate purchasing structures seem to be very sensitive to displays of leadership from the corporate top. If the top management cannot succeed in other areas at corporate level, then, in our opinion, they will certainly not succeed in the field of purchasing (see Box 11.2).

Box 11.2 Using purchasing to create a competitive advantage

Research has shown that initiatives in the field of corporate purchasing coordination need to fit in with the level of coherence in the corporation and with the level of maturity within the purchasing function in the subsidiaries involved.[8] The extent of coherence indicates the extent to which the corporation is led as a single entity. Big differences between subsidiaries in the area of management style, vision, strategy and culture indicate a low level of cohesion. The extent of purchasing professionalism is reflected in the status, role and organizational position of purchasing within the company, as well as in the degree of automation of purchasing processes, the level of the purchasing staff and the degree of cooperation with suppliers.[9] A low level of coherence within the corporation and minimal purchasing maturity make purchasing coordination a fruitless task. In these situations decentralized purchasing will usually be the rule. If both parameters are at a moderate level, the purchasing coordination will often have hybrid structures. Centrally deployed commodity teams are then often combined with voluntary coordination initiatives. If both parameters are at a high level, then a centre-led coordination structure is most appropriate. These initiatives are then realized by commodity teams, where the specialists from various business units work together under close supervision and with a mandate from top management. See also Chapter 5 for a more detailed explanation on this topic.

Organizing purchasing excellence is not about copying best practices found elsewhere. Best practices and models can inspire the CPO and give direction. The CPO will mainly have to ensure that the selected models and working methods fit within the specific company context and management culture. History, context, competencies, ambitions and leadership will determine the optimal solution. This solution, therefore, is different for each company and is also dynamic over time.

It can never hurt to occasionally use a tour guide in the form of a management consultant, as long as they are not left to plan the trip all by themselves. It is good to be at the helm yourself and to keep an eye on the final destination, while not overestimating your own seamanship!

11.5   Conclusion

In many large companies purchasing as a discipline has evolved into a strategic business function. Certainly in a multinational company that consists of many business units, competitive advantage can be gained through pooling common materials and service needs and requirements. Through leveraged purchasing power a better negotiating position vis-à-vis the suppliers and important cost savings can be obtained. However, making these savings sustainable is not easy. This is due to the fact that corporate governance structures in purchasing are subject to change. As both case studies from Corus and NAM have illustrated, corporate purchasing strategies and structures are not there on their own; rather, they are influenced and determined by changes in corporate strategies and structures. As in most companies these are subject to continuous change, the implication is that, as a result, corporate purchasing strategies and structures are changing with them. Bearing this in mind, a CPO should be flexible in implementing his or her strategies and plans for strategic commodities. Keeping to the original plans, which were developed and established two or three years before, is a path doomed to fail.

When implementing his or her corporate purchasing strategies and structures, the CPO should keep a sharp eye on the company politics that may hamper the implementation process. Corporate purchasing initiatives in most cases interfere with the autonomy of the individual business unit managers, who often feel that they benefit insufficiently from these initiatives. For this reason, it is important to continuously check whether BU managers are still in line with and in support of the corporate purchasing initiatives. Otherwise, they will find a number of ways to obstruct them.

Against this background we may conclude that designing and implementing corporate purchasing strategies and structures are highly sensitive and political matters. Apart from excellent communication and transparency in decision making, key parameters in deciding on the optimal corporate structure are purchasing professionalism and corporate coherence. Since corporations may differ a great deal in terms of these parameters, different strategies are pursued and different structures are to be found in the business landscape. On top of that the management of purchasing processes, and particularly the changes within them, requires effective leadership. All these factors explain why one CPO will be more successful than another.

Notes and references

[1] The author would like to thank Herman van den Hoogen, purchasing manager at Corus; Toon Liefkens, senior discipline lead for joint venture and infrastructure management at Shell EP Europe and former procurement manager of NAM; and Philip van Beek, chairman of the corporate purchasing committee of the Dutch Railroad company, for their valuable contributions to this chapter.

[2] Leenders, M.R. and Johnson, P.F. (2000) *Major Structural Changes in Supply Organizations*, Center for Advanced Purchasing Studies: Tempe, AZ; Leenders, M.R. and Johnson, P.F. (2002) *Major Changes in Supply Chain Responsibilities*, Center for Advanced Purchasing Studies: Tempe, AZ.

[3] Chandler, A.D. (1962) *Strategy and Structure: Chapters in the History of the Industrial Enterprise*, MIT Press: Cambridge, MA.

[4] Royal Hoogovens and British Steel merged in 1999. The new company was named Corus.

[5] Purchasing segments relate to homogeneous material needs, i.e. products. Examples of purchasing segments may be raw materials, packaging materials, production equipment, MRO materials etc.

[6] Figures relate to fiscal year 2003. Due to the fact that NAM is a subsidiary of Shell and Esso (Exxon), no financial data are available.

[7] Rozemeijer, F.A., Van Weele, A.J. and Weggeman, M. (2003) 'Creating corporate advantage through purchasing: Toward a contingency model', *International Journal of Supply Chain Management*, Winter, pp. 4–13; Rozemeijer, F.R. (2000) *Creating Corporate Advantage in Purchasing*, PhD thesis, Eindhoven University of Technology, Faculty of Technology Management: Eindhoven.

[8] Rozemeijer *et al.* (2003) *opere citato.*

[9] Van Weele, A.J. (2005) *Purchasing and Supply Chain Management*, 4th edn, Thomson Learning: London, Chapter 5; NEVI (2002), *Nederlandse bedrijven op weg naar Purchasing Excellence, Resultaten project 1*, NEVI: Zoetermeer.

Chapter 12

FROM BUYING TO SUPPLY MANAGEMENT AT NORDIC CONSTRUCTION COMPANY (NCC)

Björn Axelsson

This chapter deals with a process to substantially improve and upgrade the strategic sourcing function at one of the biggest construction firms in Scandinavia, the Nordic Construction Company (NCC).[1]

12.1 Change initiatives in the construction industry

The construction industry has a long history of initiatives aiming at upgrades of the purchasing function. Afterwards, these initiatives have in many cases been considered failures. This is not only true for the company under study here, the Nordic Construction Company (NCC), but also for Swedish construction firms in general. We have several indications that this is also an internationally valid experience. An in-depth analysis of a major change initiative in this industry may, thus, provide some useful insights and lessons on possible pitfalls and breakthroughs in such processes.

The first section briefly looks at previous change efforts regarding sourcing in the construction industry in general and at NCC in particular. In the following sections, a four-year change initiative at NCC (1997–2001) is described. We divide it into three subsections. First of all, we describe the background and the point of departure situation of NCC. We then present the areas of change addressed during the process and discuss what changes were created within these areas, as well as indicating how they happened. The third part describes some critical events in the process, such as what made the eventual breakthroughs happen; what created the deadlocks; what went well; what went wrong? We also look briefly at what has happened since the time period under study. Finally, we draw our inferences from the case to see what kinds of lessons of general interest we could learn from it.

Past experiences from change processes and possible reasons for failures

The background of previous change initiatives implies, among other things, that NCC had several employees with a so-called BOHICA attitude (Bend Over Here It Comes Again) as far as initiatives to foster changes in purchasing and supply issues were concerned. A new initiative would, thus, need to convincingly demonstrate that this time it was going to be 'for real'. Some of the likely reasons for the failures provide additional understanding of the challenge.

The structure of the construction industry with many work sites that move from one place to another is one contextual factor that is likely to make a difference, for example in comparison with manufacturing industries such as automotive and electronics. Serving permanent work sites (like factories) with purchasing and supply services allows more stability and, most likely, makes it easier to realize particular objectives. Furthermore, it seems that there is also a certain culture fostered in the construction business, which is entrepreneurial in the local context. The work sites often have a strong project leader with performance responsibilities that include financial bottom-line results for that specific project. This fosters strong local units even more. This is often a positive feature, but it is not always a perfect ground for centrally organized efforts to improve (compare Chapter 5 and the factors that determine the level of centralization).

The structures of the supply and demand markets also play a role. In supply markets there are basically two stereotypes: in many markets there is a monopoly or oligopoly situation (e.g. concrete, steel, insulation material etc.), in other areas there is a great number of firms, often local ones close to the regional operation with no single firm capable of serving major systems or major geographical areas. The supply markets have developed market structures and habits of carrying on their business in ways that, by and large, do not foster new ideas. There are huge numbers of rules and regulations as well as corporate and personal networks that foster a 'business as usual' orientation. Customers of the construction industry, the demand side of firms like NCC, may have been too weak in making their voices heard and pushing demands for improvements. In addition, the industry has a history of governmental subsidies. Even though the subsidies are basically gone, much of the culture remains.

The above indicates some of the difficulties of developing purchasing operations in this industry. But there are still other possible reasons for the previous failures. One relates to how the companies have tried to make it happen, the very process of change. Most previous efforts towards purchasing development have followed a 'guerrilla approach'; that is, the effort has been piecemeal (see Figure 3.3 in Chapter 3).

In such an approach, some parts of the organization have tried to do something different. It could be the introduction of new ways of handling a logistics issue, or buying functions according to a 'systems approach' instead of buying specific, separate products. Such initiatives have in many cases not been enough to make the change also happen elsewhere, on a large scale, and to really make an impact on the company as such in subsequent stages.

A second reason could be that the firms in this industry seem to have had too narrow a focus, such as just changing one separate aspect. Such single-dimensioned approaches include 'just':

- Employing a new purchasing manager.
- Redesigning the organizational structure.
- Introducing and intensifying the exploitation of new and improved information and communications technology (ICT).
- Training the purchasing officers and educating them.
- Revising the purchasing strategy, developing the necessary documents to convince the organization.
- Employing some new staff.
- Introducing new and more motivating career paths.
- Developing the exchange processes in relation to one or a few selected suppliers and within product areas of great potential.

Thus, the efforts have been too marginal in scope and too 'local'.

The reasons mentioned, whether right or wrong, represented the understanding by some of the key individuals in NCC, and were also parts of the 'industry wisdom' related to these issues before the change process started.

In particular the recruitment team, in charge of finding a CPO at NCC for this new change effort, held this opinion.[2] This new initiative was strongly supported by top management and aimed to learn from history. Still, it would be wrong to say that it was without problems and/or was 'just' a success. This remark applies both to the four-year transformation period that will be our main focus and to what has followed afterwards. This notion should bring even more excitement to the NCC case as a learning experience.

The new initiative

The overall vision of the company, in this phase of its development, was to create an international, sizeable construction firm. Therefore it was growing and had grown at a very fast rate, predominantly via acquisitions. That was also one of the important prerequisites for changes in purchasing and supply management. CEO Jan Sjöqvist said[3]:

> The logic of our business was to, in various ways, take advantage of our size. In sourcing, almost everything was done locally. We were convinced that there should be plenty of opportunities to take advantage of economies of scale, not least in purchasing.
>
> We were looking for a CPO who had a good theoretical understanding as well as relevant practical experience from modern ways of operating in purchasing,

The CPO should also act as 'upstream business developer' by contributing to innovative solutions on business concepts in dialogue with suppliers. To fully exploit scale economies, he or she should also be supportive in identifying and exploiting synergies from internal integration. 'The assignment was to make a dramatic change of the entire purchasing and supply structure, it was a very open and challenging assignment,' said Mr Sjöqvist. In addition, this time there should be no doubt that top management supported the initiative. 'We had a very dedicated and united board of directors, everyone agreed to this initiative,' he continued.

12.2   Part 1: Points of departure

Mr Sjöqvist declared: 'The search for this new CPO took some time, but we were surprised to see how many top-quality people we could choose from, who were all interested in facing this challenge.' The outcome of the selection process ended up in NCC choosing Klas Frisk from Volvo Trucks as their CPO for the newly created and very strategic role. 'This was the first phase. We had managed to get one of the very best Swedish CPOs on board,' Mr Sjöqvist continued.

Mr Frisk brought with him, and expressed from the beginning, some strong beliefs and opinions that formed an important context for the whole transformation process. One such belief was that NCC should make an explicit effort not only to learn from history but also from others, preferably from the best. With the new CPO followed also an explicit intention to utilize experiences gained from research and theories in the field of purchasing and supply management. Some of the influences were the following:

- To apply supply management concepts such as supply chain management practices and a segmented view of supply needs. Not all goods and services should be acquired based on the same purchasing methodology. This meant for example that classical, transactional purchasing and relationship-oriented purchasing should co-exist. The segmentation view meant trying to do the right things in each context (see Chapter 4 for a more detailed discussion of the various approaches). Another aspect, in line with this, that had a major impact was distinguishing and segmenting suppliers according to impact and risk.[4]
- Emphasizing the need to take advantage of ICT to support coordinated activities. This should be a natural step as the technology brings with it so many enabling possibilities (see Chapter 8 for further insights).
- Actively listening to and inviting (and possibly also employing) representatives from other companies to learn from them and their experience.
- Trying as much as possible to do without consultants. It was considered a strength if as many as possible of the new designs for structures and processes were developed from inside the firm. Besides, the process would generate more learning that would stay in the company (compare our discussion in Chapter 3 on utilizing consultants in change processes).
- Preparedness and ability to cooperate closely with internal R&D units, involving also suppliers in systematically managed processes to improve products and processes.

Some of these ideas were explicit already before the employment of the new CPO, some became more explicit during early stages of his participation in the process.[5]

By recruiting Mr Frisk, NCC got a manager with experience from a leading firm in terms of purchasing philosophy, experienced in sourcing advanced systems in the forefront of technological development.

Klas Frisk declared his expectations of this new job assignment as follows:

> I was recruited for a job that meant quite a lot of strategic change. At Volvo we had a truly global approach to purchasing and a strictly managed process, a work mode, with semi-weekly meetings at various places all over the world. I thought I should be able to benefit from this experience and introduce some similar practices. I was also aware about the previous failures regarding change processes in the construction industry.
>
> My idea was to really make sure that there was a genuine interest from top management as well as a strong commitment to the mission, not least for supplier development programmes in cooperation with our R&D department. Furthermore, I wanted to go for a holistic approach and not just change one or two isolated aspects.
>
> I also planned to use some time to carefully make a diagnosis of the situation.

Why was it considered a vital issue to develop purchasing at NCC?

It is generally known that purchasing frequently accounts for some 50–70% of the revenue of a typical manufacturing firm. In later investigations, the figure for NCC turned out to be as high as 73% for the business area of building and 76% for the business area of civil engineering. This figure was higher than expected and, to some extent, a surprise to those involved. A strongly increasing share of this consisted of various kinds of services and goods augmented with bundles of services. This high figure made it clear, early on in the change process, that it would be a vital issue to explicitly relate the corporate strategy to the sourcing strategy as well as the sourcing strategy to the operational activities within sourcing. The basic principle could be illustrated as in Figure 12.1.

This principle may look self-evident, but in practice it is not. It is known that the connection between sourcing strategy and corporate strategy is not always that automatically and explicitly created and maintained.[6] The same was true for NCC. There were corporate and business unit goals, but no expressed objectives for purchasing and supply. Klas Frisk considered it important to try to clarify the links in Figure 12.1 and have them developed into purchasing policies, procedures and processes. He was used to a work mode where almost everything ('maybe too much') was measured and followed up. To achieve a proper view of the links in Figure 12.1, a better understanding of the context and thereby the possibilities and necessities of a change process was needed. Moreover, it should be built on a foundation of facts and figures!

FIGURE 12.1   Sourcing in its strategic setting.

Context

NCC is one of the largest construction groups in the Nordic countries. In 1997, when the development process to be dealt with started, NCC had more than €3.5 billion in sales revenue. It had over 20 000 employees and a market share of 35% of all construction business in the Nordic market. The group was organized in six business areas (civil engineering, housing, building, industry, real estate and investment) and had four subsidiaries located in Denmark, Finland, Norway and Germany. The group's headquarters was (and still is) located in Stockholm. NCC shares are listed on the Stockholm stock exchange.

Historically, NCC has transformed itself from being a small local constructing company in specific parts of Sweden to a leading construction and real estate company in the Nordic and Baltic markets. In the late 1990s, NCC was one of the fastest-growing companies within the region and even more so within the industry, mainly due to acquisitions. It was a dramatic growth process that tripled the turnover in about five years. The company had been generating profits for about 30 years, even though the profits had been considered too low by the shareholders and the stock-market experts. The low profits in combination with the new size and – thereby – possible synergies were important reasons for a more strategic and systematic approach towards improvements in purchasing and supply.

Purchasing within NCC – status at the point of departure and future vision

The development of NCC's purchasing expenditures over the last three decades showed a trend that was very clear: the proportion of the company's external costs had increased significantly in relation to internal costs. In 1997, the entire NCC Group purchased construction materials and services for over €2.5 billion. Over €1.5 billion (61%) of these external costs were accounted for by NCC Sweden, the rest by NCC's four international subsidiaries.

The NCC vision expressed then was that the group should become the leading construction and real-estate firm in Scandinavia and the Baltic States with regard to volume, profitability and quality, as well as environmental friendliness. NCC should also represent innovativeness in terms of products delivered, but also in its ways of solving problems – and in the ways it used new materials and methods. Related to this was a strategy formulated in five guidelines. One of these was to identify five functional areas of priority. Purchasing and supply management was one of these five priorities. The vision statement clearly showed that purchasing was expected to play a crucial role in the future NCC. These aspects of the vision were developed early on after the recruitment of Mr Frisk and the idea to recruit him should be understood based on this mindset. Klas Frisk reflected:

> These statements were very good news for me. One of the first things I had done was to get in touch with the purchasing manager in charge before me. He had now taken up an appointment as a CPO at one of our suppliers. He explained what he had experienced as his good practices and difficulties. He also gave his view on various individuals in the management group of the company, not least in relation to purchasing issues. I even interviewed his predecessor who had been in charge some ten years before. I felt that these people could identify with my situation and speak freely since they nowadays were outsiders. Interestingly, they actually told two very different stories.

The statements mentioned above seemed to imply that the ground was laid for a dedicated change venture. Before we get into the process of change, however, it is useful to know more about the specific context of the purchasing and supply function. Again, Klas Frisk:

> In order to have an idea of the staff I had at my disposal and the expectations addressed to the purchasing function, I decided to make a survey of the purchasing staff. Another portion of information was generated from the series of interviews with business area managers, members of the corporate board of directors and other key informants. This was carried out to learn more about the staff and its capabilities and to learn how the users, the internal customers of the services from the sourcing function, looked upon it – and also their expectations of its future performance.

What came out of the interviews with the business area and other managers was among other things the following. Purchasing and supply had a role in conducting some key processes inside the company, for example supplier selection, issues in focus in bargaining and production, quality control, cost and delivery. But there was much to be desired in terms of a systematic approach; supplier selection processes, as known in for example Volvo, did not exist, and there seemed to be a lot more to do in terms of integrating efforts. Some of the staff also clearly declared that the CPO should stay away from these matters. In retrospect, Klas Frisk interpreted this as a sign of the 'Marlboro man' syndrome. There was a strong culture of 'doing it on your own and in your own way,' he said. It also turned out that the business area managers in general had rather vague pictures of the sourcing operations. They wanted more and better – but only expressed in very broad terms.

Some more facts generated by these initial studies, mostly from interviews and the survey among the purchasing staff, and partly from other activities to get to know the company, included the following:

Suppliers
In 1997, NCC had some 74 000 suppliers in total. Roughly 1500, that is around 2% of these suppliers, accounted for 77% of total purchase volume. Sweden as a geographical market accounted for over 70%. This pattern is to some extent explained by the fact that most purchases are voluminous and weighty products difficult to transport over large distances. In addition there were, for many products, no suppliers with a country- or region-wide business scope. It also turned out that the company frequently bought many of its products in various parts of the market channel, from the producer, from wholesalers, from retailers and so on.

The relationship between NCC and its suppliers had been, more or less exclusively, driven by prices of fixed and defined products. Due to inflation, the suppliers usually asked for annual price increases. NCC, in its turn, fought these in the negotiations but also managed quite well to pass the price increase on to its own customers.

Purchasing staff
In 1997, the purchasing staff numbered 200 people in total. At headquarters in Stockholm, there were no purchasing staff. From the start Mr Frisk was promised

the opportunity to employ one senior buyer and a young assistant. He soon hired one experienced purchaser, with dedicated responsibility for international coordination. All the rest of the purchasing staff worked in different purchasing departments in the – more or less – autonomous business units, mostly as project buyers in regional offices.

> I had a promise from the CEO that I would get an opportunity to present the situation and my desires (and arguments) for the operation I was hired to build up. He stood with his promise as he saw the potential for improvement. This made it possible to gradually develop a dedicated team of purchasing staff. To begin with I had one experienced purchaser and a young assistant with no prior experience of purchasing at my side. In due time it developed into a group of ten people.

Some characteristics of the people in purchasing include the following:

- A low level of education – fewer than 10 people had an academic degree. They had poor skills in foreign languages.
- Recruitment from inside – almost everyone had previous experience of operational construction activities.
- Long experience in the construction business, but almost nobody with experience of other industries.
- Older people, average age around 50, older than the average age structure of the company.

A mapping of attitudes and skills of the staff initiated by Mr Frisk was one of the first priorities. This led to the conclusion that a vitalization was urgently needed. There seemed to be an attitude of complacency and no real recognized need to try to do better. Other conclusions were that there was a great need to create team spirit in purchasing and a 'mental framework' based on recent theories on supply issues. There was also a need for new influences from outside, from other industries and from education. This included not least insights into sourcing principles and theories. It seemed to be a staff in great need of new ideas and inspiration.

Some early initiatives by the change agent

As CPO, Klas Frisk had some important principles that he brought along from his previous jobs:

> In the company I came from, and in my general experience, decisions should be taken based on solid facts. In the case of NCC, most of the essential facts about purchasing had yet to be found or investigated.

Mr Frisk soon also hired a young assistant and they started to gather information. The fields of desired information concerned among others the following questions:

- *'What have we done?* This meant looking backwards and reflecting on the history. What has worked out well and what has failed?' For example, they made contact with some people with a long-term perspective on the developments.
- *'Where are we now?* This means solid facts. What do we purchase from whom? How much and at how many places within the firm is the specific item

used? Could we identify some patterns in our purchasing activities?' For example, this meant carrying out a study of purchasing staff mentioned before and interviews with business area managers about their attitudes towards purchasing, opinions about the functioning of it as well as expectations for future performance. Furthermore, it meant finding out all basic facts in terms of volumes of different items, suppliers utilized – a so-called spend analysis.

- *'Where do we want to go?* What is our assignment? What future goals does the company have and how do these influence us?' The initial role description for the CPO was complemented by the views of business area managers and some tentative overall strategy was formed.

- *'How will we be able to get there?* What kind of activities will take us to the positions decided?' Some initial thinking about what would be needed to make purchasing and supply as a function ready to make a real contribution to the competitive power, including improved profitability, came out of this.

- *'How do we get it done?* Who is responsible for which activity?' This meant some initial thinking about staffing and organizational issues.

It turned out to be much more demanding than anyone had expected to find the answers to all these questions. As indicated above, there was not such a good systems support (ICT and or defined processes) available, and in order to stay firm to the principle of fact-based decisions there was a great need for more and better information. Quite a lot of effort was devoted to developing this platform in the early phases of the process. All these questions were considered vital in order to lay the ground for future activities, even though it meant loss of momentum when it came to implementing new activities and procedures.

Mr Frisk perceived very strongly that after no more than six months, he needed to show results and present a clear direction of actions for the future. But it seemed to be inherent in the NCC culture not to be that eager to find facts. Similar experiences had been had by the accounting and control function. There seemed to be a lack of interest among managers of various levels to reach transparent figures.

The first priority once relevant figures for various commodities were established was to go and negotiate the total package with suppliers. As NCC had recently merged with another company, Siab, the short-term priority was to investigate the respective companies' purchasing patterns and to negotiate from the new volumes and knowledge. This was done in parallel with the long-term efforts aimed at building a new infrastructure for purchasing and supply activities.

Some general problems identified early on

Even though it was difficult to find accurate answers to many of the things that Klas Frisk (and others who wanted to see a more radical change) asked for, it was still possible to draw some tentative conclusions. Some of the problems identified in the early stages of the change process have already been indicated, not least the problems related to the purchasing staff. But there were also a number of other issues to take into consideration:

- Coordination and integration were a problem. For a company spending more than €2.5 billion annually on materials and services, the sheer volume of transactions was overwhelming. The company had multiple business units spread geographically over five countries and six industry sectors, each with its own purchasing department. Even the purchasing activities of the specific business units were on many occasions not coordinated. There were different autonomous purchasing organizations within the company. Many of these would have contracted with the same supplier, yet each contract was locally negotiated. Many sites did not realize that other sites within the company were using the same suppliers. The result was different pricing and contract conditions, an overall reduction of negotiation leverage, and an extensive amount of redundant contract development activity.

- Another area targeted for improvement was purchasing authorization. Field drafts were used extensively in the business units. Any employee could place an order with a supplier of his or her choice and have the item delivered just about anywhere. In 1997, NCC received about 1.5 million invoices. Personnel within purchasing departments were busy controlling and paying these invoices and they often had to deal with complaints from vendors who were not being paid on time. There were also complaints from business units that they were being billed for items not received.

- Existing stand-alone electronic purchasing and accounts payable systems were ineffective (and only sporadically existing). There was no integration of data between purchasing and accounts payable. In addition, the systems were maintenance intensive, with no online capability. Other problems included the inability to consolidate payments, the existence of multiple data files, the issuing of multiple cheques to vendors, and the manual processing of approximately 1.5 million invoices annually, of which roughly 40% consisted of purchases without a written order.

Management thus did not have the corporate-wide information needed to identify and correct problem areas and budget preparation. There was no way to identify the corporate-wide high-volume commodities, analyse commodity costs and track volume with specific vendors. It was not uncommon that the buyers had to ask the suppliers for such facts. This was very different from what Mr Frisk was used to. Thus, NCC was lagging behind other industries in terms of ICT maturity.

NCC had identified purchasing as a possible source of competitive advantage, one that could give the company a favourable cost structure and allow it to price its services and products appropriately. However, by the mid-1990s, NCC lacked the necessary control over its purchasing activities to be able to take corporate-wide actions. It should be acknowledged, however, that this was not a unique situation for NCC. It seems as if this period was a time to wake up for companies in many industries. Our introductory case with the dramatic development of IBM took off at the same time – and so did many others (Chapter 1).

It should also be acknowledged that there were a number of very positive things present in the NCC case too. Sourcing was an area identified as one of coming strategic importance. It had very explicit support from top management and the new CPO was appointed a member of the board of directors. Besides, it is a positive thing that so many things could be improved! It could be worth noting that, most likely, a diagnosis of this point of departure in relation to the maturity model (Chapter 2) should, for most of its operations, position NCC on level 2. The aims were to climb upwards and the corporate management, not least the CEO, wanted it to happen fast! And it was not totally focused on lowering cost: there was a broader approach.

From now on we will describe some of the steps taken during the following four to five years. We will not provide a rigorous chronological story. Instead we are going to highlight some of the most critical steps taken.

12.3   Part 2: Areas of change and ways to create that change

In the subsequent discussion of the core of the change process, we will primarily focus on what was done in the various areas of change and what changes were created. Later, we will partly return to some chronology when we discuss a number of critical events that occurred and were dealt with during this process.

As a general starting point, a holistic approach was applied. It was thought of as a key aspect to see to it that necessary changes in several areas were synchronized. These included organizational aspects, technology (ICT), people, systems and management practices. Let us first look at some organizational measures undertaken.

Organizational changes

Several organizational changes were introduced (Chapter 5 discusses the various ways to organize sourcing activities in more detail). Some came rather early, while others occurred later during the four-year period. From the start, the new CPO was assigned a position on the corporate board of directors and he reported directly to the CEO. This was one of the structural aspects that Klas Frisk saw as demonstrations of the dedication of corporate management to improvements in purchasing. The previous CPO had had a more restricted role and less time devoted to corporate-wide/joint operations. The changed role gave Mr Frisk a formal position, signalling that something new and powerful was to be expected.

The organizational design measures described below became major ingredients in the NCC 'journey'. They were meant to build specialist knowledge for each substantial product/service and related supply market (the commodity champions and teams) and to improve integration between units and countries (purchasing council, steering groups). The purchasing board of directors came in quite late in the process as a way to put extra pressure on business area managers to drive integration issues that had not worked well enough.

Commodity champions and commodity teams

Looking at its cost position and value chain, NCC decided to change its purchasing policy and strategy in a drastic way. Mr Frisk says:

> I thought that the decentralized and dispersed purchasing practices applied hitherto meant limited possibilities to really have an impact on the suppliers and to make use of the total NCC purchasing body. The lack of coordinated volumes was one aspect. Another, at least equally important one, was the limited possibility to build knowledge and expertise. The

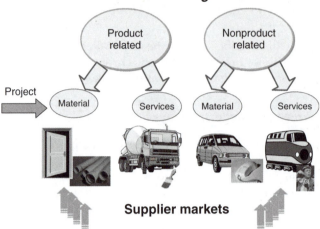

FIGURE 12.2   NCC – segmentation model.

supplier is a specialist in his product, but our purchasers could only know very little about every single product they purchase.

This was a message frequently repeated in various forums among purchasing staff, as well as among business area managers and the like. It was accompanied by a simple segmentation model based on the principles outlined in Figure 12.2.

This was a way to clarify that suppliers of for example business travel, a nonproduct-related service, are specialists on just that and that they know their supply chain. NCC had no dedicated purchasing specialists on each commodity. Instead, it had to cover several fields. This figure was efficient in bringing that message through. 'When we started to communicate it this way, it was genuinely understood,' said Mr Frisk.

Having made the analysis of staff competencies, Klas Frisk managed to get support for a competence development programme (centrally funded). Several new managers and staff were recruited, some of them from outside of the construction industry – and with a much better conceptual and strategic understanding than average existing staff. NCC developed a centre-led purchasing system approach, with commodity champions and teams. The very best people among the purchasers were or would be appointed as commodity managers. These managers were there to take a value-chain-wide view. The champions should make deals and carry out development projects with suppliers. They should be specialists within their commodity area, they should 'live' in and 'feel the pulse' of the market.

The commodity champions should lay the ground for the actual everyday buying, executed by business units or directly by so-called project purchasers in service of the project sites. This idea required, as indicated above, some new and very capable people. It took some time to get the first ones installed, even after the agreement on going in this direction had been reached. This led to some criticism of Frisk. However, when the core part of the process, as analysed here, was finished, more than ten full-time commodity manager positions and several part-time positions were in place and a joint development programme for these strategic purchasers was also in operation. Some of them were physically located at specific business areas, others in the central staff. Mr Frisk said:

> There was some frustration before we got this going. First because of the costs of hiring some new people, which was a necessity. Secondly, we had some difficulty in explaining to the business areas what these people would do. All products were already bought in 'satisfying' ways – what more could these people do? This caused resistance and was a challenge for us. The best way to explain turned out to be by developing real and good business cases performed by a team and to communicate them as role models. We were fortunate to find some good cases early on. I was convinced that with roughly 20 commodity managers in place, we would have been a very capable organization to carry out our sourcing mission.

It should be mentioned that several commodity teams were already in operation, in practice, before they were actually appointed to these roles. The commodity or category team was defined as 'a systematic process to manage/reduce complexity by segmenting supply purchases by industry; optimizing across businesses; and extending internal resources through the use of supplier category specialists'. Klas Frisk explained:

> The role of the commodity sourcing team was to build the business case for optimization across NCC's five business areas and operations in four countries. The idea was that the commodity sourcing team should be built around the company's corporate purchasing industry or commodity experts. Here we should also find representatives for technology and support staff to coordinate with the R&D process, production people as well as experts in financial issues and other areas. They should also coordinate with the manager of supplier quality assurance, the category operations managers (project purchasers) who are responsible for coordinating the operations side, including logistics, planning, vendor-managed inventory and associated issues, and a few other people. It should be admitted that we didn't reach that vision other than in a few cases during the time period under study.

Still other specialists may participate, on an *ad hoc* basis, to lend their expertise or express their views. These teams should be a strong support for the everyday job of the commodity manager. It should be mentioned that, however nice and logical these organizational arrangements and the search for good business cases may sound, this was not easily accepted. It turned out that not all stakeholders were convinced of the benefits of this approach, even in spite of the examples and the communication around them. There were also negative interpretations from some project purchasers who felt degraded into second-class purchasers. Some of the negative feelings were due to the fact that a substantial share of what project purchasers bought were services that were not easily suited to simple 'call-off' ordering.[7] This implies that some employees resisted because they did not agree to the basic idea, but there were also other reasons such as a loss of individual control and decision power (compare the discussion in Chapter 10 on various ways to interpret such activities). Without the good examples, the efforts to establish this organizational principle would have been even more difficult.

Project purchasers

Before these changes the purchasing operations had been dominated by project purchasers, operating primarily as supply controllers very close to the specific construction projects. They carried out the 'serve the project' aspects. The problem was that they had very limited opportunities to build knowledge and to operate on a corporate level. Klas Frisk commented:

> These people were in charge of reaching agreements in a great variety of products and services. It was like in athletics if a decathlon athlete were confronted by a specialist (the supplier's staff) in each game. They would have very little chance to do a good job in relation to every commodity they bought. We needed to complement – and in some cases convert – these people with/to commodity champions and commodity teams. This was the basic idea behind the new roles and structures.

Some early questions in the process, preceding the decision to go for specialization by commodity, had been: should the purchasing function be organized to support a particular business unit, thus cutting across many commodity groups? Should the purchasing function be organized around a commodity or 'category', thereby cutting across many business units? As has already been disclosed, the latter became the choice.

The NCC corporate purchasing council (CPC)

In order to move to a higher level of strategic involvement, the purchasing organization broadened its scope through the internal transfer of purchasing-related activities to a corporate purchasing department, located at NCC headquarters in Stockholm. To ensure that all major purchases of products and services were handled on a genuinely professional basis, NCC formed a corporate purchasing council (CPC) made up of representatives from several functions (for a detailed discussion on coordination mechanisms see Chapter 5). While considering important inputs from key functions and users, the role of the CPC was to decide on and to ensure that purchasing issues in different business departments were handled in consistent ways with the overall goals and strategies of the entire NCC Group. Klas Frisk was the council leader and really the 'general manager' of the council. Other CPC members were the deputy CPO, the manager of international sourcing (with the function of coordinating all international efforts), five purchasing directors representing the five business units (housing, civil engineering, building, industry, real estate and investment) and four managers representing the international subsidiaries. This was a decision forum, not merely a matter of experience sharing. It was meant to support these purchasing directors in their efforts to implement the new strategy operatively consisting of commodity managers, commodity teams and project purchasers. Again, Klas Frisk:

> This was a way to involve key people throughout the purchasing organization. Purchasing needed to be visible and coherently implemented in each business area, otherwise it will not take off. That was the idea behind this move. They should also be in dialogue with their respective business area managers who needed to be informed, in all aspects of sourcing today and in the future. The business area managers had also to get to know the meaning of concepts such as supplier development, supply chain management, global purchasing etc.

Members of CPC were supposed to have a high level of commitment and be missionaries to the rest of the group – preaching for the importance of coordinated and cross-functional purchasing in the entire NCC group. In forging the contracts, the commodity team was often quite active and the corporate purchasing council was informed of progress and key issues. Only after the contract started to run, however, were the agreed issues to be proven.

Most of it worked well but 'in due time it turned out that some members of this body, back in their everyday practice, counteracted decisions taken,' said Mr Frisk. 'This made me both disappointed and angry,' he continued.[8]

These purchasing managers of course had other loyalties in the organization too (e.g. to project managers, to suppliers that might lose a customer and so on) – and they were not always prepared to push the new purchasing strategy strongly. 'Remember also that several previous efforts to change had failed; what if a person loyal to this initiative gets into too much fighting and it later turns out that we wouldn't succeed after all?' said Mr Frisk. Therefore much effort had to be put into this process, especially as this operation was an international one including the development of cross-border agreements. Activities and agreements in Sweden, Finland, Noway, Denmark and Poland had to be coordinated in an organization created by mergers and acquisitions and with a strong decentralized culture overall.

In order to strengthen the implementation power on the level below the business area purchasing managers and to put pressure on the people involved in the operative everyday activities in the various supplier relations, several small steering groups for important supplier relations were created. This consisted of the key account from NCC and from the supplier, complemented by a top line manager from NCC and someone similar, most often the CEO, from the supplier. This group met once or twice every year to make sure that the specific relationship of their responsibility actually developed according to agreements and expectations. They made plans for future developments of the relationship and took decisions on important steps to take. Also the CEO of NCC, Jan Sjöqvist, was involved in several such supplier relationships.

Altogether this was an organizational design that should facilitate not only everyday business operations but also the tackling of more strategic issues.

NCC group purchasing board

After two years of progress in many areas but lack of progress in others, not least due to problems in getting strong support from some of the business area managers and thus in making the business area purchasing managers fulfil their mission, some additional steps had to be taken. Klas Frisk explained:

> I had all the support from the CEO I could ask for. I was a member of the corporate management team and we decided on several important issues, but, at least in some areas, only a portion of what was decided really happened. My interpretation – and I was quite sure about this – was that for some reason, the business area managers, once back in their respective organizations, did not really want and try to support the implementation of what had been decided. My conclusion was that we needed a complementary and more powerful decision body for purchasing and supply issues. That was the thinking behind the NCC group purchasing board. A dialogue with the CEO led to the appointment of

the head of the largest business area to accept the role as the chairman of this body. It is interesting to note that he had, in my mind, been the most reluctant person regarding the proposed changes in order to promote purchasing development. I think this appointment by our CEO was made in line with the principle: 'If you can't beat them, make them join you!'

This organizational body worked very well and it turned out that the chairman, once identified with the mission, became a very strong actor promoting, from that moment on, the new purchasing strategy. Nevertheless, it was not a smoothly functioning process. There were still some obstructive activities where for example in one exceptional case the purchasing manager from one business area even refused to send its staff to training programmes, expressing the opinion that they were 'too theoretical and thus not useful'.[9]

Additional support for the process was created when the CEO decided to make key purchasing ratios a part of top management's internal bonuses. This gave even stronger support to the implementation of the new strategy (compare discussions in Chapter 9 regarding measures to take in order to motivate individuals). Already before this, purchasing was an issue, via key ratios, at the meetings of the corporate executive committee, but now its presence was likely to become stronger. Among others, the CPO presented key performance indicators of the purchasing development process bi-monthly at the committee meetings. These could vary somewhat from one year to another. The five key indicators one specific year were the following:

- Number of international company-wide agreements.
- Amount of purchases for which company-wide agreements exist.
- Compliance: how much of the purchasing volumes potentially covered by company-wide agreements are actually bought via those agreements.
- Price reductions through NCC-wide contracts, as compared to local contracts or without contracts.
- Supply-base reduction.

For all these measures, there were specific targets. Some important criteria behind them were that they should be relevant, few, simple and ICT supported. The developments of these indicators versus the targets were presented on a one-page overview with some explanatory comments. The company managed – at last – to make its systems provide this information, thereby making it possible to track the development of each of the five key performance measures. Mr Frisk said: 'It is tough to expose yourself to such measurements (and targets), but it is a great way to give visibility and orientation to the venture you are managing.' It also acted as a great support in the 'top-down' aspects of the change process. It provided points of reference in managing the process.

Comment on organizational changes

All these organizational changes took quite a lot of time to introduce, but after three years they were all put into action. Most of the significant commodities had a designated champion by then, and the teams were on their way to generating a deeper level of expertise as well as developing methods of operating their business. The changes meant that around 15 new staff members were recruited to the company, five of whom worked with nonproduct-oriented purchases.

During these years of change they also managed to build a quality system that enabled NCC, as the first Swedish construction firm, to qualify for the ISO 9001 and 14001 certificates. That had meant a lot of efforts in the purchasing part of the firm and was facilitated by the ongoing developments in purchasing and supply. These efforts and achievements also helped Mr Frisk and the responsible corporate quality manager to get to know one another and develop their personal networks.

Everything that has been mentioned as organizational change has not been an easy process. The CEO of that time, Jan Sjöqvist, said:

> I think Mr Frisk was taken by surprise by the culture of NCC. In Volvo there were not that many people you needed to confront and convince once a decision was made. NCC was a much more decentralized company with strong and entrepreneurial project leaders. When you are in change management you always find some people who do not like what you are doing. Mr Frisk came into several fights based on conflicting interests and had to do a lot of internal fighting. But he gradually learnt how to make his way through.

Some people in the organization found the new purchasing structure threatening, or believed that it would encroach on their territory, or did not believe in it. Most of all it was a debate on topics such as 'How much more will this cost?' 'What will be the value of the contribution of these specialists?' 'Why so much talking, why can't we just keep on doing our business?' This created a need for purchasing management to be better able to demonstrate the (potential) value of its contributions. Mr Frisk commented:

> We developed several interesting business cases that were documented and communicated. But we also put a lot of efforts on new processes and procedures to get away from maverick buying and the like. Such measures led among others to that we could take away an 'invoice-controlling factory', i.e. tens of people doing nothing but controlling incoming invoices. Such actions had a significant economic impact.

Thus organizational changes, organizational design as well as a stricter purchasing process all had effects.

Changes in information and communications technology

During this development process, there was also a radical improvement in the possibilities of using information and communications technology (ICT). Early on, internal communication was primarily done via e-mail and increasingly through the intranet, to which a number of important databases were connected or in the process of being built. Through this, it gradually became possible to communicate more effectively within one or more group(s) of actors. The World Wide Web has to an increasing degree been put into use, to collect information and possible new sources of supply.

This was only the start of a long-term development process, and was still far from perfect. But the development process of the sourcing function benefited from it, even though it did not have to make it happen all by itself – many others have pushed this issue within the firm. Gradually, it became possible to use the intranet for making important tools available, like the purchasing handbook, contracts with suppliers, analyses of supply markets, the 'red and green' list of chemicals, courses to take, application forms and so on. Interestingly, both the head of the ICT department and the CPO were in charge of units in strong development. As their desires coincided, they got along very well. Towards the end of the period studied NCC was awarded the annual prize for innovativeness issued by the national body for stimulating improvements in purchasing and logistics. The prizewinner herself was one of the new recruits from outside the construction industry.

During these years NCC passed through a development similar to many other firms when it came to the implementation of new technology. This development supported the general development in purchasing.

Development of the people in sourcing

After collecting the facts about the actual status of the educational skills of the staff in sourcing, a strategy for improvement was decided on (see Chapter 7 for a more detailed discussion on developing skills and competencies). One important aspect was to try to recruit new people; another was to try to develop the existing staff.

Sourcing management tried its very best to attract (and finance) people with a different background than the present employees. Gradually they managed, step-by-step, to attract interesting people from other industries as well as from other internal positions within the company. Likewise, a number of newly educated people were also recruited. It became evident that these made a significant difference. Klas Frisk said:

> I wanted to find basically three kinds of profiles, preferably combined in one person. On the one hand, it was important to find people with a background in interesting industries from which we buy. We noticed that the early recruitment of a previous marketer from a business travel services firm could provide a superior contribution in terms of field knowledge. We systematically tried to find people we needed, based on such background aspects. But we also wanted people with experience of applying modern purchasing practices. For such reasons, well-respected companies with a modern view on purchasing were important targets. In addition, we looked for young, newly employed and hungry people.

Development of the existing staff meant a lot too. One important step was to design a competence ladder in four steps: a one-day introduction, a basic programme of 11 days, the purchasing management platform, plus specialist programmes for commodity managers and project purchasers respectively.

The joint basic programme was thought of as something of substantial durability and with content, which 'really could make a change'. The programme was split into three blocks and 11 groups of 20 people each had 11 days on campus. Altogether it meant the production of nearly 2500 individual course days in 1.5 years. The aim was to establish a joint perspective on sourcing thinking and provide an arena for discussions about the new strategy. The CPO managed to make the CEO and all business area managers actively promote the programme by involving them in a video that was shown when every individual programme started. This had strong symbolic value, signifying that business area managers stood behind the change process (even though that had not always been the case elsewhere). Between blocks 1 and 2, participating purchasers were requested to carry out a product-market analysis according to identical instructions, including models for analysis. Through these assignments, NCC created around 70 product-market descriptions and analyses, in a more or less identical way. The model was based on general management theories, actually a combination of a five forces analysis[10] and network/value chain mapping.[11] In Figure 12.3 we can see an illustration of such an analysis.

Between blocks 2 and 3, participants were requested to carry out a supplier analysis according to the new model for supplier evaluation that had been developed during the change process. Again, this resulted in 70 supplier analyses according to a unified protocol. All of these were later used and improved by the commodity champions and put into a joint electronic format for use and continuous upgrading. They were put into a database connected to the intranet, but not everyone had access to it. Klas Frisk said:

> I think this was one of our great achievements. We combined education with building market knowledge as well as initiating the systematic use of electronic databases. We also put demands on creativity. Each group of purchasers working with a specific supply market was challenged to identify at least five options to improve the ways in which each specific item/service was purchased. The purchasing staff were also trained in writing and presenting. They all got a lecture on presentation techniques and when they presented their study they had to apply this lesson. The written material was judged based on content as well as readability (and critical perspective) and creativity (i.e. suggestions for improvement), and the purchasers were also judged on presentation and discussion skills.

Later on, the analyses generated from these exercises were developed into a strategic plan. An estimate of possible improvements in terms of lowering costs or providing better value pointed to a potential for improvement of a substantial percentage of total purchasing spend. It became a 'hot' item to be invited to present to the board of directors.

All these changes warranted the development of NCC's courses and training programmes that would allow purchasing professionals to perform their roles effectively in years to come. For example, with the move to cross-functional teams, team building, communication skills and ICT affinity would require greater emphasis. With a focus on such things as value chain management, reducing cycle time, negotiating in a partnering arrangement and greater cultural awareness in dealing in a continuously changing global economy, there was a strong need for competence development initiatives.

People involved in strategic sourcing would need expertise in competitive analysis, while those more involved in day-to-day operations of the function would require a greater affinity with information system technology. The mentioned competence ladder that was developed identified these needs and forged suitable contents.

Comments on changes in people
The efforts in developing existing staff and bringing in new people from outside were quite successful. Much of the debate, along the lines of 'that's not applicable in our industry' and 'we have tried that before, it's no good', could be reduced.

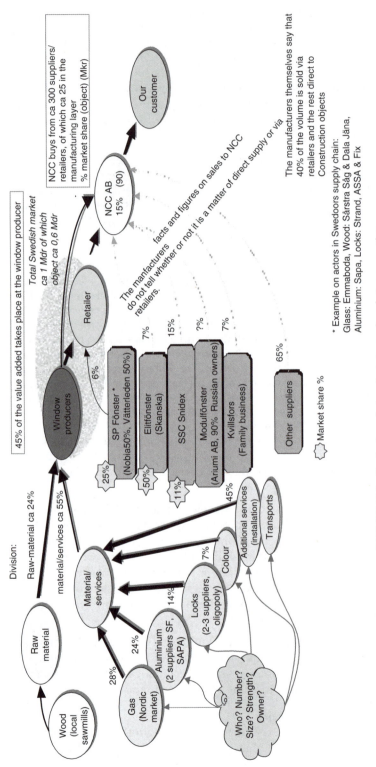

FIGURE 12.3 Product-market analysis in a value-chain perspective.

The new staff were generally strong in argumentation skills and could witness to good practices taught and practised during course sessions and in relation to task assignments, both related to the development programme and in everyday business activity. Of course, this was not true for each and every individual. There were still a number of individuals who basically bought like they always bought. In general, however, the initiatives taken at NCC seem to have been a good way to develop people's attitudes and skills.

It should also be mentioned, as an interesting illustration, that Mr Frisk actively took part for one day in each block in all programmes, either by being 'on stage' or actively commenting on the market and supplier studies done. This way he also got a good picture of his staff and could identify people with interesting potential. Furthermore, he learnt a lot about the supply markets at the same time.

Changes in systems and procedures

It was mentioned earlier that the company also had shortcomings as far as systems and procedures were concerned. The shortcomings meant that some systems and processes were totally missing or did not fit well (enough) with the new mission. One example is the process of selecting suppliers. The new approach was to design a subprocess for product-market analysis (see above) and a subprocess for supplier evaluation. These were two of the most important ingredients in the new model for supplier choice.

Two other tools for ensuring that the process of goal setting and achievement permeated the purchasing group were to identify 'best practice' programmes and to create a system for performance measurement. The best practice initiative identified vital activities, set performance goals for each activity and aggressively benchmarked performance. Some of the areas that have been targeted include:

- Supply base reduction.
- Supplier review and analysis benchmarking.
- Implementation of selected intensified cooperative relationships.

This was communicated within the organization as well as to individual suppliers and the supply markets in general. One way to achieve the latter was the introduction of an annual 'Supplier Day', in which invited representatives from the 100 most important suppliers took part. This gave a good opportunity to communicate new policies and procedures and to get responses. In conjunction with this there was also the election of the 'Supplier of the Year', based on creativity and innovativeness, for example that it has introduced new and valuable working methods or products. At the time, this was a new activity within the Swedish construction industry and it generated a great deal of positive feedback from the invited suppliers.

Comments on changes in systems and procedures
Also in this case the change had to start almost from zero. The processes had to be designed and accepted by various stakeholders. It took some time to get it all in place, and the benefits were frequently questioned.

There was a need both internally as well as externally to get to understand not just the new purchasing strategy, but the basic ideas behind it. To meet that need, purchasing management in cooperation with the NCC University produced a booklet. This 'blue book' was a 30-page explanation of the thinking behind the developments in purchasing. It was printed and 2000 copies distributed. Purchasing also became visible in the official company annual report to the stock market (and other groups taking an interest in it). In this report, purchasing had one page at its disposal; previously it had nothing. It was also explicitly mentioned in the foreword by the CEO. All these practices were part of the communication and rhetoric surrounding purchasing.

Changes in managerial practices

In addition to what has already been mentioned, a number of specific practices were put into operation. One was that each strategic agreement with a supplier should include a vision for cooperation: what should be achieved? How are the benefits of cooperation going to be realized?

Another aspect of the management practices to be mentioned here is innovation through continuous improvement. Three fundamental principles were considered important for the success of this, in line with personal goal setting and active learning. These principles were:

- Failure would not be punished.
- Follow up on performance, reflect and correct.
- Create new routines in the case of frequent deviations.

The goal was to learn and to go on. Indeed, the key question in these situations was: 'Did you learn something?'

Changes in relation to suppliers and supply structures

It has already been mentioned that NCC had very many suppliers and that the supply markets typically either consisted of a very fragmented structure with many small and locally oriented firms or a very concentrated structure with a monopolist or a few dominating actors. Mappings of supply structures showed that quite frequently the markets were dominated by one or two very strong suppliers up the supply chain.

The changes in relation to suppliers and supply structures included reducing the total number of suppliers, deciding in what part of the supply chain to settle the deal, and how to approach the commodity in question. Klas Frisk commented:

> We had to decide on issues such as should NCC as a large firm buy elevator installations including the equipment from rather small entrepreneurs who were not likely to be able to exercise very much purchasing power, as we did? Or should we as heavy users when considering the totality of our operations buy the equipment from the global elevator suppliers and only the installation service from the service provider? To me the answer was obvious, but I realized that – logical as it might be – it wouldn't be an easy change to make. And it wasn't.

In the change efforts in relation to supply markets, NCC used more or less all the alternatives presented in Chapter 4. It managed to reduce the number of suppliers considerably (50%), it progressed quite well in focusing on the level in the supply chain at which the deals should be settled: at the first tier, the second or third tier and so on (compare Figure 12.3). It also managed to develop several frame agreements on a country-wide as well as Scandinavian basis. In doing so, it frequently also tried to change the way of operating the joint (supplier and customer) business.

One country-wide agreement that came quite early in the process was with the MRO supplier Totalpartner. In this case NCC took the initiative to develop a new actor, where some previously independent MRO distributors in cooperation with NCC created a new company with country-wide coverage and with developed forms of operating, for example concerning assortment, logistics, administrative routines and so on. NCC and Totalpartner even had a joint purchasing team, with joined forces, to approach the suppliers of Totalpartner. This was a success story and it made Totalpartner one of the winners of NCC's annual awards for outstanding creative suppliers. The motivation was 'for excellent supply compression and braveness'. Still, it was not a change process without friction. It was a tough job to make it all come true in the buyer–supplier relationship itself, but maybe even more so inside the supplier. The manager in charge at that supplier at the time, Mr Gustaf Eckhardt, explained this:

> It was one of the most exciting periods of my career. We really had a challenge and we saw the potential of these changes, not just because of increased volumes, but because of the new designs of our business processes. In meetings with the suppliers and also internally, when all of us involved penetrated the ideas and the potential joint improvements, everyone agreed. But then, back in the everyday operative activities when people actually had to change their behaviour, we had a hell of a mountain to climb. To me it was, for some period, a full-time job to stand up internally and defend the measures decided on. So many people were so upset about having to change their behaviour including, for example, breaking old business relationships.[12]

The new concepts are fully alive and also considerably developed today. The ideas were right and in due time they were accepted. But Mr Eckhardt emphasized how demanding a change process intended to develop purchasing could be also for the suppliers who somehow get involved and – not least – for the change leader(s) at the supplier's site. It takes at least two, preferably more, winners to make a breakthrough of innovative new ideas.

In this case both NCC (and indirectly NCC's customers), the supplier, Totalpartner and some of Totalpartner's suppliers saw a significant business potential. That enabled the change even though it was not an easily won step. Other cases of changed operations initiated by NCC included making strategies to attack or get around suspected cartels and escalating and increasing the scope of the business in some relationships, for example concentrating on one supplier of oil and including car rentals in the scope of the joint business. Many such activities were taken, but hardly ever without any kind of resistance from someone inside NCC, inside the supplier or on the industry level. Strategic change is, thus, not only an internally oriented issue in order to develop organizational designs and so on. Also inside the supplier and in various supply networks such changes create tension and changes in conditions to influence, changes in economic outcome as well as gains and losses of power.

12.4   Part 3: What happened later?

In 2001, after four years, a radically new situation arose. The owners of NCC had become discontented with the revenues delivered. They decided to change corporate top management. A new CEO was appointed and his mandate was very clear. The shareholder value of NCC needed to be increased! But the mandate was in other ways contrary to the previous management. They had been urged to create a major construction company of European size. Now, it was more of a downsizing and 'stick to your knitting' approach.

The strategy to build an internationally integrated construction firm would be partly abandoned. Foreign operations that did well could stay in the corporation, but everything that needed a lot of hands-on coordination as well as all 'noncore' businesses should be sold off. Furthermore, the corporation needed to become much more lean. According to the new management, the corporation in general had been designed for a much more qualified mission than it had to fulfil.

The new CEO started the slimming process close to himself. More than two thirds of all staff in the corporate centre were laid off. This meant that whole functions such as the corporate units for quality management, environment management and even central R&D were closed down. The qualification for the ISO 9001 certificate was considered not important and NCC left such obligations. Very few of the central units remained.

The central purchasing and supply management unit, altogether 15 people, which had been built up from zero by Mr Frisk and had been working with the creation of the infrastructure described – the organizational design, the processes, development of people as well as making strategic and central deals with suppliers – was also to be closed down. It was said to be 'not requested by the organization'. This also meant that Mr Frisk and all his staff at the corporate level had to leave the company. The previous vice-CPO, these days working in another function in one of the business areas, became responsible for purchasing and supply in the biggest business area and with certain responsibilities for corporate/joint purchasing issues.

There are several interpretations of why some units were closed down and others remained, ranging from 'not providing enough value' to a result of a desire by the new management to 'clear the table' and get rid of all units that were too closely related to the previous management team. In any case, the new strategy and the subsequent reduction and decentralization of functions and people were implemented in powerful ways.

There were many layoffs all over the organization and the management principles of top management changed from a more administrative, decision- and document-based strategy as well as a cross-divisional mode, to a much more field-based, hands-on action approach. The emphasis was on eliminating 'waste' and making operational activities and actors 'heroes'. This meant that NCC rapidly seemed to return to the previous 'business as usual' methods. The international agreements were much less in focus. Integration between business areas could still take place, but was not supported by the organizational and processual infrastructure developed.

In retrospect: What really happened?

Today, some years after the dramatic change of strategy at the company, there is an interesting pattern to observe. In terms of resources and management attention, the first steps after the dramatic turnaround seemed to downplay purchasing to the low level it had before the start of the change process. Gradually, however, it became evident that purchasing would also come to play an important role under the new regime.

The basic principles of working with commodity managers were soon reinstalled (or actually in practice never left). In due time, a need was also felt for integration and more international operations. After two years, a new purchasing manager with specific responsibility to develop NCC's international purchases was recruited. She, too, came from the automotive industry! Also some decision forums came back because of the need to handle issues of integration and internationalization. It seems more and more as if there is an acceptance that the analysis of the situation originally made by Mr Frisk and his team was correct. But there are some diverging opinions as well.

The process of increased attention to purchasing and supply was strengthened even more in 2003 and 2004. The development of this function has been selected as one of three areas of highest priority. The latest top 100 managers' conference was totally devoted to purchasing and supply management issues. A taskforce has been created that should identify and develop new sources of supply. All employees involved in management training programmes have to choose something related to purchasing, when there is any assignment of topics to develop.

The CEO is actively involved in the taskforce and also takes action, for example when someone does not buy in accordance with frame agreements, he – personally – acts on that, searches and confronts the individual in question. He pays weekly visits to construction sites and requests opinions from the people on the operative levels. If there are complaints, for instance about some frame agreements, the responsible business area manager will get to know it from the CEO personally. The CEO will give the background and ask for clarification: is it a bad agreement or are there other explanations? He will also ask for a prompt action plan.

So basically the company is back to where it was when the process was interrupted in 2001, and in several areas clearly ahead of that position. It has a somewhat different orientation. It seems to undertake fewer efforts in creating steering groups and other organizational measures, and more towards hands-on activities. Implementation, making the good ideas materialize, is heavily emphasized. This is not to say, however, that the previous purchasing management did not do a hands-on job. But in relative focus and in rhetoric, this seems to be the case. There is a basic acknowledgement that what was done during Mr Frisk's days was correct. But the process of implementation had shortcomings, largely because of a culture inside the company that decisions from 'up there' (the board of directors and CEO) were not really interpreted as compulsory. To some employees they were considered more as a 'hint' or a general recommendation. That has changed today!

There are also more efforts to support the operational staff in doing business and giving active support at local levels as well, for example on how to negotiate and settle deals. This has helped to build and strengthen the legitimacy of and respect for the support organization of today.[13]

Success or failure?

Was this process a success or a failure after all? During four years the CPO and his team managed to put purchasing and supply issues on the corporate agenda more powerfully than before. They managed to get a lot of the basic infrastructure needed for a purchasing and supply operation in line with steps 4 and 5 in the maturity model from Chapter 2.

They also managed to develop a number of business cases to demonstrate the basic concept and indicate the improvement potential. They established several key measures, for example number of suppliers, share of total purchases in accordance with developed frame agreements, and these developed quite nicely. Furthermore, they measured and regularly reported five key ratios to the corporate board of directors, among which were the developments of supplier reduction, prices, invoice reduction and share of purchases based on frame agreements.

They all went in the right direction: the number of suppliers had been reduced from 74 000 to 36 000 and the number of invoices reduced by 30%, doubling the average amount per invoice. The volumes bought according to NCC agreements went from 10 to 31% and the obedience to negotiated agreements also increased substantially. The relative cost developments on NCC agreements were estimated at an annual improvement of circa 5%. Purchased volumes across country borders also showed a steadily increasing trend. Altogether, these were a number of convincing developments!

An effort was made to estimate savings over a three-year period. The purchased volume varied between €1.3 and €1.7 billion per year, implying roughly €4.5 billion over the three-year period. Calculating the increases of products bought in line with contracts, times €4.5 billion, times the expected average improvement, amounted to an estimated total cost reduction of €45 million in savings over these three years. In addition to that, some €10 million were estimated benefits from the international agreements. This exceeds by far the investment made in staff and other measures. Other economic effects came from time savings (labour-cost savings) due to fewer invoices and many other changes. This was the internal estimation made, trusted by the board of directors. Mr Frisk said:

> Problems with estimated savings are twofold. First, there are always some uncertainties in estimations made and they can be questioned from various points of departure. In this case, however, we felt that we were on the safe side. Secondly, you would need to tell positive news to strengthen the process of change, but you don't always want to let your suppliers know about it. It goes without saying that they want some share in conjunction with next negotiations if they know.

The progress mentioned hardly ever occurred immediately. Normally it came after some struggle in processes of muddling through. One important aspect of creating change is to build coalitions (see Chapter 3). Mr Frisk gave his view:

> From the beginning I felt the support of our CEO. Gradually I managed to win the confidence also among other units, e.g. business area industry and real estate, our purchasing management in Norway and Denmark etc. In some areas, however, I didn't fully manage even though the measures described. e.g. the creation of the corporate board of directors with one of the previously resisting managers as chairman etc., made me turn some of these from resisting people to supporting ones. I am sure I could have done more and better but I wasn't dissatisfied with those developments. In change processes you cannot expect everyone to applaud everything.

Thus, there were a lot of achievements and there was also substantial support for the venture. Still, when the new management came in, one early conclusion based on field dialogues, between the new CEO and business area informants as well as production-related people, was that there was little understanding of the contribution of the central part of the purchasing organization. From that point of view, the change process failed. It still had not really reached an acceptance all the way through the organization.

One should, however, also remember that there was a radical shift in corporate strategy at this time. Very many things had been achieved, especially when it came to the building up of the basic infrastructure. But the estimated payoff was not evident or generally known (or accepted as a fact). When asked whether or not this change process should be considered a success, the initiator, the CEO Mr Sjöqvist, referred to the figures mentioned above and responded:

> I consider it most of all successful. We had managed to get so many important structures in place. We had managed to create savings by bringing down the number of suppliers and, not least, the huge amount of invoices to take care of. We had several success cases in how to influence supply markets and to apply an international perspective. All this was in line with our aims to take advantage of being the big firm. Before this process started we behaved as a small firm in all local markets. This view changed dramatically. We had invested a lot in this field and had a very promising development under way. If it had got one or two more years extra, I am convinced that we could have harvested even more significantly from all the efforts we made.

Some three years after the dramatic interruption of this change process, when many of the basic ideas and ways of operating (parts of what have been referred to as infrastructure) are back and in line with those of the core part of the change process studied here, the described process may be judged more positively also among a broader audience. As so often when one is to judge in terms of success or failure, it is a matter of *when* and *by whom* the evaluation is done. It could hereby also be of interest to again return to the introductory best practice case from Chapter 1, the IBM case. The results demonstrated were arrived at after seven years of intensive efforts towards strategic change!

What could have been done differently? Some critical events during the process

As has been indicated, many of these activities and actions took place in parallel. When they are presented as summaries of content and result they may appear to be free from friction. That is not the case. It was always a process of muddling through and many paths proved not to be possible to walk.

Any major organizational change is traumatic to individuals accustomed to either a status quo or 'having their own way' in departments 'doing their own thing'. There were many individuals in the purchasing organization as well as outside of it (staff in IT, quality, R& D, finance and so on) who got a broader scope (job enrichment) and responsibilities during this process. In general, they were positive to the new ideas. Others saw a loss in influence and scope. Nobody likes to give up power or autonomy and it is normal to encounter resistance of various degrees in individuals charged with both instigating and accepting change. 'Turkeys don't vote for Christmas' is a common saying that captures much of such resistance. There still are and often have been barriers to change in various aspects: inside the purchasing function, between different functions, in relation to different internal business areas and in relation to individual suppliers, as well as to entire markets of actors within a certain product-market. At the same time, much has actually been achieved and we have still not seen the end of the story.

When asked about possible events that had or could have had a major impact on the process described, Mr Frisk identified some critical events that he thought could have made a difference. He described a list of, roughly, 20 such events. Some of those are the following:

> A very early critical event was when I first met the management group as the new CPO. I had then learned that there had been a conflict between the previous CPO and the president of the largest business area. My predecessor had left and, in retrospect, I realize that most members of this group looked upon the recruitment of me as the solution of that conflict. That was their mental framework. That I was expected to fill a much more proactive role had not been communicated or understood. It took me by surprise and none of us acted instantly on this. Maybe this laid the ground for much tension to come.

> Another event was when the head of development of managerial resources, Mr Björn Wootz, and myself presented the results of the initial enquiry on expectations by corporate top managers and the diagnosis of staff competence in front of the board of directors. It was scheduled for half an hour, but went on for three hours. That was dynamite! At least it demonstrated a mismatch in perceptions as well as expectations on performance in relation to capabilities.

> A similar thing happened several years later when I presented the analyses of the 40 supply markets and our estimates for potential improvements. It was to some parts questioned, but it arose interest and made a strong impact. We could demonstrate what the improvement potentials were in a very structural way.

> Two very important positive events were when we made the first major deals according to the new model of operating with suppliers. One had to do with travel management. We had employed a responsible commodity manager from that specific industry. We made a deal with one supplier for all of Scandinavia which included several augmented service components – and we managed to achieve substantial price reductions. The other was the MRO agreement with one supplier, Totalpartner, covering Sweden and also including an attractive bundle of services. Before we had hundreds of agreements based on local supply chains in this field. There were of course many other deals also related to direct materials. But these two were very useful to communicate as role models. They helped demonstrate our intentions. But one should also be aware that such changes challenge many and strong interests. Some potential suppliers for example dared not be a part of this process because of possible bad effects in several other relations.

There were several instances of nonobedience to decisions made. This was both on business area manager level and among purchasing managers at certain regions of the country. With my background from Volvo Trucks I was used to a culture where decisions made at the top level, while sometimes delayed and somewhat altered, were also expedited. Here we had discussions, took decisions jointly – and nothing happened. It took me some time to realize that and to develop ways to cope with it (several of the organizational measures described should be understood in light of this). During that vacuum my legitimacy probably got somewhat eroded and I had to involve in internal political fights that not only generated friends. The real breakthrough that sent the share of purchases in line with agreements skyrocketing was when we introduced this as one of the bases for personal bonuses among top managers. That's the kind of thing you can do if your CEO supports your ambitions.

Another area had to do with staffing. In one of the business areas, we had as a purchasing manager a superb person who did it all right and with a fantastic drive. He got headhunted for another firm. The business area manager was not in favour of the change process within purchasing. The new recruitment made by the business area manager was not at all to the level of the previous purchasing manager. In the early stages of strategic change during which you start building new structures and a new culture, you may be very dependent on a few key individuals. In retrospect, thus, the loss of this excellent person was a critical event. I sometimes think that the choice of person to replace him was a deliberate move by the business area manager to employ a new individual with the wrong attitude. I can also think of several critical incidents that were positive in terms of finding the right candidate for the job, both external and internal recruitments. Such things could make huge differences.

In retrospect I also think that we tried to cover too large an area considering the resources we had. But, on the other hand, we knew that piecemeal approaches had failed in earlier attempts to develop purchasing in NCC.

This indicates that during a process like this, there are hundreds of upcoming events interpreted in a certain way, often based on incomplete information, that could all make a substantial difference. If X would not have happened, much could have been different. It seems, however, as if the structural measures – spend analysis, organizational designs and so on – were all appropriate. An especially interesting feature in this case was that all this was done without outside support from specialized consultants. Still it was not a perfect world.

When asking the head of the NCC University, in charge of the development of management resources, Björn Wootz, who all the time was involved in this process as a discussion partner to Mr Frisk and other actors inside the company, some complementary views come to the surface. Mr Wootz pointed to the process described and said that most of what was done was right. But one thing failed. That had to do with 'winning a genuine acceptance and liking for the new ideas out in the field'. He pointed to the traditionally very decentralized operations of a construction firm.

In order to change, Wootz emphasized, one has to understand the 'why' and 'how' on a detailed level, and in relation to that be able to show convincingly why a new way of operating should be preferred. He thought that this aspect, somehow, was underestimated or not genuinely understood by Mr Frisk. When confronted with this view Mr Frisk pointed to certain circumstances:

I and the vice-CPO had decided to divide our respective foci. He had a background as among others a project manager and had a strong legitimation in that part of our organization. My job was primarily to concentrate on the top levels and the vice-CPO on operative levels. Still, the changes were most of all identified with me and I spent a considerable amount of time meeting people also on operational levels, but I admit it could have had an even higher priority.

To be better off in terms of understanding and interpreting the culture of a construction firm, Mr Frisk had also asked for an internal mentor, the head of one of the business areas. He was a person who knew 'everything' about the construction business in which he had been for decades. Mr Frisk said:

It was great to have regular coaching meetings with him, to get his points of view and discuss coming decisions as well as events that had occurred. From him, a highly respected person with genuine understanding of this specific business, I got several important insights. This was a conscious effort on my side to faster and better get to learn this industry.

Mr Frisk also took part in practical purchasing negotiations and the creation of business cases, but that could also maybe have been done more extensively. The 'headquarters part' of the implementation, which could have been sufficient in other organizations, was handled well. But in this company, this was not enough.

We have noticed that there was a very strong commitment to this change process from top management. Mr Sjöqvist was also asked what he, as acting CEO, would have done differently if he could run this process once again:

I managed to get the best possible purchasing expertise in place and he made a superb job also as a change agent. He was a good pedagogue and communicator and possessed the toughness needed. But, in retrospect, all the political infighting in such a major change process takes a lot out of the involved key actors. They get burned somehow.

I think I should have supported Mr Frisk with an expert on managing change in large corporations and have such an expert take care of that part. This would have allowed Mr Frisk to fully concentrate on the development of the purchasing content of the change.

One more thing that could have been done differently relates to the systems and managerial techniques. The greatest resistance to the change came from the middle management levels, especially the project managers responsible for every construction project. They have bottom-line economic responsibility for each project. The benefits of e.g. utilizing our frame agreements and limiting the number of sources utilized had, most of all, indirect effects in relation to their operation. Those effects did not become visible and easy to calculate in relation to the specific project. Those effects appeared later, in other forums, e.g. in administrative savings due to fewer invoices and kickback agreements from loyalty to the frame agreements. In order to deal with this we had towards the end of this process developed a system to give immediate, up-front kickbacks to make these economic effects instantly visible. I wish we had developed it earlier. I think that would have increased the speed of the change process. Another similar improvement would have been to connect the development in the purchasing area to top managers' bonuses earlier. It was the right thing to do, but the timing of it could have been better.

Mr Wootz, who was closely involved in the process described and is still with the company – and still involved in the present, possibly even more focused change process – was asked the same questions. He expressed the following view:

The idea of genuinely winning acceptance from middle management and the operative levels is one way to success. Carrots based on knowledge and understanding of concepts and intentions are fine and we could have done better on that. But what we see happen now makes me convinced that in an organization like NCC it is also very much about exercising power. You have to demonstrate your dedication and be willing to sacrifice and also punish. Sticks are needed to complement the carrots!

We exercised some power also in the process managed by Mr Frisk, but relatively speaking I think we believed too much in explaining the message relative to demonstrating our dedication in terms of exercising power. Nowadays everyone knows that there will be severe consequences for those individuals counteracting corporate principles. But maybe I am getting cynical as years go by.

These reflections show that change is not only a matter of doing the right things but also at the right time. Furthermore, it is a combination of structural measures and handling a political process. And also it could be difficult to act both as the change agent and the specialist in charge of the operative parts of the operations, especially in major change processes in large corporations.

One more aspect has to do with the role of leadership style in change processes (see Chapter 6). Also in retrospect, Mr Sjöqvist thinks in terms of designs of processes and infrastructure – staffing with change experts, timing and designing reward systems and so on – which is basically managing through the use of various kinds of structural measures. The descriptions of the style of the new CEO, even if they are fragmentary, demonstrate a very different approach. What is right or wrong, good in a short- or a long-term perspective, in specific contexts and so on we do not know. But this illustrates that leadership as such really matters. It seems as if the implementation forces are stronger today and reach further. If so, in what ways are the activities of today facilitated (or hindered) by the actions taken during the focused part of the process as described here? This is interesting in principle but outside the scope of this analysis. It should be noted that the notion of the impact on leadership is, of course, also valid for other actors in other positions exercising leadership, such as the activities and action patterns by Mr Frisk. There are thus several actors involved and many choices to make as well as ways to carry out the strategizing process (see Chapters 3 and 6). The differences will result in varying outcomes.

Reflections by the change agent

After leaving NCC, Mr Frisk worked as a consultant with change management as his speciality. He then joined the Swedish national railways (SJ AB) as its new CPO. What does Mr Frisk say in retrospect? What would he have done differently today? What has he learnt from the NCC experience, in relation to his work now at SJ?

When I took on my new job it soon turned out to be a similar situation as in NCC. Actually this was one reason why I got the job. There was a very unclear organizational structure, poor statistics and processes. I did, again, start by getting the facts by making spend analyses, competence evaluations, mapping expectations from management, the purchasing staff and other stakeholders. From that, I made calculations of improvement potentials in various purchase areas and connected these to the investments in personnel and technology needed. So far, a very similar approach to begin with. But I made it deeper, more detailed and with stronger focus on developing the business cases.

What I have done differently is that I have tried to listen more. Very early on my assistant and I did in-depth interviews with each individual (there are not as many in this organization). I have also early on communicated that this diagnosis work will take some time. This was in order to buy some time free from expectations on immediate action. It was also a way to be better able to, with some better patience, get my staff and new environment prepared for the changes. In this job I have decided to always take 'the bad guy task' when and if it is needed in certain business cases, e.g. when we leave a major supplier who has worked with us during many years. One more feature is that I bring in specialists as temporary consultants, for example to support us in certain business deals. It could be one of the best production engineers I have ever worked with (from earlier employment). They run excellent business cases, stimulate and teach my new staff best practices. I have also brought in consultants to help us develop specific commodity strategies, to give top-class examples and present role models. This is much easier to do here because the attitude is different. In NCC, the attitude was more based on the uniqueness of that industry and a world-champion attitude to carrying out the job.

Apart from this, I think I possess the same values but adapt my behaviour. We create stronger and better-documented business cases. We put more emphasis on carrying out economic estimates on improvement potentials etc. Many things are different and call for adaptations. I do not have the same immediate access to top management in this job as in NCC. That makes one difference. SJ AB is also a typical services firm with no production of its own, which also makes it different, and there are additional differences. But the three major lessons learnt regard the importance of communication on all levels, being as specific as possible in suggested savings and presenting as early as possible some good business cases that demonstrate the new ways of operating this business.

12.5   Conclusion

We have described some aspects of a development process, trying to go from purchasing to supply management. At first, it might appear as a textbook example of what to do and how to do it. But if so, that is an oversimplified impression. Throughout the process there have been a lot of critical decisions to take and a lot of sensitive interpretations to make. The process was close to collapse a number of times. One reason had to do with history. These kinds of efforts have been tried before. Can anyone trust that it will endure this time? Other reasons have been due to general resistance to change in conjunction with poor statistics, which in turn has made it difficult to communicate points of departures as well as successive improvements.

It seems very much as if the involvement and dedication of top management to support this change were the most important prerequisites for the – eventual – success. In addition to that we find important the power of endurance, never giving in and – as an important part of that – a dedicated team of key actors who basically run the process. We have noticed the significance of facts and good examples to communicate concepts and successive progress. Also the understanding of the organization as a 'political system', pointing to the necessity of always trying to involve people and make them a part of the process, seems to be a key to success in change processes.

In addition we have also noticed the need for a systemic solution; that is, being prepared to change not only one isolated issue, but a combination of them. All this is easy to say but difficult to perform!

Notes and references

[1] This process was followed very closely for four years, from the initial phase until it entered into a new phase of its development. The author has followed the process partly as an academic in documenting much of it, partly as a consultant involved in, most of all, training programmes. Later, in writing this chapter, a follow-up was made on what has happened since.

[2] Source: Björn Wootz, director of the NCC University, who was involved in setting out the demands and expectations put on the incoming purchasing director.

[3] Jan Sjöqvist was the CEO of NCC during the process under study.

[4] Kraljic, P. (1983) 'Purchasing must become supply management', *Harvard Business Review*, September–October, pp. 109–17.

[5] Klas Frisk was acting CPO with the title vice-president purchasing during the process described. In the documentation of the case, he was interviewed several times. The critical reader may argue that this strong reliance on the key actor in the case will give a biased view of the entire story. We have tried to limit those effects by also interviewing and verifying the case with other informed people. One of these was Björn Wootz, the director of the NCC University, the internal unit responsible for management development. Wootz was very close to the process and is still with the company (2004). Also the acting CEO, Jan Sjöqvist, has been interviewed and has given his comments on the case. As explained earlier, the author has also been involved quite intensively with the company on numerous occasions.

[6] Narasimhan, R. and Das, A. (2001) 'The impact of purchasing integration and practices on manufacturing performance', *Journal of Operations Management*, Vol. 19, pp. 593–609; Jonsson, S. (1998) *Den strategiska försörjningsprocessen*, Licentiate thesis, Linköping University: Linköping.

[7] This was emphasized in an interview with Björn Wootz.

[8] We have not, in this study, investigated the reasons for this by interviewing the other party. We think we could live with that, as the primary reason for this study is to illustrate a process of change, not to fully investigate who was right and who was wrong in the specific process.

[9] This was one incident that took place towards the end of the period studied. Mr Wootz emphasized this as a rather significant event when the change process got challenged from below.

[10] Porter, M.E. (1998) *Competitive Strategy: Techniques for Analyzing Industries and Competitors*, Free Press: New York.

[11] Axelsson, B. and Wynstra, F. (2002) *Buying Business Services*, John Wiley & Sons Ltd: Chichester; Gadde, L.-E. and Håkansson, H. (2001) *Supply Network Strategies*, John Wiley & Sons Ltd: Chichester.

[12] Telephone interview with Mr Gustaf Eckhardt on January 27 2005.

[13] This view was presented by the new head of purchasing, Kent Ericsson, in general discussion (not a regular interview). It has been verified by Mr Wootz.

Chapter 13

THE SUPPLY FUNCTION'S ROLE IN A MAJOR CORPORATE TURNAROUND: LESSONS FROM THOMSON

P. Fraser Johnson and Michiel R. Leenders

This chapter builds on earlier chapters and identifies opportunities to use the supply function and suppliers in major corporate turnarounds at large companies. Using the example of Thomson (formally Thomson Multimedia), ten specific areas are identified where senior executives can use the supply function and suppliers to improve overall performance. In addition, implementation challenges of creating supply and supplier opportunities in a turnaround are also identified.

At some point in their evolution, most companies face serious problems and the need to execute a strategy designed to reverse declining fortunes. Declining profitability or significant financial losses are caused potentially by a number of factors, either external or internal to the organization. Turnaround management is the systematic and rapid implementation of a range of measures to make a major improvement in the performance of an organization. Turnarounds are associated with situations where major stakeholders, creditors, shareholders and senior management consider the performance of the organization unsatisfactory. Turnarounds usually result in drastic management action, such as downsizing or debt restructuring, a sense of urgency to change performance and, in the end, significant changes to the organization.

The importance of the supply function to firm performance is well recognized.[1] However, the focus of much of the literature has tended to be on strategic supply management issues. In contrast, this chapter will focus on the contribution of supply in major corporate turnarounds in large companies. Since the supply function and suppliers can significantly affect a company's competitive position, they can play a vital role in a corporate turnaround.

We have studied supply organizations at more than 20 large companies in North America and Europe.[2] From this group, Thomson stood out as the best example of effective use of the supply function as part of a major corporate turnaround, and is the focus of this chapter. While the supply function cannot take sole credit for the improvement of Thomson's performance, its contribution was significant.

This chapter describes the role that the supply function can play as part of a major corporate turnaround and ten specific elements of the Thomson turnaround strategy involving supply are identified. The chapter also identifies the implementation challenges of creating supply and supplier opportunities in a turnaround. Managers can gain insights concerning the role that supply can play in a corporate turnaround situation and the implementation challenges that they can face. The lessons from Thomson are also applicable to any manager attempting to implement a major change to his or her supply organization.

13.1   Turnaround management

There are a number of well-documented corporate turnarounds. For example, DaimlerChrysler is currently undergoing its third turnaround since Lee Iacocca's efforts in the late 1970s.[3] Nortel Networks is one of the many technology companies struggling to reverse declining fortunes. Meanwhile, Jurgen Dormann is leading the turnaround efforts at Switzerland-based ABB.

For the purposes of this chapter, a corporate turnaround situation is defined as one that meets each of the following four criteria:

1.   The corporate performance of the organization is considered unsatisfactory by major stakeholders, such as shareholders, the board of directors, banks and lenders, and senior management.
2.   Drastic management action is necessary to reverse the poor performance.
3.   There is a sense of urgency associated with the need to improve the performance.
4.   The turnaround plan results in significant changes to the organization.

If management is able to recognize the problems early, a corporate turnaround can be put into effect before bankruptcy protection is required. Symptoms may include declining market share, profit margin erosion, defections of important customers to competitors, negative cash flow, increasing administrative costs as a percentage of revenue and customer dissatisfaction.[4] For example, Levi Strauss has taken action that it hopes will reverse a five-year trend of declining sales in the US.[5]

The literature indicates that a successful turnaround plan requires major changes to the company that touch several areas simultaneously.[6] However, as discussed in Chapter 2, barriers to change within firms can be substantial. Consequently, two major challenges of executive leadership are convincing other stakeholders of the need for change and getting commitment to the turnaround plan.

Single-element solutions, such as restructuring the balance sheet or rebranding products, frequently fail to address the company's problems adequately. The successful turnaround manager looks for opportunities in all parts of the company, with the objective of addressing underlying problems in marketing and sales, operations, finance, supply chain and human resources. Possible tactics include restructuring debt, negotiating new lines of credit with lenders, closing facilities and offices, reducing headcount, extending payment terms, forgoing debt repayments, eliminating unprofitable product lines and customers, increasing prices, changing market focus, increased outsourcing and expediting the introduction of new products or services.[7]

Four principles can be identified for a successful turnaround: new competent management with full authority to make all necessary changes, an economically viable core business, adequate financing during the turnaround period and a positive attitude and motivated people.[8] However, despite management's best efforts, success in a turnaround cannot be assured and implementation is fraught with uncertainties. Managers are advised to objectively assess the opportunities for the likelihood of a successful turnaround.[9] Louis Gerstner took on the daunting challenge of revitalizing IBM in 1993, following his successful tenure at American Express and RJR Nabisco (see also the IBM case in Chapter 1).[10] While IBM's fortunes have improved, at least for the time being, many other efforts have been far less successful. Turnaround efforts at US retailer JC Penney and technology services firm Unisys have been underway for some time, without signs of definitive success or failure. Other turnaround efforts at firms in the US steel industry in the 1980s and the airline industry following deregulation failed primarily because of weak overall market conditions.

Turnarounds are accompanied by a sense of urgency. Short-term and long-term plans are established and shared with key stakeholders (e.g. board of directors, employees, lenders, suppliers and customers). Benchmarks are set, such as cost reduction objectives and cash flow targets, which are intended to define the success or failure of the plan. The new corporate turnaround strategy and objectives help create recognition for the need for change and provide a sense of urgency.

The sense of urgency is further reinforced by many changes that are made in the company, especially in the top management ranks. The arrival of a new CEO and trusted lieutenants, as was the case at Xerox in 2000 when the CEO was replaced and a new senior management group was installed, underscores that it will no longer be 'business as usual'.[11] The new management team brings a fresh perspective and is usually the architect of the turnaround strategy. Some managers have made a career out of handling turnarounds, such as Maury Myers, who managed firms in the airline, freight services and waste management industries, and Robert Burton from Moore Corp. Frequently, turnaround managers depart after the turnaround plan has been successfully executed and the company is on solid ground, preferring to leave the day-to-day management of the going concern to others.[12]

13.2   Supply's role in corporate turnarounds

Most authors have said little about the role of the supply function and suppliers in turnaround management.[13] These books tend to focus on supply activities related to cash flow management, such as stretching payables. However, some authors have recognized the critical role that supply can play in some turnaround situations, and suggested several possible opportunities to use supply as part of an overall turnaround plan[14]:

- Elevate the role of supply within the organization and inject new talent into the supply group as required.
- Make sure that suppliers are world class. If necessary, look internationally for suppliers with superior quality, lower costs or more sophisticated technology.
- Engage in value analysis as part of cost reduction efforts.
- Combine purchases of common parts and services for price leverage.
- Standardize purchases wherever possible.
- Simplify and streamline systems to improve efficiency and improve information flows.
- Invest time in vendor identification and qualification.
- Set vendor price reduction targets.
- Purchase raw materials on a consignment basis.
- Consider total cost of ownership factors, such as costs for transportation and returns as a result of poor quality.
- Evaluate opportunities for outsourcing.
- Formulate a short-term and long-term plan for the supply function.

Examples exist where supply has been an integral part of a major corporate turnaround. One such example is DaimlerChrysler, where top management, including CEO Dieter Zetsche, expects the supply function and suppliers to play an important role in the turnaround of the company. In the competitive North American automotive market, with limited opportunities for significant short-term sales growth, cost reduction efforts at DaimlerChrysler are a key part of the turnaround plan. Since the company spends approximately $40 billion with suppliers, declaring that it would pay suppliers 5% less resulted in a $2 billion annual cost saving.[15] While this heavy-handed approach has caused problems between DaimlerChrysler and its suppliers, the company has plans for a further 10% reduction in purchased costs by working with suppliers to eliminate waste in the supply chain and through value analysis and value engineering efforts.[16]

Xerox, like DaimlerChrysler, has attempted to rein in supply costs as part of its turnaround strategy. Efforts include negotiating cost reductions on direct and indirect purchases, assessing lease versus buy options to free up cash and extending supplier payment terms to relieve cash flow pressures.[17] As was the situation at DaimlerChrysler, senior management involvement and support played a key role in the implementation of strategies at Xerox regarding the involvement of suppliers and the supply function in the corporate turnaround.

The potential for significant contribution by the supply function in a turnaround situation is immense. However, most of the evidence regarding the role of supply in major corporate turnarounds is supported only by anecdotal examples, such as the DaimlerChrysler and Xerox situations described here. Consequently, this chapter documents how and where the supply function and suppliers can make a substantial contribution in a corporate turnaround.

13.3   The Thomson example

In what has been described as one of Europe's most successful corporate turnarounds, the supply function at Thomson played a critical strategic role in reversing the fortunes of the company.[18] Specifically, we identified nine areas of supply involvement at Thomson as part of the turnaround: early involvement in new product development, continuous improvement, cost reductions in indirect purchases, revenue enhancement, inventory management, global commodity management, quality, new management talent and cross-functional execution. In addition, executive leadership was identified as an enabler to the effective use of the supply function and suppliers in the turnaround. This chapter provides a detailed account of the participation of the supply function at Thomson in the company's turnaround and provides lessons for managers.

Thomson in 1997

Thomson's history goes back well over 100 years to 1879, when Elihu Thomson, a high-school science teacher in Philadelphia, teamed up with his colleague, Edwin Houston, to create Thomson-Houston, a fledgling electrical company. In 1893, Compagnie Française Thomas-Houston was established in Paris. These companies went through many changes, acquisitions and divestitures over the following years. Acquisitions included the Telefunken, Dual, Thorne and Ferguson brands in Europe and RCA and GE Consumer Electronics in the US. In 1995 Thomson Consumer Electronics changed its name to Thomson Multimedia.

In 1996, Thomson was a multinational consumer electronics firm with revenues of approximately $6 billion.[19] The company had experienced extensive losses in the late 1980s and the 1990s, including a loss of more than $500 million in 1996. That year the French government, Thomson's sole owner, concerned over its mounting debt and the continuing financial drain, announced its intention to sell the company for one French franc to Daewoo, the Korean conglomerate, provided that Daewoo was willing to assume Thomson's debts. Massive protests by employees prevented the sale. Consequently in 1997, Thierry Breton was brought in as chairman and chief executive officer with the express purpose of transforming Thomson into a profitable and private company.

Thierry Breton's five-year turnaround plan, dubbed TMM2002, had as its objective the return to profitability, elimination of debt and privatization. He believed that Thomson had core corporate strengths in its dominant position in a variety of consumer electronic fields. He also saw an opportunity to increase the emphasis on technology and services because of the convergence of telecommunications, computers and electronics.

Thierry Breton asked Charles Dehelly, who had worked with Breton during the turnaround at the French computer manufacturer Bull Group, to come and join him at Thomson in early 1998. In his position as senior executive vice-president for operations coordination and business performance, Dehelly was given functional responsibility for sourcing and supply chain management as well as for two key corporate-wide initiatives, the Spring and Safe programmes. The Spring

Cost Reduction Programme, started the day after Breton became chief executive officer, was a massive corporate cost-cutting initiative, eliminating all costs that did not provide value for the consumer. It included a total reorganization of Thomson's sourcing practices in relation to products and components purchased from outside, which represented a significant part of the sale price of Thomson's products. The purpose was to reduce the number of suppliers and generate substantial cost savings. In addition, Spring also sought to reduce indirect costs and overheads.

The Safe Reengineering Programme, started in mid-1997 just before Dehelly joined Thomson, focused on reengineering business practices. The objective of this programme was to improve the processes involved in manufacturing, distribution and marketing of products and services, making them more cost effective and more responsive to customer demands. Under the Safe Reengineering Programme, Thomson restructured its industrial base and supply chain and modernized the organization of its salesforce to adapt it to changing market conditions and opportunities.

Breton's programme called for a radically different organizational structure in which business units were created, largely focused on product or service lines, supported by key corporate functions. Breton reorganized internal activities along vertical lines, forming eight strategic business units (SBUs), in order to ensure total integration from research and product development to distribution of finished products. The management of each SBU was responsible for the profitability of the entire range of products and services sold by the SBU. He also fashioned four key partnerships with technology leaders in affiliated fields and insisted that these partners would not only share technologies with Thomson, but also take ownership stakes.

Jean-Philippe Collin

Charles Dehelly found his earlier exposure to the high-tech business a true learning experience, including his appreciation of the supply side, which reported to him at Bull Group. He believed that a number of supply practices in high technology could be transferred to Thomson. He was convinced that proper measurement of supply performance and contribution to the bottom line and balance sheet was critical to supply effectiveness. Therefore, when Breton recruited him in early 1998 to help him transform Thomson, he believed he had a significant opportunity to bring his ideas into action.

During his first year on the job Dehelly became convinced that he needed a new head for the sourcing function. He wanted someone with a non-Thomson background, but with sound supply experience in automotive or high technology. He found the person he was looking for: Jean-Philippe Collin.

The supply organization that Jean-Philippe Collin took over in January 1999 had already started to change in response to Dehelly's initiatives in 1998. The previous CPO, who had been an operations executive before moving to supply in 1995, had moved to the position of chief information officer and head of IT with the arrival

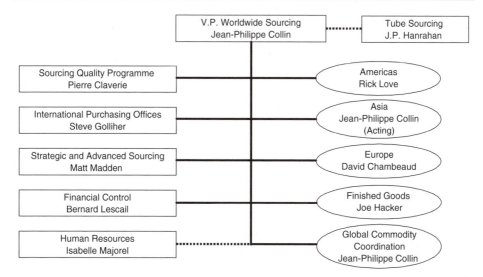

FIGURE 13.1   Corporate sourcing organization.

of Collin. The latter had valuable supply experience at IBM in the US and as head of supply for a major European automotive parts manufacturer.

Thomson's supply organization before 1997 had been part of the corporation's manufacturing organization. Its primary focus was on serving manufacturing's needs around the world. The yearly materials acquisition plan, refined by Pat Keating's group at RCA in the US, was a very detailed, carefully orchestrated process for direct production requirements. When Keating took over corporate Thomson supply responsibility for several years prior to 1997, he introduced this planned approach as a model for all Thomson's sourcing units. With a small central corporate group in France, the bulk of the supply organization was located at Thomson's manufacturing and laboratory sites around the world.

With the support of Dehelly, Collin undertook to restructure the supply organization, increasing the level of centralization and expanding its role in several areas (see Figure 13.1). Under this new structure and new vision for Thomson, the supply organization acquired a significant set of new responsibilities and was meaningfully involved in its corporate turnaround.

13.4   Supply's role in Thomson's turnaround

The following section describes the role of Thomson's supply function in the company's turnaround. Executive leadership and visible support are identified as enablers to the effective use of the supply function and suppliers in the turnaround at Thomson. In addition, nine areas of supply involvement are identified: early involvement in new product development, continuous improvement, cross-functional execution, cost reductions in indirect purchases, revenue enhancement, inventory management, global commodity management, quality and new management talent (see Table 13.1).

TABLE 13.1 Areas of supply involvement in corporate turnarounds

- Early involvement in new product development
- Continuous improvement
- Cross-functional execution
- Cost reductions in indirect purchases
- Revenue enhancement
- Inventory management
- Global commodity management
- Quality
- New management talent

←———— Executive leadership ————→

Executive leadership and visible support

Supply involvement in Thomson's turnaround started with an understanding by top management, Charles Dehelly in particular, of the potential significant impact of the supply function and suppliers on the business. Furthermore, Dehelly could articulate a clear vision for the supply function. He was heavily involved personally in all major supplier initiatives and had direct contact at the top management level with Thomson's key suppliers.

Thomson's supplier conference was one such example. In April 2000, Thomson held its first ever worldwide supplier conference at its Paris headquarters. The president and all of the heads of the strategic business units made presentations to the top executives of Thomson's key suppliers from around the world. Several suppliers also made presentations on key Thomson initiatives which they had pioneered, such as consignment arrangements and quality improvement projects. Also, five supplier awards were presented for outstanding contributions to Thomson.

Jean-Philippe Collin had been the driving force behind this conference and Dehelly confessed that his earlier doubts about the need for it were ill founded. The function was deemed an outstanding success and Thierry Breton, who had initially planned on staying for only part of it, attended the full day.

Early supply involvement in new product development

In 1997, Thomson was taking 40% longer to develop and ship product compared to its major competitors. Breton and Dehelly took steps to improve its performance in this area. The Thomson supply organization had traditionally focused on negotiating supply agreements and vendor management activities following product design. Dehelly expected the supply function and the company's suppliers to play an important role in improving the company's time to market performance.

Recognizing that the opportunity to add value required significant supply involvement during the development and specification for new products and services, Collin started the Advanced and Project Sourcing Programme. Its purpose was to tie supply and design closer together, avoid premature supplier commitments and create a team responsibility for margin and profitability. Suppliers were asked to commit up-front capacity and volume obligations, cost reductions and quality targets.

Continuous improvement

A key initiative that Dehelly promoted was the Product Model Cost Follow-up Process in which, for key products, a team composed of a business unit manager, the product manager, the sourcing manager, an accountant, a product manager and a designer met monthly to track all costs for a particular product. They then determined prices and costs for the period ahead and reviewed actual performance to target and causes for deviations. The objective was to improve margins and to make everyone jointly responsible for product or service success, avoiding a silo mentality and lengthy and costly delays in corrective action. Figure 13.2 provides an outline of the process.

Once sales of a new product started, regular tracking meetings as part of the Product Model Cost Follow-up Process with the business unit manager, the product manager, production sourcing, development and accounting assured a team focus on ways and means of meeting sales demands profitably. Opportunities for cost reductions included value analysis and reverse engineering to change the design and functionality of the component, improving quality, changing tolerances and changing the logistics processes. Thomson expected its suppliers to suggest ways to reduce costs, challenge specifications and match the price and cost pressures for the market. Collin expected single-digit to double-digit yearly deflation in prices and provided a financial incentive to managers to beat the net sales price index used by Dehelly to forecast and drive supply cost targets.

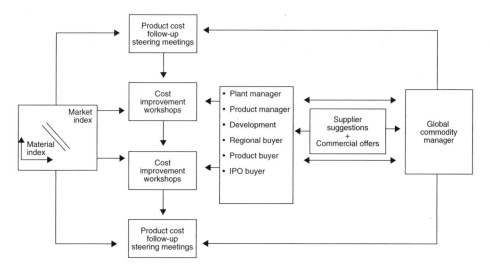

FIGURE 13.2   Product Model Cost Follow-up Process.

Cross-functional execution

Dehelly recognized that cross-functional orientation was critical to the success of the company's turnaround. Prior to 1997, the supply function was not meaningfully involved in key business processes such as product management and new product development. However, Dehelly expected supply to participate with other functions as an equal player and to be consulted in major business activities. The Advanced and Project Sourcing Programme and the Model Cost Product Follow-up Process were two examples of how supply worked effectively with other functions on key programmes and activities.

Cost reductions in indirect purchases

With an annual spend in nonproduction purchases (NPP) of $1.2 billion, Charles Dehelly saw greater supply involvement in NPP as one key thrust. Prior to 1997 NPP purchases were largely decentralized and had relatively low involvement by supply personnel. Specific initiatives to involve supply more significantly included travel, facilities, maintenance, capital equipment, advertising and other marketing expenditures, transportation and logistics, consulting and investment banking services for IPOs. About 150 individuals outside of the supply organization were identified across the corporation's locations worldwide as nonproduction purchasers who needed training and support.

Whereas under the previous corporate organizational structure supply's involvement in outsourcing was minimal, under the new regime Dehelly insisted on a major supply role in all insourcing and outsourcing initiatives for both production and nonproduction purchases. For example, a major transportation logistics outsourcing venture for all of Thomson required major supply involvement. Moreover, whereas transportation and logistics had previously not been supply's responsibility, the outsourced contract would be managed by supply.

Recognizing that transaction costs were an important component of NPP, Jean-Philippe Collin believed that e-commerce applications could help lower the cost of acquisition and reduce working capital requirements. Using a business-to-business (B2B) solution based on SAP technology, he hoped to reduce acquisition costs by 60% and leverage combined multicompany spending.

Revenue enhancement

Whereas the supply markets for electronics had been reasonably soft during the previous years, this changed drastically in 1999. The continuing strength of the US economy, coupled with improvements in Europe and recovery in Asia, created a very strong consumer demand for electronics. The supply side had difficulty coping with this surge in demand and shortages occurred in a variety of components. Thus, Jean-Philippe Collin and his team not only faced the challenges of creating an effective supply organization and process, but also the simultaneous pressures of market shortages, which in themselves took close to 50% of their time. Taking steps to monitor 'supply market share' and ensure availability of critical components, the supply function was able to help the organization meet its revenue growth targets.

Charles Dehelly commented on the challenges facing Thomson:

> Thomson Multimedia anticipates double-digit growth in 2000. We need a committed supply base to support this growth and our cost reduction targets. In the long term, we require suppliers that can provide technology breakthroughs, accomplished with speed and innovation, and operational excellence, with best-in-class performance in terms of cost, quality and delivery performance. Our success will also be our suppliers' success.

Inventory management

Another major initiative involved working capital improvement. Dehelly commented:

> It came as quite a surprise to some supply people that I expected them to worry about the balance sheet by insisting on measuring their return on capital employed performance.

Thus, Thomson embarked on a major effort to have suppliers provide consignment stock and to protect Thomson from price reductions on inventory on hand.

Dehelly felt that 'supply was disconnected from the balance sheet' and he insisted that Collin take steps to improve the use of capital employed by supply. As a result, Collin created a small group to help build an efficient supply chain, including working with site materials management and buyers to define and deploy vendor-managed inventories.

Global commodity management

When Collin arrived in January 1999, there was one person working in global commodity management. Given the large number of common requirements and suppliers, along with the geographical spread of manufacturing and laboratory facilities, Collin deemed it essential to increase the staffing of global commodity management. Therefore, by July 2000 the number of coordinators had grown to ten persons, each assigned worldwide responsibility for a specific group of common requirements. A major challenge for each global commodity coordinator was the appropriate melding of local and regional concerns and interests with global ones. Until July 2000, Collin put himself in charge of this initiative.

Quality

The purpose of the Sourcing Quality Assurance Programme was not only to assure the quality of purchased requirements, but also to develop and manage an appropriate supplier evaluation system that was fact based and time sensitive. With a focus on total cost of ownership, this programme was also concerned about incidents, anything that interrupted operations at any location, the degree of supplier responsibility for those occurrences, and preventive measures. Care was taken to tie this programme directly to quality initiatives at both the local and global levels to assure effectiveness. The new global quality organization consisted of 59 people.

New management talent

During the tough financial times corporate spending on training had been deeply curtailed. Collin saw training of supply staff as an essential step in the building of an effective supply organization. The addition of younger and less experienced people to the supply organization further reinforced this need. Overall, the staffing levels in the supply organization were increased to accommodate Dehelly and Collin's initiatives.

13.5   Outcome of the turnaround

In December 1996, Thomson had accumulated approximately $2.5 billion in debt (FF15.5 billion). The following year, the French government recapitalized the company with $1.8 billion (FF11 billion) as part of Breton's turnaround plan. Technology partners were asked to take ownership stakes. NEC, Microsoft and Alcatel each acquired 6.8% ownership, with Thomson and DIRECTV bought in for 5.2%. Employees were offered the chance to buy 5.5% and an initial public offering (IPO) in November 1999 sold a further 17%.

The sale of shares, coupled with Thomson's return to profitability, by 1999 had eliminated all corporate debt. Thomson's stock, which had sold at €21.50 at its initial public offering in November 1999, had more than tripled by July the following year. In 2000, the company reported revenues of $8.2 billion, an increase of one third from 1996, and a profit of $350 million, compared to a loss of more than $500 million in 1996.

In October 2000, the French government sold a 17.7% equity stake for approximately $1.8 billion (FF11 billion) to recoup its 1997 investment, leaving it with approximately 34% of the company, which represented an approximate market value of $3.5 billion. Just three years earlier, the French government had been prepared to sell its 100% stake in the company for 1 franc.

Although much remained to be done by 2000, the evidence of a quick and successful turnaround was impressive.

13.6   Conclusion

This chapter used Thomson as an example to illustrate the role of the supply function and suppliers in a successful corporate turnaround. We identified executive leadership and support as key enablers and documented nine additional areas of supply and supplier involvement in the turnaround (see Table 13.1). A key element was the enabling role that top management played, creating an environment where the supply function and suppliers were expected to have a significant impact on the turnaround of the business. The senior executive to whom the supply function reported, Charles Dehelly, could articulate a clear vision for the supply function in the turnaround. His vision and direct personal involvement were critical to creating a situation where supply could be meaningfully involved in important business activities as part of the turnaround at Thomson.

Unfortunately, some executives view supply as a tactical function, ignoring its potential strategic role. Consequently, in many companies the supply function plays a secondary role. However, the Thomson example illustrates that the strategic use of the supply function and suppliers can improve organizational performance. While the lessons here are certainly applicable to turnarounds, they also apply to any manager interested in extracting the maximum financial and strategic benefits from his or her supply function and suppliers. While the opportunities described in this chapter can be applied when formulating supply strategies for almost every organization, obstacles to change may represent the most significant challenge.

The supply function and suppliers can influence a firm's performance in many ways. Unfortunately, many managers focus only on issues related to supply's impact on the income statement, such as supplier cost reductions and the budget and staffing levels of the supply function. The Thomson example is useful in demonstrating the potential of the supply function and suppliers to make a contribution in several areas, namely the balance sheet (e.g. inventory investments), revenue and sales growth (e.g. revenue enhancement), customer satisfaction (e.g. quality and continuous improvement) and corporate strategy (e.g. congruence with corporate goals and objectives). Not only must managers recognize the full range of opportunities to use their supply function and suppliers effectively, they must also be prepared to commit appropriate resources in achieving their objectives, namely organizational talent. This extends beyond just the people and should include business processes and structure (see Chapter 5).

Notes and references

[1] See for example Carter, J.R. and Narasimhan, R. (1996) 'Is purchasing really strategic?', *International Journal of Purchasing and Materials Management*, Vol. 32, No. 1, pp. 20–28.

[2] Leenders, M.R. and Johnson, P.F. (2000) *Major Structural Changes in Supply Organizations*, Center for Advanced Purchasing Studies: Tempe, AZ; Leenders, M.R. and Johnson, P.F. (2002) *Major Changes in Supply Chain Responsibilities*, Center for Advanced Purchasing Studies: Tempe, AZ.

[3] Iacocca, L. and Novak, W. (1984) *Iacocca: An Autobiography*, Bantam Books: New York; Gardner, G. (1996) 'Chrysler: The cat with nine lives', *Wards Auto World*, Vol. 32, No. 5, pp. 67–70; Stundza, T. (2001) 'How Chrysler will cut costs', *Purchasing*, February 8, pp. 30–32.

[4] Murray, E.J. and Richardson, P.R. (1998) 'Leasing successful business turnarounds: Lean and mean or lean and keen?', *The Financial Post*, May 6, p. 4.

[5] Cuneo, A.Z. (2000) 'Ailing Levi Strauss refits U.S. strategy', *Advertising Age*, Vol. 73, No. 28, pp. 73–4.

[6] Apri, B. and Wejke, P. (1999) *International Turnaround Management: From Crisis to Revival and Long-Term Profitability*, Macmillan Business: Basingstoke.

[7] Finkin, E.F. (1987) *Successful Corporate Turnarounds*, Greenwood Press: Westport, CT.

[8] Bibeault, D.B. (1982) *Corporate Turnaround Management*, McGraw-Hill: New York.

[9] Seidemann, R.S. and Sands, D.A. (1991) 'Determining the likelihood of a turnaround', in DiNapoli, D., Sigoloff, S.C. and Cushman, R.F. (eds), *Workouts and Turnarounds: The Handbook of Restructuring and Investing in Distressed Companies*, Richard D. Irwin: Homewood, IL.

[10] Gerstner, L.V. (2002) *Who Says Elephants Can't Dance?*, HarperCollins: New York.

[11] Moore, P.L. (2001) 'She's here to fix the Xerox', *Business Week*, August 6, pp. 47–8.

[12] Bibeault, D.B. (1982) *Corporate Turnaround Management*, McGraw-Hill: New York.

[13] Bibeault (1982) *opere citato*; Goldstein, A.S. (1994) *The Business Doctor: How to Turn Your Headache into a Debt-Free Money Machine*, Garrett Publishing: Deerfield Beach, FL; Apri, B. and Wejke, P. (1999) *International Turnaround Management: From Crisis to Revival and Long-Term Profitability*, Macmillan Business: Basingstoke.

[14] Finkin, E.F. (1987) *Successful Corporate Turnarounds*, Greenwood Press: Westport, CT.

[15] Meredith, R. (2001) 'The Anti-Iacocca', *Forbes*, Vol. 168, No. 4, pp. 50–54.

[16] Stundza, T. (2001) 'How Chrysler will cut costs', *Purchasing*, February 8, pp. 30–32.

[17] Avery, S. (2001) 'Aggressive sourcing slashes $199 million at Xerox', *Purchasing*, March 22, pp. 36–9.

[18] Tieman, R. (2000) 'French consumer electronics company undergoes astonishing recovery', *Knight-Ridder Tribune News: Evening Standard*, London, September 6.

[19] All financial information is presented in US$.

Chapter 14

STRATEGIC CHANGE TOWARDS GLOBAL SOURCING: ERICSSON IN CHINA

Tony Fang and Björn Axelsson[1]

The choice of sourcing strategy is of great importance for a firm's competitiveness and is therefore a means for strategic change. The international outlook of the firm and the subsequent scope of its sourcing decisions are vital components. In our purchasing maturity matrix discussed in Chapter 2, global sourcing enters as one important part of the sourcing patterns at levels 5 and 6. Large manufacturing as well as retailing firms increasingly have adopted a global sourcing approach and report considerable development of sourcing benefits from it.[2] One important ingredient in this achievement is a fundamental change of the nature of supply markets on a global basis, where China plays an increasingly important role.

Similar developments can also be identified in other parts of the world. For example, eastern Europe is approached for the purposes of manufacturing; India is targeted for sourcing ICT-related services such as software programming and call centres. While patterns vary from firm to firm, industry to industry and country to country, today's overall trend is that of moving from home-country and single-country sourcing to a borderless global sourcing of production and know-how.

14.1   Change in sourcing patterns as strategic change

The choice or change of sourcing strategy is closely related to the themes discussed in Chapter 4 of this book. Changes in sourcing patterns are very much about changing relationships with suppliers. It could be 'just' a matter of exchanging a portion of the total number of suppliers the company deals with, for example someone else from the same industry or geographical market. It could also be to alter the ways in which the company carries out its purchases (the amount of business directed towards a certain supplier, the work mode applied and so on). A third aspect of a changed sourcing strategy is to stay with the same supplier and follow that one, or bring the supplier along to another geographical supply market. Multiple changes of sourcing policies that have a geographical dimension are thus possible.

Strategic changes derived from new geographical markets suggest that one can go to the most advanced suppliers in the most developed economies. This could mean to stay close and get access to the most significant processes of new technological developments wherever necessary. Referring to Figure 4.2 in Chapter 4, it could be a matter of high involvement for a shorter (development) period followed by a low-involvement, high-volume production period with another supplier, maybe from a low-cost country. It could also be that the supplier from the low-cost country in the initial phases needs a period of high involvement to learn to perform according to standards and methods asked for. It could thus for a shorter or longer time mean paying a high price for the services bought and putting a lot of effort into the relationships with specific suppliers, because it is worth it.

Strategic changes could also mean immediate increased efforts to source from low-cost markets. Cost reduction through low-cost sourcing has been a central concern among managers and in the sourcing literature.[3] This is not surprising at all. The potential benefits are huge. China, for example, offers some of the lowest labour costs in the world, in some cases at just 3% of European manufacturing wages, and it may retain its labour cost advantage for a considerably long period.[4]

As illustrated by Box 14.1, there is a significant cost difference in outsourcing operations from a European or US context compared with a low-cost country alternative.

Box 14.1   Cost comparisons

The purchasing manager of a major automotive company presents the following calculation, where A is the European/US cost for producing a vehicle and B is a low-cost country alternative.

	A	B
Materials, costs of components	40	40
Capital cost (equipment)	10	10
Salaries for staff	25	6
Other costs, services bought for localities, transportation, services etc.	20	20
Demanded profit margin	5	5
Total	100	81

In this illustration, the estimated differences come only from lower labour costs included in the firm's operations, most of all its production. The services to that production bought from a local market are assumed to be cheaper too. But on the other hand the low-cost producer will have to be debited for several services that are not needed given the framework of producing and using the product in a European/US context. That means increased transaction costs, e.g. for overseas transportation, longer lead times, higher risks etc. The sum of all such services is assumed to be equal between the two alternatives. In order to be a supplier to a major automotive (or any other) firm, a high-cost country supplier needs to compensate with increased productivity. If only the price of the product is taken into consideration, the necessary improvement would have to be 25% (95/76). It should be observed that we calculate with the same material and equipment costs for the components used. That does not need to be the case, as will be discussed below.

So far, cost concern has been concentrated on the downstream part of the supply chain; that is, the final production link of that chain. However, it is increasingly evident that China is not only attracting labour-intensive manufacturing industries but is quickly moving to become a centre for R&D, innovation and high tech.[5] This creates even more excitement to the phenomenon. As time passes we will increasingly witness strategic changes of sourcing patterns, in some of today's low-cost countries, from low-end product manufacturing sourcing to R&D-oriented sourcing through the firm's entire supply chain. By doing so, not only will the costs of labour for a certain production activity be lower, but also other internal labour costs (e.g. costs for R&D staff) plus all the external labour costs at different levels in the supply chain could be lower, leading to additional cost reductions of any components as well as of equipment being utilized. Given competition in global markets, companies will have no choice but to gain the cost leadership already in the early phase of R&D and product development. Sourcing 'brains' and expertise in the early part of the supply chain is and will thus be critical to the firm's overall competitiveness.

Changes towards global sourcing are multifaceted

Changes in sourcing patterns mean not only reorientation of several activities, for example ordering products from a new counterpart. Differences in communication patterns (language), changes in transportation and logistics, as well as changes in quality control systems and so on also follow. There are examples of purchasing organizations recruiting immigrants from east European countries to their domestic purchasing organizations in order to be better off in communicating with suppliers from their respective countries of origin.

One should look at a sourcing organization as a system consisting of people, organization, processes and procedures, reward mechanisms, technology and so on. The global sourcing venture may not necessarily force changes of all purchasing staff and all organizational measures, but a portion of the staff and a portion of processes and procedures need to be adapted to the new challenges. For more experienced firms, a change from international purchasing to global sourcing may be a smaller step compared with the companies having very little experience in international business to start with.

Ericsson as a case

This chapter discusses the sourcing of production as well as R&D and product development in China, an emerging pattern of sourcing undertaken increasingly by large multinationals. By focusing on Ericsson we will be exposed to the sourcing of advanced products, expertise and talents. The chapter is framed as a matter of strategic change where Ericsson has demonstrated a radical change according to our classification in Chapter 3, be it proactive or reactive in nature. Ericsson is a multinational telecoms and mobile communications manufacturer of Swedish origin.[6] Some of the questions to be addressed are: why is Ericsson interested in sourcing in China? In what ways could it be considered a strategic move? What should be considered when undertaking sourcing in China? What could, in general, be learnt from this experience when it comes to going for global sources in a move towards strategic change?

In the case, we look at the background and state of the art of Ericsson's sourcing operations in China. We also attempt to describe their experience and analyse what we can learn. The case is viewed as an illustration of strategic change in global sourcing and how this will help improve the strategy of sourcing organizations and capabilities. This case focuses on the sourcing of hardware and software within R&D and product development in high-tech areas such as radio base stations, switchers and so on rather than consumer products (e.g. mobile phones). Before presenting our case, we briefly discuss literature about sourcing and China.

14.2   Background

Global sourcing

We adopt a working definition of 'global sourcing' as the management of flow of components, finished products, know-how and human resources (and services) across nations and regions in serving foreign and domestic markets.[7] Although sourcing has been driven primarily by cost concerns in many firms, technology and quality considerations should be viewed as equally significant to cost concerns.[8] Sourcing permeates the interfaces between R&D, manufacturing and marketing.[9]

Global sourcing requires the integration of requirements between units, in order to identify common purchases, processes, technologies and suppliers that can benefit from a coordinated sourcing effort. It often involves implementation of global commodity teams and global information systems. Often it goes along with an international procurement office (IPO) in a certain geographical area (e.g. Eastern Europe or Asia-Pacific) aimed at, among other things, soliciting quotes or proposals, negotiating supply contracts, expediting shipments, performing supplier visits and building up a qualified supply base in that area (see also Chapter 5). When companies start aligning and coordinating their designing, manufacturing and sourcing functions globally, they enter the global sourcing stage.[10]

Moving towards a global approach will consequently cause impacts on organizational designs, technology support as well as the human resources involved. Some have even argued that the 'human factor' such as culture, perception of trust, language and communication, human resources and personal relationships is the most important factor in securing successful global sourcing and supply chain management.[11]

China: 'The workshop of the world'

China has emerged as one of the most dynamic elements in the global economy.[12] During the 1990s, US$300 billion foreign direct investment (FDI) went to China. In 2002, China overtook the US as the world's largest FDI recipient.[13] The FDI in China increased by US$53.5 billion in 2003. Today, some 480,000 foreign-invested enterprises including more than 400 companies from the Fortune 500 are operating on Chinese soil.

China is known as the 'workshop of the world'[14] (see also Box 14.2). Even some of the manufacturing lines earlier located in Southeast Asian countries such as Malaysia and Singapore are also moving to China.[15] China's 'insatiable appetite' for seemingly unlimited industrial manufacturing is believed to be one of the key factors behind today's sharp rise in oil and other raw materials and transportation prices in the world market. With this background we could argue, in the same way as we discussed ICT (Chapter 8), that global sourcing, particularly sourcing in China, is a necessity in order not to lose sight of the competition!

Box 14.2   China in the world economy

Size of economy (GDP):
- $1467 billion
- At market exchange rates: 4% global output (no. 7)
- At purchasing power parity (PPP): 13% global output (no. 2)

Share of global growth 2000–2003:
- 30% of GDP growth (PPP) (<20% until 1992)
- 30% of imports growth
- 60% of growth in fixed investment
- 35% of growth in oil consumption

Trade balance 2003:
- +$125 billion with US
- +$25 billion with EU
- −$25 billion with Japan
- −$75 billion with Singapore, South Korea and Taiwan

Worldwide production share:
- 65%: photocopiers, microwave ovens, DVD players, shoes
- 50%: digital cameras
- 40%: personal computers
- 25%: refrigerators
- 19%: ships

Source: *Economist*, October 2, 2004; *Link*, September 2004.

The high concentration of FDI and international business in China has contributed to driving up its technology and competition levels; it has contributed to making China one of the world's most demanding markets. Many companies have set up their research centres in China. Motorola and Samsung have adopted the same global strategy when launching new mobile phones: first in China and Korea, then Europe and the US.[16] China seems to have become the ultimate testing ground for leadership skills and a company's ability to excel in global business: 'If you can make it here you can make it anywhere; if you can't make it here you can't make it anywhere.'[17]

Sourcing in China

Sourcing in China offers foreign companies opportunities to acquire high-quality and low-priced products, at the same time.[18] Today, the ratio between the costs for a European worker and a Chinese worker is roughly between 1 to 20–50; that is, it costs between 20 to 50 times as much to pay for the work in western parts of Europe compared to China. In Box 14.1 the difference was estimated at only 1 to 4, meaning that the cost of labour would only be four times as expensive in a European or US context. Still, we could indicate significant consequences. Furthermore, China can be expected to retain its labour cost advantage for a long time given its enormous pool of increasingly mobile workers, both skilled and semi-skilled.[19] Setting up an international procurement office (IPO) in China to source China-made components for their firm's global operations can be a profitable option.[20] One should not, however, forget that such organizational arrangements are investments that entail costs too.

So far, sourcing in China has been approached in the existing literature mainly from a low-cost *production* point of view. But production is just one link in the downstream of the firm's supply chain. Faced with global competition, more companies will build their cost concern into all the links of their supply chains, especially the R&D and product development part of the chains. The unique combination of low-cost and high tech that is a feature of today's Chinese market opens up new opportunities for foreign firms to fundamentally change their sourcing strategies. This is the central point to be discussed in this chapter.

Transaction costs such as the impacts of culture, language, communication and administration barriers could be as significant as production costs. Therefore, in addition to the kind of transaction costs already mentioned, cultural aspects should not be neglected when conducting sourcing in China.[21] As a purchasing director recently asked his Dutch audience at a conference: 'Who speaks Mandarin?' Very few, was the answer. Being able to speak Mandarin would help to decode the Chinese mindset and the Chinese way of doing business.

14.3   Ericsson's sourcing in China

Ericsson is one of the largest suppliers of telecommunications and mobile systems in the world and 40% of all mobile calls are made through Ericsson's mobile telephony systems. In 2003, its turnover was €16 billion and the company had 47,000 employees in more than 140 countries. Ericsson's history in China dates back to 1894 when the company made its first shipment of 2000 desk telephone handsets to Shanghai. Actually China was already on the list of Ericsson's top ten markets 100 years ago. In 1984, Ericsson delivered its world-famous AXE-10 to Beijing, which was also China's first digital switch. In 1985, Ericsson opened its first representative office in China. Since then, Ericsson's China activities have experienced explosive growth and the company is now a major player in the Chinese telecommunications infrastructure.

Why sourcing in China?

The forces driving Ericsson to source in China have changed fundamentally during the past decade. For most of the 1990s, foreign telecoms manufacturers approached China to seek local production mostly out of marketing and political considerations. They had to be in China because at that time the Chinese legal framework directed foreign firms to sourcing locally to reach the required percentage of local content. In the words of the sourcing director of Ericsson:

> If we look back a few years, we more or less had to be here in order to be able to sell our products in this market. For sales reasons we must have local contents in our manufacturing. The Chinese were talking about localization.

Even though it was basically the sales side that originally brought Ericsson to China, cost reduction has certainly also been a major factor:

> Then of course you have the cost perspective to manufacturing, the cost of labour, not only the cost of labour in the last part of the supply chain, but in the entire supply chain. We have first-tier suppliers, second-tier suppliers, third-tier suppliers, all the way down to the iron and mine, where they produce steel so to speak. So it's a long chain. And all that supply chain has its cost advantage. Most of the materials and products are available in China from the manufacturing point of view. That leads to significantly lowering our manufacturing costs.

Since the turn of the twenty-first century, the supply markets in China have undergone strategic changes. Local Chinese suppliers have become increasingly professional, for they have gained a wealth of experience in working with large multinational firms in recent years. Many have formed strategic alliances with foreign firms and, as a result, improved substantially the quality of their supply work. The country's distribution infrastructure has also been improved. More importantly, more and more international suppliers and logistics firms with various niche competencies started establishing themselves in the Chinese market.

> Cost concern is not the only reason [for sourcing in China]. I think the situation during the last couple of years is changing dramatically again. We can establish ourselves here with design activities and then develop our products. Thereby we gain two things. One is that we get lower R&D cost, because the salaries for engineers are much lower here. The cost for an R&D organization here becomes much lower than, for example, in Sweden or in the US. It also gives us the opportunity to develop products together with Chinese suppliers and/or international suppliers that are present in China. This gives far better cost advantage compared to designing something in Sweden or the US and then just transferring it to China for manufacturing.

Given China's growing importance in the global economy and international business (see Box 14.2), there is a strategic motive to come to China as well. Although there are still very strong sales motives to be in the market, nowadays the most important sales motives are somewhat different from before. In the words of the sourcing director:

> It's worth mentioning that there are also other reasons that we are here, not just for costs and transfer of competence. To be present here gives access to local market knowledge. We have to be aware that China is one of the biggest markets for Ericsson. This has been the case for many years. We need to be present here to understand what the Chinese customers want from us.

Ericsson's sourcing director expresses his view of China as the hub in Ericsson's global supply networks. Some products are adapted to the local Chinese market, but most products and processes that are designed, developed and produced in China are geared for Ericsson's global markets. This means that not only does Ericsson operate low-cost production and R&D to develop competitive products for the local Chinese market and produce certain components cost effectively in China and have them shipped to production facilities in Sweden and the rest of the world, the company also exports complete products to the rest of the world from China.

As such, Ericsson's sourcing in China thus seems to have been driven by four factors:

- The cost concern for manufacturing, R&D and running a sourcing organization.
- The opportunities to work with local suppliers in China as well as international suppliers present in China.
- The closeness to the Chinese market to gain local market knowledge and understand the Chinese customers' needs and wants.
- China's importance in Ericsson's global supply networks.

China as a dynamic supply market

China as a supply market has become increasingly competitive. Ericsson has steadily increased its sourcing volume since the strategic change took off in the second half of the 1990s. Many of Ericsson's international suppliers followed Ericsson to China. The sourcing director said:

> In the late 1990s, we pushed our existing supply base to follow us to China because we had to be here for the reasons I mentioned before. So we told our western suppliers that either you follow us to China or your market share will decrease. Many of these suppliers and even some small Swedish suppliers said 'OK, we take the chance to go to China with Ericsson.' So they started to set up joint ventures and other activities in China. We are still doing a lot of business with many of these companies. By providing an existing customer base, Ericsson actually helped these suppliers to develop their business in China.

Today, Ericsson considers its supply structure in China as strong and satisfying. Ericsson's suppliers serve not only Ericsson but also its competitors from both the global and the Chinese markets.

> This is actually good for the growth of the suppliers. This means that you have requirements coming not only from Ericsson but also from other companies. They will become more professional if they have tough requirements from a number of different sources.

Ericsson does not import anything from outside China unless it is more efficient than sourcing locally. The ideal situation, according to the sourcing director, would be to have everything sourced in a low-cost region all the way. It means that the entire supply chain should be located in low-cost regions. The sourcing director emphasized that nowadays, thanks to the rapid development of China, one can actually source almost everything in China.

The selection of suppliers is based on criteria such as quality, operational systems, turnover, product knowledge and cost. Ericsson works with many suppliers in China, both international and local. The supplier quality can vary a great deal. It is therefore necessary to have a good quality system in order to get stable quality. Therefore Ericsson has involved itself in quite a number of supplier development projects. At the same time, it has also been observed that the pace at which the Chinese are learning and improving is so fast that China is believed to be able to deliver any top-quality product comparable to any world standard in the not too distant future.

Ericsson's suppliers are organized in a multitiered structure in which Ericsson has a commercial relationship with all the first-tier ones. Depending on the specifics of each project, Ericsson may enter into a commercial relationship with a second-tier supplier. One success factor, when it comes to negotiating a good price when sourcing in China, is competition. If competition is emphasized continuously, the costs can be held at lower levels, the sourcing director explained. As long as suppliers make a profit they will be able to lower their prices. If the suppliers have similar production costs, then the purchasing price will generally be the prevailing market price, which has a very small profit margin.

Ericsson's IPO in Beijing

In April 2003, an international purchasing office (IPO) was set up in Beijing as an integral part of the Ericsson China R&D Institute. The IPO focuses on R&D-oriented sourcing. At the corporate strategy level, China emerges as one major global hub for supply and R&D. The increasing importance of the China market is reflected in the Ericsson China organization and in the scope of responsibilities devoted to this market.

Finding and dealing with suppliers

One of the IPO's missions is to find competent local Chinese suppliers. For historical reasons Chinese suppliers are not as good as international suppliers in having their voice heard. So how can one find and deal with Chinese suppliers?

> This is a very relevant question. There are a number of ways. One way is of course various governmental bodies. They have good connections with the local suppliers in their respective regions and we attend different fairs and trade shows arranged by the government. Another efficient way of finding local suppliers is to recruit experienced sourcing staff.

Apart from one expatriate, the rest of the Ericsson sourcing organization staff consists of local Chinese. Chinese employees are familiar with the local market and can therefore provide substantial support in various ways, for example in establishing contacts with new suppliers, negotiating, following production, making sure that products meet quality standards and overseeing transportation and shipping. One way of keeping sourcing costs low is to try to use multiple suppliers and increase competition among them:

> Whatever you are buying, competition is razor sharp so the only way to keep the right price level is to constantly make sure that competition exists.

Dealing with suppliers is also a question of regular exchanges, including on quality issues. The quality level in many local Chinese suppliers is considered to be behind that of western suppliers. For companies involved in sourcing advanced products, such as Ericsson, there are however a number of suppliers that are able to produce the more advanced products. In the telecommunications industry there is a high dependency on having extremely good producers and also on sourcing them in the best possible way. One aspect of that is whether to buy several separate components or systems of integrated components. Many times the latter has proven to be preferred, but then the suppliers need to be able to increase their scope of responsibility. The Ericsson strategy is expressed accordingly:

> We try to buy more complete products. At this point, the number of suppliers in China that can supply finalized products is, however, lower than in Europe and USA.

A shift from producing solely low-complexity items to producing more complex items in the future could reduce costs for companies sourcing in China. But it could also increase the risk of losing intellectual property: high technology can be at risk of being copied by competitive Chinese firms or by former employees who leave the company. This is also part of the picture from sourcing in China, and something companies should be aware of.

At the same time, the Ericsson representative emphasized the fast learning capacity of the Chinese suppliers and the tremendous improvement in quality among local Chinese suppliers in recent years. Chinese firms are aware of the importance of quality; they are widely discussing quality measures and methodology.

Ericsson's strategy is to work closely with Chinese suppliers to improve their supply quality:

> We are quite sure that we are getting low-cost manufacturing and low-cost design here. But we are also very well aware that we have to work with the quality aspect and delivery performance.

This is a way to continuously try to develop the supplier and to capture improvement potentials.

Dealing with cultural issues

Dealing with international suppliers means also dealing with cultural diversities. One ingredient in Ericsson's framework to cope with such diversities is to let local Chinese employees do business and negotiate with local Chinese manufacturers:

> The key to succeeding in China is to let Chinese do business with Chinese ... Having Chinese engineers in our company thinking in the Chinese way means that it is easier to work with local Chinese suppliers. We prefer having Chinese engineers to sending western engineers to China.

Be aware of the cultural differences that exist and learn as much as possible about Chinese history. At the same time, be open-minded in interpreting actions and behaviour in light of the changing Chinese society.

Sourcing from 'Day Zero'

Integrating sourcing with design seems to be Ericsson's secret for many successful product development projects. The sourcing director explained the interdependent relationship between design and sourcing and emphasized the significance of conducting sourcing in the early part of the supply chain:

> One part of that R&D organization is sourcing. We firmly believe that it's impossible to do effective and efficient R&D and product development unless sourcing is an integral part of it. Also the other way around, you can't do sourcing unless the development and design resources are involved. So it's an interdependent relationship between design and sourcing. That's why we are co-located. That is our recipe for successful product development.

It would be too late to conduct sourcing solely in the production link of the supply chain. Sourcing must start from 'Day Zero'. In the words of the sourcing director:

> We need to involve the suppliers from the very beginning. When you involve suppliers you have to involve sourcing. Because you need to consider the commercial aspects from the very beginning. Otherwise you would not reach the target cost really. The target cost is a combination of smart design and efficient negotiations. Wherever we set up design activities that involve suppliers we put sourcing engineers in place.

This mode of operating is very similar to the way Ericsson handles suppliers in other parts of the world. The company has reached a level of sophistication, which is far from a stage where it was basically shopping around. Now it has regular activity patterns, developed organizational designs and operations synchronized with the local market as well as with the rest of Ericsson's organization.

14.4   Case comments

This comment consists of two parts. First, we provide a brief resumé of the changes introduced in activity patterns by Ericsson and the effects of these. Next, we discuss cultural issues in general and specifically in relation to China.

The activity and organizational changes

This case demonstrates some of the possible benefits but also challenges of global sourcing. Over the years Ericsson has gradually increased its commitments in China. The country was initially considered (and operated) mainly as a sales market. China is today one of the top two sales markets for Ericsson. It became in the early 1990s a source of low-cost production. This, in turn, has gradually developed into an integral part of the company's R&D-oriented technology sourcing and product development.

We have learnt that China is much more than a mere low-cost market for sourcing production capabilities for Ericsson. The dynamism of the Chinese market offers opportunities to undertake both low-cost and high-tech-oriented sourcing. We don't know the accumulated impact but we could consider a simple calculation.

Let us for pedagogical reasons, as pure speculation, assume that for the rest of Ericsson's production a share of 20% would be sourced from China. If so, the generated savings on pure labour costs would be at least 15% in relation to total production costs. The more activities that are performed in the low-cost market, the higher the degree of cost savings (see the illustrative product calculation in Box 14.1).

There are, however, also limiting factors such as transport, logistics and overall administrative costs. Still, such cost items seem to be small in comparison with the potential savings. If we had the relevant figures and could put them into the DuPont scheme in Chapter 2, we could read the dramatic effects of this on the ROI figure. It is, of course, a necessity for a company facing fierce global competition to apply a global sourcing strategy. This is maybe not primarily to generate better ROI figures, but to avoid having them totally deteriorate.

Still, success does not come without serious efforts to learn how to deal with the new supply market and to coordinate internal production, marketing and development efforts. The company has created facilities for production, learnt to deal with the supply market and adapted its behaviour, created a logistics system and so on. Going for global sourcing is thus, not least in this case, a major act of strategic change!

This move was evidently good for Ericsson, but would it be good for other companies? There is always a tradeoff between lower prices and higher risks and high transaction costs.[22] In the introductory part of this chapter, we indicated that intensified efforts towards global sourcing would also have potential benefits for other firms, maybe also small and medium-sized enterprises (SMEs). In order to be competitive it could be hazardous not to tap favourable new sources. As always there is, however, a tradeoff between costs, risks and benefits. It needs to be a certain scale, a certain size, to be worthwhile. But today we witness ever more frequently SMEs also entering into a more active sourcing strategy, albeit from a generally lower level.[23]

Cultural issues

International business means doing business across borders. This entails both geographical and psychic distances. The latter concept covers aspects like language differences, law and regulations as well as religion and institutional differences. Culture is a mental construct formed by behaviour and habits resulting from the ways the differences mentioned contribute to established habits and attitudes.

One very important concept is the prevalence of so-called ethnocentrism. This means that representatives from any culture find their own habits and attitudes natural. They have normally been rewarded, in that culture, for a behaviour that fits with others' expectations. This phenomenon means that when an individual with a specific 'learnt behaviour' – that is, one specific culture – meets an individual from another culture with other 'normal' habits, he or she will interpret that other individual from the frame of reference of his or her culture. This means that representatives from other cultures always will appear to be somewhat strange (not normal).

There are basically two ways to deal with cultural differences as described in the literature. One way is to establish stereotypes of the respective culture that are as accurate as possible, learn as much as possible about it and adapt one's behaviour accordingly. Some of the best-known general attempts to build such stereotypes are the models by Hofstede and Trompenaars.[24] They both develop a number of dimensions where cultures could differ, such as power distance (high or low), individualism vs collectivism and so on. Cultures score differently in various dimensions and from such patterns we can establish the stereotyped patterns of various cultures.

The other way to deal with culture, where the basis is built on a critique of the principle of stereotyping, is to adopt a different agenda. Stereotyping does more bad than good and forces our view of individuals, who are all unique, to fit into a certain format. The other approach is to be culturally competent, to listen and be aware of differences, and to move beyond cultural stereotyping to capture cultural paradoxes and diversities.[25]

China is described as a 'relationship-focused' culture.[26] This means that Chinese people expect to see their suppliers and partners in person much more often than would be necessary in 'deal-focused' markets, such as western Europe. It takes time to build up a high degree of trust that is person specific but crucial in doing business in China. There exists a rich literature on Chinese communication styles, the Chinese way of negotiating and so on based on basic cultural values[27] such as Confucianism[28] and other changing aspects of the Chinese society from which sourcing managers could benefit intellectually.

Several sources indicate that negotiations are crucial to the Chinese.[29] For instance, the Chinese are always ready to discuss a deal; renegotiation can crop up at any moment; the Chinese are focused on sales and sales figures and they judge success in relation to direct sales. We have learnt from the case study that Ericsson partly deals with such issues by letting local employees do business and negotiate with local Chinese manufacturers. In addition, the Chinese tendency to renegotiate also suggests that no door is closed in China and anything is possible and one must not give up easily when facing difficulties in this market.

14.5   Conclusions

Global sourcing is a natural step in the increased professionalism of purchasing and supply management. For those firms that have not yet started on that road, it should come as no surprise that such practices could give access to 'untapped goldmines'. This is true both for the 'obvious' low-cost sourcing alternatives, as well as for more qualified sourcing alternatives from qualitatively unique, high-cost markets.

Lessons learnt on strategic change towards global sourcing

In the introduction to this chapter we raised some questions. The first regarded the reasons for Ericsson showing an interest in this supply market. The second question concerned the ways in which this could be considered a strategic move.

There are several reasons for Ericsson to have a strong presence in this market, the potential to get access to low-cost labour for production purposes being just one. Closeness to a sales market of growing magnitude seems to be equally as important and – furthermore – access to qualified labour (R&D engineers) at relatively low cost is also of importance. It is almost self-evident that this must be of strategic importance to Ericsson. The company has made a lot of efforts in the market and it has a significant impact on its total business venture.

The third question was what should be considered when undertaking sourcing in China. We have seen that it needs to be a serious effort. It takes a lot of energy invested in learning from experience to deal with this market. Therefore it needs to be of a certain scale. We have also noticed the need for a presence in the local environment to be able to strengthen visibility and make relevant judgements. Also bringing locals into the organization has been mentioned.

The fourth question concerns what could be learnt from this experience when it comes to going for global sourcing. It is clear that such a move calls for several developments and adaptations. In the case of Ericsson we have described the local organization for production, sourcing and R&D. The bigger the scale, the more demanding the organizational challenges. But it should also be noticed that these organizational arrangements are reflected in other markets too. In a global perspective there will be a global design of the organization, including division of responsibilities and tasks, reporting and managerial systems and so on. Also staffing on a global scale becomes a different issue.

For the company that has not yet started to systematically utilize international suppliers and sourcing markets, the step towards truly global sourcing is a big one. But already international sourcing of selected items could make a major difference. However, international – and even more global – sourcing demands many new capabilities. It has to do with dealing with foreign languages and cultures, understanding and managing foreign suppliers, finding ways to solve the logistics aspects, negotiating, contracting and so on.

For a company like Ericsson that has been present all over the world for almost a century, this is less problematic. Still, it does not come without efforts to move from a sales organization that understands and is capable of dealing with customers, to sourcing and coordinating suppliers and even utilizing suppliers as development resources. The intensified efforts of Ericsson during the last ten years have meant a lot of investment in sourcing technology, talented people and know-how.

Lessons learnt about sourcing in China

Global sourcing means a much more active approach to sourcing efforts. The company that starts operating in this direction could harvest a lot, but it needs to be prepared to work hard, to have the courage to make mistakes and learn from them, to be willing to take commercial risks and invest, to find partners and build trust. Such changes are truly strategic and they also call for significant efforts of strategic change!

Some more hands-on findings derived from the case and other related experiences can be summarized as follows[30]:

- China offers opportunities for sourcing both low-cost production and high-tech components and processes. Thus the entire supply chain can be made more effective and powerful. To be competitive sourcing should start from the very early phase of product development. Large firms like Ericsson have, as has already been pointed out, also started conducting advanced sourcing for the purposes of R&D, innovation and product development of strategic importance through tapping potential talents and expertise in China.

- China is not one homogeneous market. Different regions within China vary in terms of salaries, regional support, educational level and economic development. Therefore, companies should consider the needs of the company's operations in relation to the specifics of the various regions. The unique sourcing opportunity in Chengdu, Sichuan province, where radio competence has always been developed, provides strong proof of this. There are several places with unique competencies like that one.

- It seems to be a good idea to establish local offices and let the Chinese deal with the Chinese. It is good to be present locally and to hire staff locally. The Chinese have a better knowledge of the market and master the language and hidden implications, which makes the purchasing process more effective.

- It is necessary to be prepared to invest time and effort in building strong, trusting relationships. In business relations with the Chinese, it is of high importance to understand the need to build and nurture relationships. Good relationships with suppliers can overcome difficulties and can be a success factor in price negotiations.

- It is important to make sure that suppliers meet the company's quality standards as far as production and working conditions are concerned. The quality of items that are produced in China can vary. Likewise, working conditions in Chinese factories can vary. This has not been dealt with in the text above, but it is paramount to make sure that the suppliers meet company standards. Further, it is a good idea to inform suppliers about the structure of the market as clearly and comprehensively as possible, as most Chinese suppliers still have limited knowledge about foreign markets and cultures. Purchasers must be very clear in their instructions, since mistakes caused by misunderstandings can otherwise happen.

- Finally, the pattern that is reflected by the necessity for Ericsson to be present in this customer market also has a mirror image. Ericsson has, for example, asked many of its international suppliers to move to China. These companies have, in turn, developed their sourcing networks in China with the help of Ericsson China organizations. Thus, more and more firms are moving to China not only to tap the low-cost advantage, but to gain strategic access to the global suppliers' network that is emerging there.

In preparing this chapter, we are convinced that China is on its way to becoming a global hub of sourcing, industrial networking and idea generation, and that both management practice and (academic) research regarding the benefits and problems of leveraging the inherent possibilities are only just taking off.

Notes and references

1 This chapter benefits partially from an unpublished paper written by Tony Fang, David Ohlsson and Josefin Sporrong from Stockholm University School of Business. We would like to thank David and Josefin for their efforts.

2 For example, Swedish furniture retailer IKEA has managed to lower its total cost for products landed into its stores by about 35% in less than a decade. A significant share of this improvement is due to sourcing from low-cost countries, most of all from China (speech by S.-O. Kulldorf, IKEA's CPO responsible for global sourcing, December 12 2003).

3 The focus on global supply markets among business firms is also reflected in the literature. In recent years there has been a growing interest in global sourcing, e.g. Kotabe, M. (1992) *Global Sourcing Strategy: R&D, Manufacturing, and Marketing Interfaces*, Quorum Books: Greenwich, CT; Kotabe, M. (1993) 'Patterns and technological implications of global sourcing strategies: A study of European and Japanese multinational firms', *Journal of International Marketing*, Vol. 1, No. 1, pp. 26–43; Trent, R.J. and Monczka, R.M. (2002) 'Pursuing competitive advantage through integrated global sourcing', *Academy of Management Executive*, Vol. 16, No. 2, pp. 66–80. The literature has covered aspects such as which companies tend to source in foreign, particularly global, markets and why. But it also deals with ways on how to get organized for global sourcing, demands on human resources, finding and developing distribution channels, dealing with new cultures etc.

4 Hemerling, J., Momin, Z. and Rupf, I. (2002) *'Rethinking "Made in China": Cars and parts'*, Working paper, Boston Consulting Group: Boston, MA.

5 Kärrberg, P. and Almström, D. (2002) 'The deceptive wireless dragon of the Middle Kingdom', *BrainHeart*, November, pp. 56–8; Hökerberg, J. (2004) 'Made in China = world-class', *Dragon News*, Swedish Chamber of Commerce in China/Swedish Chamber of Commerce in Hong Kong, pp. 4–11; Sigurdson, J. (2004) 'Information and communication technologies (ICT) in China: An emerging global force', in Sigurdson, J. (ed.), *Conference on China's New Knowledge Systems and Their Global Interaction: Summary of Papers*, VINNOVA: Stockholm, pp. 57–64.

6 The case is largely based on the first co-author's personal interview with the director of sourcing, Ericsson China, conducted in Beijing on March 15 2004.

7 Developed from Kotabe, M. and Murray, J.Y. (2004) 'Global sourcing strategy and sustainable competitive advantage', *Industrial Marketing Management*, Vol. 33, pp. 7–14.

8 Alguire, M.S., Frear, C.R. and Metcalf, L.E. (1994) 'An examination of the determinants of global sourcing strategy', *Journal of Business and Industrial Marketing*, Vol. 9, No. 2, pp. 62–74.

9 Kotabe, M. (1998) 'Efficiency vs effectiveness orientation of global sourcing strategy: A comparison of U.S. and Japanese multinational companies', *Academy of Management Executive*, Vol. 12, No. 4, pp. 107–19; Kotabe and Murray (2004) *opere citato*.

10 Trent and Monczka (2002) *opere citato*.

11 Handfield, R.B. and Nichols Jr., E.L. (2004) 'Key issues in global supply base management', *Industrial Marketing Management*, Vol. 33, pp. 29–35.

12 Lardy, N.R. (2002) *Integrating China into the Global Economy*, Brookings Institution: Washington, D.C.; Nolan, P. (2001) *China and the Global Economy*, Palgrave: Hampshire; Panitchpakdi, S. and Clifford, M.L. (2002) *China and the WTO: Changing China, Changing World Trade*, John Wiley & Sons Ltd: Singapore.

13 *China Daily* (2003) 'Adjust foreign investment policy', April 29; Kynge, J. (2003) 'Consumers fuel Chinese growth', *Financial Times*, April 16, p. 1.

14 Roberts, D. and Kynge, J. (2003) 'How cheap labour, foreign investment and rapid industrialization are creating a new workshop of the world', *Financial Times*, February 4, p. 13; Chandler, C. (2003) 'Coping with China', *Fortune*, pp. 66–70.

15 Sigurdson (2004) *opere citato*.

16 Kärrberg and Almström (2002) *opere citato*.

17 Schlevogt, K.-A. (2002) *The Art of Chinese Management: Theory, Evidence, and Applications*, Oxford University Press: Oxford, p. 18.

18 Matteo, M.D. (2003) 'Sourcing in China', *China Business Review*, September–October, pp. 30–32.

19 Hemerling *et al.* (2002) *opere citato*.

20 Nordstrom, D. (2000) 'Sourcing in China: A different kind of IPO', *China Business Review*, September–October, pp. 30–31.

21 Liu, L. (2002) 'China: The next offshore sourcing frontier?', Gomtner Research, COM-14-9027; Qu, Z. and Brocklehurst, M. (2003) 'What will it take for China to become a competitive force in offshore

outsourcing? An analysis of the role of transaction costs in supplier selection', *Journal of Information Technology*, Vol. 18, pp. 53–67.

22   Liu (2002) *opere citato*; Qu and Brocklehurst (2003) *opere citato*.

23   Agndal, H. and Axelsson, B. (2004) *'Upstream internationalization: How do SME-firms meet their foreign suppliers?'*, Paper presented at the IPSERA conference, Catania, Italy, April 4–7.

24   Hofstede, G. (1991) *Cultures and Organizations: Software of the Mind*, McGraw-Hill: London; see also Trompenaars, F. (1994) *Riding the Waves of Culture: Understanding Diversity in Global Business*, Irwin: Chicago; Ulijn, J.M., Lincke, A. and Wynstra, F. (2004) 'The effect of Dutch and German culture on negotiation strategy: An exploratory study to compare innovation and operations contexts', *International Negotiation*, Vol. 9, No. 2, pp. 202–28.

25   Herlitz, G. (1989) *Kulturgrammatik*, Konsultförlaget: Uppsala; Usunier, J.-C. (1993) *International Marketing: A Cultural Approach*, Prentice Hall: New York; Osland, J.S. and Bird, A. (2000) 'Beyond sophisticated stereotyping: Cultural sensemaking in context', *Academy of Management Executive*, Vol. 14, No. 1, pp. 65–79.

26   Gesteland, R.R. (2002) *Cross-Cultural Business Behaviour*, 3rd edn, Copenhagen Business School Press: Copenhagen.

27   See e.g. Fang, T. (1999) *Chinese Business Negotiating Style*, Sage: Thousand Oaks; Pye, L.W. (1992) *Chinese Negotiating Style: Commercial Approaches and Cultural Principles*, Quorum Books: New York; Bjerke, B. (1999) *Business Leadership and Culture*, Edward Elgar: Cheltenham; Gao, G., Ting-Toomey, S. and Gudykunst, W.B. (1996) 'Chinese communication processes', in Bond, M.H. (ed.), *The Handbook of Chinese Psychology*, Oxford University Press: Hong Kong, pp. 280–93.

28   Confucianism is a 2500-year-old Chinese philosophical tradition that has exerted a fundamental influence on the Chinese and East Asian modes of thinking and ways of behaving. The influence of Confucianism on the Chinese style of business can be studied from the six basic Confucian values: (1) moral cultivation; (2) importance of interpersonal relationships; (3) family and group orientation; (4) respect for age and hierarchy; (5) avoidance of conflict and need for harmony; (6) the concept of Chinese face (*mianzi, lian*); see Fang (1999) *opere citato*.

29   Fang (1999) *opere citato*; Pye (1992) *opere citato*; Bjerke (1999) *opere citato*.

30   This case study is part of a larger research project on Swedish firms in China. In this section we utilize more informants than in the rest of the chapter.

Part IV

REFLECTIONS

Chapter 15

SYNTHESIS AND REFLECTIONS

Björn Axelsson, Frank Rozemeijer and Finn Wynstra

This book has dealt with a topic of increasing interest and importance. In the first two chapters we provided the rationale for the need in most firms to be aware and take steps in order to develop and improve their purchasing activities. Regardless of what level on our maturity model the specific firm is positioned, there are always possibilities to improve in purchasing and supply management. Of course, the greatest improvements and those that are easiest to capture should be available to those firms who have not yet made any such efforts. It is like starting to improve one's ability to swim. The untrained will start from a very weak position and will soon be able to improve a lot. The world champion can still be better, but it takes more effort and the relative improvement may not be equally significant.

15.1   A short summary

The key theme of the book could be summarized in two words: strategic change. We have tried to explore today's understanding of strategic change as such, and relate it to our understanding of development in purchasing and supply management (Chapters 1–3). We have studied several areas of significant potential for change in the field of strategic sourcing (Chapters 4–10). These areas signify the potential content of change:

- Developing the supply base by new ways of dealing and cooperating with suppliers (Chapter 4).
- Organizational design including modern forms of organizing applied to purchasing and supply management (Chapter 5).
- Different ways to exercise leadership and build culture in organizations in general and specifically in sourcing organizations (Chapter 6).
- Competence development and learning in organizations; changing by growing the total set of capabilities specifically in strategic sourcing (Chapter 7).
- Leveraging performance by utilizing ICT, again with special attention to purchasing and supply management (Chapter 8).
- Applying the up-to-date level of understanding of performance measurement to impose change in relation to purchasing (Chapter 9).
- Coping with and possibly overcoming individuals' resistance to change (Chapter 10).

All these areas have been described and analysed with reference to points of departure for strategic change. They were selected to cover most of the strategically important areas related to (strategic change in) purchasing and supply management.

We clearly declared that for practical reasons we dealt with them one by one but that in practice they should all be integrated – as also illustrated by the subsequent chapters on case illustrations. In Chapter 4, for example, we discussed the interdependence between the external and the internal dimensions of the role of purchasing and supply management. The increasing possibilities and applications of ICT have not only affected how suppliers can be and are dealt with, but also how the purchasing function can be organized. Competence development and performance measurement are important tools in facilitating and stimulating changed behaviour in supplier relations.

The picture that emerges is one of significant knowledge bases highly relevant to changes in the field under study. The leaders of change should benefit from such understanding, even though it could be a giant step to go from understanding the science of change to practising the art of change!

The process of change was a second aspect of the overall theme. We learnt in Chapter 3 some of the general routes to implementing change and some of the possible resistance and enabling situations. In Chapter 10 we provided insights about the individual involved in and exposed to change and possible reaction patterns, including resistance, as well as reasons behind such patterns. The main lesson from this chapter is that to foster strategic change in purchasing, change leaders have to understand individual behaviour as an instrument in strategic change. Interventions to invoke individual behavioural change can be derived from behavioural theories, but should be applied with knowledge of causes of resistance, individual personalities and the specific context.

Chapter 11 provided an exciting overview of what kind of measures those people resisting change could put into operation, clearly demonstrating that change is rarely a straightforward process or easy to carry out. From this chapter we may conclude that designing and implementing strategic change in purchasing are highly sensitive and political matters. Some in-depth case studies of varying nature followed. They all demonstrated rather complex and demanding change processes, especially the NCC and Thomson cases (Chapters 12 and 13) demonstrating intriguing processes of change. These cases showed the need for a systemic solution; that is, being prepared to change not only one isolated issue, but a combination of them. Also, it seems very much as if the involvement and dedication of top management to support this change were the most important prerequisites for possible success. In addition to that we stress the power of endurance, never giving in and – as an important part of that – a dedicated team of key actors who basically run the process. Also the understanding of the organization as a 'political system', pointing to the importance of always trying to involve people and make them a part of the process, seems to be a key to success in change processes.

The final chapter explained that a company that starts with sourcing in China could harvest a lot, but it needs to be prepared to work hard, to make mistakes and learn from them, to be willing to take commercial risks and invest, to find partners and build trust. The case of Ericsson shows that such changes are truly strategic and also require significant effort in terms of strategic change.

15.2   Lessons learnt

In our opinion, the following are the three most important lessons.

First, there is no such thing as an easily described plan for change that will hold true all the way till the final goal is reached. Nevertheless, plans are needed to prepare for the uncontrollable processes that follow. Chance favours the prepared mind! We also learnt that processes of change are never identical. Furthermore, they consist not only of the areas of change and the logical deduction of activities needed to be performed to make the goals materialize. Admittedly, it could be equally important to manage the political aspects of the change. The illustrations from Dutch purchasing managers of the various ways in which change could be counteracted (Chapter 11) gave a convincing illustration of this.

The NCC case (Chapter 12) is also an interesting example. There had been efforts before the one that is the focus of our study to dramatically change the purchasing and supply function. They had all failed, not least due to lack of support from top management. The process under study had very strong support from above with the CEO heavily involved with and committed to the process. The leading coalition had learnt from history and made an excellent design for the change process. Still, it was not such a clear-cut success as one would have expected.

There were several other variables constituting the context that had significant impact. Today after a 'loss-of-momentum period' they are back, as it seems, stronger than ever. All the structural elements are back: the same market situation, the same organizational structure, a CEO who supports the change and so on. Yet this time, it seems to reach further. The reasons could be discussed, but a general increased preparedness and understanding of necessity in combination with – most of all – an even more dedicated CEO probably explain the most, not in the least his very active leadership, close attention to detail and his lack of hesitation to exercise power.

Second, there is a need for a holistic approach. As demonstrated in the Thomson and NCC cases (and indirectly by the Ericsson case) one cannot only focus on one aspect of the change process such as a new organizational design. Too much in today's purchasing organizations is integrated and mutually interdependent. Various mixes of measures are needed and the potential change in organizational design needs to be complemented by and adapted to changes in leadership, usage of ICT, developing an adequate mix of key rations and other techniques from modern management accounting and so on. Furthermore, the timing of when to introduce what kind of measures and their sequencing are key aspects too.

Last but not least, in order to be effective, strategic sourcing should be strategically aligned with the whole organization. Implementing sophisticated purchasing practices alone is not enough to create superior organizational performance. Purchasing and supply management is an integral part of a larger system, therefore purchasing directors should also look at the larger picture of the organization, including other business and functional strategies, processes and linkages. The effects of strategic sourcing practices cannot be isolated and linked to outstanding organizational performance. It is the fit between purchasing and the whole organization that does the trick.

Other lessons are that a single company cannot survive in the long run unless it is able to adapt and change. Some of the changes are merely adaptations to changing conditions, others should be more proactive. The first means to find measures to match and adapt to changing conditions. The other, proactive changes are more a matter of taking the lead for change: the proactive way of being ahead of the need for adaptations, to drive customers and competitors into new needs, requests and delights. This demands much more bravery and foresight as well as influences from the vision of the firm, the ability to mobilize a company that is not in crisis and so on.

Furthermore, we learn that companies cannot afford not to try to leverage the potentials available to them. The firm that does not utilize ICT, does not have a proper and professional leadership in place, or does not take advantage of global sourcing opportunities when competitive advantages from such practices are in reach, is likely to suffer significantly from this. Therefore firms need always to be in a process of change of some continuous or revolutionary type!

The above leads us into the general wisdom that firms need to be alert to survive. As purchasing constitutes such a large part of the total corporate operation, no company can consider it a second-class function. Purchasing and supply needs to be taken seriously and to always be a candidate for change, be it strategic changes or more continuous and modest ones.

15.3   Future challenges

It is always challenging to reflect over the future. Our way of doing it is to raise the following question: 'If we were to write a new book similar to this one in ten years' time, which themes would we add then?' We think that there could be some themes that are likely to be unavoidable in ten years' time. First, we think that globalization processes will imply that processes of strategic change will increasingly have an international and multicultural flavour. This demands new skills from all the people involved (e.g. language, culture etc.). In Chapter 14 we touch on this theme, but in a future book we would most likely put a lot more emphasis on managing change in intercultural settings.

Secondly, outsourcing will increasingly become a real strategic challenge in the near future. In the 1980s we saw the debate on the 'hollow company', when an increasing number of manufacturing operations were being outsourced. Currently, we have much of the same debate in the area of business services and the service sector in general (see also Chapter 1). Knowing what to outsource when, to whom and how is becoming an important 'dynamic' capability for firms and nonprofit organizations alike (see Chapter 7). As such, outsourcing capabilities – in a growing number of organizations and sectors – will complement and sometimes even replace more traditional, 'internal' organizational core competencies.

Further, we expect increasing attention to human resources development (HRD) in the area of purchasing and supply management. HRD involves human resource strategies and dedicated personnel focusing on identifying, hiring and developing high potentials in purchasing. More and more companies are willing to invest in setting up professional training programmes, action learning programmes, management development programmes and executive coaching for people involved in purchasing and supply management processes. These training programmes will increasingly become cross-functional and cross-enterprise (i.e. suppliers and customers will join these programmes).

We also expect deeper integration with suppliers and customers (e.g. information sharing, decision making, collaborative planning), ongoing development and innovation on a collaborative basis among all participants in the supply chain, strategic cost management across the value chain (e.g. identifying costs and focusing efforts to reduce those costs jointly), asset sharing between organizations and shared technology development and shared revenue generation. These trends will require suppliers to take a greater cost management role by providing services in R&D, manufacturing, order fulfilment and system integration.

Finally, we expect to see significant change in the way that the purchasing and supply management function will be involved in the value creation process. Referring back to our maturity model in Chapter 2, we see the creation of value as the ultimate objective of any business function or process. In the case of strategic sourcing, this means a focus on issues like leveraging supplier relations in new business development, and replacing or complementing a focus on total cost of ownership with one on total value of ownership. It also means that the strategic sourcing function will be interacting more intensively not only with functions like R&D and new business development, but especially with the marketing function. In some sectors, like fashion retailing, this may already be common practice, but we foresee similar developments in other sectors as well.

In short, we expect continuing and significant changes in the years to come. We hope that the ideas, frameworks and insights provided in this book may help in interpreting and dealing with the challenges of this permanent process of strategic change.

INDEX